PERSONAL
FINANCIAL
PLANNING

Christmas Greetings
from
Ian. and Rae

The Chapman & Hall Series in Accounting and Finance

Consulting editors

John Perrin, Emeritus Professor of the University of Warwick and Price Waterhouse Fellow in Public Sector Accounting at the University of Exeter; Richard M.S. Wilson, Professor of Management and Accounting at the University of Keele; and Richard Pike, Professor of Finance and Accounting at the University of Bradford Management School.

E. Clark, M. Levasseur and P. Rousseau
International Finance

H.M. Coombs and D.E. Jenkins
Public Sector Financial Management
   (2nd edn)
(Also available: *Teacher's Manual*)

J.C. Drury
Management and Cost Accounting (3rd edn)
(Also available: *Students' Manual, Teachers'*
Manual, Spreadsheet Applications Manual,
Guidance Notes and Disk, OHP Masters, Dutch
Students' Manual*, see also Gazely)

C.R. Emmanuel, D.T. Otley and K. Merchant
Accounting for Management Control (2nd edn)
(Also available: *Teachers' Guide*)

C.R. Emmanuel, D.T. Otley and K. Merchant
   (editors)
Readings in Accounting for Management Control

M. Ezzamel and D. Heathfield (editors)
Perspectives on Financial Control: Essays in
   memory of Kenneth Hilton

A.M. Gazely
Management and Cost Accounting Spreadsheet
   Applications Manual

P. Hancock
An Introduction to Taxation

D. Henley, A. Likierman, J. Perrin, M.
   Evans, I. Lapsley and J.E.H. Whiteoak
Public Sector Accounting and Financial Control
   (4th edn)

B.W. Koch
European Financial Reporting Practices

R.C. Laughlin and R.H. Gray
Financial Accounting: method and meaning
(Also available: *Teachers' Guide*)

T.A. Lee
Income Value Measurement (3rd edn)

T.A. Lee
Company Financial Reporting (2nd edn)

T.A. Lee
Cash Flow Accounting

T.A. Lee
Corporate Audit Theory

S.P. Lumby
Investment Appraisal and Financial Decisions
   (5th edn)
(Also available: *Teachers' Guide*)

R.W. Perks
Accounting and Society

A.G. Puxty and J.C. Dodds
Financial Management: method and meaning
   (2nd edn)
(Also available: *Teachers' Guide*)

J.M. Samuels, F.M. Wilkes and R.E.
   Brayshaw
Management of Company Finance (5th edn)
(Also available: *Students' Manual*)

J.M. Samuels, R.E. Brayshaw and J.M.
   Craner
European Financial Statement Analysis

C.M.S. Sutcliffe
Stock Index Futures

B.C. Williams and B.J. Spaul
IT and Accounting: The impact of information
   technology

R.M.S. Wilson and Wai Fong Chua
Managerial Accounting: method and meaning
   (2nd edn)
(Also available: *Teachers' Guide*)

*The *Dutch Students' Manual* to accompany the third edition of *Management and Cost Accounting* by Colin Drury, is not published by Chapman & Hall, but is available from Interfaas, Onderzoek en Advies, Postbus 76618, 1070HE, Amsterdam. Tel. (020) 6 76 27 06.

PERSONAL FINANCIAL PLANNING

AN INTRODUCTION

Thomas McRae

University of Bradford Management Centre, UK

CHAPMAN & HALL

London · Glasgow · Weinheim · New York · Tokyo · Melbourne · Madras

Published by Chapman & Hall, 2–6 Boundary Row, London SE1 8HN, UK

Chapman & Hall, 2–6 Boundary Row, London SE1 8HN, UK

Blackie Academic & Professional, Wester Cleddens Road, Bishopbriggs, Glasgow G64 2NZ, UK

Chapman & Hall GmbH, Pappelallee 3, 69469 Weinheim, Germany

Chapman & Hall USA, 115 Fifth Avenue, New York NY 10003, USA

Chapman & Hall Japan, ITP-Japan, Kyowa Building, 3F, 2-2-1 Hirakawacho, Chiyoda-ku, Tokyo 102, Japan

Chapman & Hall Australia, 102 Dodds Street, South Melbourne, Victoria 3205, Australia

Chapman & Hall India, R. Seshadri, 32 Second Main Road, CIT East, Madras 600 035, India

First edition 1995

© 1995 T.W. McRae

Typeset in 10/12pt Palatino by Saxon Graphics Ltd, Derby

Printed in Great Britain by Hartnolls Ltd, Bodmin, Cornwall

ISBN 0 412 62660 8

A catalogue record for this book is available from the British Library

Library of Congress Catalog Card Number: 95-67594

♾ Printed on permanent acid-free text paper, manufactured in accordance with ANSI/NISO Z39.48-1992 and ANSI/NISO Z39.48-1984 (Permanence of Paper).

Contents

To Lydia Maisie

Preface

This book is intended as an introduction to personal financial planning for those who are starting out on a career as a personal financial adviser.

Exhibit 1.1 in Chapter 1 shows the wide range of subject matter covered by the discipline of personal financial planning. Personal financial planning is a continent rather than a country. No one individual, no matter how assiduous, can be an expert over such a wide range of topics. Specialization is essential. The personal financial adviser (PFA) must build up a network of contacts so that she or he can access specialist information when required.

The wide range of subjects covered in personal financial planning raises problems for anyone attempting to write an introductory book on the subject. Which topics should be included and which left out? What depth of treatment should be accorded to each subject?

One complete book could be devoted to each chapter in this book and still not cover every aspect of the subject. Several key topics, such as personal taxation, investment theory and pension planning, would need several books to do the subject full justice.

I have attempted to solve this problem by introducing the key ideas on the subject matter within each chapter and then suggesting further reading at the end of the chapter for those who wish to pursue the subject to a deeper level.

In my opinion the main limitation on the quality of current courses on personal financial planning is the excessive emphasis on facts and the very limited emphasis on analysis. Regulatory rules, legal limitations and devices for limiting tax liability are very important to a PFA, but are of limited use if employed within a poorly constructed overall plan. Personal financial planning is holistic. Each individual plan on investment, insurance, pension and housing etc. can only be optimized within an overall plan for the individual. Overall holistic planning requires the PFA to acquire an analytic overall approach which balances each independent plan against one another to find the optimal balance.

We have tried to emphasize the analytical approach to plan design in this book.

In July 1994 the magazine *Moneywise* commissioned the Gallup polling organization to ask a representative sample of 1046 adults in Great Britain what they thought about the honesty and competence of personal financial advisers. The results were not good. Some 50% of the persons polled considered that clients of PFAs were frequently sold the wrong investments; only 28% were quite or very confident that a PFA would be 100% honest! A further 20% claimed that they had been given poor investment advice by PFAs in the past.

All of this suggests that the training of PFAs could be improved somewhat. Several organizations are making sterling efforts in this regard, but the lack of books specifically designed for training personal financial advisers – a gap in the market that this book is intended to fill – is currently a serious limitation to the improvement of the training process.

The book is based on the material presented to students attending the 'Personal Financial Planning' elective offered within the MBA programme at the University of Bradford Management Centre.

I would be grateful for advice from trainers of personal financial advisers as to any improvements in the structure of the book and particularly for any suggestions as to additional material which should be included which would widen its coverage of the core knowledge required by a personal financial adviser.

TWM, July 1995

The personal finance profession

1

THE GROWTH IN THE PERSONAL FINANCE PROFESSION

In recent years the profession which provides personal financial advice has shown one of the fastest rates of growth of any profession operating in the advanced industrial world. In the UK, some 19 000 persons now earn most of their income from providing advice on personal finance, while in the USA there are currently around 200 000 personal financial advisers[1] offering their services to the public. In addition to the full-time professionals, some 250 000 persons in the UK working in such institutions as insurance companies, banks, building societies, stockbrokers and estate agents, spend some part of their working time providing advice on personal finance.

Advising on personal finance is now a major economic activity in the UK.

WHY HAS THE PROFESSION OF PERSONAL FINANCIAL ADVISERS (PFA) GROWN SO RAPIDLY IN RECENT YEARS?

The most obvious reason for the recent increase in demand for personal financial advice is the rapid growth in real personal incomes of workers in advanced industrial countries in recent years.

Up until around 1950 most families, even in Europe and North America, had little income to spare after paying for basic necessities. From about 1950, and certainly after 1960, most families living in what is often called 'the rich North' found that the proportion of their income required for basic necessities such as food, clothing and accommodation diminished substantially, leaving a surplus which could be spent either on luxuries and entertainment – or saved. Exhibit 3.7 in Chapter 3 illustrates the distribution of total personal expenditure in the UK in recent years. Note how the proportion spent on necessities has diminished.

---

[1] See Block, Peavy and Thornton (1990, chapter 1).

This growth in the proportion of income saved by the individual earner in turn stimulated the demand for advice on investing this surplus, and so the profession of personal financial adviser was born.

This substantial growth in personal saving also stimulated the growth of financial institutions. By the end of the 1960s personal saving had become the main source of funds for investment in the UK. A huge amount of personal saving, much of it channelled through contributory pension funds and life assurance funds, provided UK financial institutions with immense financial power and influence on the UK economy.

The selling of a wide range of financial products such as pension schemes, life policies, health insurance and unit trusts created a highly competitive market. This fierce competition persuaded the large institutions to pay substantial commissions to agents to encourage these agents to sell their products rather than those of their competitors. Many of these agents, in time, developed skills in providing financial advice to clients and so these agents gradually began to evolve from being salespersons selling financial products into a new profession of personal financial advisers providing financial advice. In time, some of these advisers no longer accepted commission but became exclusively fee-based. However, we should not forget that the commissions on the sale of financial products provided the initial financial stimulus which fertilized the growth of the personal finance profession.

Unfortunately this ambivalent approach of PFAs to their clients (are we salespersons maximizing commission, or PFAs giving impartial advice?) has led to all sorts of problems in recent years. We shall return to this important issue in Chapter 11.

Around 5000 of the PFAs in the UK work in small private practices providing advice on investments, insurance and pensions. A large majority of the PFAs working in small firms take some commission on their sales to clients. Another major group of PFAs work within the large financial institutions, such as the banks, building societies and insurance companies. These advisers sell only the products of one company but may provide impartial advice on other aspects of personal finance. These advisers may return any commissions received on external products to their client. A third group of PFAs work in financial services companies which are devoted to providing personal financial advice. Many professional accounting firms and legal firms run a personal finance wing. Some companies are exclusively devoted to providing financial advice. Financial services companies such as Allied Dunbar and Towry Law provide a wide range of services which include not only personal financial advice but also indulge in such activities as portfolio management and devising and selling new personal financial products.

Recent changes in the law now require all PFAs to declare that they are either an 'independent' financial adviser who must, by law, provide impartial 'best advice' to a client or are 'tied agents' who are devoted to selling the products of one particular company. We shall elaborate on this division in the profession in Chapter 11.

The provision of personal financial advice is gradually evolving into a profession, but the rate of evolution is slow. There is no recognized controlling body in personal finance which sets standards for its members as there is with other professions such as medicine and law. There is no properly organized examining body, although applicants for PIA membership must pass, at the very least, the Financial Planning Certificate set by the Chartered Insurance Institute or possess some equally recognized or superior qualification in finance. Some professional institutes do require that exams in personal finance be taken as a condition of membership.[2]

Personal financial planning is not yet recognized as a university subject in the way that, say, business finance and government finance are, but a start in this direction has been made.[3] The basic problem in organizing a professional body to represent personal financial planners is the ambivalent attitude of many PFAs towards their role as either a salesperson or an impartial professional adviser. So long as PFAs continue to receive the bulk of their income from the commission they earn from selling financial products rather than from the fees they earn from providing financial advice they will have difficulty in persuading the community in general that they are a profession rather than a sales organization. The fault is not entirely with the profession. There is some evidence that the British public is unwilling to pay the fees required to buy proper financial advice, which would be of the order of £60 to £120 an hour if no commission were received by the adviser. A Gallup poll in July 1994 found that 46% of those polled considered that financial advice was worth less than £25 an hour; 20% thought £50 an hour was 'reasonable'.[4]

WHAT DOES A PERSONAL FINANCIAL ADVISER DO?

A PFA devises a set of personal financial plans for his or her client. These plans differ from client to client, but most clients will require financial plans to be drawn up on such things as devising a suitable investment portfolio, house purchase, life, health and general insurance, pension

[2] For example, the Society of Financial Advisers, the Institute of Financial Planning and the Association of Independent Financial Advisers. The students of these associations are normally required to take the Financial Planning Certificate set by the Chartered Insurance Institute as a preliminary to membership.
[3] The MBA programme at the University of Bradford Management Centre offers an elective designed to train personal financial planners. It has been taken by 25 to 30 students in recent years. The City University, London, has instituted a Professorship in Personal Finance. Several of the 'new universities' such as Bournemouth University, Hallam University, Sheffield and Glasgow Caledonian University have set up degrees in Financial Services which include modules on personal finance.
[4] *Moneywise*, July 1994 p. 32

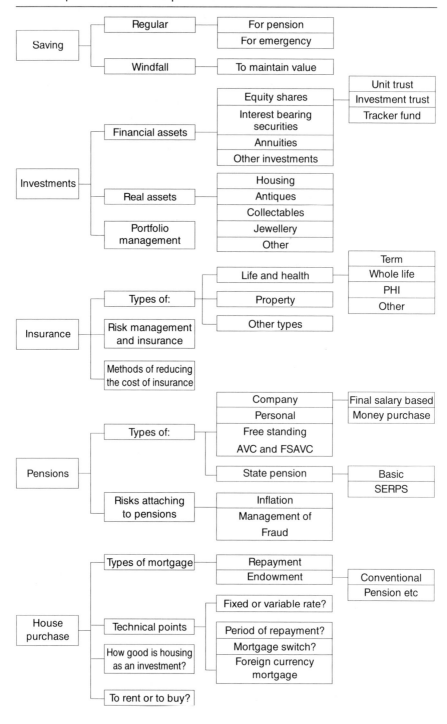

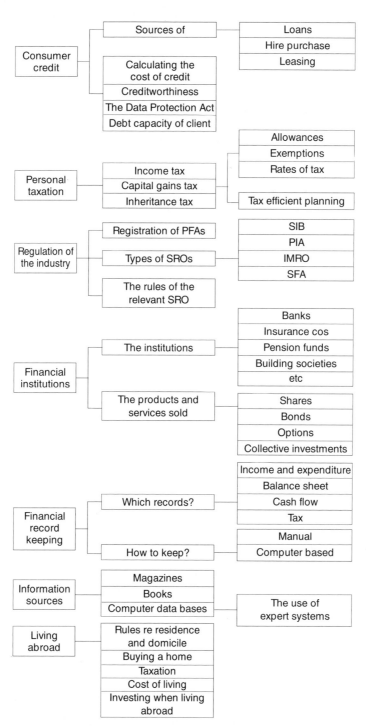

A personal financial adviser needs to acquire knowledge covering a very wide field to construct an efficient financial plan for her client. No individual PFA can hope to be expert over the entire field so it is important to build up a network of experts with whom to consult when devising a plan. This advice applies particularly to the field of taxation.

Exhibit 1.1 A taxonomy of personal finance.

planning, personal tax planning including inheritance planning,[5] planning for school fees, debt scheduling and cash planning. This list by no means exhausts the variety of personal financial plans that may be requested by a client. Exhibit 1.1 illustrates the wide range of subjects on which a personal financial adviser might expect to be consulted. The list is formidable and presents a challenge no less demanding than that faced by a solicitor, accountant or doctor.

First, PFAs are required to find out about their client. In addition to listing the obvious information such as name, address, etc. a PFA must make up an inventory of the client's income, assets and liabilities, insurance contracts, pension rights, marital status, dependent relatives, future job intentions, health condition, etc. This is explicitly required by the Securities and Investment Board (SIB) and the other regulatory authorities such as the Personal Investment Authority (PIA) which monitor the personal finance profession. A PFA cannot simply sell a financial product to a client without first finding out about the client's financial and personal situation.

The two basic duties of a financial planner are first to advise a client on building a portfolio of investments sufficient to provide an adequate income in the future, particularly on retirement, and second to secure the client against the 'slings and arrows of outrageous fortune'. In other words to carry out a 'risk analysis' on the current and likely future situation of the client to identify possible hazards they might face such as death, serious illness or loss of job and then to devise methods of hedging against the consequences of these negative events.

With regard to security of income, the PFA should know that academic research over the last 40 years has demonstrated that it is not possible to foretell the financial future – in other words it is not possible to consistently outguess an efficient financial market. Research has also shown, however, that a portfolio of assets can be constructed which will stabilize the value of a portfolio of investments against changes in the fortunes of individual companies and the economy. Income from an investment portfolio can be protected but not maximized.

As was noted above, all PFAs must decide whether they wish to work as an independent financial adviser providing impartial best advice to clients, or as a tied agent selling the products of one company. A tied agent can also be a financial adviser, but the choice of products available to such an adviser is restricted. A tied agent may not be directly regulated but works for a company which is registered with the PIA or IMRO or some other regulatory body.

All PFAs must also decide whether they are salespersons maximizing income from commission, or professional advisers giving the best advice available for a fee. This is not the same distinction as that between an

---

[5] Many PFAs may, wisely, decide to pass on this responsibility to a specialist tax consultant.

independent and tied agent. As we shall see in Chapter 11, an independent adviser must provide best advice; a tied agent also provides best advice, but within the restrictions set by the company for whom he or she sells products.

The problem of advising on personal taxation is a difficult one. Personal tax is so complex and the legislation so extensive and ever-changing that it is very difficult for a PFA to keep continuously up to date on every aspect of the subject. Taxation of foreign income, for instance, is particularly complex. All PFAs must have a basic knowledge of the current tax legislation and procedures in their own country, but few will have the time to maintain a truly up-to-date detailed knowledge of the tax system. The wisest course may be for a PFA to subcontract this aspect of business – that is, to find a good tax adviser to work with on a continuous basis. Once a financial plan has been drafted it can be submitted to the personal tax adviser to be checked out for tax efficiency.

HOW DOES A PFA LEARN THE SKILLS REQUIRED?

This question, oddly enough, does not have an obvious answer. Almost all the professions in the UK and in most other industrialized countries have developed a well-organized professional structure which includes a training programme and an examination system which leads directly into the profession. In such professions, this system guarantees a certain basic competence on the part of practitioners. The letters 'MB ChB', 'RIBA' or 'ACA' tells a client that, at least at some time in the past, the adviser has shown a reasonable competence in the skills required in his or her profession.

No such universally recognized professional organization exists to control and monitor the personal finance profession. The various regulatory organizations set up under the 1986 Financial Services Act check that those PFAs registered with the organization possess some two years' basic experience in advising on personal finance and have passed a minimum qualifying examination in the subject, but no qualifications are awarded by them. Several attempts have been made to organize a profession of PFAs[6] but these attempts have met with only limited success to date.

A registered PFA can practise with no professional qualifications if he or she has the requisite experience; many practitioners have no qualification other than having passed the first-level CII examination. It should be pointed out, however, that a similar situation holds in the accounting profession. Auditors of public limited companies must be qualified accountants, but accountants who prepare accounts etc. for private clients and give advice on tax need not be qualified. Society assumes that if clients are wise they seek out the advice of qualified accountants but they need not do so.

[6] See note 2 above.

We now return to our original question. How can a person seeking to become a personal financial adviser gain knowledge sufficient to become skilled in the practice of his or her profession? Exhibit 1.1 illustrates the wide field of knowledge required by any person operating in the personal finance field. It can be seen from this exhibit that the knowledge required to practise as a PFA is very extensive, certainly as extensive as that required by an adviser on corporate finance or international finance. We suspect that this fact is not widely appreciated by the general public.

How do the other professions operating in the finance industry measure up on personal finance? Many accountants advise on personal finance but, if we exclude personal taxation, there are few questions on personal finance in the professional accounting examinations. The examinations in banking and stockbroking set excellent questions in their own specialist areas, but few questions are set directly on personal finance. The Chartered Insurance Institute has set up the Financial Planning Certificate as a part of its qualifying examination. This certificate is used as part of the entrance qualification by the Society of Financial Advisers and the Institute of Financial Planning.

Thus if a potential PFA were to take qualifications in accounting, banking, insurance, property management and stockbroking, he or she would have a reasonable level of professional competence – but, of course, this is a nonsense. A great deal of the information learned in these examinations would be of little use to the PFA.

A proper programme of training and examination in personal finance is urgently needed to protect the public against incompetent advice from ill-trained financial advisers.

SO WHAT IS TO BE DONE IN THE MEANWHILE?

The best course to be pursued by those wishing to become a PFA is to start in insurance or banking or accounting and gain a qualification and expertise in one of these sectors of personal finance. From there they can move across into personal finance work by joining one of the larger national firms providing advice on financial services, firms such as Frizzells or Noble Lowndes. In other words, the potential PFA will work as an apprentice, learning a trade in the traditional way by doing. Many of the PFAs who are now well established in the personal finance profession started work in accounting firms or merchant banks working on tax or corporate finance and only later moved into the personal finance arm of their particular organization. The most common entry point to the profession seems to be as an independent insurance broker.

SOURCES OF INFORMATION ON PERSONAL FINANCE

Many excellent sources of information on personal finance are provided on a regular basis in the daily, weekly and monthly press. The financial institutions need to advertise the sale of their financial products to the public, especially of any new financial products they may have devised. This is achieved by passing detailed information about these products to financial journalists, who publish the information in their regular columns in the media. A great deal is written on personal finance – several popular journals on personal finance are published each month, along with several 'personal finance' supplements in the newspapers. If a PFA scans the weekly and monthly journals plus the personal finance columns of the newspapers on a regular basis, he or she should be able to keep up to date on current developments in personal finance. A PFA needs to maintain a set of files on all aspects of personal finance and to keep an indexed, up-to-date personal cuttings file of this information.

Books are more problematic. A large number of books on personal financial management are published in the USA but these have such a strong American bias, especially on tax and law, that they are of very limited value to a PFA working in the UK.

Most of the books on personal finance currently available in the UK are aimed at individuals who wish to do their own financial planning. Mitchell (1993) is an excellent example of this genre. The accounting firm Robson Rhodes provide a useful listing of things to remember on various aspects of personal finance. Many excellent and very detailed books are published on personal tax for the tax professional, but most of these are much too detailed for the needs of the PFA. The *Daily Mail* tax guide provides a useful introduction to personal tax in the UK, and Allied Dunbar have issued a series of books on various aspects of personal financial planning. These books cover a wide spectrum of knowledge from personal tax planning to retirement planning. Gee have published a useful compilation of facts for financial intermediaries.

An annotated bibliography of magazines, journals and books on personal finance is provided at the end of this book.

Several university degree courses are offered with a strong emphasis on banking, insurance and financial services but none, in the UK, are devoted exclusively to personal financial planning. However, the Bradford University MBA programme offers an elective on personal financial planning and several of the new universities have introduced courses on financial services which include modules on personal finance.[7]

HOW IS THE PERSONAL FINANCIAL PLANNING PROFESSION REGULATED IN THE UK?

A number of well publicized financial scandals in the 1980s, such as that suffered by Norton Warburg, forced the government of the day to consider a revision of the way in which the financial markets in the UK were

---

[7] See note 3 above.

regulated. The initial study was contained in the Gower Report (1984) on 'Investor protection in the UK'. This report led to the Financial Services Act of 1986 which set up a number of organizations to oversee the regulation of the various financial markets in the UK. These regulating bodies are called SROs, self-regulating organizations.

The body in overall control of financial regulation in the UK is called the Securities and Investment Board (SIB). The SIB in turn oversees the various bodies which monitor the various specialist sectors of the UK financial market. Three organizations monitor some aspects of the work of the personal finance sector. These are the PIA, IMRO and the SFA.[8]

All independent PFAs must apply for registration with a regulatory authority such as the PIA before they can practise as an investment adviser. The only exception to this rule arises if the PFA is already a member of an organization, like the Law Society, which is recognized by the PIA. Some other professional organizations recognized by the PIA are the various Institutes of Chartered Accountants and the Insurance Brokers Registration Council. Once an applicant is registered with the PIA, the PFA must read the extensive rule books published by the PIA and the SIB which set out how investment advice should be given to a client, the records that must be kept and how investments should be managed. These rules must be obeyed, or the PFA will lose her or his registration with the PIA and so will not be permitted to operate as an investment adviser or manager. The more important of these rules are set out and discussed in Chapter 11.

Some PFAs who are not independent but work for financial organizations are registered with IMRO.

The rules set down by the regulatory organizations cover such things as the necessity of finding out about the client's background, how to conduct various relationships with the client, how to advise on the degree of risk attached to an investment, a warning on the need to give 'best advice' to a client, the need to keep proper books of account which must be audited, the need to keep clients' funds separate from those of the PFA, the need to have taken out adequate indemnity insurance, and so forth.

Most of these rules are no more than applied common sense which a competent PFA would have been likely to have followed even had the regulatory bodies not been set up to monitor his or her performance.

THE INVESTOR'S COMPENSATION SCHEME

One of the more controversial aspects of recent legislation governing the regulation of the personal finance industry has been the introduction of

---

[8] PIA (Personal Investment Authority), IMRO (Investment Managers Regulatory Organization) and the SFA (Securities and Futures Authority).

the Investor's Compensation Scheme in 1988. This scheme is designed to compensate private investors who lose money by reason of the incompetence or fraudulent practice of their personal financial adviser.

The maximum amount of money an individual investor can claim under the scheme in any one case is £48 000. The scheme is run by the SIB and is funded by a levy on existing PFAs registered with the relevant SRO. The annual levy imposed on PFAs under the scheme depends on the total compensation paid to claimants by the SIB in the preceding year.

Unfortunately a very substantial number of claims on the scheme have been lodged with the SIB – the cost exceeded £10 million in 1992. This has resulted in the compensation fund teetering on the edge of bankruptcy since its inception. In effect, the competent and honest PFA is subsidizing the incompetent or dishonest PFA who is inadequately insured.

The cost of this levy has persuaded many independent PFAs to give up being independent advisers and become tied agents who are not in the scheme. It has even been suggested by some financial commentators that the ICS will end up by wiping out the entire profession of independent financial advisers! 'By increasing fees [the ICS] will drive more independent advisers out of business... leading to the destruction of FIMBRA.'[9]

This is probably an exaggeration, but the number of independent advisers has been substantially reduced in recent years. This may be related to the rising annual cost of the ICS levy.

The 'Clucas' Report, financed by the SIB, has attempted to find a solution to this problem but so far little has been done to remedy what is universally regarded as a most unsatisfactory situation.

We will discuss the ICS in more detail in Chapter 11.

COMMISSION ON PRODUCTS SOLD

The commission paid by the providers of financial products to PFAs is negotiated between the parties involved. The commission paid is usually a fixed percentage of the premium paid or of the value of the product sold. A high level of commission, say 25% of the premium, is received by the agent for a certain number of months, say 16 months, after sale of the product, plus a smaller percentage thereafter.

LAUTRO, while in existence, provided a table of suggested rates called 'standard rates'. PFAs who were not receiving these rates were required to inform the client of the actual rate of commission being received.

As from 1 January 1995, all commission received must be declared to the client.

[9] Ian Harper, *CA Magazine*, September 1993.

The rates vary between companies but an example might be as shown below.

Endowment assurance

Term	25% Commission paid for:	2.5% Commission paid for:
10 years	16 months	8 years 8 months
15 years	24 months	13 years

Whole life assurance

Age	25% Commission paid for:	2.5% Commission paid for:
40 and under	48 months	thereafter
55	41 months	thereafter
65	31 months	thereafter

Single premium insurance bond

First year	3% commission	+ 0.5% thereafter

PROBLEMS IN PROVIDING PERSONAL FINANCIAL ADVICE

Personal finance is a complex subject. Devising viable financial plans for clients throws up a whole range of problems for the assiduous PFA.

The first problem arises out of the sheer complexity of the knowledge base as illustrated in Exhibit 1.1. Each branch of personal finance inter-links with every other branch so that advice on one area such as pensions can impinge on other areas such as investment policy, insurance needs, inheritance tax planning and suchlike. It is difficult to give sound advice on any one area of personal finance without checking out the impact of this advice on every other aspect of the personal financial plan.

A second problem arises from the fast-changing environment of personal finance. It is not easy to keep up with all of the changes which occur in new products, new laws, new taxes and so forth. A fully comprehensive updating service on personal finance does not exist,[10] although a regular review of the popular and trade journals should cover most key changes.

A further problem arises from the difficulty experienced by some PFAs in interpreting the regulatory rules set forth by the SIB and the PIA.

---

[10] However, Tolley's *Compliance Monitor* provides an update service on regulatory changes announced by the SROs.

Some of these rules are worded in a way which can leave doubt as to their precise meaning. What exactly is 'best advice'? How does one know it is best advice? What exactly is 'integrity and fair dealing'? What is meant by 'fair'? How much buying and selling of shares must be carried out before a PFA can be accused of 'churning' a portfolio? How can a PFA prove that he or she was 'well informed' about a client's situation when offering certain advice? We may think that we know the answers to these questions, but it will take a court case or two to arrive at a set of legally binding definitions.

The last but by no means least of the problems faced by a PFA is the wide variation experienced in the expectations, honesty and co-operation of the client. For example, some clients have totally unrealistic expectations as to the amount of income which can be generated from their assets. As we will learn later in this book, the return from an asset is closely linked to the risk attached to that asset. High return means high risk, low risk means low return. A client who demands that a PFA must find a very secure asset which will also provide a high income is being unrealistic. Alas, many such clients exist. These are the ones who are pushing up the claims on the Investor's Compensation Scheme, since in time they will succeed in finding a PFA who offers to satisfy their impossible demands.

The honesty of the client is another problem faced by every PFA. Every personal financial plan is based on a set of facts and assumptions, most of which are provided by the client. If the client provides incorrect information to his or her adviser, the plan can be a nonsense. This is why the PFA must always take care to write down the assumptions on which the plan is based and get the client to sign the agreed list of facts and assumptions as being correct. The PFA is then absolved from blame if, for example, a client claims to be perfectly healthy in an assurance contract when, in fact, they had a serious heart attack some years previously.

Finally there is the problem of persuading the client to expend the time and effort to collect all of the data needed to draw up a proper set of financial plans. The PFA will want to see a list of the client's investments, the current mortgage deed, the most recent tax assessment, the most recent annual pay summary, a list of current insurance contracts and possibly the contracts themselves to check for possible hidden benefits or exclusions, a copy of the company pension scheme rule book, and so on. Some clients are more efficient than others at filing and indexing such things so the effort required to collect them varies from client to client.

The PFA will give a new client a questionnaire to fill in to assemble the relevant information about the client and their family. A thorough questionnaire can run to 20 or 30 pages. Some clients may object to providing such detailed information about themselves, while others may not be able to find the time to fill in the questionnaire completely or, much worse, accurately.

PFAs must always remember that they are not social workers but professional advisers who take their instructions from the client. They must do what they are asked to do, no more and no less. They must do the best they can with a disingenuous, dishonest or lazy client. PFAs are not alone in this regard – lawyers, doctors, architects and accountants face the same problem.

WHAT HAVE WE LEARNED IN THIS CHAPTER?

1. The number of people practising as personal financial advisers in the UK has increased dramatically in recent years.
2. Financial institutions such as banks, insurance companies and building societies have also grown rapidly in the UK since the end of the Second World War.
3. Both these trends are due to the same factor, the increasing surplus of income over basic expenditure enjoyed by the working population of the country over this period.
4. A major portion of the income of PFAs comes from the sales commission earned on financial products sold. This fact sets up a conflict of interest between the PFA's role as a financial adviser and his or her role as a salesperson.
5. PFAs must decide whether they wish to be an 'independent financial adviser' selling a wide range of products from many different companies or a 'tied agent' selling the products of only one company. They must also decide whether they wish their income to be fee-based or commission-based.
6. The job of a PFA is to devise a set of financial plans on investment, insurance, pensions etc. for the client.
7. The financial markets in the UK are monitored by a group of self regulating organizations (SROs) set up by the Financial Services Act of 1986. The SROs which monitor the various aspects of the personal finance profession comprise the SIB, the PIA and IMRO. PFAs must register with one of these organizations if they wish to provide advice on, to manage or to sell investments in the UK. It is also possible to register with the PIA indirectly via a professional organization such as the ICAEW or the Law Society.
8. The Investor's Compensation Scheme has proved to be a major problem for the personal finance industry in the UK. Too many financial advisers have found themselves in financial difficulty.
9. The qualifications required to practise as a PFA in the UK are not onerous. A registered PIA member must, at the very least, have passed the Financial Planning Certificate of the Chartered Insurance

Institute. The training facilities available to those persons wishing to become PFAs are inadequate at present in the UK. The most common route into advising on personal finance is through a financial institution such as an insurance company, a bank, a building society or an accountancy firm.

10. The literature on personal finance is rather limited. While many excellent journals are published regularly on the various aspects of personal finance, only a few books and updating services deal directly with personal finance.

11. The PFA faces some special problems. Keeping up with the rapidly changing personal finance environment presents a challenge to every PFA. The SIB and PIA rule books are ambiguous in some respects. The PFA needs to build up a good relationship with his or her client, a relationship which encourages frank discussion. This is not always easy to do.

FURTHER READING

DTI (1985): a detailed impartial report on the state of the industry in 1985. The basis for much of the later legislation.

Gower (1984): the key report which persuaded the government to act to protect investors in the UK.

Matatiko and Stafford (1985): a rather old book now, but unique in presenting developments in the UK economy which have impacted on personal saving, spending and investment.

Mitchell (1993): an excellent introduction to the basics of personal finance. Not an academic book. Intended as a do-it-yourself for those who would like to manage their own finances.

Vaitilingam (1993): a useful guide to the jargon of the financial world.

See bibliography on p.311 for a full annotation of these books.

TUTORIAL QUESTIONS: THE PERSONAL FINANCE PROFESSION

1. Why did financial institutions in the UK show the fastest rate of growth among large UK business organizations from 1960 to 1990?

2. The profession of personal financial advisers has also shown rapid growth in the UK in recent years. Are the reasons for the growth in this profession the same as the reasons for the growth of the financial institutions?

3. It has been claimed that 'All those so-called personal financial advisers are really just salesmen in disguise'. Do you agree? Why do you think that this complaint has been made? What is the essential condition that differentiates a PFA from a salesman (or saleswoman!)?

4. What are the two basic duties of a financial planner?

5. 'The job of a PFA is to devise a set of personal financial plans for clients'. Suggest six financial plans that a PFA might be asked to devise.

6. 'Income from an investment portfolio can be protected but not maximized.' Explain this statement.

7. What qualifications must be acquired before an individual can practise as an investment adviser in the UK?

8. Name four of the self-regulating organizations that monitor the operation of the financial markets in the UK. What specific activities in the financial market does each of these SROs monitor?

9. Describe the facilities provided to the public and to their members by any one of the 'old' professions such as medicine, law or accountancy? What structures, in your opinion, need to be set up to provide proper facilities for personal financial advisers?

10. How can an individual who is practising as a PFA keep up to date with the latest developments in personal finance?

11. Which self-regulating organization monitors the work of small-scale financial advisory firms in the UK?

12. What are the names of the two regulatory bodies which merged to form the PIA in July 1994?

13. What is the 'Investor's Compensation Scheme'? Why has this scheme come under such intense criticism by investment advisers in recent years?

14. Why is the 'contract letter' sent by an investment adviser to a client before taking on an engagement of such importance?

Suggested solutions to odd numbered questions are provided at the back of this book.

Personal finance record keeping

2

INTRODUCTION

One of the more difficult tasks faced by PFAs is to persuade the client to keep adequate financial records. Many clients are very busy people and for most clients at least one evening a month will need to be devoted to the job of maintaining an adequate set of financial records. The client must be persuaded to sacrifice this amount of time to enter the current financial transactions for that month into his or her financial records.

The sophistication of the financial records maintained by clients can vary all the way from simple annotation in pencil of the monthly bank and credit card statements to a full-blown computer-driven personal accounting system.

The key point which needs to be put across to a client is that the quality of advice provided by a PFA depends to a large extent on the adequacy of the information supplied to the PFA by the client. An up-to-date and comprehensive record of past financial transactions is very useful to the PFA trying to provide sound financial advice.

THE BASIC RECORDS THAT NEED TO BE KEPT

The financial records which need to be kept by individuals to control their financial affairs are very similar to the financial records which need to be kept by a small business.

The six basic sets of records which need to be maintained are:

1. A personal balance sheet of assets and liabilities.
2. An income and expenditure account for each period.
3. A long term cash flow budget.
4. A listing of current insurance contracts.
5. A file containing all current tax documents.

6. A copy of the pension scheme rule book.

THE CLIENT INFORMATION SHEET

Before collecting information about the client's financial affairs, a PFA is required by the PIA rules to collect information about the client's background. This covers the family situation, work situation and any special or unusual factors which might be relevant to devising a financial plan.

Exhibit 2.1 sets out a simple client information sheet which covers most of the key non-financial facts which need to be collected by a PFA.

THE BALANCE SHEET

Exhibit 2.2 sets out an example of a personal balance sheet. On one side is listed all of the assets owned by the client, on the other side is listed all the liabilities of the client. The difference between these two sides of the balance sheet represents the net worth or 'equity' or wealth of the individual. This net worth figure presents the PFA with a snapshot of the client's wealth at a given point in time.

Where assets of one class are made up of a number of items, for example a share portfolio composed of a number of different shares, only the total value of the portfolio should appear in the balance sheet. A breakdown of the individual list of shares should be shown in an accompanying schedule.

In order to prepare a balance sheet, the assets must first be identified and then valued. In some cases the valuation of an asset is easy – for example, it is easy to value a loan or a publicly quoted share,[1] in other cases the current value of an asset may be more difficult to measure. For example, the value of a share in a privately owned company or the value of a plot of land can present valuation problems. Insurance valuations may be helpful in estimating the value of assets of imprecise value. The PFA needs to remember that the relevant value to the client is the sale value if sold by the client, net of all selling costs. The value of the asset as listed in a sale catalogue supplied by a dealer is not the relevant value to use, since this is the value at which the dealer sells, not the value at which the dealer buys. Chapter 5 expands on this problem of valuing real assets.

There is less of a problem in valuing debts owed by the client, as these are invariably quoted in money value. The major types of debt are the mortgage debt incurred in buying a house and the bank loans or hire purchase loans taken on to buy consumer goods, for instance cars.

Apart from the family home, the major asset owned by most individuals consists of the cash-in value of their pension funds and insurance

---

[1] If the client has a micro-computer and a modem, his or her shares can be continuously updated in value by using a package such as 'Updata', which links into the stock exchange system via teletext.

NAME _____

ADDRESS _____
_____
_____

TEL. NO. _____

FAX _____

SEX

FEMALE		MALE	

DATE OF BIRTH

DAY	MONTH	YEAR

MARITAL STATUS

UNMAR.		MARRIED	
DIVORCED		WIDOW(ER)	

NAME OF SPOUSE (AGE) _____

CHILDREN

	NAME	SEX	BIRTHDAY
1.			
2.			
3.			

OCCUPATION _____

EMPLOYER NAME
         ADDRESS _____
_____

PARENTS STILL LIVING

FATHER	MOTHER
DATE OF BIRTH	DATE OF BIRTH

SPECIAL RESPONSIBILITIES

      HANDICAPPED RELATIVE _____
_____

      AGED PARENTS _____

      OTHER _____
_____

SOLICITOR: NAME _____
               ADDRESS _____
               TEL. _____

ACCOUNTANT: NAME _____
               ADDRESS _____
               TEL. _____

BANK: NAME _____
               ADDRESS _____
               TEL. _____

Exhibit 2.1   A client information sheet.

CLIENT: JOHN SWALES

PERSONAL BALANCE SHEET

	Current market value
Financial assets	
Liquid assets	
Cash	−1333
Building society deposit	25 000
Total liquid assets	23 667
Fixed interest stocks	
Govt stocks: see List A	36 541
Commercial bonds: see List B	15 329
Other: premium bonds	5000
Total fixed interest stocks	56 870
Equity stocks	
Equity shares: see List C	75 333
Total financial assets	155 870
Real assets	
House and land (Mortgage of £40 000)	220 000
Land: Site for holiday cottage in Wales	40 000
Other real assets: see List D	21 000
Total real assets	281 000
Total value of assets	436 870
Less: liabilities	
Endowment mortgage on house	40 000
Short term bank loans	5000
Hire purchase debts	750
Total value of liabilities	45 750
Net worth of Mr Swales (Equity) Pound Sterling	391 120

Exhibit 2.2   A personal balance sheet.

policies. We do not recommend evaluating these assets and placing them on a personal balance sheet. The temptation to cash in such assets can be very great at certain times in life and the consequences of such an action can be catastrophic for the financial future of the individual client. We suggest it is better to leave well alone.

Another valuation problem can arise from what are called 'contingent liabilities', such as future school fees. For example if the client's daughter is enrolled at a private school, then fees are likely to be paid in the future but are not legally committed. Until these payments become legal commitments they are best ignored in the balance sheet, although they must be included in any future long term cash flow budget.

THE INCOME AND EXPENDITURE ACCOUNT

Exhibit 2.3 sets out a typical income and expenditure account of a client for a given period. In this case the period chosen is one year.

In theory, income and expenditure accounts should be prepared once a month, consolidated monthly during the year into a cumulative statement to date and these totals compared to an income and expenditure budget consolidated up to this date. This control procedure is the ideal state of affairs but like most ideals it is seldom implemented. A monthly income and expenditure account which can be compared to the previous year should provide most clients with sufficient information to control their expenditures.

The precise classification of expenditures and income will depend on the particular characteristics of the client. A variation on the set of expenditures set out in Exhibit 2.3 should suit the majority of clients.

Income data should be listed gross of all deductions and these deductions such as tax and pension contributions, which should be listed separately to arrive at the net cash flow received into the client's bank account each month.

The usual sources of data on income are the monthly payslips from an employer and the dividend and interest vouchers from the paying organization. These must, by law, provide all of the relevant data on tax and other deductions. Collecting data on income is usually not a problem since most income is paid directly into the client's bank account.

The usual sources of data on expenditures are the monthly bank statement and the regular credit card statements received by the client. Most substantial payments nowadays are paid either by cheque or by regular bank payment, although it is not unknown for clients to pay many bills by cash, for tax reasons. If a client pays substantial sums in cash there can be problems in preparing accurate expenditure accounts. This topic touches on the delicate question of the honesty of the client, a subject we shall return to later.

NAME: JOHN SWALES

ANNUAL INCOME AND EXPENDITURE ACCOUNT 1992–1994 + BUDGET

		1992	1993	1994	Budget 1995
Income		Pounds Sterling			
Basic salary		42 000	48 000	55 000	60 000
Commission etc		13 500	14 100	17 740	14 000
Dividends and interest		6700	7400	8100	8530
Other income		540	720	870	900
Total income		62 740	70 220	81 710	83 430
Less:	Taxation	18 822	21 066	26 147	27 532
	Other deductions	5500	5700	6000	6500
Net cash inflow		38 418	43 454	49 563	49 398
Expenditure					
Mortgage (net of tax)		4400	4200	4000	4000
Household	Rates	800	1100	1200	1200
	Gas	1230	1476	1754	1800
	Electricity	582	603	660	700
	Food/Meals out	3720	4110	4237	4500
	Repairs	561	1448	754	800
	House insurance	550	597	684	684
	Security	600	600	600	700
	Other	593	619	631	700
Total household		8636	10 553	10 520	11 084
Transport	Fares	1800	1875	2040	2000
(Mr Swales has	Mrs Swales' car	2100	2300	3000	2500
a company car)	Car licence	120	120	140	140
	Petrol	385	402	420	500
	Insurance	230	270	330	400
	Repairs	120	430	220	300
Total transport		4755	5397	6150	5840
Communication					
	Postage	75	85	123	120
	Telephone	611	688	744	800
	Computer	311	750	320	600
Risk hedging					
	Insurance	430	430	430	430
	Medical care plan	321	333	375	402
Children		1800	4000	5000	5000
Personal	Clothing	2300	2000	2400	2400
	Holidays	3200	5334	4000	4000
	Entertainment	1788	1889	2000	2000
	Subscriptions	700	750	800	900
Sundry	Cash expenses	2400	2500	3000	3500
Total expenditure		31 727	38 909	39 862	41 076
Net saving		6691	4545	9701	8322

Exhibit 2.3 An income and expenditure account.

Clients should be encouraged to make all substantial payments through a bank account by cheque or by other bank payment. This procedure provides an automatic record of expenditures, while payment by credit card also provides some legal advantages. If the goods bought are not delivered or are defective in some way when delivered, the cardholder may be able to proceed against the credit card company.

THE LONG-TERM CASH FLOW BUDGET

The bottom line in personal financial control is the long term cash flow budget. A cash flow budget can be prepared for one month ahead, for one year ahead or annually for up to five years beyond the life expectancy of the client as estimated from actuarial tables. Exhibit 2.4 provides a set of life expectancy tables for men and women in the UK as at the end of 1990.

UK LIFE EXPECTANCY TABLES: 1990

	LIFE EXPECTANCY				MOST LIKELY LIFESPAN	
	MEN		WOMEN		MEN	WOMEN
AGE	YEARS	MONTHS	YEARS	MONTHS	AGE	AGE
20	53	4	57	6	73	77
25	48	7	52	10	73	77
30	43	11	48	1	73	78
35	39	3	43	6	74	78
40	34	6	38	10	74	78
45	30	0	34	3	75	79
50	25	7	29	9	75	79
55	21	6	25	5	76	80
60	17	6	21	2	77	81
65	13	11	17	2	78	82
70	10	9	13	6	80	83
75	8	1	10	5	83	85
80	5	11	7	7	85	87
85	4	3	5	6	89	90
90	3	0	3	10	93	93
95	2	2	2	9	97	97
100	1	9	2	1	101	102

The life expectancy table shows that a man retiring at 65 can expect to live for about 14 years and a woman retiring at 60 for 21 years.

However in recent years both men and women are tending to retire at around the age of 60. This can present a financial problem to the male retiree since the man will now live, on average, for 17.5 years. He may not have planned for this.

The problem is that inflation at about 5% can reduce the real value of a pension by one half in 15 years. It is essential to make an allowance for inflation in pension planning. Also see Exhibit 7.5.

Exhibit 2.4   How long can we expect to live?

The cash flow budget estimates the inflow and outflow of cash annually over the relevant period. Exhibit 2.5 sets out a 'lifetime' cash flow budget for a Mrs Margaret Gee, a 73-year-old widow with one married son. Her life expectancy at age 73 in 1995 is estimated to be some 12 years. The long-term cash flow budget runs to the year 2007 when Mrs Gee, if she survives that long, will be 85 years of age. We have assumed an average rate of inflation of 4% per annum.

The figures set out in Exhibit 2.5 can only be compiled after extensive discussion with the client. The PFA needs to find out about such things as the current income and net assets, the future expenditures, the likely date of retirement, the pension rights, the responsibility of the client for relatives and a host of other matters.

Preparation of a long-term cash flow budget is the most demanding job undertaken by a PFA on behalf of a client. The client also needs to be persuaded to undertake a great deal of work in collecting relevant financial and other information for the PFA.

Exhibit 2.5 is based on a 'most likely' scenario. In other words, it is based on a series of events which the client thinks are most likely to happen. The PFA will also, if they are wise, prepare several other scenarios based on less optimistic assumptions – the 'worst case' scenario being based on the assumption that the client will fall seriously ill or die in the near future, leaving several dependent relatives.

The number of scenarios prepared by the PFA depends, of course, on the amount of money the client is prepared to pay for financial advice. However, we shall find in Chapter 10 that the use of computer-based decision support systems can greatly reduce the chore of preparing different scenarios.

The preparation of a cash budget, month by month, for the year ahead is a much simpler task. If the client keeps good financial records this is a relatively easy job. This cash budget can then be used as a norm. As the actual financial data accrues month by month from the bank and credit card statements the actual income and expenditure can be compared to the 'norm' to throw up any substantial differences which will alert the client to impending cash flow problems. Any substantial items of expenditure which are known to be due during the coming year, such as a wedding or a new car or school fees, will be built into this annual cash flow budget.

Once the annual cash budget of income and expenditure has been completed, the estimated month-end surpluses or deficits can be examined to see if surplus money for investment will become available in any month or if future cash deficits need to be financed. Plans to invest the surplus cash can then be drawn up or alternatively plans can be made to finance the deficits out of the sale of assets or the acquisition of new debt.

BUDGETED ANNUAL LIFETIME CASH FLOW

Name:	Margaret Gee		
Occupation:	Retired		
Age:	73	Widowed	Children	1
Assumed inflation:	4% per annum		
Currency unit:	£		

Age	73	74	75	76	77	78	79	80	81	82	83	84	85
Year	1995	1996	1997	1998	1999	2000	2001	2002	2003	2004	2005	2006	2007
Income													
Pension	2500	2600	2704	2812	2925	3042	3163	3290	3421	3558	3701	3849	4003
Dividends	3700	3885	4079	4283	4497	4722	4958	5206	5467	5740	6027	6328	6645
Other income	3600	3816	4045	4288	4545	4818	5107	5413	5738	6082	6447	6834	7244
Total income	9800	10301	10828	11383	11967	12581	13228	13909	14626	15380	16175	17011	17891
Less:													
Tax	1960	2060	2166	2277	2393	2516	2646	2782	2925	3076	3235	3402	3578
Total deductions	1960	2060	2166	2277	2393	2516	2646	2782	2925	3076	3235	3402	3578
Gross cash flow	7840	8241	8663	9106	9574	10065	10583	11127	11701	12304	12940	13609	14313
Expenditure													
Accommodation	500	525	551	579	608	638	670	704	739	776	814	855	898
Repairs	800	840	882	926	972	1021	1072	1126	1182	1241	1303	1368	1437
Utilities	600	624	649	675	702	730	759	790	821	854	888	924	961
Food	1920	1978	2037	2098	2161	2226	2293	2361	2432	2505	2580	2658	2737
Transport	500	510	520	531	541	552	563	574	586	598	609	622	634
Clothing	500	500	500	500	500	500	500	500	500	500	500	500	500
House insurance	300	315	331	347	365	383	402	422	443	465	489	513	539
Rates	990	1030	1071	1114	1158	1204	1253	1303	1355	1409	1465	1524	1585
Recreation	900	909	918	927	937	946	955	965	975	984	994	1004	1014
Medical and health	300	330	363	399	439	483	531	585	643	707	778	856	942
Subs and gifts	200	200	200	200	200	200	200	200	200	200	200	200	200
Other	200	208	216	225	234	243	253	263	274	285	296	308	320
Total expenditure	7710	7968	8238	8521	8817	9127	9452	9792	10149	10524	10918	11332	11766
Net surplus/deficit	130	273	424	586	757	938	1131	1335	1551	1780	2022	2277	2546
Total surplus/deficit	130	403	827	1412	2169	3108	4239	5574	7125	8905	10927	13204	15750

Assumptions: It is assumed that the cash flow will remain constant after the age of 85

Exhibit 2.5 A lifetime cash flow statement.

The annual cash budget allows the client in consultation with his adviser to plan ahead and control the cash flow month by month.

Finally we should note that this approach to cash planning of comparing actual to budget is an ideal system which, alas, is seldom employed in practice at the personal planning level.

An alternative strategy might be for the PFA to keep these records on behalf of the client. This approach is employed by many small businesses which arrange for an accountant to prepare monthly accounts. Unfortunately the cost of such an approach is likely to be beyond the financial resources of all but a few seriously rich clients.

INSURANCE, TAX AND PENSION

The client should be encouraged to keep up-to-date files on all other basic financial records. These include insurance policies and past insurance claims, all documentation referring to tax matters, particularly the annual P60 salary form from the employer and any tax assessments, and a copy of the company or personal pension plan, including the latest rules and rights of the contributor.

KEEPING THE FINANCIAL RECORDS

Up till now we have discussed the records which should be kept by the client, but how are those financial records to be maintained and stored? What are the mechanics of record keeping?

There can be no possible doubt that if clients are computer literate then they should be encouraged to keep their personal financial records on a home computer. As we shall see below, computer-based records bring many advantages to both the client and the PFA.

Unfortunately the vast majority of clients, especially older clients, are not computer-literate and if the PFA insists on their learning about computers as a preliminary to keeping financial records, then few clients will keep these records.

A much simpler alternative, which may well be perfectly adequate, is to keep a set of annotated records on income and expenditures each month. This record can be created by simply annotating the individual items on the monthly bank and credit card statements and copying the totals onto a prepared income and expenditure sheet. If the bank and credit card statements are already well annotated by the bank then all that is required of the client is to scribble notes defining each item of income and expenditure onto the statements themselves and then totalling them by account into an income and expenditure sheet each month. Exhibit 2.6 illustrates an annotated bank statement.

NATIONAL BANK

Statement of account with National Bank Plc
Erewhon

Mr E. NOON
17 Arcadia Avenue
Erewhon
EW17 9RH

	Sheet Number	174

All entries to	30 Feb 97
Account No	56381

Date	Particulars	CODE	Payments	Receipts	Balance (When overdrawn marked OD)
					1489.92 Balance
1 Feb	BRITISH GAS	S/O	50		1439.92 Gas
	EREWHON MDC	D/D	55.2		1384.72 Rates
2 Feb		263	34.92		1349.80 Books
7 Feb	DALTON PLC	BGC		1977.39	3327.19 Salary
	EREWHON	C/P 1			
	DATE OF WITHDRAWAL	5 Feb	40		3287.19 Cash
		223	7		3280.19 Papers
15 Feb	BARCLAYS BANK	C/P 1			
	DATE OF WITHDRAWAL	14 Feb	30		3250.19 Cash
24 Feb	RTZ			175.88	3426.07 Dividends
		265	8.74		3417.33 Petrol
		266	29.5		3387.83 Shoes
30 Feb		267	3500		–112.17 Deposit (car)

The items and balance shown should be verified. Details of rates and calculations of any interest charged are available on request to this branch. The bank is not liable for loss or delay caused directly or indirectly by industrial action or by circumstances beyond its control.

Many clients do not have the time to prepare a monthly income and expenditure statement. Simply annotating the monthly bank and credit card statement can prove to be a simple but effective substitute. This data is posted from here to an income and expenditure classification sheet.

Exhibit 2.6   An annotated bank statement.

Formal systems of preparing such a set of manual records are offered by several publishers. For example Trakka Systems offers 'Money Trakka'. This manual system allows the user to keep records of all assets, liabilities, monthly income and expenditure, tax, insurance and pension details etc.

Listing income is less of a problem. Income can be easily listed from payslips, dividend and interest warrants. The income should be shown gross, with the deductions, mainly tax, listed separately.

The key point is to persuade the client to adopt a systematic approach to record keeping by listing the individual items of income and expenditure from the statements each month and then classifying them by account.

PERSONAL FINANCE COMPUTER PACKAGES

In recent years a wide range of pre-programmed computer packages have become available which make the job of keeping personal financial records a relatively painless process. The one essential precondition to using these systems is that the user is computer-literate. This simply means that the user is familiar with the basic processes of using a computer which is pre-programmed with a suitable package to achieve the required results – it does not mean that the user needs to be able to write a computer program.

The simplest approach to maintaining financial records on a computer is to use a spreadsheet program. These programs, much beloved by accountants, are designed to process numerical information easily. The best known spreadsheet packages are 'Lotus 1-2-3', 'Quattro' and 'Excel'. However, these are powerful and expensive programs which provide far more power than is needed for maintaining personal financial records. A shareware program called 'As-easy-as' is very much cheaper and is adequate for keeping personal financial records.

Exhibits 2.2 and 2.3 are examples of a balance sheet and income and expenditure account prepared using Lotus 1-2-3. Accounts prepared using any of the other spreadsheet packages mentioned would look much the same.

In recent years a series of computer packages have been on offer which are specifically designed to process personal financial records. These packages have already sold over eight million copies in the USA alone.

The best known of these personal finance packages which are available on the UK market are called 'Quicken', 'Microsoft money', 'Moneywise' and 'Moneybox'. The first two of these packages were developed in the USA but have recently been redesigned for the British market. Moneywise and Moneybox were developed in the UK.

Some of these packages were initially designed for small business bookkeeping, rather than for personal finance. We would recommend those packages such as Money and Quicken which are intended exclusively for the use of individuals to keep personal financial records rather than company accounts. However, clients who are running a small business can have two for the price of one if they buy Moneywise or Moneybox. Quicken can also be used by a very small business for keeping its accounting records. 'Moneysmith 3' is a shareware product which can be adapted to keep personal financial records.

Once the monthly data have been keyed into the computer and stored in the computer data base, an almost limitless range of financial schedules can be produced with very little effort. A few strokes on the keyboard can generate a current balance sheet and net worth, an investment schedule, a debt schedule, a cash flow statement, a bank reconciliation, an income and expenditure account between any two dates and even, in some cases, an estimate of income tax due or reclaimable to date!

'Money' provides a useful range of additional financial tools for calculating such things as choosing between different mortgage schemes, comparing loan terms, estimating the interest to be paid on an account and estimating retirement income under various assumptions plus an investment tracker to monitor a portfolio of shares.

Easy access to such a wealth of personal financial information is invaluable both to the client and to the PFA; however, all of this information is bought at a price. The catch is that the information needs to be keyed into the computer each month from the bank statement, credit card statement and other sources. This task will require the client to set aside at least a couple of hours a month. In addition the client must know how to handle a fairly sophisticated computer package. Personal finance computer packages are sold on their simplicity and user friendliness. To the computer buff it is all very simple, to the occasional computer user the instruction manual and operation of these programs might appear a formidable obstacle.

A client with a limited knowledge of computing should be advised initially to work with a cheap spreadsheet, which is very simple to use, and then to move on to a specialist financial computer package such as Money or Quicken. The writer understands that many personal finance computer packages are bought but not used.

Exhibit 2.7 provides some basic information on the attributes of some popular personal finance computer packages.

ADVANTAGES OF PERSONAL FINANCE COMPUTER PACKAGES

A computer-based personal finance recording system brings with it the following advantages.

1. A single entry of a transaction can update many separate but related files. This saves time and reduces recording errors.
2. The calculations are extremely rapid and accurate.
3. Access to quite complex patterns of financial information can be organized very rapidly by the computer-literate user. For example, long runs of data over many periods can be compared, and trends of income and expenditure identified.
4. The results of any financial analysis can be printed out very clearly and in a wide range of formats.
5. The computer hard disk provides a very compact store for all of the client's financial information. This can be quickly and easily copied onto a floppy disk for safe keeping.

NAME OF PACKAGE:	'Quicken'	'Money'	'Moneywise'	'Moneybox'
PRODUCER:	Intuit	Microsoft	Sage	Moneybox Software
APPROXIMATE PRICE:	£55	£30	£55	£40
SYSTEM CAPACITY NEEDED:	386, 2m RAM 5m hard disc	386, 2m RAM 3m hard disc	386, 2mRAM 5m hard disc	386, 2m RAM 3m hard disc
SUPPORT	Unlimited	30 days' unlimited	30 days then Sagecover available	Unlimited help available

FACILITIES PROVIDED BY THESE PACKAGES: (All of these packages do not provide all these facilities)	
	1 Six different account types can be maintained: bank, cash, credit card, assets, liabilities. Including shares and mortgage.
	2 Automatically enters regular payments such as direct debits.
	3 Produces balance sheet, income and expenditure account, net worth statement, monthly budget statement, cash flow and investment portfolio.
	4 Can reconcile bank statements with cheque stubs.
	5 Can work between any two dates.
	6 A single entry can update several accounts.
	7 A specific transaction can be accessed instantly.
	8 Data can be analysed into a wide range of patterns.

OTHER FACILITIES WHICH MAY BE AVAILABLE:	
	1 A cheque printing facility.
	2 A VAT summary can be produced monthly.
	3 A simple tax return can be produced (Quicken).
	4 A loan payment and mortgage calculator.
	5 A foreign currency conversion facility.
	6 Password protection.
	7 A facility for producing reports in graphic form.
	8 A Pension and saving planner.

The table illustrates some of the more important facilities provided by the various computer based personal finance planning packages.

Exhibit 2.7   Some personal finance computer packages.

The main disadvantages have already been noted.

1. The client must be computer-literate.
2. The data need to be keyed into the computer each month.
3. A safety regime needs to be worked out to preserve the data if the original computer files, or even the computer itself, are stolen or destroyed.
4. The records need to be preserved from prying eyes. In other words, some sort of simple security system, such as a password system or an encryption system, needs to be built into the program.

In conclusion, a computer-based personal finance recording system is much superior to alternative systems, but a price has to be paid in the form of the learning curve.

If the client finds the use of a computer a daunting prospect, then suggest a manual system like 'Money Trakka', which is comprehensive in its coverage.

WHAT HAVE WE LEARNED IN THIS CHAPTER?

1. Adequate financial records must be kept by a client if the client wants to receive regular useful financial advice from his PFA. The PFA may find that there can be problems in persuading a client to keep such records on a regular basis.
2. The five basic sets of records which need to be kept by a client are a balance sheet, an income and expenditure account, a long-term cash flow budget, and an up-to-date file of insurance contracts, tax and pension documents.
3. Valuing debts is easy. Valuing assets may present more of a problem. It is best to ignore the cash-in value of pension funds and insurance policies when calculating a client's net worth.
4. The simplest method of recording income and expenditure is to annotate monthly bank and credit card statements. This is the least a client can do. A computer-literate client may prefer to keep a full set of personal accounts using a personal finance computer package.
5. The bottom line in personal financial planning is the long term cash flow statement. A fully developed cash flow statement would estimate the major cash inflows and outflows of the client up to a date five years beyond his or her estimated lifespan. At least two cash flow statements should be calculated, one based on a 'most likely' scenario and the other based on a 'worst case' scenario. Cash flow statements can also be calculated for the immediate relatives of the client on the assumption of his death at different ages.
6. Personal finance computer packages bring many benefits to the user but to be able to use such packages the client must be both computer-

literate and willing to devote the time, at least one evening a month, to keying in the basic data. If the client is very rich, the PFA can arrange to personally keep the client's monthly financial records up to date.

FURTHER READING

Begg (1994).

See bibliography on p.311 for a full annotation of this book.

TUTORIAL QUESTIONS: PERSONAL FINANCE RECORD KEEPING

1. Suggest five basic records that need to be kept in order to monitor the financial affairs of a client.
2. The PFA needs to collect certain non-financial facts about a client before providing financial advice to the client. Which non-financial facts about a client do you think are important to a PFA?
3. What is meant by the financial 'equity' of an individual? How is this important figure calculated? What is another more commonly used word for the 'equity' of an individual?
4. A client owns 2000 shares in British Gas PLC, 1000 shares in a private company operating in Leeds and five acres of land in the Yorkshire Dales. How would you go about valuing these assets for your client?
5. Why are sale catalogue valuations not suitable for valuing the assets of clients?
6. Why is it not wise to put the cash-in value of a pension fund or assurance policy onto a client's balance sheet unless specifically asked to do so?
7. Suggest six major classifications of expenditure which should cover the bulk of the expenditures incurred by a client.
8. Two documents which provide information about the inflow of income to a client are a payslip and a dividend warrant. What financial information will be listed on these documents?
9. Why should clients be encouraged to make all significant expenditures using a cheque or credit card?
10. Why is the long-term cash flow budget the 'bottom line' so far as personal financial advice is concerned?
11. What was the life expectancy of a 45-year-old woman and of a 70-year-old man in 1990?
12. What key questions would a PFA need to put to a client before compiling a long-term cash flow statement?

13. If an annual cash flow budget identifies a substantial deficit at some point within the year, what are the alternative options available to the client to cover the deficit?
14. Suggest a simple system of monthly financial record keeping which would suit a client who cannot devote a great deal of time to the subject.
15. What tax records should the client keep to assist the PFA in the annual review of the client's affairs?
16. Suggest four key advantages provided to a client who keeps financial records on a personal computer rather than maintaining them by hand.
17. What are the key attributes of a personal finance computer package which might recommend them to a PFA?
18. Suggest two simple security systems that would assist in concealing from prying eyes the private financial records held on a computer.

Suggested solutions to odd numbered questions are provided at the back of this book.

The UK
financial system

3

THE GROWTH OF THE FINANCIAL INSTITUTIONS

A financial system provides many useful services to the community, but the efficient conversion of savings into investment is the primary one.

The United Kingdom has evolved one of the most sophisticated financial systems in the world. There are few financial products or services which are not offered within the square mile of the City of London. Every personal financial adviser needs to acquire a sound working knowledge of these products and services if he or she is to provide a worthwhile service to clients.

The most important change in the UK financial system over the last 50 years has been the increase in personal savings as a proportion of total saving. The rapid growth in recent years of the personal financial advice industry is a direct consequence of this development.

Before the Second World War, most of the saving in the UK was carried out by large companies, a few rich individuals and the government. Since 1945 in both the UK and all the other industrialized countries of the world, the bulk of saving has been provided by millions of small savers. For the first time in history the mass of the people have earned enough money to cover their basic needs whilst leaving a surplus which they do not need to consume immediately. This surplus is saved for use in the future. This significant social change has resulted in a quite dramatic shift in the way the UK financial system is organized.

Although the bulk of saving is effected by millions of small individual savers, these savers, unlike business or government, lack sufficient knowledge of finance to invest their own savings efficiently. All of these small funds of saving need to be consolidated and invested in such a way that the funds are secure and yet earn a reasonable return for the investor.

This gap in the knowledge of the small-scale saver has been filled by the evolution of large financial institutions and the advent of the personal financial adviser. Since 1945 there has been a dramatic increase in both the number and the size of those financial institutions which devote their energies to collecting and investing the savings of small scale savers. Exhibit 3.1 illustrates the growth in the size of the liabilities of the financial institutions in the UK between 1982 and 1992. Financial institutions have been around in the UK for over 400 years, but their growth and influence has increased out of all proportion in the last few years.

It should be noted that a large proportion of the regular savings made by the small-scale individual saver is compulsory saving, not voluntary

YEAR	1992	1992	1987	1982
ASSETS	£bn	%	£bn	£bn
Tangible assets	94	3.5	71	43
Financial assets				
Bank lending	914	34.5	629	373
Company securities	694	26.2	344	117
Deposits with banks	368	13.9	254	153
Government securities	106	4.0	95	63
Other assets	476	17.9	218	85
	2652	100.0	1611	834
FINANCIAL LIABILITIES	£bn	%	£bn	£bn
Deposits with banks	1291	48.7	863	532
Life assurance and pension funds	694	26.2	381	156
Deposits with building societies	216	8.1	137	68
UK company securities	143	5.4	91	31
Unit trust units	61	2.3	35	8
Bank lending	102	3.8	65	20
Other	145	5.5	39	19
	2652	100.0	1611	834

Note the substantial increase in the assets and liabilities of the financial institutions over this period. The substantial increase in the real wages of workers in the UK over the period since 1950 has provided a substantial surplus on incomes which can be saved. This surplus has been channelled into the insurance companies, pension funds and building societies. Thus the volume of funds controlled by these societies has expanded dramatically in recent years.

Source: *Financial Statistics*, HMSO, (various years).

Exhibit 3.1   The growth in the funds held by financial institutions.

saving. Compulsory saving is mainly effected via regular contributions to pension funds and insurance policies. The growth in the composition of personal savings in the UK from 1966 to 1991 is shown in Exhibit 3.6.

THE FINANCIAL INSTITUTIONS

Exhibit 3.2 shows the flow of long-term funds between the major financial institutions operating in the UK.

The financial institutions are conventionally classified into deposit taking institutions, provident institutions, institutions which manage portfolios of assets, and a disparate group of other financial institutions which provide a wide range of specialized financial services.

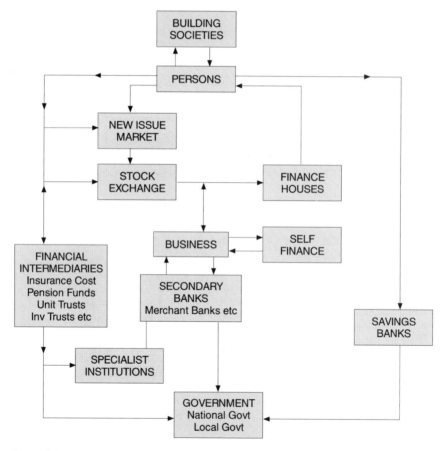

Most of the savings in the UK are generated by PERSONS. The savings are channelled through the financial institutions via the stock exchange to the business sector. The building societies and government also receive substantial amounts of personal saving.

Exhibit 3.2   The flow of long term funds through the financial institutions in the UK.

DEPOSIT-TAKING INSTITUTIONS

The major deposit-taking institutions in the UK are the commercial banks, which handle their customers' short-term deposits and also provide various types of loans and other financial services. The Bank of England is the government's banker and also keeps a watchful eye on the entire financial scene on behalf of the government. The discount houses play a specialized role in the money markets and the National Giro facilitates the rapid payment of bills between customers.

The secondary banks, for the most part, play a specialized role in the market which is of limited interest to the PFA, except that many of the merchant banks, which act as the PFA to many of the wealthiest people in the UK, manage large portfolios of securities on behalf of their clients.

Among the other deposit-taking institutions, by far the most important to the small investor are the building societies. The growth of the building society movement in the UK since 1945 is a remarkable story. These institutions, rather than the savings banks as in other countries, have become the main depository of the voluntary savings of small-scale investors in the UK.

Before 1985 the building societies, almost single-handedly, financed the remarkable growth in house ownership in the UK. The fact that they chose to pay variable rates of interest rates on their deposits and to charge variable interest on their loans appears to have been the key to their success. This strategy detached them from the wide swings in market interest rates which damaged the growth of some competing institutions both in the UK and elsewhere.

Hire-purchase companies are finance houses which take money on short-term deposit from business and lend it, mainly, to individuals, to assist in buying consumer goods.

PROVIDENT INSTITUTIONS

Insurance companies pool the risks faced by their customers and compensate those few who occasionally face losses out of the small payments of the many who pay the regular premiums. They also provide savings facilities for their customers. We shall expand on the important role played by the insurance companies in encouraging investment in Chapter 6.

The pension funds have accrued vast sums of money under their management. The trustees of these funds manage the investments on behalf of the many employees who make regular contributions into the funds. Some funds are managed by the companies who employ the contributors, other funds are farmed out and administered by independent specialist pension fund management groups, who may run many pension funds on behalf of many companies.

Lloyd's of London is a specialist insurance underwriter which operates through syndicates. It is famed for its ability to underwrite risks which other insurance companies are not prepared to accept. It has run into funding problems in recent years, however, because of the irresponsible underwriting policies pursued by the managers of a few maverick syndicates.

PORTFOLIO MANAGEMENT INSTITUTIONS

We noted above that some financial institutions manage pension funds on behalf of companies. Many organizations in the City of London specialize in administering large portfolios of securities. The best known of these are those which manage the funds invested in unit trusts and investment trusts. (Unit trusts are called 'mutual funds' in the USA.)

Following the end of the last world war in 1945, the unit trust pioneers devised an investment scheme which allowed the small private saver in the UK to invest in a diversified portfolio of equity shares at relatively low cost. It has been argued that the unit trusts diversify their portfolios too widely and churn their shares too much, but it cannot be denied that over the last 40 years or so the unit trust movement has protected their investors' interests against the ravages of inflation. Many other investment schemes failed to do this.

The investment trust concept is much older than that of the unit trust. Investment trusts were first set up in the nineteenth century to fund foreign ventures but have come to the fore as a popular saving medium in the UK only in recent years. An investment trust buys a fixed number and mix of shares and then sells further shares in this fund of shares to the general public. Investment trusts, unlike unit trusts, are allowed to 'gear' their portfolio – in other words, they can take on debt and use the debt to buy more shares for the fund. As in all gearing operations, if the equity shares bought earn a higher return than the interest paid on the debt, then the shareholders in the investment fund benefit; if not, the shareholders in the fund lose out. Investment trust shares are quoted just like any other share quoted on the Stock Exchange.

The basic idea behind both unit and investment trusts is to diversify the risk attached to any individual share among many shares. The specific risks attached to individual shares in the portfolio are diluted via diversification of the risk among all the shares in the portfolio. The current buying and selling values of unit trust units and investment trust shares can be found at any time by perusing the financial columns of the popular press.

OTHER SPECIALIZED FINANCIAL INSTITUTIONS

Many other specialized financial institutions have been set up in recent years, but few of these are likely to be of much interest to the PFA. Most of these institutions provide finance for sectors of the economy which might have difficulty in raising finance from conventional sources. One example of a specialist institution which might be of interest to the PFA is the venture capital company. These companies provide finance for small companies that wish to expand. Some private equity plans (PEPs) invest funds in such companies, so venture capital companies might be of interest to the PFA when devising a mix of investments for a client's portfolio. Venture capital shares are likely to be high-risk, high-return shares.

Other examples of specialized financial institutions are institutions which provide finance for farming, and for exports, the frontiers of technology, developing countries and so forth.

THE MAJOR FINANCIAL MARKETS

The two major financial markets in the UK, each of which is subdivided into several minor markets, are the capital market and the money market. The capital market provides long-term finance for loan periods beyond one year, while the money market provides short-term funds, mostly for periods of under one year.

The insurance companies, pension funds and building societies are the major providers of funds to the capital market. The commercial banks and the discount and finance houses are the major providers of finance to the short-term market.

The Bank of England, a sort of Big Daddy, looks after the financial interests of the government, keeps the system liquid and generally keeps a wary eye on the goings-on in all the many sub-markets within the UK financial system.

Foreign banks and institutions are playing an increasingly important role in the UK financial system. This has made the control and monitoring of the system much more difficult in recent years, since the culture of these institutions has proved to be very different from the traditional British financial culture.

CONTROLLING THE FINANCIAL MARKETS

A financial market will only be efficient if a proper control mechanism is in place which can detect fraud or gross negligence.

The Bank of England plays the key role in controlling the UK financial market. As we noted above, the Bank of England is the government's banker, supplying the government with adequate funding to meet its liabilities. The Bank is also a lender of last resort in the event of the banking system running short of liquid funds. Last but by no means least the Bank of England supervises and monitors the operation of the other institutions operating within the system, particularly the commercial banks.

By tradition, the various financial markets operating within the UK financial system have policed themselves. Most of the key players within the system have, in the past, worked within the golden square mile of the City of London, where everyone knew everyone else and dubious practices were quickly detected.

In the 1980s the UK market was opened up to foreign competition, and as a consequence this self-policing approach became subject to criticism. Under the provisions of the Financial Services Act of 1986 the Securities and Investment Board (SIB) was set up as a regulatory body. The SIB began functioning in 1988, and under its supervision a number of other self-regulating organizations (SROs) were established to set standards and identify fraud and gross negligence within the various subsectors of the UK financial market. Exhibit 3.3 illustrates the relationships and roles of these self-regulating organizations.

So far as the PFA is concerned, the two most important self-regulating bodies are the SIB and the Personal Investment Authority (PIA). The PIA was previously divided into two bodies, FIMBRA and LAUTRO. FIMBRA

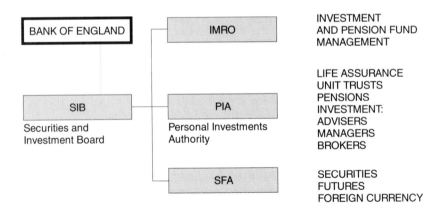

The UK financial market is regulated by a group of self-regulating organizations which monitor the proper operation of the market. These organizations are paid for by the institutions which they monitor.

The situation in the USA is quite different. There the Securities and Exchange Commission is an arm of the US government, paid for and monitored by the government of the day.

Exhibit 3.3 The self-regulatory organizations which monitor the financial markets in the UK.

monitored those who advise on, sell or manage investments, and LAUTRO monitored the sellers of life assurance and unit trust products. Now the PIA regulates all of these activities.

The operation of and the rules imposed by these two important regulators will be described in more detail in Chapter 11.

SERVICES PROVIDED BY THE FINANCIAL MARKETS

The financial markets provide a myriad of services to the community, but not all of these services will be of interest to the personal financial adviser. Exhibit 3.4 illustrates the wide range of financial services provided. We have classified these services into six groups: raising capital, managing funds, providing markets, absorbing risks, providing a payments mechanism and providing specialist financial advice.

FINANCIAL SERVICES PROVIDED TO INDIVIDUALS					
Raising Capital	Managing Funds	Financial Services	Providing Markets	Absorbing Risk	Payments Mechanism
House Mortgages	Funds Management	Taxation Advice	Stock Exchange	Insurance	Cheque Clearing
Consumer Durable Loans	Cash Management	Investment Advice	Estate Agency	Pensions Management	Giro Payment
Hire Purchase	Saving Schemes	Credit Advice	Forwards Futures Options Swaps	Forwards Futures Options Swaps	Credit Debit Cards
Leasing Assets	Trustee Management	Mortgage Advice		Guarantees	Banker's Drafts
		Pension Advice			Traveller's Cheques
		Insurance Broking			Electronic Payment
		Legal Advice			
		Property Advice			

This table illustrates some of the financial services provided to individuals by a fully developed financial market.

Exhibit 3.4   The range of services provided by the financial markets in the UK which can be used by PFAs.

RAISING CAPITAL

So far as the personal financial sector is concerned by far the most important providers of funds are the building societies and mortgage corporations which provide a wide variety of loans for the purchase of property.

The commercial banks provide a range of short-term loans for buying everything from freezers to holidays abroad, and finance companies provide hire purchase facilities for buying consumer goods, particularly motor cars and household goods.

Cars and other assets can be leased rather than bought via the facilities provided by leasing companies, but, for tax reasons, this facility is used more by business than by the private individual.

The PFA can provide useful advice to clients on how to select products and services from among the wide range on offer. For example, there are many types of mortgage products available. A mortgage needs to be matched to the particular needs of the client. Again, the cost of consumer credit varies a great deal between different sources of funds. The client should be encouraged to use their creditworthiness to reduce the cost of credit and should be warned, for example, that hire purchase is usually a very expensive source of funds because of the high proportion of defaults suffered in this line of credit.

MANAGING FUNDS

There are many institutions, most of them in the City of London, which are only too happy to manage a portfolio of assets for a regular management fee.

If a client does not wish to manage his or her own portfolio – usually the case – then the PFA can advise on the selection of a reliable portfolio fund manager, or possible the PFA is one of the few licensed to conduct this activity as well. The cost and competence of portfolio fund managers varies a great deal. Since comparative measures of performance of these firms are published regularly in the financial press and elsewhere,[1] the PFA should be able to find an institution suited to the particular needs of the client without too much difficulty.

PFAs can provide their own fund management service, but this requires a special licence from the PIA, who will require evidence from the applicant of competence in this type of work.

There is a school of thought which believes that, rather than investing the client's money in a managed fund of individual shares, the better policy would be to invest it in a 'tracker fund',[2] which mimics the All-

---

[1] See the computer-based financial information system, 'Micropal'. Rankings are published regularly in the magazine *Money Management* and elsewhere.
[2] See Chapter 5 for a more detailed discussion of the benefits or otherwise to be derived from investing in a 'tracker fund'. A list of such funds is provided in Exhibit 5.5.

Share Index. This reduces the cost of buying and selling shares which inevitably occurs with a managed fund, while providing an income not far short of that achieved in the managed fund. We shall return to the subject of tracker funds in Chapter 5.

PROVIDING MARKETS

If there are sellers and buyers around who wish to trade products such as ordinary shares, antique clocks, traded options or postage stamps, then one thing is certain: markets will develop in these products.

Markets are currently available in the UK for trading hundreds of financial and real assets. Unfortunately it is sometimes difficult for an outsider to access these markets directly – the outsider may have to trade through a broker, who will charge a fee.

Some markets are run in a specific place at a specific time; the best known of these are the auction markets such as Sotheby's, which trade art and antiques. Some markets do not exist in a physical sense, but are organized through brokers who put buyers in touch with sellers. The estate agent who organizes the buying and selling of houses provides a good example of this genre. The Stock Exchange in London, perhaps the best known of all markets, no longer trades from a specific location – the electronic revolution in communication has switched trading to the computer screen and the telephone. Some markets only exist in the advertisement section of a 'collectables' journal.

One of the more useful services which a PFA can provide to a client is to tell them if a market exists for trading in the range of assets owned by the client, where the market is found, how trading takes place and how much it costs to trade.

ABSORBING RISK

Risk is unavoidable. No matter how cautious a person may be, he or she will face risk; the future is always uncertain.

There are several financial institutions which have been set up to absorb this risk factor from the individual. In return for a fixed regular premium, the individual passes the uncertain risk of loss to a much more wealthy institution which is better able to bear the cost of misfortune, should it arise.

Insurance companies are not the only institutions designed to absorb risk, but they are the oldest and the biggest. The insurance company organizes a large group of persons who pool their individual risks at a relatively small individual regular cost. Relative to the cost of the possible misfortune which might occur to the individual, the cost of insurance is usually quite small. The annual cost of insurance seldom exceeds 2% of the estimated value of the asset insured, although exceptions to this rule exist. The insurance cost depends on the calculations made by the insurance actuary and the insurance underwriter regarding the risks and the costs involved.

Chapter 6 is devoted to a description of the various aspects of insurance which should be of interest to the PFA.

There are other risk absorbers operating in the financial market. Banks and some other institutions will, for a fee, absorb risk by providing guarantees on the due performance of certain acts by their customers. Such guarantees are sometimes needed when, for example, one is renting accommodation or trading abroad. The pension funds and insurance companies also absorb risk by guaranteeing such things as the minimum value of a pension to be received from a certain age.

Other risk absorbing institutions exist, but they are less likely to be of interest to the PFA. For example, the markets which trade derivatives, such things as options, forwards, futures and swaps, are directly concerned with absorbing risk and may be recommended as a hedging device by the PFA in certain circumstances – for instance, to cover the foreign exchange risk attached to a foreign loan. See Galitz (1994).

PROVIDING PAYMENT MECHANISMS

One important recent development in the UK financial market has been a growth in the number of mechanisms available to the individual for paying bills. Thirty years ago, except for foreign transactions, the individual buyer could choose between only two methods of payment, cash or cheque. Today, the choice includes a wide range of payment mechanisms including cash, cheque, giro payment, credit card, debit card, bankers order or traveller's cheque.

Since the cost and security of payment varies a great deal between these methods, the PFA needs to be aware of the advantages and disadvantages of each payment method. For example, if payment is made by credit card, certain advantages accrue to the buyer since the seller cannot receive cash until the goods are dispatched to the buyer, and when using some credit cards, insurance of considerable value is provided free if the product or service is charged to the card. Sometimes, however, a cash discount is lost if payment is made by credit card. The debit card removes money from the buyer's account much more quickly than a cheque or credit card.

There are many factors to consider when deciding on the payment mechanism to use. The cost of paying bills in a foreign currency is a particularly treacherous subject. The costs are high and vary widely between the different methods available. Giro payment is usually the cheapest method of payment.

The payment mechanism employed by a debtor is not a trivial matter.

SPECIALIST FINANCIAL ADVICE

In addition to the range of services discussed above there is a veritable raft of services available to the PFA seeking specialist advice. As shown in Exhibit 1.1, no PFA can possibly be expert in every aspect of personal finance. From time to time the PFA will need to consult with other specialists in the field. The successful PFA will, over the years, build up a network of contacts who can provide advice on topics as diverse as inheritance tax, split-level trusts, loss of employment insurance and even such arcane matters as the taxation of trusts and the current state of the market in netsuke.

Taxation is the most common topic on which advice is sought. It is difficult to keep up to date with personal tax legislation unless one devotes one's whole professional life to this topic. The PFA needs to acquire a sound grasp of personal tax but it is probably a wise precaution to ask a specialist tax adviser to check out any personal financial plan for tax efficiency before it is finalized.

Advice on legal matters is another area where the PFA must seek help. Stockbrokers are available for providing information on the latest stock market trends, estate agents can advise on trends in the housing market and mortgage availability, insurance brokers can provide advice on the latest and most economical insurance schemes, and so on.

However, it is best to shop around for advice from several sources before opting for any particular course of action. The advice from some specialist advisers may not be impartial – some products pay a higher commission than others.

THE PERSONAL SECTOR BALANCE SHEET

THE ASSETS

Exhibit 3.5 shows the balance sheet of the entire personal sector in the United Kingdom for some recent years. The figures are estimates prepared by the government's statistical department.

Note that the total value of assets owned by individuals in the UK is almost equally divided between real assets and financial assets.

Almost 90% of the value of real assets owned by individuals in the UK consists of property. The breakdown of financial assets is more interesting.

We note that in 1992 insurance and pension rights made up 27% of the total assets and 50% of the value of financial assets owned by private individuals. These rights are not accessible, at least they are not accessible except at a high cost. They only become accessible when the individual reaches a certain age or a specific event occurs, for example retirement or death.

Deposits in building society accounts are the financial asset of next highest value, at 13%. These assets are normally accessible quickly and provide the personal sector with a useful source of liquidity.

PERSONAL SECTOR BALANCE SHEET

	1976	1986	1992
	£b	£b	£b
Real Assets			
Residential Buildings	142.3	620.6	1091
% of Total Assets	42.9	42.3	41.9
Other	38.1	96.9	122
% of Total Assets	11.5	6.6	4.7
Total Real Assets	180.4	715.5	1213
% of Total Assets	54.4	48.9	46.5
Financial Assets			
Insurance & Pensions Funds	41.5	329.2	704
% of Total Assets	12.5	22.5	27.0
Building Society Deposits	25.8	115.5	187
% of Total Assets	7.8	7.9	7.2
Shares	19.5	91.1	144
% of Total Assets	5.9	6.2	5.5
Unit Trusts	1.8	16.7	24
% of Total Assets	0.5	1.1	0.9
Govt Securities	5.9	23.8	18
% of Total Assets	1.8	1.6	0.7
Bank Deposits	20.7	71.8	168
% of Total Assets	6.2	4.9	6.4
Nat Savings	8.5	33.1	43
% of Total Assets	2.6	2.3	1.7
Trade Credit	8.4	28.0	44
% of Total Assets	2.5	1.9	1.7
Other	19.3	39.4	61
% of Total Assets	5.8	2.7	2.3
Total Financial Assets	151.4	748.6	1393
% of Total Assets	45.6	51.1	53.5
Total Assets	331.8	1466.1	2606.0
Financial Liabilities			
Housing Loans	29.0	154.0	338.9
% of Total Liabilities	60.7	64.2	69.5
Bank Loans	6.1	44.1	83.1
% of Total Liabilities	12.8	18.4	17.0
Trade Credit	7.7	24.0	38.3
% of Total Liabilities	16.1	10.0	7.8
Other	5.0	17.6	27.6
% of Total Liabilities	10.5	7.3	5.7
Total Liabilities	47.8	239.7	487.9
Net Personal Sector Wealth	284.0	1226.4	2118.1
Gross Domestic Product	124.7	378.8	596.2

	1976	1986	1992	% increase in ratio 1976–92
Net Personal Sector/GDP	2.3	3.2	3.6	56.0%
Total Assets/GDP	2.7	3.9	4.4	64.3%
Financial Assets/GDP	1.2	2.0	2.3	92.4%
Residential Buildings/GDP	1.1	1.6	1.8	60.4%

Source: *UK National Accounts* (Blue Book) (various editions, 1989–93)
Publisher: CSO HMSO

Exhibit 3.5   The balance sheet of the personal sector in the UK economy.

The asset of next highest value is investment in shares and related assets. When unit trusts are included, this accounts for 12% of financial assets. Most of these shares are represented by the shares of public companies quoted on the London Stock Exchange. Considering that shares account for only 12% of financial assets, and a mere 6.4% of all privately owned assets, it seems that the UK has a long way to go before it can truly be called a share-owning democracy.

The only other substantial investment by the personal sector is the money placed on bank deposit. This again accounts for around 12% of financial assets. A substantial proportion of these deposits are held as liquid funds which can be accessed reasonably quickly in an emergency.

If we study the trend in asset holding by the personal sector in the UK from 1976 to 1992, we find that there have been some shifts in the mix of asset ownership over the period. The proportion of the value of assets held in the form of real assets has fallen because of the fall in the relative value of 'other real assets', such as cars, furniture and so on. The proportion held in the form of financial assets has increased from 45% to 53% over the 16-year period. This is the result of the substantial increase in the relative value of insurance and pension funds built up cumulatively over the period. It is worth noting that these funds have been built up mainly by compulsory, rather than voluntary, saving. The proportion of personal wealth held in the form of National Savings and holdings of government stock has halved over the period.

We conclude that the composition of the asset portfolio of the personal sector in the UK in recent years has moved gradually into financial assets and away from real assets. The proportion invested in housing, however, has remained stable. The only major change has been a substantial increase in the proportion of total assets invested in insurance and pension funds.

FINANCING OF THE ASSETS

Since housing is the major asset held by the personal sector it is not surprising to find that housing loans make up the largest portion of the financial liabilities of the personal sector, at 70% of total liabilities. Bank loans are also substantial, accounting for a further 17%. Trade credit, including hire purchase, accounts for a mere 8% of the liabilities of the personal sector.

The trend over the period shows an increase in housing loans and bank loans and a fall in trade credit.

THE NET WORTH OF THE PERSONAL SECTOR

If we deduct the liabilities of the personal sector from the assets owned by it, we find that the net worth or 'equity' of the personal sector comes to the substantial sum of £2118 billion. That is around £38 000 for each person in the UK.

The British people own a substantial stake in their own country. The duty of the PFA is to help these many stakeholders to look after the value of their individual stakes.

PERSONAL SAVING AND CONSUMPTION

Exhibit 3.6 sets out the total income, savings and expenditures of the personal sector for selected years between 1966 to 1991. These figures are not adjusted for inflation, since we wish to concentrate on the ratios between the amounts spent and saved.

UK Personal Income, Savings and Consumption 1966–91

Code	Personal Disposable Income	Consumers' Expenditure	Total Personal Savings (PDI – CE)	Contractual Saving
	PDI	CE	TPS	CS
Year	£1 000 000			
1966	26629	24195	2434	1147
1969	31731	29154	2577	1464
1974	55733	53781	1952	921
1979	122988	119949	3039	2426
1984	208266	203468	4798	4472
1989	341778	347570	–5792	8098
1991	403999	393461	10538	9759

Ratio	CE/PDI %	TPS/PDI %	CS/PDI %	NCS/PDI %
1966	90.9	9.1	4.3	4.8
1969	91.9	8.1	4.6	3.5
1974	96.5	3.5	1.7	1.8
1979	97.5	2.5	2.0	0.5
1984	97.7	2.3	2.1	0.2
1989	101.7	–1.7	2.4	–4.1
1991	97.4	2.6	2.4	0.2

Note the sharp decline in voluntary savings in 1989. This phenomenon was due to the sharp rise in nominal house prices during this period. Note also the steady increase in, and importance of, contractual savings during the period.

PDI = Total personal income less tax and social security contributions

CE = All expenditure by persons

TPS = PDI less consumers' expenditure

CS = Contributions to contractual pension schemes and life assurance schemes

NCS = Non-contractual saving (i.e. voluntary savings)

Source: CSO Blue Books 1966–93: HMSO

Exhibit 3.6   The growth of personal income, savings and expenditure in the UK 1966–91.

We note that the ratio of consumers' expenditure to personal disposable income (CE/PDI) has remained relatively stable over the 25-year period, the extremes being 90.9% in 1966 and 101.7% in 1989.

On the other hand, the ratio of non-compulsory savings to personal disposable income (NCS/PDI) shows some fluctuation over these same years. Had it not been for the stability of contractual saving over the period, the savings ratio would have fluctuated more widely. The sudden jump in house prices between 1984 and 1989 seems to have been the major cause of the fall in voluntary saving in 1989. The substantial rise in the value of their homes, allied to the fixed money value of the mortgages financing the home purchase, seems to have persuaded many home-owners to forgo saving and take part in a spending spree during this period.

The proportion of total personal saving which is contractual seems to be increasing year by year in the UK – a fortunate circumstance, since it will stabilize the savings ratio in the years ahead.

HOUSEHOLD EXPENDITURE IN THE UK

Exhibit 3.7 provides details of the changing pattern of household spending in the UK between 1976 and 1990.

We note that the proportion of total expenditure spent on food, alcohol, tobacco, clothing and fuel has declined over the period, tobacco and food quite markedly so. Only the proportion spent on housing, transport and the catch-all category 'other goods and services' has increased.

Item of Expenditure	Year			
	1976	1981	1986	1990
	%	%	%	%
Food	19.2	16.3	14	12.7
Alcohol and Drink	7.6	7.3	6.9	6.6
Tobacco	4.1	3.6	3.2	2.7
Clothing and Footwear	7.7	6.7	7.1	6.1
Housing	13.6	14.9	15.5	14.5
Fuel and Power	4.7	5.1	4.6	3.7
Household Goods and Services	7.6	6.9	6.7	6.7
Transport and Communication	15.4	17.2	17.1	18.4
Recreation and Education	9.2	9.4	9.4	9.3
Other Goods and Services	10.8	12.5	15.5	19.4
Totals	100	100	100	100

The expenditure pattern of households has remained surprisingly steady over the 15 year period. Only the proportion spent on transportation and 'other goods and services' has risen by a substantial amount. The proportion spent on food and alcohol has fallen and most other forms of expenditure have remained constant. Note that the percentage spent on housing has not risen by as much as might have been expected.

Exhibit 3.7   A detailed analysis of household expenditure in the UK.

CONCLUSIONS

The UK has developed one of the most sophisticated financial markets in the world. PFAs need to know the characteristics of the various products offered by this market if they are to provide competent advice to clients.

An efficient financial market should provide a safe haven for savings, an efficient method of converting these savings into investment, a mechanism for hedging risks, a set of markets for trading financial instruments and real assets, a payments mechanism and last but by no means least a mechanism for controlling and monitoring these interlocking systems. The UK financial market provides the community with both a long-term capital market and a short-term money market.

A plethora of financial services is available to assist PFAs in constructing financial plans for their clients.

An efficient PFA will build up a network of contacts to supplement their own knowledge of the workings of the financial system. No single person can hope to be expert on the vast field of knowledge now required by a PFA when called upon to design an efficient personal financial plan.

WHAT HAVE WE LEARNED IN THIS CHAPTER?

1. The primary function of a financial market is to convert savings into investment. In the UK there has developed one of the most efficient financial systems in the world.
2. The financial institutions in the UK can be classified into deposit-taking institutions, provident institutions, institutions which manage large portfolios of financial assets, and other specialized financial institutions which assist farmers, entrepreneurs etc.
3. The two major financial markets which have evolved in the UK are the money market, which handles short term money, and the capital market, which handles long term investment.
4. By tradition the UK financial market is self-regulating – there is no government watchdog like the SEC in the USA. However, the Bank of England keeps a wary eye on all financial markets in the UK on behalf of the government. The major watchdog in the UK is the SIB, which watches over the PIA, IMRO and the SFA. The PIA is now the main self-regulating body which is empowered to monitor those who advise on personal finance.
5. The financial markets provide a wide range of services which are useful to both the PFA and their clients. These markets can assist in raising capital, managing investment portfolios, providing markets to buy and sell financial products, absorbing risk from the client and providing a wide range of payment mechanisms.

6. The major assets held by the personal sector are housing, insurance and pension rights, shares and building society deposits. The major change in the composition of the assets of the personal sector in the last 15 years has been the rise in the value of insurance and pension rights. Housing loans and bank loans make up the bulk of the financing of the personal sector. The proportion of total debt owing to trade creditors has declined in recent years.
7. The net worth of the personal sector in the UK is around £2000 billion – a substantial sum.
8. The ratio of consumers' expenditure to personal disposable income has remained relatively stable over the past 25 years. However, the percentage of income saved has fluctuated quite widely. This may have been influenced by the wild gyration in house prices in the late 1980s. The proportion of total saving which is contractual is increasing year by year.

FURTHER READING

DTI (1985): a detailed impartial report on the state of the industry in 1985. The basis for much of the later legislation.
Gower (1984): the key report which persuaded the government to act to protect investors in the UK.
London Business School (1993): a study of the costs of regulating the UK financial system, including a comparison with the cost of regulation in some other countries such as the USA and France.
Matatiko and Stafford (1985): a rather old book now, but unique in presenting developments in the UK economy which have impacted on personal saving, spending and investment.

See bibliography on p.311 for a full annotation of these books.

TUTORIAL QUESTIONS: THE UK FINANCIAL SYSTEM

1. Explain why the financial institutions have grown to such a size in the UK and in most other industrialized countries in the last 40 years.
2. A financial market provides at least six basic services to the community it serves. What are these six basic services? Give one example of the type of service provided in each class.
3. Financial institutions are conventionally classified into four groups. What are these four groups? State which groups the following institutions would fall into: an insurance company, a building society, a hire purchase company, an investment trust.
4. What are the main differences between the operation of a unit trust and an investment trust? How are unit trust units and investment trust shares encashed?

5. The financial markets in the UK are divided into two basic sectors. What are these two sectors? What is the basic function of each of these sectors?

6. What role is played by the Bank of England in the UK financial market?

7. What principle of regulation is traditionally employed in the UK financial market? What is the role played by an SRO in this control process? Which SRO is most likely to monitor the work of a PFA?

8. Fewer and fewer markets are now sited in a specific location. Why is this so?

9. Describe three financial organizations which operate in the UK that are designed to absorb risk from the individual. What device does each of them sell to absorb the risk?

10. What advantages accrue to a debtor who pays a bill by using a credit card rather than a cheque?

11. Describe three rights given to the owner of (a) an equity share, (b) a bond, (c) a deposit in a building society.

12. What is meant by the word 'networking' as used in the personal financial advice industry? Give three examples of networking.

13. What are the main types of personal assets owned in the UK? What is the breakdown of these assets between real and financial assets? Can you identify any major changes in the pattern of personal asset ownership between 1976 and 1992? What proportion of the personal assets held in 1992 is liquid assets? Can you identify any major changes in the pattern of the personal financial liabilities over the period 1976 to 1992? (Study the tables provided in the chapter.)

14. How did the ratio of total housing loans to the market value of houses change in the UK between 1976 to 1992? Is this change in the ratio likely to have an effect on personal spending in the period since 1992? Why do you think house values in the UK jumped so dramatically between 1984 and 1989?

15. The Conservative government in the UK has made much of the 'great expansion in share ownership from 1980 to 1990'. How important are equity shares in the asset base of a typical British family? What percentage of the income of a typical British family comes from dividends on shares? (Typical annual gross UK household income in 1993 = £19 000.)

16. What was the value of the total wealth owned by the British people in 1992?

17. Use the tables provided in the chapter to answer the following questions:
    (a) It has been claimed by the Conservative government that the income of individuals in the UK rose in real terms by 20% over

the period 1980 to 1990. What effect did this increase have on personal saving and personal expenditure over the period?

(b) What role does contractual saving play in total personal savings in the UK economy?

(c) Why do you think that voluntary saving fell by such a large margin in 1989?

18. Look at Exhibit 3.7. How has the spending pattern of the British people changed over the period? Can you think why these changes have taken place?

Suggested solutions to even numbered questions are provided at the back of this book.

Personal
taxation

4

THE IMPORTANCE OF PERSONAL TAXATION IN FINANCIAL PLANNING

Personal taxation is a very important aspect of personal financial planning. The reason for this is that certain personal expenditures can be charged against personal tax and so, in effect, the government contributes towards the cost of the good or service bought with this expenditure. In addition most forms of personal income are taxed by the government at different rates, and certain types of income are zero-rated. If the taxpayer can alter his or her tax situation so that a lower rate of tax is applied to their income, substantial savings can be achieved.

The rates of tax applied to personal income in the UK vary between 15% and 40% of the income received, thus by suggesting a suitable tax stratagem, the PFA can reduce the tax bill of the client by a substantial margin.

For example, if £100 000 is invested at 8% per annum then £8000 a year, gross of tax, is earned from the investment. However, if the £100 000 is invested in a lump sum pension fund in such a way that the £100 000 can be charged against income which is being taxed at the highest rate of tax – 40% – then a tax refund of £40 000 will be received by the taxpayer over time. This rebate of tax reduces the cost of the investment to only £60 000. The gross income is still £8000, so the annual rate of return is increased from 8% to 8000/60 000 = 13.3% – a substantial increase in return on the original 8%.

Another example of a possible tax saving arises if a husband leaves to his wife an estate worth £500 000. In such a case, probably no inheritance tax is paid. If the wife dies soon after her husband and leaves her estate to her children, then £(500 000 – 154 000) × 40% = £138 400 tax is payable in inheritance tax. The children inherit £361 600. If, on the other hand, the husband, on his death, leaves £154 000 of his estate to his children and £346 000 to his wife then still no death duties are payable, but when his wife dies only £(346 000 – 154 000) × 40% = £76 800 is paid in inheritance tax. The children inherit £423 200 between them – a saving of £61 600 in tax compared to the first option.

The rules of tax can be quite complex; the taxation of foreign income is particularly complex.

Every PFA must have a sound knowledge of the personal tax regime which is applied in the country in which he or she is operating, but it is difficult for a PFA to keep up to date with all of the continuously changing minutiae of personal taxation. The laws and rules of personal taxation are in a state of perpetual flux, and even tax specialists have difficulty in keeping up to date with all the latest changes in the tax laws, allowances and regulations.

Personal and company taxation is an eternal battle between the tax inspectors and the tax consultants. The government of the day introduces some new tax legislation, often to plug loopholes in the existing tax law, and the tax consultants immediately get to work on the new legislation to find ingenious new loopholes to save their clients money.

It is difficult for anyone who does not devote their full time and energy to tax matters to keep up to date with all their ramifications. Thus, although a PFA must know the basic law of the land and rules with regard to tax on personal income, expenses and assets, he or she may well consider it a prudent policy to work in association with a full-time tax specialist when designing personal financial plans for clients. The PFA should design a set of plans, including basic tax optimization, and then hand these plans over to a personal tax specialist to fine tune them for maximum tax efficiency. The question is whether the same planning objectives can be achieved at lower cost by utilizing a more subtle tax strategy.

Reducing the tax liability of a client to a minimum figure is a perfectly legal activity – there is nothing wrong with avoiding tax legally. Anyone who pays more tax than they need to pay is either a saint or a fool. A competent PFA must know the basic rules of calculating a client's tax liability and also be aware of the better-known and lawful stratagems available for reducing the client's tax bill. However, the PFA must guard against devising plans which are exclusively tax-driven. For example, a PFA must not put a client into an unsuitable, high-risk investment scheme just because it provides large tax benefits if it is otherwise unsuited to the client's needs.

Tax evasion on personal income which is legally subject to UK tax is, of course, illegal and punishable with high fines and possible imprisonment. Some investment schemes, particularly some foreign-based tax schemes, walk a narrow tightrope between legal tax avoidance and illegal tax evasion. This grey area has been called 'tax avoision'.

PERSONAL TAX IN THE UK: INCOME TAX

There are three types of personal tax paid by those persons domiciled in the UK: income tax, capital gains tax and inheritance tax.

Let us first examine income tax.

The Inland Revenue allocate personal income into several classes or schedules, each schedule being treated rather differently by the tax authorities. The various schedules of income as defined by the tax authorities are set out in Exhibit 4.1. The class to which a source of income is allocated can be a matter of some importance. For example, earned income is given more tax concessions than unearned income.

Certain types of income are not subject to any form of tax in the UK. These types, which are few, are listed in Exhibit 4.2. The reasons for the exemption from tax are varied. In the case of PEPs, TESSAs and SAYE, the government exempts these sources of income from tax because it wishes to encourage share ownership or saving by persons with lower incomes. Most of the other cases would either involve double-taxation of the same income – maintenance payments, for example – or tax being charged on persons with very low incomes who would pay little or no tax in any case.

Schedule	Definition
A	Income from land and buildings including rents
B	Abolished in 1988
C	Income from government securities
D	Divided into six cases:
Case 1	Trades
Case 2	Professions and vocations
Case 3	Interest received, annuity payments, annual payments
Cases 4 and 5	Overseas income from investments and business income
Case 6	Any other profits not included in other cases
E	Wages and salaries
Case 1	Work done in UK by UK resident
Case 2	Work done in UK by non-UK resident
	Work done abroad by UK resident. Income paid in UK
F	Dividends and other distributions paid by companies

The schedule under which income is taxed is important since the allowances and concessions differ between schedules. Items allowed against tax under Schedule D may not be allowed against tax under Schedule E.

Exhibit 4.1   Classes of income as defined by the Inland Revenue.

Type of income exempt from tax

1. Compensation for loss of office (up to £30 000).
2. Covenanted payments made under a voluntary non-charitable deed of covenant (but many restrictions apply).
3. Dividends paid out of personal equity plans (PEPs).
4. Interest from save as you earn schemes (SAYE).
5. Interest on National Saving certificates.
6. National Savings bank interest up to £70 per annum.
7. Rent received from a tenant under the 'rent a room tax free' scheme.
8. Payments in kind so long as the employee is earning less than £8500 per annum.
9. Interest paid under a tax exempt saving TESSA scheme.
10. Maintenance payments, e.g. alimony, made under a court order.
11. Scholarship income while studying.
12. Social security benefits received.

The table lists most of the important types of income which are not subject to tax in the UK. The reasons for the exemptions is either that the government wishes to encourage this type of investment or that the money is taxed once already or that the money is paid to poor people by the government to provide a reasonable standard of living and to tax it would be silly.

Exhibit 4.2   Income not subject to tax in the UK.

Once the total world income of an individual from all sources has been calculated, certain tax 'allowances' are available which can be set off against this total, to arrive at the 'taxable income'. The current allowances which can be offset against earned income are listed in Exhibit 4.3.

Various rates of tax are then applied to each ascending 'slice' of 'taxable income'. These rates are changed quite frequently; at the time of writing they were:

On the first £3200, a rate of 20% is charged

On the next £24 300, a rate of 25% is charged

On the remainder, a top rate of 40% is charged.

These rates are likely to change in the future.

The top rate of tax paid by a taxpayer is important. This rate is called the 'marginal' rate of the taxpayer, and many tax allowances can be set off against income at this top marginal rate. For example, at one time mortgage interest on any size of loan was allowed as a charge against income tax at the taxpayer's marginal rate. Thus when the top rate of income tax was 60%, as it was at one time in the past in the UK, a mortgage on which interest was charged at 10% per annum effectively cost the taxpayer on a high income only $10\% \times 0.4 = 4\%$ per annum! Some

	Value 95/96	Value 94/95
Personal Allowances	£	£
Age below 65 years	3525	3445
Age 65–74 (1)	4630	4200
Age 75 and over (1)	4800	4370
Married Couples Allowances		
Age of elder spouse below 65 (2)	1720	1720
Age of elder spouse 65–74 (2)	2995	2665
Age of elder spouse 75 and over (2)	3035	2705
Other Allowances		
Widow's bereavement allowance (2)	1720	1720
Personal allowance for child (2)	1720	1720
Blind person's allowance	1200	1200
Inheritance tax exempt limit	154 000	150 000
Capital gains tax exempt limit	6000	5800
Age allowance income limit	14 600	14 200

(1) Excess above the basic personal allowance is reduced by 50% of income above £14 600 adjusted for reduction made in the personal allowance because income exceeds £14 600.

(2) Tax relief is restricted to the 15% tax rate band for these allowances in 95/96. The maximum PEP investment allowed is £6000 in any one year.

The Table shows some of the allowances which can be set against the taxable income of the individual for the tax years 1995–96 and 1994–95. These allowances will reduce the tax charge.

How the values of these allowances are calculated is a profound mystery to tax experts. The allowances for bereavement and blindness seem derisory.

Exhibit 4.3   Some income tax allowances for tax years 1995–96 and 1994–95.

single payment pension plans allow the lump sum premium to be charged against current income tax at the highest 40% marginal rate.

A typical personal tax computation is set out in Exhibit 4.4. Ms Walthorn earns an annual salary of £40 000, interest on government stock of £4000 paid gross of tax, £6650 of dividends paid net of tax at 25%, plus a rent of £6000 from Mr Amble, a lodger in her home. Her total income subject to tax is thus £56 650. She is allowed to deduct a personal allowance of £3445 from this total. Her taxable income is thus £53 205.

This taxable income is taxed in three slices at increasingly higher rates. The first £3000 at 20%, the second slice of £23 700 at 25% and the remainder at 40%. Thus the total tax due is £16 795. However, during the year her employer has already deducted PAYE under Schedule E on her £40 000 salary. Thus at the end of the tax year she is still due to pay tax at 40%, her marginal rate, on the £6000 of rent on the £4000 interest received gross of tax on government stocks, plus an additional 15% on the dividends

Tax computation for Ms Walthorn 1995–96

Ms Walthorn works as a business executive with the Arlenia Travel Corporation.

She is 40 years of age and unmarried. She has no children. She lives with Mr John Amble who works as a stockbroker in the City of London.

Mr Amble pays Ms Walthorn a rent of £500 a month. He has full use of the house.

Ms Walthorn currently earns a salary of £40 000 a year from the Arlenia Corporation and enjoys additional income of £4000 a year received gross of tax from government stocks, plus dividends of £5320 from Tarmac PLC. The tax credit on the dividends is £1330.

Income tax computation for the year

Income	Schedule	£
Salary	E	40 000
Interest received (gross of tax)	C	4000
Dividends (£5320 + £1330 tax credit)	F	6650
Rent from Mr Amble	A	6000
Total Income		56 650
Less: Allowances		
Personal allowance	3525	
Total allowances		3525
Taxable income		53 125
Income tax payable at 20% on first £3200		640
Tax on dividends of £6650 at 20%: payable at source		1330
Income tax payable at 25% on next £(21 100 – 6650)		3613
Income tax payable on remaining untaxed income at 40%		11 530
Total tax payable	£	17 113
Average tax rate paid £17 113/£56 650		30 %
Marginal rate paid		40 %

Ms Walthorn pays £17 113 of income tax on her income. The tax on her salary will be deducted by her employer under PAYE and forwarded monthly to the Inland Revenue. She has received the interest on government stock gross of tax. Tax at 20% was deducted by Tarmac from the dividends paid to her.

The tax on the government stock and the tax on the rent received from her tenant and additional tax at 40% on income above £24 300 not already taxed will need to be accounted for at the end of the financial year. She will receive a tax assessment from the Inland Revenue in due course. This income will be taxed at her highest marginal tax rate of 40% since she has used up all her lower tax bands at 20% and 25%.

Ms Walthorn cannot take advantage of the 'rent-a-room scheme' to avoid tax since Mr Amble has full use of the house.

Exhibit 4.4   Example of a personal tax computation.

received. The company paying the dividend has already deducted 25% from the dividends paid to Ms Walthorn.

BASIC, MARGINAL AND AVERAGE RATES OF TAX

The basic rate of tax is the standard rate of tax charged on normal incomes. Currently in the UK this rate is 25%. This is the rate paid on most of the income earned by most people in the UK.

The marginal rate of tax, as we noted above, is the rate charged on the 'top' slice of income. Currently in the UK this rate can be as high as 40%.

The average rate of tax is the total tax paid divided by the total income. In the above case, this is £17 113/56 650 = 30%.

INCOME TAX SCHEDULES

We noted above that the tax authorities allocate personal income to one or other of various classes, or 'schedules'. The most common schedules to which income is allocated are Schedule D and Schedule E.

Self-employed persons working in a trade or profession are taxed under Schedule D. Thus anyone who runs their own business is taxed under Schedule D. Many items of expenditure which can be offset against income taxed under Schedule D cannot be offset against income taxed under Schedule E. Therefore, if it is possible to choose between schedules, it is better to arrange matters so that a client is taxed under Schedule D rather than Schedule E.

A self-employed client who pays tax under Schedule D may need to arrange for business accounts to be prepared once a year. These accounts will be sent to the Inland Revenue, but unless the firm has a revenue in excess of £90 000 they need not be audited. The tax inspectorate works out the tax bill for the year and sends the bill to the self-employed person. The rules in preparing these accounts and tax assessments are quite complex and beyond the scope of this book.

Some interest and annuities are also taxed under Schedule D.

Employees, that is clients who work for someone other than themselves, are taxed under Schedule E. Normally Schedule E tax is deducted by an employer on a regular basis under the PAYE (pay-as-you-earn) scheme; the tax is deducted and recorded on the monthly payslip. Very few deductions are allowed against income assessed under Schedule E therefore it is difficult to reduce a Schedule E tax bill. As we noted above, Schedule D income offers much more scope for legal reduction of the tax bill.

Company distributions of income in the form of dividends etc. are taxed under Schedule F, and income from land and property is taxed under Schedule A.

PERSONAL TAX IN THE UK: CAPITAL GAINS TAX

If an individual in the UK sells an asset for more than they paid for it, then they may be liable for capital gains tax (CGT). The tax rate charged on capital gains depends on the individual's marginal tax rate before charging the CGT.

Husbands and wives are taxed separately for CGT purposes. This can provide much scope for reduction of the tax on a family.

In any one year the first £6000/5800 of capital gains are exempt from CGT. This is a substantial sum and it means that in the great majority of cases profits on asset sales are not subject to CGT.

Note that any unused capital gains allowance cannot be carried forward to be offset against capital gains in future years. However, capital losses can be carried forward and offset against capital gains tax due in future years.

Any surplus profit above the CGT allowance is subject to tax at a rate depending on the marginal tax rate of the individual in that year. If the marginal tax rate paid in that year is 40%, the capital gain is taxed at 40%. If the marginal rate in that year is 25%, the CGT rate is 25%; however, if a taxpayer has used up only part of one band, say the £3200–£24 300 25% tax band, he or she can use up the remainder of the band on the balance of any capital gains tax liability. Once this is used up, the balance of capital profit will be taxed at the next highest band, which is currently 40%.

An example of a CGT assessment for 1994/95 is set out in Exhibit 4.5.

Mr Wilson made an ostensible capital gain of £60 300 on the sale of his Victorian painting; however, the calculation of the capital gains tax payable is not as simple as this. First, something called an indexation allowance – see Exhibit 4.7 below – needs to be worked out, second the capital loss on another sale needs to be allowed for, third the annual exemption of £5800 needs to be deducted and finally his marginal rate of tax needs to be calculated. The calculation of CGT is complicated!

Exhibit 4.5 shows the indexation allowance, which allows for inflation, to be £15 367. The capital loss of £5000 on the sale of the antique silver is deducted, then the £5800 annual CGT exemption is deducted, and finally the marginal rate of tax is calculated.

Mr Wilson's lowest 20% band has been fully utilized by his earned income and £17 500 of the 25% tax band up to £23 700 has also been used up so there is only £(20 700 – 17 500) = £3200 of the 25% band left to tax the capital gain of £34 133 at the basic rate of 25%. Thus the first £3200 of the capital gain of £34 133 is taxed at 25% and the balance £(34 133 – 3200) = £30 933 is taxed at the highest 40% tax rate. The total CGT payable is thus £13 173.

Mr Charles Wilson bought a Victorian painting for £50 000 in December 1988. He sold the painting for £120 000 on 25 April 1994. The selling costs incurred on the painting were £9700. In January 1995 Mr Wilson incurred an adjusted capital loss on the sale of antique silver, of £5000.

The taxable income of Mr Wilson for the year ending March 1995 after deducting all tax allowances turns out to be £20 500.

What is Mr Wilson's liability for capital gains tax?

CALCULATIONS

Revenue from sale of painting		£
Gross revenue		120 000
Less: costs of sale		9700
Net revenue		110 300
Original cost of asset sold	50 000	
Indexation allowance		
$((144.2 - 110.3)/110.3) \times 50\ 000$	15 367	65 367
Chargeable gain on sale of painting		44 933
Capital loss on sale of silver		5000

COMPUTATION OF CGT TAX PAYABLE

Chargeable gain on sale		44 933
Less: capital loss on sale		5000
Net chargeable gain		39 933
Less: CGT exempt amount (94/95)		5800
CGT chargeable on	£	34 133

The tax rate applied to this CGT charge depends on the marginal rate of tax paid by Mr Wilson on his other income. In this case Mr Wilson's taxable income after all allowances have been deducted is £20 500. Therefore Mr Wilson has used up the lowest 20% tax rate band and £17 500 of the 25% band. He therefore has £20 700 – 17 500 = £3200 of the 25% rate band left to use up before paying 40% on the balance due for CGT.

His CGT charge is thus:	£...
£3200 charged at the 25% rate	800
£30 933 charged at the 40% rate	12 373
£34 133	
Total CGT charge on sale of painting	£13 173

The CGT charge is reduced first by the capital loss which was incurred during this period and then by the indexation allowance and then by the exempt allowance of £5800 for 94/95. The charge of £34 133 is treated just like normal income tax. Since the 20% has been used up, the balance is charged at the 25% rate up to £23 700 and then the remainder is charged at the 40% rate.

Note that Mr Wilson has already used up his 20% income tax band and £17 500 of his 25% band.

Exhibit 4.5   Calculation of a capital gains tax charge.

ASSET SALES EXEMPT FROM CGT

Certain assets are exempt from CGT, the most important being that of the family home. The family home can be sold at a considerable profit and yet no CGT is payable. This only applies to a first home; the profit on the sale of a second home is not exempt from CGT. Other assets exempt from CGT are listed in Exhibit 4.6. The most important exemptions are life assurance policies and assets passed on to a beneficiary at the time of death.

ASSETS EXEMPT FROM CAPITAL GAINS TAX

Primary private residence (first home if more than one owned)
National saving certificates
Premium savings bonds
Proceeds of life assurance policies
Government securities
Securities issued by public corporations
Most fixed interest stocks
Most 'private chattels' such as a motor car or furniture

Also:

Assets held at the time of the owner's death
Assets given to a charity
Assets given to a national institution
Assets given to a spouse unless the couple are living apart
The disposal of a business. 100% of profit on sale eliminated up to £150 000
(Tapering relief available thereafter).

The profits from the sale of many assets sold by an individual taxpayer are exempt from paying CGT. The most important of these exemptions is the private residence of an owner-occupier. The proceeds from a life assurance policy are also exempt from CGT.

A concession by the Inland Revenue allows the cost of the asset to be indexed for inflation. The falling value of money relative to other goods. This avoids the owner having to pay tax on artificial inflationary profits.

Exhibit 4.6   Assets exempt from capital gains tax.

INDEXATION OF THE VALUE OF ASSETS SOLD WHICH ARE SUBJECT TO CGT

A further benefit to the taxpayer is that the bought value of an asset can be indexed to allow for the impact of inflation. In other words, the amount of tax payable under CGT is reduced by an indexation allowance applied to the cost of the asset. Were it not for this indexation allowance, CGT would be paid on an increase in the value of an asset due to inflation; such an increase in value is not a real increase, it simply reflects a fall in the value of money.

An example of indexation for CGT purposes is provided in Exhibit 4.7.

Mrs Thomas buys 10 000 shares in AXT PLC for £12 000 in 1988. She sells them for £25 000 in 1993. However part of this £13 000 'profit' simply reflects the 34% fall in the value of money between 1988 and 1993. Once the indexation allowance is applied, the profit falls from £13 000 to £8938, the first £5800 of which is exempt from CGT. So Mrs Thomas only has to pay CGT on £3138, at her marginal rate of income tax. If her marginal rate is 25% she pays £3138 × 0.25 = £784.50.

INDEXING THE COST OF AN ASSET

Let us suppose that Mrs Helen Thomas bought 10 000 shares in AXT PLC on 3 February 1988. The net cost of the shares was £12 000. On 18 February 1993 Mrs Thomas sold the shares for £25 000. How can the indexation allowance reduce the CGT Mrs Thomas must pay on the profit on the sale? Assume Mrs Thomas sells no other chargeable assets during this year.

The key statistics are:

RPI for February 1988	103.7
RPI for February 1993	138.8

Therefore the indexation allowed on the cost price is:

((138.8/103.7) × 100) − 100	33.85 %
Cost price	£12 000
12 000 × 33.85% =	£4062

Therefore the CGT due on the sale is:

Proceeds of the sale	£25 000
Less: cost of the shares	£12 000
Net unadjusted proceeds	£13 000
Less: indexation allowance	£4062
Chargeable to CGT	£8938
Exemption allowance for year	£5800
CGT to be paid on	£3138

An asset can rise in value because of the fall in the real value of money. Thus when the asset is sold, the 'profit', that is the excess of the selling price over the cost, is not a real profit but simply a reflection of the fall in the value of money over the period.

Taxing such an unreal profit would be unfair, so the Inland Revenue allows the seller of the asset to adjust the cost price upwards by an indexation allowance.

The indexation is based on the retail price index (RPI), which the government publishes every month. The cost price is uplifted by the ratio between the RPI when the asset is bought and the RPI when it is sold.

Exhibit 4.7   Calculation of the indexation allowance to reduce capital gains tax liability.

Retirement relief from CGT on the disposal of a business on retirement is a very important concession by the Inland Revenue to business owners. The matter is too complex to pursue here.

Other complex CGT provisions apply to gifts and assets held in trust. See Slevin (1993) and Mellows (1992) for a more detailed discussion of these provisions.

PERSONAL TAX IN THE UK: INHERITANCE TAX

This tax is applied to the value of assets transferred to others either during the lifetime of the owner as a gift or, more usually, on the death of the owner of the asset.

The deceased is assumed to be domiciled in the UK. If domicile is uncertain the tax situation can be complicated.

Currently, the 1995/96 rate of tax payable on the first £154 000 of value transferred is nil. On transfers above this value, the rate is 40% of the value of the remainder of the estate at date of death.

Transfers of assets between husband and wife are exempt from inheritance tax. For example, if the family home is in the name of the husband and it is left to the wife on the death of the husband, no inheritance tax is payable on the transfer value, no matter how large the estate may be.

GIFTS

A gift made by an individual during his or her lifetime may be subject to inheritance tax, even if the donor dies many years after the gift is made.

Not all gifts are subject to inheritance tax. For example, gifts to a spouse, wedding gifts up to £5000 by a parent to a child and many other forms of gift are exempt, including £6000 of gifts over a two-year period.

The current rules are that if an individual dies within seven years of making a substantial gift which is not exempt from inheritance tax, the tax to be paid is as follows:

Years before death	Inheritance tax is paid at the following rate
1–3	100% of amount due
4	80%
5	60%
6	40%
7	20%
8	nil

If a donor wishes to hedge the risk to the donee of the donor dying within the seven-year period, he or she should be advised to take out a stepped endowment insurance policy or some alternative to hedge this risk.

The inheritance tax rules regarding the tax to be paid on the transfer of business assets to trusts and the tax liability of trustees for assets held on behalf of beneficiaries are rather complex. See Mellows (1992) for a detailed discussion of the subject.

SOME SCHEMES FOR REDUCING THE INCIDENCE OF PERSONAL TAX

Many highly ingenious people spend a good deal of their time thinking up schemes designed to reduce the burden of personal tax on their clients. The richer the client the greater the scope for reducing personal tax. Clients who live and work in several different countries provide much scope to tax advisers for reducing their total tax burden.

Several 'tax information services' exist which distribute information on tax reduction schemes to PFAs for a regular fee.

In order to provide the flavour of what is possible a few examples of these tax reduction stratagems are listed below.

1. Buy rather than rent a home.
    Reason: There is no capital gains tax to be paid on the profits from the sale of a home which is the primary residence of the owner. Interest paid on a mortgage on this primary residence is allowable against tax at a 15% rate up to a £30 000 mortgage.
2. Arrange a substantial pension.
    Reason: The Inland Revenue are very generous in giving allowances to those setting up a good pension for themselves. (This may relieve the State from responsibility for looking after the pensioner in later life.) The pension contributions may be set against tax at the highest marginal rate. Lump sum payments to set up a pension are also allowable against tax. Certain lump sum terminal payments are tax-free.
3. In writing a will, once it is ensured that the wife is in a sound financial position on the death of her husband, then leave the remainder of the estate up to £154 000 to others, possibly the children, or set up an absolute or discretionary trust to hold the remainder of the estate on behalf of the children.
    Reason: If this is not done the zero rate of inheritance tax on an estate valued at between £0 and £154 000 on the death of the owner of the assets is wasted. The recommendation is particularly important if husband and wife should die at the same time or shortly after one another. Trusts can, at the very least, delay the payment of tax and may reduce the marginal rate of tax payable.
4. Total assets of the family estate should be split roughly equally between husband and wife.

Reason: As for 3. above. On the death of either spouse the full zero-rated band of inheritance tax up to £154 000 will be used up against that part of the estate of the dead spouse left to the children (or others). If this is not done, the children could be landed with a heavy inheritance tax bill on the death of the second spouse. Remember that assets left in excess of £154 000 are taxed at 40%.

5. If the client is running a business consider incorporating the business if the client's income from the business exceeds the basic rate band of tax – currently £3201–£24 300 at 25%.
   Reason: The client will pay tax on the profits from a small business at only the 25% rate up to £150 000 of profit. (There are other considerations here, though.)

6. Take income in the form of goods and services rather than cash.
   Reason: The tax on accommodation, use of car, lunch vouchers etc. may be zero or lower-rated than the marginal rate of the taxpayer. The rules are complex here, the tax is situation-dependent, but benefits are available.

7. Set up or take part in a profit-related pay scheme.
   Reason: Half of the profits derived from such schemes are tax-free (FA 1989 s.61 and Sch. 4) up to £4000 a year.

8. Pass revenue-generating assets to your spouse if the spouse has a low income.
   Reason: The spouse may not be using up all of his/her personal tax allowance. An individual can earn up to £3525 before they have to pay any income tax. Also one spouse may pay tax at a lower marginal rate than the other spouse.

9. Sell some assets which are standing at a profit over cost each year to use up the maximum annual capital gains tax allowance.
   Reason: A capital gain of £6000 can be made each year before CGT is payable. If this allowance is passed over for a year it is lost for ever, and eventually tax may have to be paid at the highest marginal rate of 40% on the capital gain. Thus if capital gains of up to £6000 are available they should be utilized each year to absorb the capital gains tax allowance in that year. The divisibility and cost of selling and buying back the asset is also relevant here.

10. If an employee is about to retire, he or she might consider taking a tax-free 'golden handshake' of up to £30 000 rather than negotiate a part-time job for a few years as a supplement to retirement income.
    Reason: The employee will have to pay tax on an income of, say, £10 000 a year for three years which is earned from the part-time job while he or she can avoid tax on the first £30 000 of a 'golden handshake'. The employer would be losing work from the employee for the three years, though, and may have other ideas!

11. If an employee or a self-employed person is contributing towards a pension scheme but the annual contribution is less than the maximum permissible (for example 30% of net relevant earnings in the case of a self-employed person aged 51), then the individual might consider increasing the pension contributions to the maximum possible under a free standing additional voluntary contribution scheme, assuming the cash is available. An employed person can pay in up to 15% of gross salary.

    Reason: Pension contributions are allowable against tax at the employee's highest marginal rate, say 40%. This might well turn out to be the best investment available for surplus cash, when the return on the net of tax contributions is worked out. Note that 25% of the pension to be received on retirement can be commuted into a lump sum.

12. Increase life insurance cover to the maximum possible under a free standing additional voluntary contribution scheme.

    Reason: An employee in a death-in-service scheme can increase his or her life cover to 2.5 times salary under an AVC scheme. This is likely to be cheaper than alternative forms of life cover available to the employee.

13. Place some of the assets of the individual client into a private equity plan (PEP) up to the maximum possible amount each year.

    Reason: No income or capital gains tax is paid on income or capital gains arising from assets held in a PEP, so long as the assets are held in the PEP for a period of five years. However, if the total capital profit on assets held each year is less than £6000 the benefits flowing from the PEP are much reduced. We recall that capital gains must exceed £6000 in any one year before CGT is payable.

14. Save via a tax exempt saving scheme (TESSA).

    Reason: Same as 13. above. No tax is paid on the income from the scheme if capital is left in the scheme for five years.

15. Give careful consideration to the date when a financial transaction takes place.

    Reason: For example, CGT paid is based on the taxpayer's marginal tax rate in the year the asset is sold. If the marginal tax rate of the owner of the asset will be lower in a later year, e.g. after retirement, then postpone the sale until a later year. There are many other cases where the date of a transaction can affect the tax paid. For example, when the Inland Revenue altered the income base for Schedule D assessment from the previous year to the present year in 1994/95 this move opened up limited opportunities to reduce the total tax payable.

16. The use of trusts.

    Reason: A trust is a legal device whereby person A transfers some assets to person B for the benefit of person C. Many tax schemes for avoiding, reducing or delaying CGT and inheritance tax payment are built around trusts. These schemes can only be safely set up by using the services of a competent lawyer, since an error in even one word of the deed can wreck a scheme.

Many other tax-reducing schemes are available; they change from year to year as the tax laws change. The above are listed to give the reader a sampler of what is possible.

WHAT HAVE WE LEARNED IN THIS CHAPTER?

1. Personal taxation is a very important aspect of personal financial planning. If a payment is allowable against personal tax the government is, in effect, subsidizing this activity. The rate of tax payable on income can sometimes be shifted to a lower rate by employing various stratagems.
2. The PFA must always be careful to differentiate between tax avoidance, which is legal, and tax evasion, which is illegal.
3. There are three major taxes on the individual in the UK: income tax, capital gains tax and inheritance tax.
4. It is important to differentiate between the basic rate, the average rate and the marginal rate of tax paid by a client. The marginal rate is often the important rate so far as the value of allowances is concerned.
5. Income is allocated to various tax schedules, such as Schedule D and Schedule E. The allowances and concessions are not the same under all schedules. For example a client can benefit by being taxed under Schedule D rather than under Schedule E.
6. Not all assets sold at a profit are subject to capital gains tax. A house which is a first home is one major example of a tax-exempt asset. A reasonable amount of capital gains can be made in any one year before capital gains tax is payable.
7. So many ways of avoiding inheritance tax have been devised by tax specialists that inheritance tax has been called a voluntary tax!
8. A wide range of perfectly legal methods of reducing personal taxes have been devised by tax specialists. It may be wise for a PFA to hand over to a personal tax specialist any personal finance plan they have devised so that it can be checked out for tax efficiency under current tax legislation.

FURTHER READING

Barlow *et al.*: covers tax aspects of inheritance law.
Butterworth (1993): a comprehensive source of information on international tax.
Mellows (1992): a standard reference book on the taxation of executors and trustees. Intended for specialists.
Slevin (1993): an introduction to the complexities of the capital gains tax. Rather technical.

Sharp, I.N. (1994) *Self-Assessment: Dealing With The New Income Tax Regime,* ICAEW

Sinclair (latest edition): a readable yet pretty comprehensive guide to UK personal and company taxation. Lots of tips about the more publicized methods of reducing the personal tax bill of clients.

Sinclair and Silke: a remarkably comprehensive 'introduction' to a difficult subject. Somewhat legalistic in approach.

Tingley: a new edition is published after every budget. A basic introduction to UK income tax, capital gains tax and inheritance tax. An eminently practical book. Some advice is given on how to reduce the personal tax burden.

See bibliography on p.311 for a full annotation of these books.

TUTORIAL QUESTIONS: PERSONAL TAXATION

1. Describe the three main types of personal tax paid by individuals in the UK. What is being taxed in each case?
2. What is the difference between tax avoidance and tax evasion? Give an example of each. What is meant by the term 'tax avoision'?
3. Describe the different classes of income assessed under Schedule D and Schedule E. Why is it advantageous for the income of an individual to be assessed under Schedule D rather than under Schedule E? Dividends on ordinary shares are allocated to which tax schedule? Are these dividends paid gross or net of tax?
4. Exhibit 4.2 lists various items of income which are not subject to tax in the UK.

   Explain why the following items are exempt from tax:

   casual gambling profits, premium bond winnings, educational grants, income support, compensation for loss of office up to £30 000.

   Can you identify any overall tax philosophy behind these exemptions?
5. Work out the annual income tax to be paid by Mr and Mrs Jones in the following situation.

Mr Jones: Salary		£50 000
Mrs Jones: Salary		£10 000
Dividends:	Mr Jones	£4000
	Mrs Jones	£6000

   Approximately how much tax would already have been paid to the Inland Revenue at the end of the tax year?
6. What is the 'marginal' rate of tax? Why is the marginal rate of tax paid by a taxpayer on her annual income important in tax avoidance schemes? Why is the marginal rate of tax not so important now as it used to be?

7. Mr Wiles takes out a mortgage worth £40 000. The gross of tax rate of interest paid by Mr Wiles is at 12% a year. Mr Wiles works as an employee and earns £40 000 a year.

    How much interest does Mr Wiles pay, net of tax, on his mortgage? If Mr Wiles earned only £15 000 a year, how much interest would he pay, net of tax, on his mortgage?

8. Capital gains tax is charged on what sort of a gain? Give an example. How much capital gain can be earned in any one year before CGT is payable? Under what conditions might investing in 100 Krugerrands provide tax advantages compared to investing in a gold ornament worth exactly the same amount of money?

9. Mrs Dodson, a 50-year-old widow, wishes to sell a family heirloom, a marble statue, for £200 000. The statue was bought by her father, now deceased, in 1985 for £120 000. Inheritance tax has already been paid on this work of art. Mrs Dodson's pension income for the year is £15 000. She has no other income. Calculate what capital gains tax Mrs Dodson will have to pay on the sale of this statue.

10. Miss Mitford and Mr Nicholson are both left £120 000 net of inheritance tax by a deceased relative. Miss Mitford, who is a wine buff, invests her £120 000 in 1200 bottles of Chateau Latour 1973 at £100 a bottle. Mr Nicholson invests his inheritance in a modern photo-painting by David Hockney, which also costs £120 000.

    Five years later when both the wine and the pictures are valued at £300 000, Miss Parry and Mr Miles decide that they want to sell their acquisitions.

    Required: Discuss the CGT tax position in either case. Assume that both Mr Nicholson and Ms Mitford earn sufficient income to take their marginal tax rates into the 40% band. The inflation index has moved from 100 to 130 during the five-year period.

11. Name three forms of transfer of assets which are exempt from inheritance tax. If a wife who owns assets with a market value of £400 000 on her death leaves £250 000 of her assets to her husband and £150 000 to her daughter, how much inheritance tax is payable in total?

12. Mr Witherspoon donates shares with a market value of £200 000 to his son on 13 February 1995. He dies on 12 March 1999 leaving £600 000. The shares which he donated are now worth £300 000. How much inheritance tax must be paid on the gift by his son?

13. Mr Pollard dies leaving a home worth £250 000 and ordinary shares worth £120 000 to his wife. A year later Mrs Pollard makes a gift of the house, which is now worth £220 000, to her daughter Jenny aged 38. At the same time she makes a gift of the equity shares, now worth £150 000, to her son Jonathan aged 33. Mrs Pollard is invited to live with her son and daughter for six months each year. Mrs Pollard dies five years later.

Required: How much inheritance tax is paid by the Pollard family on Mrs Pollard's estate?

14. Mr and Mrs Jameson live in rented property. Mr Jameson owns gilt-edged stock worth £100 000 and shares worth £200 000, his only assets; his wife owns no assets. They have an only son Donald, aged 24. Work out the inheritance payable by the Jameson family in the following two situations:

   (a) Mr and Mrs Jameson are involved in a serious car crash. Mr Jameson dies a year later still owning all the shares and gilt-edged stock. The stock and shares are left to his wife Sheila in his will. The stock is now worth £120 000 and the shares £180 000. Mrs Jameson dies two years later, when the shares are worth £220 000 and the stock £110 000. In her will she leaves everything to Donald.

   (b) Same as above, but Mr Jameson leaves half his stock and shares to his son Donald, the other half going to his wife.

Mrs Jameson's marginal rate of income tax is 25%. Donald is at university reading to be a doctor. He has no income except for his government education grant.

Suggested solutions to even numbered questions are provided at the back of this book.

Personal investment

5

INTRODUCTION

In Chapter 1 we noted that the lifetime cash flow of an individual is not constant. The flow is negative for most of the first 20 years of life, then the flow turns strongly positive for most of the next 40 years. The flow then tends to turn negative again. For approximately one half of our lives we have a positive flow and for the other half of our lives a negative flow.

The main objective of investment planning is to shift this lifetime cash flow from one period to another. The primary aim of the individual investor is to create a positive cash flow after the age of 60 by investing part of the positive cash flow generated between the ages of 20-odd and 60.

This shifting of the cash flow in time is illustrated in Exhibit 5.1. This exhibit shows the net cash inflow and outflow over the lifetime of an employee. This particular individual attended school and college up to the age of 23. During these years the cash flow was negative. The person then took up employment at age 23, enjoying a successful career and ending up with a salary in excess of £50 000 a year. They then retired at age 58.

The net cash flow was positive between the ages of 23 and 58, then it turned negative. However, sufficient income was saved over the period from age 23 to 58 to cover the negative cash flow between the ages of 58 and death at age 82.

In Chapter 7 we will discover that pension planning is concerned with converting this saved and invested income into an adequate pension after retirement.

TYPES OF INVESTMENT AVAILABLE

Anything which can carry value through time is an investment. Thus the number of investment vehicles available to a PFA are legion. However,

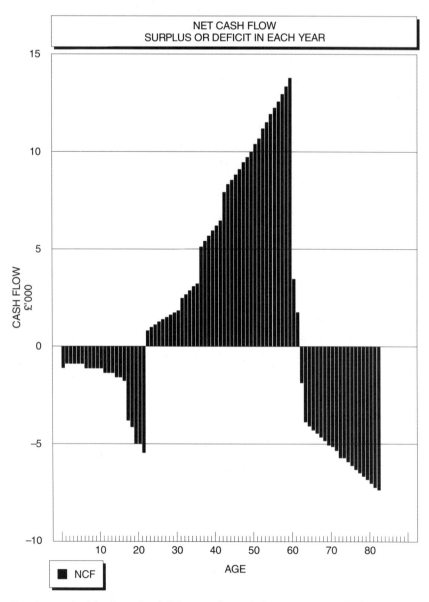

The above schedule shows the deficit or surplus cash flow over a person's lifetime of 82 years. In the early and later years the individual spent more than he or she earned. In the middle years a cash surplus was available for investment. The income from this cumulative investment provided sufficient cash to cover the later cash flow deficit.

Once the individual earns an income he or she will save from 8% to 12% of their net cash flow in order to provide an adequate pension after retirement at, say, age 60.

Exhibit 5.1   The surplus and deficits on a lifetime cash flow.

we can divide all investments into one or other of two broad classes: financial assets and real assets. Exhibit 5.14 and Appendix B to this chapter illustrate the wide range of investment choice available to a PFA.

A financial asset is a document, normally a legal contract, which provides the owner with the right to some kind of future cash flow. Being embodied in a piece of paper, the legal contract, a financial asset is easily stored and protected.

Ordinary shares, bonds, building society deposits, annuities, share options etc. are examples of financial assets. Some financial assets, such as ordinary shares, can be traded on an active market; others, like building society deposits, cannot.

A real asset is a physical asset the use of which the owner enjoys in his own right. Some examples of real assets available to an investor are a house, an antique clock, a set of Japanese netsuke, a bar of gold, an Impressionist painting.

A real asset might well possess aesthetic qualities which appeal to the owner of the asset even if no cash is generated until the asset is sold. This is sometimes called the 'psychic' income flowing from the asset. It is somewhat unlikely that a financial asset, such as a commercial bond or a futures contract, will provide its owner with psychic income.

The key point in the comparison is that a financial asset is held exclusively for the future cash flowing from the asset. A real asset may be held for many reasons among which the future cash flowing from the asset may be a relatively minor one.

THE RISK VERSUS THE RETURN ON AN INVESTMENT

The theory of investment is saturated with opinions as to how, where and when money should be invested to maximize the return on the investment. Most of these nostrums have been discredited long ago by scientific analysis. The one theory of investment which has withstood the rigours of careful scientific testing is the theory that there is a close relationship between the risk attached to an investment and the return from that investment.

Exhibit 5.2(a) illustrates this relationship. The x axis in the diagram measures the degree of 'market' risk attached to the investment, the y axis measures the return on the investment. Note that as the market risk increases, so the return on the investment also increases, in a linear fashion.

The relationship between risk and return shown in Exhibit 5.2(a) can be applied to any investment, but for the moment let us assume that the only choice available to the investor is to invest in ordinary shares quoted on an efficient stock exchange. Let us further suppose that a share of average risk is designated as having a risk of one unit of risk and that a

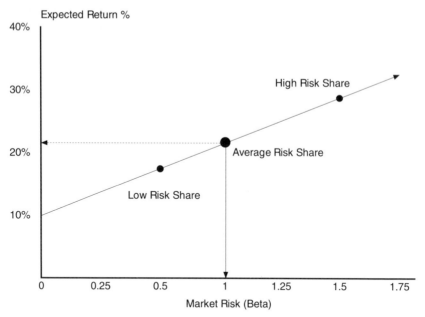

A riskless investment such as a government security provides a return of 10%. All other investments are more risky and so provide a return in excess of 10%. An equity share of average market risk has a risk factor (beta) of 1. Such a share is shown to provide a return of about 22%. A share with a beta of 0.5 provides a return of about 16%. A share whose return varies more than the market return with a beta of, let us say, 1.5 must provide a return of at least 28% – otherwise the owners of this share will sell it and buy another.

Note that the risk we are discussing here is market risk. Specific risk has already been eliminated by diversifying the portfolio of shares.

Exhibit 5.2(a)   The (market) risk versus the return on an investment.

share with a risk rating of 1.7 is approximately 70% riskier than a share with an average risk of 1. A share with a risk rating of 0.8 will be approximately 20% less risky than a share of average market risk. Exhibit 5.2(a) shows that as the risk rating rises, so the expected return on the share also rises. In this case a share of average risk, 1, has a return of 22% and a share having a risk rating of 1.5 has a return of around 28%. A share with a risk rating of 0.5 provides an expected return of around 16%. A share having no risk, if such a paragon existed (which it does not), would provide a return of 10%. Later in this chapter we will find that the type of risk we are talking about here is called 'market' risk. There is another type of risk called 'specific' risk. We shall return to specific risk later in the chapter.

Exhibit 5.2(b) shows the risk–return relationship on a range of different investments. Government stock is a low return–low risk investments and traded options are high return–high risk investments. If a PFA

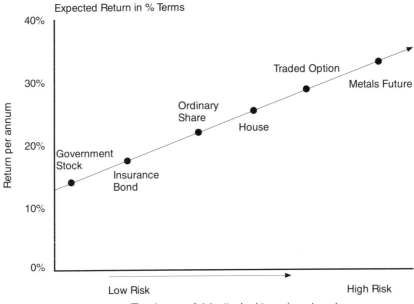

The degree of risk attached to an investment

In an efficient market the return flowing from an investment can only be increased by increasing the risk attached to the return from that investment.

In the above diagram the cash flowing from a government security enjoys a low risk and so provides a low rate of return. Company shares provide a higher return and so are more risky. Options and other derivatives can provide a very high return but for this very reason are very risky investments.

Exhibit 5.2(b)   The (market) risk versus the return on some specific investments.

recommends writing traded options to a client for investment purposes the PFA must, by regulatory rule, warn the client of the high degree of risk attached to this kind of investment.

We will return to the measurement of market risk later in the chapter, but first let us examine the concept of investment risk in more detail.

WHAT DO WE MEAN BY INVESTMENT RISK?

When we talk about risk in the context of investment theory we are talking about the risk attached to the cash expected to flow in the future from that investment. This cash flow includes the expected return from the eventual sale of the investment. The important question is whether this cash flow will be steady period by period, or will show a great variation from one period to another. The greater the variation in the periodic cash flow, the greater the risk attached to the investment. The expected variance on the period by period future cash flow provides us with one measure of risk.

The income generated by an investment can flow from two sources. First there is the income flowing from the periodic dividends, interest, rent etc. generated by the investment, that is the income from the periodic cash payments received by the owner of the investment from the company issuing the share or bond. The second source of income arising from an investment is the income received from any profit or loss on the eventual sale of the investment. So far as the investor is concerned, it makes no difference whether the income from an investment comes from the periodic payment or from profit or loss on the sale of the investment. It is all income. Income is just income, wherever it comes from.[1]

We conclude that the return on an investment, let us say a share, during a given period is made up of two parts. The first part is the dividend declared on the share during the period, the second part is the rise or fall in the capital value of the share between the beginning and end of the period.

If a share in the Tarmac Corporation is worth 240 pence at the beginning of the year, provides a dividend of 32 pence during the year and is worth 220 pence at the end of the year the return on the share for the year is $32p + (220 - 240)p = 12$ pence, a return of 5% for the year.

Exhibit 5.3 explains how to calculate the approximate yield on a share for a given number of periods, given the current price, the expected future price, the expected annual dividend and the number of investment periods. The same approach can be used for other types of investment.

It sometimes happens that the risk attached to the cash flowing from the periodic income from an investment is very low, while the cash flowing from the possible sale of that investment might be at considerable risk. For example, if an investor holds £100 000 of irredeemable government stock paying out a fixed 8% per annum and the market rate of interest rises suddenly and unexpectedly from 8% to 12% the market value of the £100 000 of government stock can be reduced from £100 000 to £66 666 overnight – a capital loss of £33 333, more than four times the annual interest payment of £8000! Guarding the capital value of an investment is an important duty of a financial adviser.

We now turn to another important question: how can the risk attached to an invested portfolio of wealth be reduced. From Exhibit 5.2(a) we see that one simple answer to this question would be to reduce the income from the investment – in other words, to invest in less risky investments!

---

[1] Incorrect measurement of income is a common mistake made by investors. They assume that income from the periodic payment is somehow more important than income from the profit on the sale of the asset. If, in a given period, a fall in the capital value of an asset exceeds the period payment generated by that asset, and these periodic payments are spent, then the investor is spending capital, not income. This is why so many British householders found themselves holding negative equity in their houses during the period 1990–94! However, we should also note that the tax treatment of income may differ between revenue receipts and capital gains. See Chapter 4 for a fuller discussion.

Average annual dividend	=	D
Current share price	=	C
Future share price	=	F
Number of investment periods	=	N
Approximate yield	=	Y

$$Y = (D + ((F - C)/N) / (F + C)) / 2$$

For example:

D =		6 pence per period
C =		110 pence
F =		150 pence
N =		4 periods

The approximate yield is:

$(6 + (150 - 110) / 4) / (150 + 110) / 2$ =   12.3%

Calculating the precise yield on an investment can be quite complicated. However, the approximate yield is often all that is required.

The above formula allows an analyst to calculate the approximate yield on an investment given the current and expected future share price, the expected annual average dividends and the number of periods the share will be held.

Exhibit 5.3   Calculating the approximate yield on a share.

However, before a PFA contemplates advocating such a drastic solution to the problem of risk reduction, they should first exhaust the benefits of an alternative strategy. This strategy is called diversifying the wealth portfolio.

REDUCING INVESTMENT RISK BY DIVERSIFICATION

Our previous discussion of risk has assumed that all of the client's wealth is invested in a single asset, for example in the shares of a single company.

This would be a very foolish and expensive investment strategy to adopt. It has been shown that a substantial fraction of the risk attached to a wealth portfolio can be eliminated by the simple stratagem of investing in a random diversified range of assets as against investing in a single asset.

Exhibit 5.4 illustrates the reduction which can be achieved in the total risk attached to a share portfolio by investing an equal amount of the total portfolio in from one up to 60 shares. Note that beyond about 20 shares the incremental reduction in total risk is very small. In other

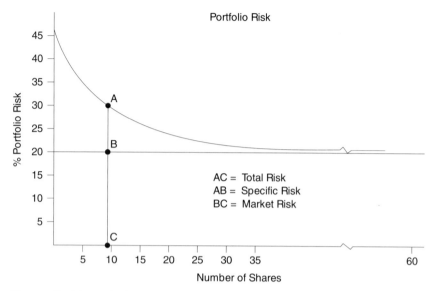

The specific risk attached to an individual share can be reduced by investing in a portfolio of shares. If the return from one share falls because of the specific risk attached to that share the returns on one or other of the other shares in the portfolio are likely to rise thus compensating for the fall.

A portfolio of twenty shares selected at random removes about 80% of the specific risk attached to the portfolio. Diversification does not reduce market risk.

AC = Total Portfolio risk   AB = Specific risk   BC = Market risk

Adapted from Correia *et al.* (1993) *Financial Management*, Juta & Co.

Exhibit 5.4   Reducing the risk on a portfolio of shares by diversifying the portfolio.

words, about 80% of the risk attached to the return on an individual share can be eliminated by the simple stratagem of diversifying the port-folio into about 20 different shares. If a stratified sample of shares is care-fully selected from several different industries the same reduction in risk can be achieved by investing in about 10 shares.

We conclude that a good part of the 'specific' risk attached to individ-ual shares in a wealth portfolio can be eliminated by the simple stratagem of spreading the wealth portfolio among a range of shares. If the portfolio consists entirely of ordinary shares, then the number of different shares required to achieve this objective need not be large. Ten shares might suffice, and a random sample of 20 shares would certainly be adequate for the UK market.

We should note that the total value of the wealth portfolio needs to be split approximately equally between these assets; this can present some individual investors with a problem. For example, most individual investors have much too high a fraction of their total wealth portfolio tied

up in a single asset, their house.[2] Also the value of each individual investment alters through time, so it may be necessary to buy and sell fractions
of the investment in each period to maintain sufficient diversification in
the portfolio.

However, the basic philosophy is simple. Diversification can eliminate
most of the specific risk attached to individual shares in a shares portfolio. The same principle can be applied to any other aggregate of assets.

We must beware that the market on which the shares are being traded
is an efficient market. London and New York are efficient markets:
emerging country markets less so.

TRACKER FUNDS

An even simpler solution to the diversification problem is to invest in what
are called 'tracker funds'. A tracker fund invests in the stock exchange
index – in other words, a tracker fund portfolio is designed to mimic the
composition of the shares in a stock exchange index. Such a fund provides
a high degree of diversification and so removes most of the specific risk
attached to the individual shares in the fund. Exhibit 5.5 lists some tracker
funds currently available in the UK. Tracker funds are available which
attempt to mimic the UK FT Index, the Standard and Poor Index of the US
market, the Nikkei Dow 225 Index in Japan and many others. A portfolio
of tracker funds can provide the investor with an inexpensive world
investment portfolio. An investor cannot hope to diversify much more
than this, until a Martian or Venusian tracker fund comes on-stream!

The reader may consider such an investment policy to be very conservative; surely the financial analysts who manage large share portfolios in
the City of London can always beat the All-Share Index? Wrong!
Academic research has shown that fewer than 10% of UK unit trusts have
consistently beaten the All-Share Index and around 75% of these funds
have performed less well than the All-Share Index.[3] A fund that invests in
a tracker index provides the additional advantage that it avoids the cost
of 'churning' shares in an attempt to maximize the total return on the
portfolio. The annual management cost is low, averaging around 0.5% of
the fund. A tracker fund will have a risk factor, or 'beta', of 1.

SPECIFIC VERSUS MARKET RISK

We have been using the term 'risk' rather loosely up till now. Where
investments are concerned we can identify at least two types of risk. First

---

[2] During the period 1989 to 1994 the nominal value of UK house prices fell, on average, by
25%. This, as we noted above, left many house owners with negative equity. In many cases
the house owner's annual income would have been negative over the entire period, if the
fall in house value had been set against the house owner's annual income!
[3] See *Investor's Chronicle*, 9 July 1993, Personal Financial Planning Survey.

Some UK Tracker Funds

	Index Over 3 Years (to July 1993)
Gartmore UK Index	1418
James Capel UK Index	1384
Morgan Grenfell UK Index	1365
Norwich UK Index Tracking	1430
Royal Life UK Index Tracking	1337
Schroder UK Index Institutional	1253
Swiss Life UK Index Tracker	1430
FT All-Share Index	1486
Average UK general unit trust	1309
Average UK general investment trust	1320
Overall average of all indices listed	1373

Tracker funds for some other foreign stock exchanges:

USA: Standard and Poor's 500 Index

James Capel American Index
John Govett MIS US Index
Morgan Grenfell US Equity Tracker

Europe: FT Eurotrack 100

Fidelity Europe Index Fund
James Capell Eurotrack 100
John Govett MIS European Index

Japan: Nikkei Dow 225 Index

Fidelity Japan Index Fund
John Govett MIS Japan Index
Morgan Grenfell Japan Tracker (FT A World: Japan)

Emerging markets

Baring Emerging Markets Index Tracking Fund

International tracker funds: FT A-World (excluding UK)

Norwich International Index Tracking Fund

Tracker funds attempt to mimic the composition of an all share index. Thus tracker funds remove almost all specific risk from the shares in the portfolio and have an average market risk. That is the portfolio has a beta of 1.

Tracker funds are available which mimic the UK, USA, European, emerging markets and world indices.

Research suggests that tracker funds provide investors with a return that beats about 80%–90% of general unit trusts which buy and sell shares over the same period.

Source: AUTIF, AIT, FINSTAT (Quoted by *Investor's Chronicle* 9.7.93).

Exhibit 5.5   A listing of some 'tracker' funds.

there is the 'specific risk' mentioned above – this is the risk attached to the income flowing from a specific investment, such as an ordinary share in Glaxo PLC or the interest on a building society deposit or the rent from a house. Every individual investment has a series of specific risks which relate only to that investment. There are, however, other risks that relate to whole groups of investments. If we limit our discussion of risk to ordinary shares, then there are risks which apply to the industry in which a company operates, the country in which an industry operates and last, but by no means least, the risk attached to the entire global market.

In recent years financial analysts have concentrated on measuring the risks which apply to all of the shares quoted on a specific share market in a specific country – for example, the risks attached to all the shares quoted on the London Stock Exchange. This risk is called the 'market risk'. The market risk attaching to a specific share – its beta – can be measured.

MARKET RISK AND THE BETA

We conclude that there are two risks attaching to a share quoted on an efficient stock exchange. First there is the specific risk involving all of those risk factors which apply only to the income flowing from the shares of one particular company. Second there is the market risk which applies to all the shares quoted on the stock exchange. What exactly is this 'market risk', and does it affect all shares equally?

The market risk consists of all of those risk factors which cause movements in the return on the whole market. These factors do not affect all quoted shares equally. The return on some shares is strongly correlated to market risk; on others it is not.

The degree to which a share is affected by the market risk is measured by the beta of the share, the relation between the return on the whole market and the return on an individual share quoted on that market. If the return on the whole market falls by 10% the return on some shares will consistently fall by more than 10% while other shares will consistently fall by less than 10%. If, when the market rises or falls, the return on a given share rises or falls by more than the market, the share is said to have a 'high beta'. On the other hand if the return on a given share rises or falls by less than the market rises or falls it is said to have a 'low beta'.

The beta measures both the variation in the return on the share and the correlation between the return on the share and the return on the market. Some shares with high variation in return, like gold shares, have low betas because of the low correlation of their returns with the market return.

Exhibit 5.2(a) actually illustrates the relation between the beta (market risk) of a share and the return on the share. A share with a beta of 1 has an 'average market risk', that is a degree of risk similar to that of the entire market. In Exhibit 5.2(a) such a share enjoys an expected return of around 22%.

If the betas of all the shares quoted on a stock market are known, a competent PFA can put together a portfolio of shares to suit the needs of an individual client. If a client wants to invest in a high return, high risk portfolio, the PFA can select shares from a list of high beta shares. Conversely if the client is retired and wants a portfolio of shares having low risk, and consequently low returns, the PFA can select a portfolio of shares from a list of low beta shares.[4]

We must also recall that the number of shares in the portfolio must be sufficient to eliminate most of the specific risk attached to these individual shares. The beta only tells us about the market risk attached to the share or the portfolio, not the specific risk.

If the wealth portfolio is invested in a tracker fund (see above) then the beta of the fund is 1 for that market and the fund will have an average risk and average return. This may, or may not, be acceptable to the client.

OTHER IMPORTANT ATTRIBUTES OF AN INVESTMENT

The most important attribute of any investment is the risk–return relationship. Investors need to be guided so that they can choose a portfolio of investments which meet their specific needs as to the risk and return involved. We will return to this particular problem later, but first we need to study some other attributes of investments which may, or may not, be important to a particular investor.

PERIODIC CASH FLOW

The specific characteristics of the cash flow from the investment are important. What is the cash flow from the investment? How often is it paid? Can the investor vary the timing and the amount of the periodic cash flow? For how many periods will the cash continue to flow?

Some investors will need no cash from their investment until the investment is sold; others, particularly retired investors, need a regular inflow of cash each month. Thus the periodicity of the cash flow is important.

CAPITAL GROWTH

Younger investors are more likely to be interested in the prospects for capital growth, rather than the security of the periodic return. Certain

---

[4] There are alternative ways of controlling the risk attaching to a portfolio of shares. For example, a PFA could advise a client who wants to increase the risk and so the return on his or her portfolio to borrow funds and 'lever' the portfolio.

investments, for example shares in 'emerging country' funds, shares in companies which have high price–earnings ratios, growth bonds, zero-income bonds and some real assets such as antique silver, give promise of capital growth while providing a low or zero cash flow.

Investments which provide high capital growth allied to low income can present tax benefits to the investor. For example, investors who have set up a discretionary trust to reduce personal taxes are likely to seek out investments combining high capital growth with low income.

SECURITY

How safe is the capital and income invested in the asset?

Neither the capital value nor the income (dividends) on ordinary shares are guaranteed. The income from fixed interest government stocks is very safe but the capital value of the stock may not be safe if the market interest rate should rise. This stricture also applies to most commercial bonds issued by large companies.[5] In non-inflationary times building society variable rate deposits provide excellent security for the capital value invested in the deposit but the income on this investment may be relatively poor and subject to wide variation as market interest rates and inflation expectations change. The average yield on building society accounts from mid-1975 to mid-1994 was 7.8% gross of tax. Income and insurance bonds can provide excellent guarantees on the security of both capital value and income, but may suffer from other shortcomings such as inflexibility, illiquidity or low returns.

Good security is an important attribute, but it must be paid for in the shape of low returns. Nothing is for nothing, in the world of finance.

LIQUIDITY

If an asset is said to be 'liquid', it means that the asset can be quickly converted into cash. Certain investments like building society and bank deposits provide high liquidity at the cost of low return. However, most ordinary shares which are quoted on major stock markets, and collective investments such as unit and investment trust holdings, can also be converted into cash quickly and easily at comparatively low cost.

Most real assets such as houses, works of art, antiques and collectables are rather illiquid and conversion into cash can be a time-consuming and costly business. Gold coins are an important exception to this rule.

Certain financial investments such as annuities and insurance bonds are illiquid and converting such investments into cash before their terminal date, even if possible, can prove to be prohibitively expensive.

[5] Interest rate risk can be hedged at a cost via interest rate options and swaps, but not by small investors. See Galitz (1994).

The key to liquidity lies in the existence of an efficient market trading in the asset. The existence of such a market, like a stock exchange or a gold coin market or a market for with-profits endowment policies, improves liquidity immeasurably.

Exhibit 5.6 provides a list of some of these markets.

BUYING AND SELLING COSTS

The difference between the cost of buying an asset and selling the same asset can be a key factor in investment choice. For example, the difference between the buying and selling cost of a diamond can be 30% or more of the buying cost, while government stock can be sold at a cost of less than 1% of the cost of the market value of the stock.

The spread between the buying and selling costs of real assets is usually much higher than that between the buying and selling cost of financial assets. In some cases the cost of sale is proportionate to the value of the asset, in other cases it is only weakly related to the value of the asset.

Object traded	Market
Vintage and classic cars	*Brooks (Auctioneers)*
Antique furniture, jewellery, etc.	*Antique fairs and specialist dealers*
Coins	*British numismatic trade association*
Commercial bonds	*Stock Exchange*
Company shares	*Stock Exchange*
Diamonds (high quality)	*CSO Valuations (De Beers)*
Endowment assurance policies	*Securitised Endowment Contracts PLC*
Futures contracts	*LIFFE Futures Exchange, London*
Gold coins	*City market*
Government stock	*Post Office. Stock Exchange*
Houses	*Estate Agents*
Investment trust shares	*Stock Exchange*
Land	*Estate Agents*
Postage stamps	*Stanley Gibbons, dealers*
Specialist antiques	*Sotheby's, Phillips etc. auctioneers & dealers*
Traded option contracts	*Traded Options Exchange, London*
Unit trust units	*Unit trust managers*
Wines	*John Armit wine investments*

A wide range of markets are available in the UK which trade a wide range of assets. Many markets, such as the stock exchange, do not exist at a physical location but trade through telephone and computer screens. Specialist dealers exist who are willing to buy or sell almost any conceivable asset. Such dealers will advertise in the trade press of the given asset in which they trade. The above represents only a random selection from among the many markets and dealers who operate in the UK.

Exhibit 5.6   Some markets for trading assets in the UK.

In some cases both the buyer and the seller have to pay a commission to the dealer – some assets have a buyer's premium of as much as 15% added to the purchase price.

The width of the buy–sell spread is a useful indication of the efficiency of the market trading in the asset.

Exhibit 5.7 provides a rough estimate of the buy–sell spread on several assets.

PROTECTION AND MAINTENANCE COST

The cost of protecting an asset against loss or damage can commit the owner to anything from employing security guards to simply insuring the asset against fire or theft.

Financial assets usually entail a relatively low protection cost. This is one of their more valuable attributes. The annual protection cost of real assets, assets such as houses, gold, jewellery and antiques can be high.

	% of Buying Price
Building society deposit	0
Government stock	1
Currency	1
Ordinary shares	2
Unit trust units	2
Commercial debentures	2
Derivatives: options, futures	2
Gold coins	3
Land	4
House (£200 000)	7
Antiques (good quality)	10
Antique jewellery	20
Vintage cars (pre-1930)	20
Netsuke	20
Collectors' coins	20
Antique silver ornaments	20
Postage stamps (collectors' item)	20
Other antiques	30
Antique clocks	30
New jewellery	40
Diamond (small)	40
Modern furniture	50
Victorian painting (not by master)	50
Modern painting (out of fashion)	90

The list provides a sample of the wide variation in the buy–sell spreads on some assets. For example, if the buyer takes the asset out of the shop where it is bought and then re-enters and offers it to the same dealer, how much would he be offered?

The spread is expressed as a percentage of the buying price.

The spread is much affected by the quality of the asset. Top quality assets enjoy much lower buy–sell spreads.

Exhibit 5.7   The buy–sell spread on some assets.

The annual protection and maintenance cost of real assets can amount to as much as 10% of the value of the asset in each period of ownership. This cost needs to be deducted from the gross income from the asset over its lifetime to arrive at the net return on the asset.[6] The same strictures can be applied to the cost of maintaining an asset in prime condition.

DIVISIBILITY

This important attribute is often overlooked. A painting, a jewel, a house or even a life assurance policy is a single indivisible unit. It is difficult, if not impossible, to sell off part of such an asset, although a loan may be raised against it. Other assets such as 1000 ordinary shares in a quoted company, 100 bottles of claret, a collection of vintage postage stamps or 100 Krugerrands can be sold off in parts. Divisibility can provide substantial advantages to the investor by allowing income and capital gains to be released gradually over time, thus providing a steady income while reducing liability to capital gains tax.

SIZE, TRANSPORTABILITY AND INTERNATIONAL MARKETABILITY

A house or a plot of land cannot be transported from one country to another, while share certificates, particularly bearer shares, a collection of netsuke, a valuable collection of postage stamps or a quality jewel can be transported quite easily across national frontiers.

The international marketability and transportability of an asset may well be important considerations if a PFA is advising on the compilation of an asset portfolio for a client living in a country with an unstable political climate.

This investment characteristic is sometimes measured as the value per unit of weight. Gold, for example is an international currency which has a value of around $350–$400 an ounce. Rare postage stamps possess an excellent value to weight ratio.

TAX IMPLICATIONS OF THE INVESTMENT

Finally, but by no means least important, are the tax implications of holding certain investments. In the UK, for example, the profit on the sale of a first home is not subject to capital gains tax. In many countries the income from certain government investments is tax-free. This exemption can provide substantial benefit to high marginal rate taxpayers. In the UK, certain government-sponsored private equity plans and tax-exempt

---

[6] The estimated annual protection and maintenance cost of an asset needs to be accrued forward at the client's average opportunity cost of funds and this terminal value then deducted from the eventual estimated sale of the asset if the profit from holding the asset is to be calculated correctly. In the author's experience this cost adjustment is seldom made.

savings schemes are very tax efficient. The tax treatment of certain types of investments which are held in a trust fund for the benefit of a third party can be crucial to efficient inheritance tax planning.

Tax efficient investment planning is an important and complex subject in its own right. A PFA may need to seek guided study from a tax expert to master the subject.

DESIGNING AN EFFICIENT INVESTMENT PORTFOLIO

If a client comes to a PFA with a substantial amount of money and seeks advice on investing it, we can now appreciate that the PFA may choose from among a wide range of investments when designing the portfolio.

Under normal circumstances the majority of investments incorporated into the portfolio will be financial assets rather than real assets. The only major exception to this rule will be the investment in a home. A client who has recently come into the country from abroad may not enjoy the benefit of owning accommodation in the UK and the PFA will advise the client, or be instructed by the client, to include a house as a recommended asset within the wealth portfolio.[7]

In Chapter 8 we will argue that property would not be a good investment but for the fact that there are tax advantages associated with housing. However, these tax advantages are only available if the client intends to live in the house, rather than rent it out as an investment.

Let us assume that the client already owns a suitable home and is well insured. The problem now is to select a mix of financial assets which will provide a secure capital base and yet generate the desired level of annual income.

The precise composition of the investment portfolio depends on the needs of the client. The needs of a 30-year-old unmarried computer programmer earning £50 000 a year and living in the Isle of Dogs in London in a flat worth £250 000 financed by an 80% mortgage are very different from those of a married and retired 63-year-old former town planner in Winchester with a pension of £1500 a month and a lump sum of £200 000 to invest for his retirement.

On one side of the investment equation the PFA must list the key characteristics of the client, on the other side he or she must list the various financial assets into which the client's money can be invested.

The secret of designing an efficient investment portfolio lies with matching one side of this equation to the other.

THE ATTRIBUTES OF THE CLIENT

The more important attributes of the client, that is the attributes which will influence the composition of the client's investment portfolio are

---

[7] But it will be advisable to finance the house via a substantial mortgage, so as not to place too high a proportion of the client's assets in one property basket.

likely to be age, health, dependants, existing wealth and the current composition of this wealth, attitude to risk, future prospects as to income and pension rights, number of years to retirement, existing life assurance policies, and last but by no means least, lifestyle. The wishes of the client with regard to inheritance tax planning may also be a factor.

SECURITY AND RISK

Whatever the eventual composition of the investment portfolio devised by the PFA may be, the diversification of the total sum among a wide range of different investments is essential. We noted above that by investing in 10 to 20 different ordinary shares quoted on an efficient stock exchange, the client can remove most of the specific risk attached to these shares.

However, although this diversification of the wealth portfolio into 20 different shares should stabilize the capital value of the fund, it may not stabilize the annual income from the fund. Thus a second key aspect of compiling a client's investment portfolio is to find out what stable regular income is required from the fund. If the need for a stable regular income is paramount, for example if the client is retired on a small state pension, then a large part of the portfolio needs to be invested in assets which provide a fixed regular income.

Note the problem. Investment in a portfolio of ordinary shares protects capital but not regular income, investment in fixed income government stocks or high income bonds protects regular income but not capital. Some compromise is needed which matches capital security to adequate income. A few investments, such as inflation indexed government stocks, are available which protect both the value of the investor's income and the value of their capital, but such investments offer a low return.

We noted above that income is related to risk. A higher income can only be obtained by adding a greater degree of risk to the future cash flow from the investment.

The risk a client is prepared to accept is normally related to the age of the client. The portfolio of a younger client who is 20 years or more from normal retirement age should contain a high proportion of ordinary shares and other assets, the value of which will grow with the economy. The portfolio of an older client, especially one who is retired or close to retirement, must contain a substantial proportion of fixed interest stocks and other investment vehicles like high income or distribution bonds and annuities which will provide a fixed regular income.

A suitable mix might be:

Age	Shares	Fixed Income
	%	%
30	90	10
40	70	30
50	60	40
60	50	50
70	20	80

The mix at any particular time will be influenced by the economic climate. Thus if it is anticipated that inflation might rear its ugly head once more, the PFA would be well advised to shift a much greater proportion of an older client's portfolio into equity-linked investments, despite the need for a regular income. Distributor bonds were designed to solve this problem.

If a client such as the young computer programmer mentioned above wishes to take on more than average risk to achieve a higher than average income from his or her portfolio, the PFA can suggest that the client borrows funds to 'lever' the returns from the portfolio.[8] An alternative approach might be to design a portfolio consisting mainly of shares with betas greater than 1, or to include high-risk investment vehicles such as warrants or traded options in the portfolio.

INTEREST-BEARING SECURITIES

If the client's primary objective is to secure a regular stable income, then a wide range of securities are available which satisfy this need.

Securities are also available which offer a floating rate of interest, usually tied to the current market rate. However, the income from such an investment is less stable since the rate of interest paid is related to the current market rate of interest, which tends to fluctuate over time. The base rate of interest in the UK has varied widely in recent years, as demonstrated in Exhibit 5.8. The exhibit also shows that the real rate of interest, however – the nominal rate adjusted for inflation – varies a good deal less than the nominal rate.

The advantage of investing in a security providing a floating rate of interest is that such an investment will tend to protect the value of the capital base.

---

[8] So long as the returns from the shares bought with the loan exceed the interest cost of the loan, the returns from the portfolio are 'levered' upwards. This strategy increases the overall risk attached to the future cash flows from the portfolio. Investing in highly levered investment trusts could achieve the same objective at lower cost, however.

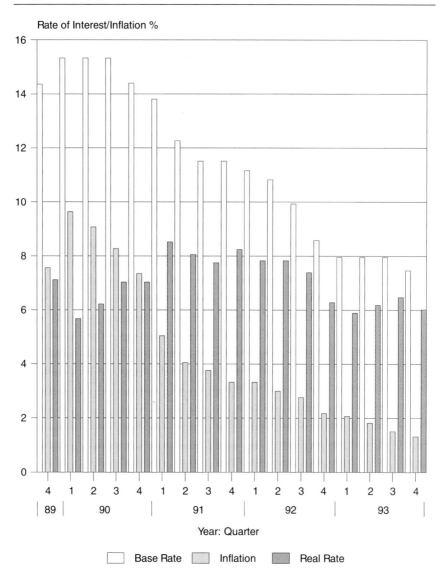

Rate of Interest/Inflation %

Year: Quarter

Base Rate ☐   Inflation ▨   Real Rate ▨

Source: Nationwide Anglia Building Society

The nominal base rate of interest fell by a substantial margin over this period. However the above schedule shows that the real rate of interest was more stable. The real rate is the nominal rate adjusted by the rise in the retail price index over the period.

Exhibit 5.8   The base rate of interest in the UK 1989–93.

Type of Investment	Rate %	Special Conditions
Government Stock		
National Savings	5%	No tax payable
Investment Account	7%–7.25%	Depending on amount invested
Income Bonds	6.25%–6.5%	Depending on amount invested
Index Linked Certificates	3.25% + inflation%	If held for full five years No income if cashed in year 1 Occasional bonuses paid
Gilts		
Index Linked	2.4%–3.26% 2.01%–3.2%	Assuming inflation of 3% Assuming inflation of 5% Yield depends on redemption date and assumed inflation
Short dated (up to 5 years)	8.5%–14.27% 4.39%–5.65%	Flat yield depending on nominal return and date of redemption Redemption yield
Medium dated (5–15 years)	6.09%–11.06% 5.25%–6.57%	Flat yield Redemption yield
Long dated (over 15 years)	5.86%–7.55% 6.05%–6.62%	Flat yield Redemption yield
Undated	5.94%–6.73%	Current yield
Building Societies and Banks		
Instant Access	0.5%–1.5%	May provide cheque facility
Notice Accounts	4%–7%	Depending on amount invested Usually requires 90 day notice of withdrawal
Term Shares	6%–8%	Depending on whether left in account for 1 to 5 years May be withdrawn with penalty May be paid on guaranteed differential above ordinary shares rate
Monthly Income	4%–7%	Depending on amount invested
TESSA Account	5%–8%	Tax free interest over 5 years Can be switched to other TESSA with alternative company for a fee

A wide range of fixed interest securities are available on the UK Stock Exchange and elsewhere. In most cases either the income or the capital invested is at risk. In the case of building society deposits the capital is safe, so long as inflation is low, but the income will vary with the current market rate. In the case of government securities the periodic income is safe but the capital value may decline if market rates of interest rise (or rise if the market rate falls).

In the case of inflation proofed investments, such as index linked bonds, both the capital and income are safe but, in consequence, the periodic income is quite low in real terms compared to other forms of investment.

Exhibit 5.9   Some interest-bearing securities available to investors in the UK (1994).

Exhibit 5.9 illustrates some of the securities in the UK which offer fixed and floating rates of interest. The index-linked certificates listed guarantee the security of both the capital and the real income of the owner of the certificates, but for this very reason the rate of return on this security is low since it is a riskless investment.

ANNUITIES

An alternative approach to providing a fixed regular income for a client is to buy an annuity from an insurance company. If a client has reached the age of 65 the PFA might consider investing a substantial part of the client's wealth portfolio in an annuity. An annuity is the traditional investment vehicle used for providing a pension; many pension funds must, by law, be converted into an annuity on retirement.

Many types of annuity are on offer. A conventional 'whole life' flat annuity pays a fixed sum of money each month or year from inception until death. The annual income paid is a percentage of the initial investment. An annuity is a kind of gamble between the annuitant and the insurance company providing the annuity. If the annuitant lives longer than the average for their class of annuitant, the annuitant wins; if less, they lose! An annuitant in poor health and who is not expected to live for a long time may thus get a very high return on a 'whole life' annuity from an insurance company. They will be offered an 'impaired life' annuity.

The return offered on a 'whole life' annuity depends on the age of the annuitant. The return offered on an annuity rises rapidly beyond the age of 65. For example, one insurance company offered the following annual income on an immediate annuity bought by a man or woman of various ages for £10 000 on 1 June 1992.

Age	Male £	Female £
55	1170	1098
60	1262	1155
65	1376	1238
70	1535	1362
75	1756	1548
80	2067	1831
90	2511	2210

Source: Stone and Cox tables.

The rates offered on annuities by insurance companies vary a great deal from year to year. The nominal rates offered almost halved between 1988 and 1994. The rates offered depend on the rates of return available on medium-dated gilts at that time.

Note that it is possible that nothing may be paid to the relatives of the deceased from an annuity on the death of an annuitant. However, most annuities are 'guaranteed annuities' and these will continue to pay out for some years after death if the annuitant dies soon after the annuity is taken out. 'Annuities certain' can be bought for a fixed period of years. Such an annuity can prove useful if the annuitant wishes to ensure that money will definitely be available to make a series of payments in the future – payment of school fees, for example.

A managed annuity allows the annuitant to vary the level of income provided by the annuity, within certain limits. Such an annuity can be invested in equity shares, unit trusts or a with-profits insurance policy.

If current annuity rates of return are low, and the rates vary a great deal from year to year, the retiree can take out a phased annuity.[9] The retiree's retirement fund, which must, by law, be invested in an annuity, is gradually released and invested in a series of annuities year by year. This strategy can improve the average return on the annuity, but the annuitant should not forget that the balance remaining in the retirement fund may vary in value over time depending on the composition of the fund and the state of the stock market.

Escalating annuities are available which increase the value of the annuity by $x\%$ a year – say by 4% a year. These annuities are more expensive than flat rate annuities.

Finally we should note that inflation-proofed annuities can be bought. As the name suggests, the income from these annuities is revalued each year to allow for any fall in the value of money (RPI). Some of these annuities are 'capped', in the sense that they only compensate for inflation up to some maximum figure, say 5% per annum. Inflation-proofed annuities are very expensive and may cost double the cost of a flat rate annuity which is not inflation-proofed. However, if the client is rich enough these annuities will provide a very secure income for life. They may become affordable once a client reaches a good age, say 75.

When a retirement fund has to be converted into an annuity on retirement it is usually possible for 25% of the terminal fund to be taken out in the form of cash. This fund can be reinvested as the retiree wishes, and so allows diversification into a wide range of alternative investments.

THE TAXATION OF ANNUITIES

The taxation of annuity income is complicated. The income on 'compulsory purchase' pension annuities is taxable like ordinary income, but with 'immediate' annuities only the interest portion of the income on the annuity is subject to income tax. The rate of tax depends on the average life expectancy of the annuitant.

[9] Recently the law has been changed and retirees can delay taking out an annuity on retiral if annuity rates are low or the income is not needed immediately.

INFLATION

Inflation, the fall in the value of money relative to the value of other goods, is a key factor in composing a portfolio of investments for a client.

This factor requires the PFA to estimate the rate of inflation over the lifetime of the client – no easy task. What is the inflation rate likely to be in the UK over the next 20 years? An examination of the rate of inflation over the last 50 years might assist in answering the question.

The average annual rate of retail price inflation over the period from 1945 to 1994 in the UK has been around 5% per annum. Exhibit 5.10 shows the rate of price inflation in the UK over the period between 1960 and 1993. Note that the inflation rate averaged 12% over the 10-year period from 1973 to 1983. The tragic consequence for pensioners when inflation destroyed the real value of fixed value pensions based on fixed rate annuities after the Second World War is well documented.

The value of an asset or income stream before allowing for inflation is called the 'nominal' value. The value of an asset or income stream after allowing for inflation is called the 'real' value. It is the real value of assets and income streams that is relevant when designing an investment scheme for a client.

A PFA must make assumptions about the likely future rate of inflation over various periods ahead. The difference between the current return

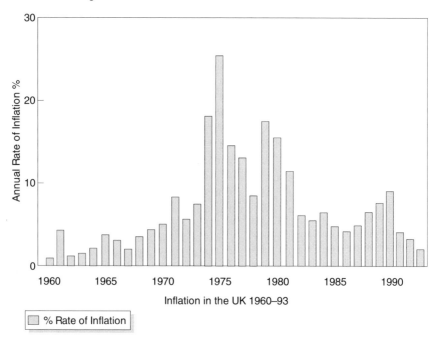

Inflation in the UK 1960–93

☐ % Rate of Inflation

Exhibit 5.10   The rate of inflation (RPI) in the UK 1960–93.

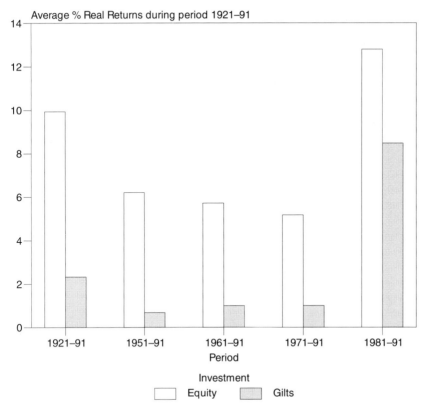

Adapted by author from BZW estimates

Exhibit 5.11   The long-term real return on gilts and equities in the UK market.

on inflation-indexed bonds and similar non-inflation-indexed bonds gives some indication of market expectations about future inflation rates.

A PFA should ensure that the client's portfolio is well protected against the possible ravages of inflation. The PFA is interested in preserving the 'real', not the 'nominal', value of the client's wealth portfolio. How can this be done?

Many studies have examined the ability of various assets to resist erosion from price inflation. The results of these studies are simple to report. The best bulwark against inflation is a portfolio of ordinary shares. The BZW (1992) study (see Exhibit 5.11) found that over the period from 1921 to 1991 ordinary shares provided an excellent real return of 9.93% before tax, after allowing for inflation. The real return from 1951 to 1991 was over 6.1%. The real return on fixed interest securities over the same 70-year period was found to be 2.22%. No other asset has provided such a consistent bulwark against inflation as ordinary shares, although over

Year	UK FT All-Share Index	Indices							UK Inflation Index (RPI)
		Old Masters Index	Impressionist Art Index	English Silver Index	Ceramics Chinese Index	Ceramics Continental Index	English Furniture Index		
1981	100	100	100	100	100	100	100		100
1982	130	106	114	122	106	95	103		105
1983	160	129	148	162	115	108	135		111
1984	192	172	181	201	143	129	181		116
1985	225	201	214	257	146	131	195		123
1986	276	185	362	285	157	140	288		127
1987	430	229	362	285	157	140	288		132
1988	340	265	598	317	195	178	379		141
1989	421	465	975	369	274	243	444		156
1990	360	478	610	374	286	250	448		166
1991	450	478	500	357	286	310	447		174
1992	432	532	498	358	264	337	438		180

Note the variance in the value of some of these real assets over time. The period from 1981 to 1989 was a boom period for real assets. Note that all of these real assets beat the inflation index over the period by a substantial margin. These figures ignore the selling and buying costs, however, which might range from 2% to 20% of the price at which the asset is bought from the auctioneer.

The FT All-Share index is not adjusted for reinvestment of dividends received. If it were, it would stand at about 520.

Sources: Adapted from indices produced by Sotheby's, Art market research, Salomans and the stock exchange.

Exhibit 5.12 Indices of the changing market value of some real assets 1981–92.

shorter periods certain real assets such as houses or silver or Impressionist paintings have far outperformed ordinary shares. These bursts of high returns from certain real assets are short-lived and are invariably followed by substantial falls in value.

Exhibit 5.12 shows a series of indices of the nominal value of certain real assets over the period 1981 to 1992, using 1981 as the base year. Note the substantial increase in the nominal value of these assets over the period, much greater than the inflation index. However, we need to remember that most real assets do not provide a periodic cash flow. On average, real assets tend to provide reasonable protection against inflation but not such consistent protection as is provided by ordinary shares.

However, it may be that a sea change is taking place in the 1990s in the balance between investing in equities and investing in fixed interest stocks, to the benefit of fixed interest stocks. It is as yet too early to judge if this is so.

RISK OF VARIATION IN THE VALUE OF INCOME AND CAPITAL

The following table shows whether the nominal investment income or the nominal capital base on certain financial assets are subject to risk of variation in value. It also examines the degree of liquidity of the asset.

Investment	Is income variable?	Is capital variable?	How liquid?
Building society deposit (variable interest)	yes	no	very
Government security	no	yes	very
Nat. Saving Certificate	no	no	not very
Bank deposit	yes	no	it depends
Normal annuity	no	none	not
Insurance bonds	no	no	not
Commercial bonds	no	yes	very
Ordinary shares	yes	yes	very

The table describes the usual attributes of these investments, but in every case exceptions to the rule exist. For example, some annuities have a terminal value on early death, and most investments, even with-profits endowment policies, can be cashed in before termination, but at a high cost to the investor.

INVESTING IN REAL ASSETS

Investing in real assets such as antique clocks, Victorian dolls, postage stamps, Royal Navy brass bells or Lalique glassware can be fun, but the evidence suggests that on average, over the long term, such real investments do not provide a higher return than financial investment in equity shares. However, real investments have performed much better than fixed interest investment over long periods this century, and have proved to be a good hedge against inflation.

Real investments usually do not provide a cash income until they are sold. The maintenance cost of many real assets – a house, for example – is high. The provision of insurance and security can be expensive. Many real assets are not divisible, and can only be transported with great difficulty. Real assets have been known to fluctuate in value by a large amount over short periods – see Exhibit 5.12.

Thus there is no real competition between financial and real assets, if risk/return is used as the criterion of choice: financial assets, particularly equity shares, are the better option.

However, few real assets are bought for income alone. Real assets such as jewellery and paintings provide a 'psychic' income over and above any cash income which they may provide. Long-term investment return is perhaps no more than a minor factor motivating most collectors.

There are two key factors to remember when advising a client on investing in real assets. First, the asset must be authenticated as genuine by a recognized authority, and a signed authentication certificate must be supplied with the asset. Second, quality is all when investing in real assets. Only the very best in any category of asset is worth buying if 'investment' is a key consideration.

The London and Provincial Antiques Dealers Association (LAPADA) can help in finding any particular antique. LAPADA provides a listing of dealers in no less than 250 specialist types of asset.

CONCLUSIONS ON INVESTMENT

An investment is any asset which can carry value forward through time. A wide range of assets are available when designing an investment portfolio. These assets can be divided into two basic categories: financial assets which provide a legal right to a future cash flow, and real or physical assets which are normally held for reasons other than for the cash flow generated by the investment. Exhibits 5.13 and 5.14 provide a panoramic view of the wide range of investments which are available to a PFA when designing a balanced wealth portfolio for her client. Appendix B describes some of these financial products in more detail.

The key idea in investment planning is to understand the relation between risk and return. The greater the risk attached to the income from an investment, the higher the return is likely to be from that investment.

Financial analysts differentiate between two types of risk attached to an investment. The first type of risk is called the 'specific' risk attached to the individual investment, the second type of risk is called the 'market'

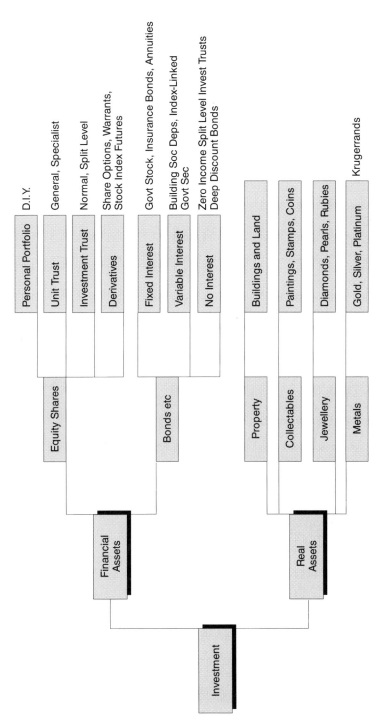

			Personal Portfolio	D.I.Y.
	Equity Shares		Unit Trust	General, Specialist
			Investment Trust	Normal, Split Level
Financial Assets			Derivatives	Share Options, Warrants, Stock Index Futures
			Fixed Interest	Govt Stock, Insurance Bonds, Annuities
	Bonds etc		Variable Interest	Building Soc Deps, Index-Linked Govt Sec
			No Interest	Zero Income Split Level Invest Trusts Deep Discount Bonds
	Property		Buildings and Land	
Real Assets	Collectables		Paintings, Stamps, Coins	
	Jewellery		Diamonds, Pearls, Rubies	
	Metals		Gold, Silver, Platinum	
				Krugerrands

Investment

The investor can choose between financial assets and real assets. The range of financial and real assets on offer are very wide, particularly the choice among real assets. However financial assets are easier to protect and maintain and equity shares have consistently provided the highest real return among the assets available for inclusion in a wealth portfolio.

Equity shares and real assets have been shown to provide the best hedge against inflation.

Exhibit 5.13 A wide choice of investments are available to the discerning investor.

Annuity: deferred
Annuity: escalating
Annuity: fixed term
Annuity: guaranteed
Annuity: impaired life
Annuity: indexed
Annuity: joint life
Annuity: managed
Annuity: perpetual
Annuity: phased
Bond: capital (government)
Bond: cash
Bond: commercial
Bond: distribution
Bond: escalating
Bond: first option (government)
Bond: fixed interest
Bond: growth
Bond: guaranteed equity
Bond: guaranteed income (sold by insurance companies)
Bond: high income
Bond: income (government)
Bond: investment, range of investments
Bond: investment, lump sum with-profits
Bond: managed
Bond: premium (government)
Bond: property
Bond: single premium
Bond: with profits
Bond: zero income
Building society deposit: (various types available)
Cash funds (interest is the only income, capital safe)
Children's bonus bond (government)
Distribution fund: normal (funds can be switched)
Distribution fund: income deferred
Endowment policies: second hand
Futures: on equity shares
Futures: stock index
Gilt edged securities (government). A wide range on offer
Indexed government stock (annual income tied to RPI)
Investment account (government)
Investment trust: warrants fund
Investment trust: geographic specialization
Investment trust: general
Investment trust: product specialization, property etc.
Investment trust: high income or capital growth
Investment trust: split level (all income and zero income)
National savings certificates (government)
Options: traded options fund
Penny share (security with very low market price)
PEP (personal equity plan): managed fund
PEP: self select fund
PEP: specialized fund i.e. emerging markets
Reverse tracker fund (makes money when market falls)
Savings certificates (7th Indexed issue) (government)

Share: cumulative preference
Share: equity (ordinary shares of publicly quoted cos.)
Tracker fund (invests in market index)
Unit trust: general fund
Unit trust: specialized by product, country, risk etc.
Unit trust: ethical, exotic, exempt, PEP, indexed etc.
Unit-linked insurance policy. Funds invested in shares etc.

If all shares, bonds, stocks and other financial products are considered, including foreign financial products, there may be something of the order of 100 000 different financial products available for potential inclusion into the portfolio of a client of a PFA!

This is why computer based data bases are essential for reviewing the wide range of financial products available at any one time. This also explains why 'managed funds' play such an important role in investment. Such funds can afford to employ specialists who concentrate in each of the various sectors.

Exhibit 5.14   A listing of some financial products available for investment.

risk flowing from factors causing changes in the return on all of the investments quoted on a specific stock exchange.

Specific risk can be greatly reduced by diversifying the total wealth portfolio between many different assets. In the case of ordinary shares, 20 shares selected at random can eliminate most of the specific risk. Market risk within a given market cannot be eliminated by diversification but by using the measured betas of specific shares an analyst can design a share portfolio to meet the desired risk–income profile of a specific investor. Portfolios can be 'levered' via loans to vary the risk–return profile of the portfolio. 'Tracker funds' provide a simple method of investing in a port-folio of average risk and return.

Several other attributes of an investment might be important in designing a portfolio to meet the needs of a specific client. Factors such as periodic cash flow, steady growth in capital value, protection cost, trans-portability etc. can influence the design of the portfolio for specific clients with special needs.

Most portfolios will consist mainly of financial assets which will be divided between ordinary shares, which have proved to be an excellent protection against inflation in the past, and fixed income investments, which provide a steady income. The age of the investor is a key factor in deciding on the debt to equity mix of the portfolio.

An annuity is the traditional investment vehicle for providing a secure income after retirement. Many types of annuities are offered to meet the specific needs of an investor.

Inflation can wreak havoc on the return from fixed income securities. Ordinary shares have been shown to be best able to withstand the rav-ages of inflation.

The PFA must design a portfolio for a client which has a built-in defence against inflation. It may be necessary to alter the composition of a client's portfolio from time to time if expectations regarding future inflation begin to change.

Many real assets have also, over the years, provided a good hedge against inflation, but real assets are inferior to equity shares in the long term as an investment vehicle, although they may well provide other non-financial benefits to the investor.

WHAT HAVE WE LEARNED IN THIS CHAPTER?

1. Most individuals have a negative cash flow for about half of their lives. Thus it is important to invest some of the positive cash flow while it is available, in order to provide an adequate income in later life.
2. Investments can be classified into two basic types: financial investments, like shares and bonds, and real investments, like gold coins and houses.
3. The key idea in investment theory is to trade off the return on an investment against the risk attached to the future estimated return from that investment. Thus to work out the financial viability of an investment we need to be able to measure both the estimated future return from the investment and the risk, variance or co-variance, attached to this future return.
4. The return on an investment consists of two parts. First, the dividend or interest paid in each period while the investment is held and, second, the gain or loss in the market value of the investment during that period. The value of the second factor often swamps the first.
5. The risk attached to an investment is defined as the variance on the periodic return on the investment. The total risk attached to a share is made up of specific risk, that is the risk attached to the returns from the specific company which has issued the share, and market risk, the risk attached to the return on all the shares quoted in the given market.
6. Company (specific) risk can be almost entirely eliminated by diversification, that is by investing in a portfolio of shares. Market risk cannot be eliminated in this way, but it can be measured. The measure of the market risk attached to a share is called the 'beta' of the share. A share with a higher than average beta must earn a higher than average return.
7. The choice between investments may be influenced by many other factors apart from risk and return – such factors as security, liquidity, buying and selling costs, maintenance cost, tax, divisibility and transportability. These are all important attributes of investments, which may influence their inclusion in a portfolio.

8. The design of an efficient investment portfolio for a given client requires the PFA to match the attributes of the investments placed in the portfolio to the attributes of the client – no simple task. Balancing security of income against security of the capital base is a key problem. Annuities are the traditional route to providing a secure future income after retirement, but whole life annuities have many limitations and alternative investment vehicles are now available to an investor requiring a regular stable return on an investment.

9. Inflation can savage the real value of an incorrectly designed investment portfolio, so a PFA must pay particular attention to the problem of protecting a portfolio against inflation. Ordinary shares have been found to provide an excellent hedge against inflation.

10. Real assets also provide a useful hedge against inflation, but often little or no cash income. Real assets, on average over the long term, are not comparable to investing in equity shares if the risk/return criterion is used as the measure of benefit.

FURTHER READING

Antique Collectors Club: a range of price guides are published regularly on a wide selection of antiques – furniture, silver, guns, porcelain, glass etc.

BZW (1992)

Chamberlain (1990)

Cheney and Moses (1993): a remarkably comprehensive introduction to choosing investments and placing them in a portfolio of shares. The book is based on US data but the principles remain the same wherever one is investing. An instructor's book with many practical examples is also available. The main book includes a computer disk with a range of investment analysis tools to assist with bond, stock and option valuation and portfolio construction. Uses Lotus 1-2-3 as the driver.

Fundtracker 2 (regularly updated), Investment Intelligence: regular comparative view of fund performance.

Galitz (1994): an introduction to most of the high-powered tools now available to financial advisers for hedging financial risk – tools such as options, futures, swaps etc. Only for the brave.

Gray (1993): a comprehensive introduction to investment for non-specialists in the subject.

Littlefair (latest year): a useful guide to investment and savings plans available in the UK.

McHattie (1992): a 'how to do it' book by an acknowledged expert on the subject of warrants.

Travers (1990): all you will ever want to know about coin trading and investing in coins. The book has a strong US bias.

Williamson (1993): an introduction to the various types of annuities available and how to choose between them.

See bibliography on p.311 for a full annotation of these books.

TUTORIAL QUESTIONS: PERSONAL INVESTMENT

1. What do you consider to be the key objectives when setting up a personal investment portfolio for your client?
2. Differentiate between a financial asset and a real asset. Provide two examples of each type of asset.
3. Ten key characteristics of an investment are listed in the chapter. Explain how each of these characteristics apply to the following investments:

   10 000 ordinary shares in Glaxo PLC.
   1000 bottles of a desirable claret wine (worth £50 000).
   A 200-ounce bar of gold.
   £50 000 in a building society deposit account.
   A vintage car (1928 Lagonda) worth £200 000.
   £50 000 of government stock paying 8% per annum gross.
   A set of Japanese netsuke ivory carvings (20 items worth £500 to £5000 each).
   A warrant to buy 10 000 equity shares in Glaxo PLC in 1998 at a fixed value 20% above today's market value.

4. From Exhibit 5.2(a) estimate the expected return on a share with a risk factor attached of (a) 1.5 (b) 0.25 (c) 0.
5. How do you think the following personal characteristics of an investor might influence the risk versus return profile of that investor?

   Age, gender, health, existing wealth (value and composition of), shape of the future income flow, dependants.
6. What is a 'tracker fund'? Give two examples. What are the benefits to be derived from investing in a tracker fund?
7. Suggest three factors which would be important in estimating the expected return on an ordinary share quoted on the London Stock Exchange.

   What is the 'beta' of a share? What do the following betas tell us about the movements in the future income from these shares?

Consolidated Goldfields	0.40
Intel Corporation	1.80
Unilever	1.05
Glaxo	1.30
British Gas	0.80

8. Advise a 25-year-old unmarried client on what value of liquid assets he needs under the following circumstances:

   Gross annual income £35 000 (net cash £24 000)
   Net monthly payment on £50 000 repayment mortgage £600

Other monthly fixed costs legally committed £300
Other essential monthly costs £550

The client owns a house currently worth £100 000. £40 000 is still due on the mortgage. He is running a bank overdraft of £2300. His only assets are furniture, a car worth £3000 and a building society deposit of £1750.
What form of liquid investment would you suggest?

9. A 55-year-old married client arrives in the UK from abroad with £200 000 to invest, neither he nor his wife has any other income or assets. He could invest in any of the following investment vehicles or a mixture of each.

A whole life annuity paying 6% for life.
A building society deposit currently paying a rate of 4% net of basic rate tax.
A commercial bond from a large quoted company paying interest at 8% a year gross of tax.
A portfolio of five equity shares currently worth £200 000 on the Stock Exchange paying £8000 a year in dividends net of tax.

If only one investment can be chosen, which one would you advise your client to invest in? If more than one is available, which mix would you advise? What factors would determine the decision?

10. A useful financial package which includes both an annuity for life and a life assurance policy on the same individual can be bought from an insurance company. Explain why both the assurance company and the individual whose life is assured might find such a package helpful in hedging financial risk.

11. Suggest two approaches to setting up a portfolio of shares if a client asks for a high-risk high-return portfolio.

12. Which types of investors would particularly benefit from the following government saving schemes:

Index-linked certificates
Premium bonds
Capital bonds
Fixed interest government securities
Tax-exempt saving scheme

13. The following investments would appeal to what kind of investor?
A PEP investment scheme, a block of gold, a Victorian painting, a time-share apartment in Acapulco, a box of Krugerrands, 100 'bearer' shares in an established Belgian company.
Compare return, risk, liquidity etc.

14. Why should any investor actively seek out an investment producing zero income such as the capital portion of a split level trust?

15. When we talk about the **return** on a share, what do mean by the word return? How do we calculate the return for a given period or periods? The following table shows the dividend, net of tax, for a period and the opening and closing values of three shares at the beginning and end of that period. Calculate the return on these shares to the shareholder during the period.

Share	Dividend	Opening value	Closing value
X	15p	100p	110p
Y	2p	120p	180p
Z	20p	100p	55p

Suppose these same figures were to cover three periods instead of one. How would this affect the return from the beginning of period 1 to the end of period 3?

16. Explain the difference between company (unsystematic) risk and market (systematic) risk with regard to the risk attached to the return on a share. Which of these risks can be eliminated? How?

17. Your client inherits a sum of £400 000 from his father, net of inheritance tax. He asks you to invest the money so as to 'eliminate all risk'. Is this possible? Approximately how many different company shares would your client need to invest in to remove about 70% of the company (unsystematic) risk from such a portfolio? Explain why this is so. Assume that he invests an equal amount of money in each share.

18. Financial analysts use a factor called a 'beta' to measure the risk attached to returns from a company share or portfolio of shares quoted on an efficient stock exchange. What does this beta actually measure? A share of average risk has a beta of what value? Why do you think it is that most gold shares, which oscillate quite widely in value through time, normally have a low beta attached?

19. If you were asked to rank the following items in order of 'riskiness' of return, measuring risk as the size of the variance on the return per period, how would you rank them?
   (a) 10 000 shares in the UK company ICI PLC, (b) a collection of antique English silver, (c) a French Impressionist painting by a well-known artist, (d) an inflation index linked government bond paying 2% a year plus the previous year's rate of inflation (e) an annuity of £10 000 a year payable until death. How would you measure riskiness of the return in each case?

20. Given the following information:

Expected average annual dividend in the future	150p
Current share price	1250p
Estimated future share price	1500p
Investment period	5 years

calculate the approximate estimated yield on this investment over the five-year period.

21. Let us suppose you have bought a portfolio of £1000 of shares and £1000 of government stock in 1951. What would have been the average annual return, net of inflation but gross of tax, on these two investments in 1991? Suppose the shares and stock had been bought in 1981, what would have been the average return in 1991?

22. Older people aim to protect the income from their investments, younger people aim to protect the capital sum. Protecting both is difficult. Which of the following investments would suit older people?

A variable interest building society deposit
Income bonds
Insurance bonds
Commercial company bonds
Redeemable preference shares paying zero dividends
National Savings certificates
Index-linked government stock paying 2% plus previous year's inflation
Zero income bonds
A managed annuity

23. A client must invest his £200 000 retirement fund in an annuity. The current rate of return on annuities is very low, only 5% for a 65-year-old man. The rate is expected to rise in the future. Advise the client how to handle this problem.

Explain your reasoning.

Suggested solutions to odd numbered questions are provided at the back of this book.

Insurance 6

RISK MANAGEMENT

Risk is endemic to life. Few of the activities in which human beings indulge do not entail some degree of risk. Fortunately most of these activities entail a risk so small that it can be ignored.

'Risk management' is the name of the scientific discipline which concerns itself with handling risk. The science of risk management is concerned with identifying future risks and working out ways of avoiding or 'hedging' these risks.

The meaning of the expression 'avoiding a risk' is obvious, but the precise meaning of the expression 'hedging a risk' is less well known. What is meant by 'hedging'?

Let us suppose that a future event is identified as likely to cause a loss if it occurs. For example, a collapse in the value of a company share or a house burning down. Such an event can be easily avoided by not investing in shares or not buying a house, but this passes up the potential benefits which can be derived from investing in shares or buying a house.

The potential loss resulting from a fall in the value of a share can be avoided by buying a 'traded put option', which gives the owner of the option the right to sell the share at a fixed price at some date in the future. If the value of the share should fall during the given period the value of the 'put' option rises, thus 'hedging' the potential loss on the share. The total value of the share plus the option remains relatively constant, The traded option has a cost, but it is a fixed **known** cost.

The above example illustrates the key idea in 'hedging'. If an event occurs which threatens a potential future loss then the solution is to set up a 'hedge' which is triggered by the same event and which provides a gain of approximately equal value. In the above example the traded option costs money, but this cost is usually only a small fraction of the current value of the share. The traded option, a small certain cost, is substituted for the possibility of a much larger future loss of uncertain magnitude.

But how do we handle the loss caused by a house burning down? A loss such as this can be covered by that classic hedge against a potential future loss, insurance. A small certain payment, the insurance premium, is substituted for the low probability of a large future payment or loss. For example an annual insurance premium of £150 may be sufficient to cover the potential loss of £100 000 which would be incurred if the home of the insured should burn down during the period when the house is insured.

WHEN TO USE INSURANCE AS A HEDGE

Exhibit 6.1 illustrates a suggested approach to handling risk. In this diagram the importance of a future event which might impose a loss on an individual is defined by two variables. The first variable is defined as the significance of the loss. The amount of the potential loss is either significant relative to the wealth of the individual, or it is not. The second variable is defined by the probability of the occurrence of the particular event. Is it likely that the event will occur, or very unlikely, within a given time period?

Insurance is the appropriate technique to use for handling a risk which falls into the lower right-hand box – all of those events which occur rarely but result in a large relative loss when they do occur. Insurance is a technique which allows a large number of people to pool their risks so that the small premium paid by thousands of individuals will be enough to cover the costs of the few unfortunate individuals in the pool who actually suffer the loss during the given period. The probability of an insured person's house burning down in any one year is very small but if the pool of insured persons is large enough then it is almost certain that one of the houses of the insured persons will burn down during the year. Insurance underwriters fix the cost of the fire insurance premium by calculating the proportion of fires which have occurred in past years in the homes of those people who insure against fire.

Returning to Exhibit 6.1, we note that there are three other boxes to consider which are not covered by the insurance hedging option.

Frequent, low cost losses fall into the top left hand box. Petty theft from a company store is a good example of such a loss. The correct strategy to use here is to change the system. The stock security system is inefficient. Insurance would be an expensive way to cover this risk – insurance companies prefer not to cover this kind of loss since the frequent claims arriving on their desk incur heavy administrative costs.

The events falling into the top right-hand box, rare low-cost losses, can be ignored. Such losses can be 'self-insured' by the individual.

Type of Event Causing a Loss

	Frequent	Rare	Frequency
Low Cost	Change System	Ignore (Self Insure)	
High Cost	Get Out of System	Insure	

Cost

The method of handling risk depends on the frequency of the occurrence of an event and the value of the loss flowing from this event compared to the wealth of the individual.

Rare low-cost losses can be ignored. If frequent high-cost losses occur, the individual involved must remove him or herself from the system. Frequent low-cost losses must be countered by changing the system. Insurance is used to hedge against rare events which result in a high loss compared to the wealth of the individual.

Exhibit 6.1   How to handle risk.

Events falling into the bottom left-hand box, that is frequent high cost losses, cannot be endured. The individual must move out of such a system. Insurance will be much too expensive a remedy, or will be unobtainable. Continuing to operate within such a system must inevitably lead to bankruptcy or worse. An example of the kind of event which could fall into this box is burglary in certain districts of certain towns in England (see Exhibit 6.6). The losses are so frequent and so expensive that the insurance companies have increased the insurance premiums to prohibitive levels, or even pulled out of insuring the contents of houses located in these postal districts. The only option available to a householder is to sell the house at low value, if it can be sold, and move elsewhere.

The remainder of this chapter is devoted to discussing events which fall into the bottom right hand box, namely those events of low probability which may cause a high loss to the individual and which will therefore use insurance as a suitable vehicle to 'hedge' the risks involved.

THE RISK AUDIT

The first duty of a financial adviser is to identify those events in a client's future life which may involve a significant loss.

How can a PFA identify those future negative events which ought to be insured against?

Fortunately most insurance companies are only too happy to assist in this task. They will provide a potential customer with a 'risk questionnaire' which reminds the customer of the risks which he or she may face and which can be insured against. A section of such a questionnaire is shown in Exhibit 6.2.

In carrying out a risk audit on a client, the first step is to identify those persons for whom the client is responsible, including the client him- or herself, and then to identify the risks to life and health faced by those persons. The second step is to list those possessions owned by the client which are at risk and which are of sufficient value to be worth insuring. The third step is to identify any other future negative events which might impose significant loss on the client should they occur. A claim for libel against the client, or injury to a third party in the client's home, are examples of this class of risk.

A Risk Analysis Questionnaire

Those for whom client is responsible

		Negative event incurring cost
Self	Richard William	Death, illness, loss of job
Wife	Alexis	Death, illness
Children		
	Sarah Jane	Illness
	John Simon	Illness

Assets owned

House	Burglary, fire, landslip, storm damage
House contents	Burglary, fire, breakage
Car	Crash, theft, fire
Caravan	Crash, theft, fire
Jewellery	Theft, loss, fire

Other events incurring loss

Libel, slander	Legal costs, damages
Third party injury	Legal costs, damages
Divorce	Legal costs

A risk analysis questionnaire attempts to identify those events which should be insured against.

The first step is to identify those persons for whom the client has some responsibility and those assets owned by the client. The second step is to identify those negative events which may occur which would impose costs on the client.

The third step is to find out if those negative events can be and should be insured against at an economic cost.

Exhibit 6.2   A risk analysis questionnaire.

The PFA can then ascertain the cost of insuring against all of those risks, and assess whether it is worth the expense. The PFA must also check that the client can afford this level of insurance. If the client cannot afford to hedge against all of these risks, the less important risks can be relegated to the self-insurance category.

TYPES OF INSURANCE

Insurance is conventionally divided into three classes namely personal insurance, property insurance and other forms of insurance. The last two are sometimes lumped together and called 'general insurance'.

PERSONAL INSURANCE

Personal insurance covers all of those risks faced by the individual, or by those for whom the individual is responsible, with regard to life or health. Some typical examples of personal insurance include life assurance,[1] which pays out on the death of the assured, endowment insurance, accidental death benefit, personal injury insurance, family income benefit, permanent health insurance, critical illness insurance, medical insurance, injury to third party insurance etc.

Such policies hedge the loss involved if the insured, or those for whom the insured is responsible, has the misfortune to suffer death or other disability.

PROPERTY INSURANCE

This type of insurance covers the risk of loss or damage to property owned by, or under the responsibility of, the insured. Examples of property insurance are insurance against loss or damage to such things as the house owned by the insured, the household contents, the motor car, jewellery etc. owned by the insured or under the protection of the insured. All such risks can be covered at relatively low cost, unless the insured has the misfortune to live in a postal district prone to burglary or theft.

Quite often, strict regulations on the protection of the property are laid down by the insurance company covering the risk. For example, jewellery may have to be stored in a bank vault and only worn for a given number of days a year. A householder may need to install a burglar alarm system before the house is accepted for cover.

OTHER TYPES OF INSURANCE

Before an event is insurable the insured person must have an insurable interest in the loss incurred, but otherwise almost all negative events can

---

[1] If an event, like death, is certain to occur the word 'assurance' is used; if an event might occur, but this is not certain, the word 'insurance' is used.

be insured against loss. Some examples of negative events which can be insured against are: being sued for libel or slander, the costs associated with holiday cancellation through illness, the bankruptcy of a personal financial adviser or lawyer, the costs resulting from rain on a wedding day, the additional costs incurred by having twins, veterinary fees, being hijacked in an airliner, the cost of divorce (after two years from initiating the policy!), and so on.

Which of these many forms of insurance is taken out by the client depends on the client's personal attitude to risk. This in turn depends on the personal circumstances of the client and the client's attitude towards money. The role of the PFA is simply to identify the potential risks and advise the client that such forms of insurance are available if the client should want to use them.

By far the most important forms of personal insurance are life assurance, health insurance, car insurance and insurance of the client's home against the costs of fire, landslip, etc.

UNDERINSURING

Underinsurance can be interpreted in one of two ways. Firstly it can mean that individuals should widen the coverage of their insurance plans. Secondly it can mean that individuals insure items for less than they are actually worth.

Regarding the first interpretation, the annual cost of insurance is seldom more than a few percentage points of the value of the item or loss insured. Research by risk analysts seems to suggest that most individuals are underinsured. In other words, if the cost of insurance is compared to the estimated cost and probability of the loss involved, then most individuals should be advised to widen the scope of their insurance cover.

With regard to the second interpretation, if the value of an item insured is undervalued by the person insured, the insurance repayment claim will be reduced proportionately. Thus it is important for a client to check that the insurance value of the property insured is revalued each year to match the replacement cost of the goods insured.

Insuring at replacement value is more expensive than insuring at cost value, but the additional expense is probably worth the cost involved since what is important to the client is the replacement value, not the cost value.

Thus far we have examined insurance in its broadest sense. Let us now examine the various types of insurance offered in more detail.

LIFE ASSURANCE

There are three basic types of life assurance. First there is what is called 'whole-life' assurance. This is an assurance policy which only terminates

with the death of the assured. The value of the policy is paid to the beneficiaries on the death of the assured, assuming that the premiums have
been maintained. Whole-life policies can be 'with-profits' or 'bare'. A
with-profits policy may cost double the cost of a bare policy.

Whole-life policies are always paid out by the insurance company
since everyone must die sometime. Thus with-profits whole-life assurance is quite expensive.

The alternative to whole-life assurance is term assurance. This form of
life assurance, as the name implies, covers the life of the person assured
for a specified number of years. For example, a man can take out a term
assurance of £50 000 for the benefit of his wife at the age of 54 for a term
of 11 years. If he should die before the age of 65 his wife will receive £50 000.
Once he reaches the age of 65 the policy terminates, so if he dies aged 66
his wife receives nothing.

Term assurance is cheaper than whole-life – see Exhibit 6.3 – since in
most cases the sum assured will never be paid out by the insurance company. Term assurance allows a breadwinner in a family to cover the

Insured: Male in good health

Annual cost of policy

	Whole Life	Endowment	Low Cost Endowment	Level Term	Mortgage Protection	Income Benefit
Term		25 years	25 years	25 years	25 years	25 years
Value	£50 000	£50 000	£50 000	£50 000	£50 000	£20 000 p.a.
Age	£	£	£	£	£	£
30	1032	1962	978	92	65	300
40	1428	2046	1050	230	165	667
50	2022	2310	1302	608	455	2011
55	2442	2562	NA	974	729	3365

Source: Stone and Cox Tables 1994. The company is the Equitable Life.

The above table shows the cost of various types of personal insurance in July 1994. The
rates vary a great deal from time to time and between companies. The Stone and Cox
tables provide a wide range of rates on a quarterly basis.

The table shows the annual cost of a healthy male taking out a £50 000 policy at various
ages. The income benefit is for £20 000. The cost to a woman will normally be about 30%
less than for a man, but it varies with age. The cost of a joint policy on the life of a man
and woman will be around 60% to 80% more expensive than for a man insuring himself.

Note how cheap term and mortgage protection insurance is compared to whole life or
endowment. The latter two are an investment scheme masquerading as insurance
schemes!

The medical prerequisites re medical inspection are set out in Stone and Cox.

Exhibit 6.3   The costs of personal insurance.

financial needs of the family on his or her death at relatively low cost when the family is financially vulnerable to the death of the breadwinner. For example a widow with two young children can take out Term assurance to provide a substantial sum to protect her children until they reach an age when they can look after themselves.

The difference between the cost of whole-life assurance and term assurance diminishes as the individual grows older. For example a 54-year-old male non-smoker can get a bare whole-life policy for only around 10% more than the cost of an equivalent 15-year term policy.

Endowment insurance is a form of term assurance which is normally used to provide both insurance cover and the finance to repay a loan at the end of an agreed period of time. The insurance is taken out on the life of the borrower for a given number of years. The endowment premiums build up a fund to repay the loan at the end of the insurance period. The most common form of endowment insurance is the with-profits endowment policy set up to cover the repayment of a mortgage to a building society or bank at the end of the endowment period.

An endowment policy is an example of a 'bundled product' – two financial products which are sold in one package, in this case an insurance product and a savings/investment product.

HEALTH INSURANCE

The UK provides a comprehensive health service for its citizens. However, many individuals decide to supplement the NHS with private health insurance, particularly for minor and chronic illnesses.[2] There is a considerable variation between the costs and benefits provided by the various health insurance schemes on offer, and so the PFA needs to take time to study the precise terms of each scheme before recommending a specific policy. Exhibit 6.4 illustrates the costs involved and the benefits provided by some medical insurance schemes.

PERMANENT HEALTH INSURANCE AND CRITICAL ILLNESS INSURANCE

If a client can afford the cost, it is wise to advise him or her to take out permanent health insurance (PHI).

This type of insurance insures the income of the client up to the age of 60 or 65. If the client falls seriously ill and can no longer work this policy provides an income up until the expected date of retirement, when, presumably, an occupational pension will be activated. The costs of PHI are set out in Exhibit 6.5.

---

[2] Studies of health provision in the UK suggest that serious acute illness is well covered by the NHS but minor illness and chronic conditions are not as well covered. It is advisable to take out private health insurance to cover such conditions.

Some Medical Insurance Plans

Plan A	Age	Cost (Monthly)
Single Person	30–34	£56 Band A hospitals 33 Band B hospitals 26 Band C hospitals
Family Group	40–44 Oldest person	£144 Band A 84 Band B 71 Band C

Full refund within hospital band for in-patients

Other Benefits

1. Includes overseas travel cover at no extra cost.
2. No policy limits on cost of specific treatments.
3. No-claims discount can reduce premiums by up to 50%.
4. Low cost option with lower benefits provides a 15% reduction in premium.
5. Special rates are offered for the over-60s.

Limitations

1. Will not cover prior or existing medical conditions.
2. Will not cover AIDS, alcoholism, drugs abuse, regular kidney dialysis, chronic long term illness or psychiatric illness.
3. Some payment limits are imposed for out-patient treatment.

Plan B	Age	Cost
Single Person	31–35	£34 Private hospital Private bed in NHS hospital 100 selected private hospitals (extra benefits)
Family	41–45 Oldest person	£87 As above

Other Benefits and Limitations

Similar to above

Plan C	Age	Cost
Single Person	30–41	£33 Various bands of hospital offered
Family	42–50 Oldest person	£71 Various bands

Other Benefits and Limitations

Similar to above.
Many discounts offered to professional workers.
If insured chooses a hospital above selected band the company makes a contribution to the cost.

A large number of schemes are on offer. BUPA has taken 50% of the UK market. PPP has 28%, WPA 6% and BCWA 4%. The above figures are taken from schemes offered by some of the smaller companies. The benefits provided are very complex. The above table simply provides a rough guide to the services offered and the costs involved.

Exhibit 6.4   The cost and benefits of some medical insurance schemes offered in the UK.

£10 000 a year cover to age 65 for a man or woman

Monthly Cost

Company		Cover deferred for 13 weeks			Cover deferred for 26 weeks		
		Age			Age		
		30	40	50	30	40	50
A	Man	15	19	31	15	17	26
	Woman	17	28	45	15	22	37
B	Man	11	18	30	10	11	20
	Woman	19	31	50	11	18	32
Inflation indexed							
C	Man	16	27	61	11	19	44
	Woman	22	40	93	15	27	66
D	Man	15	22	35	12	16	29
	Woman	22	32	50	15	22	42

PHI insures an employee's income against the possibility of serious long term illness. PHI provides the insured with a long term income of an agreed amount until the age of 60 or 65. Since women live rather longer than men the premium for women is rather higher than for men at any given age. If payment is deferred from the usual 13 weeks to 26 weeks a substantial discount is available to the insured. Some PHI policies are index linked to the RPI. Indexation is advised to cover future bursts of inflation.

Exhibit 6.5   The cost of permanent health insurance.

Critical illness insurance (CII) provides cover for the costs imposed on a family when the breadwinner is hit by very serious illness. Examples of serious illness are cancer or a heart attack. A medical examination is needed to test the health condition of the patient when the policy is taken out.

Health is such a vital part of life that all clients should be encouraged to take out the maximum insurance they can afford in this area.

HOUSE INSURANCE

The annual cost of insuring a house against fire, landslip etc. is very low – often less than half of one per cent of the market value of the house. However, the insured needs to be careful to ascertain exactly what is covered by the policy. Certain external structures such as garden walls and outhouses may not be covered by the basic insurance policy, and the owner will normally have to pay the cost of the first £1000 of any rebuilding cost caused by landslip.

When a house is bought the owner normally buys both the house and the land on which the house is built. A fire will not destroy the land on which the house is built, thus the cost of rebuilding a house will nearly

Annual Cost

Town	Buildings Cover	(£100 000)	Contents Cover	(£20 000)
	Cheapest £	Most Expensive £	Cheapest £	Most Expensive £
Aberdeen	132	190	55	80
Newcastle	132	218	136	320
Belfast	140	190	70	114
Ipswich	147	280	56	82
Cardiff	147	245	107	190
Brighton	160	280	107	148
Liverpool	160	280	268	450
London	235	400	216	400

Source: Telesure June 94

The table illustrates the lowest and highest annual premiums offered for insuring houses and the contents of these houses in various parts of the UK. Note the wide variation in cost. Some insurance companies will not insure the contents in various towns such as Liverpool, London and Newcastle. Rates quoted for early 1994.

Exhibit 6.6   The cost of insuring property and contents.

always be much less than the market value of the house and land combined. The total cost of rebuilding a house is very often considerably less than the current market value of the 'house'. The PFA should advise the client not to overinsure the rebuilding cost of the house.

In addition clients should be advised to insure both the house and the contents of the house with the same insurance company, to avoid wrangles between different insurers when reimbursing the insured for losses arising from damage to both the fabric and the contents of a house.

Exhibit 6.6 shows the annual cost of insuring a house and the contents of a house in various cities in the UK. Note the wide variation in cost between building cover in London and Aberdeen, and contents cover in Liverpool and Ipswich!

REDUCING THE COST OF INSURANCE

Various stratagems are available for reducing the annual cost of insurance. Some of these are discussed below.

SHOP AROUND

Anyone who studies the current cost of insurance premiums charged by different insurance companies for providing the same product will be amazed at the huge variation in cost. How can different sellers in a free market charge such different amounts for providing an identical service? In no other competitive market do we find such a wide variation in the price of identical products.

The answer to this conundrum lies in the inefficiency of the information processing system within the insurance market. Customers just don't know the cost of the products offered by the various companies operating in the market.

The PFA needs to 'shop around' to find the lowest 'safe' insurance premium for a client. Exhibit 6.6 provides an illustration of the wide variation in the cost of cover. There is a particularly large variation in the premiums offered in the private health and critical illness markets, where the highest cost is a remarkable 40% more than the lowest for identical cover.

The reason for this variation in the cost of insurance is twofold. First, some insurance companies pay high commission to agents to encourage them to sell their products, rather than cutting the cost of the end-product to the customer. The second reason is that not all insurance companies wish to participate in all insurance markets. Certain insurance products are quite deliberately offered at an uncompetitive price to discourage sales.

The PFA needs to search among the policies available to find that insurance policy which best meets the client's needs at a reasonable cost. On-line computer-based insurance data bases and update services such as Stone and Cox are now accessible at reasonable cost to show the comparative cost of the premiums charged by the various insurance companies.[3] The insurance policy recommended by the PFA need not be the one offering the lowest annual premium, since there is a small risk involved in the safety of payout by the insurance company and some insurance companies are safer than others. In fact an excessively low premium, that is a premium cost well below that offered by other companies, might excite suspicion in the mind of a cautious PFA.

Other techniques are also available for reducing the cost of insurance premiums to the client and the PFA needs to be knowledgeable about these and advise the client accordingly. Examples of such cost-cutting techniques are outlined below.

MAKING FULL USE OF 'DEDUCTIBLES'

If the insured is prepared to pay the first $x\%$ of a claim, a substantial discount on the annual insurance premium is usually available. Fewer claims reduces the administrative costs to the insurance company.

---

[3] TELESURE and FINIS on-line data bases are also accessible through computer and modem connection to the host computer.

SEEK OUT ANY PREMIUM-REDUCING ATTRIBUTES OF THE CLIENT

The client may have some attribute which the insurance company associates with low claims. The company will thus charge a lower premium than average to this customer. For example, elderly persons are often offered substantial discounts on motor insurance, house contents insurance is reduced for those having accredited burglar alarm systems, non-smokers are offered substantial discounts on life policies, professional workers are offered substantial discounts by some companies on certain health policies, and, most important of all, insured persons making no insurance claims for several years, are offered very large no-claims bonuses by most insurance companies.

These valuable cost-saving attributes of the insured person need to be identified and then the policies found which provide special discounts to those possessing these special attributes. The discounts offered vary a great deal between insurance companies and they are changed quite frequently. Theoretically this is a job for the insurance broker but sometimes, despite the regulations, these practitioners are not as assiduous as they might be in finding the cheapest policy, particularly where large commissions are available.

INSURE THROUGH A TRADE ASSOCIATION OR A PROFESSIONAL BODY

Special low rates of insurance are awarded to block insurance schemes arranged by professional associations, trade associations and suchlike. A client may be able to get a substantial discount by insuring through such a body if she or he is a member of such an association. The cost of medical insurance can be much reduced if the policy is taken out under a group scheme.

HOW DO YOU FIND OUT ABOUT THE COST OF INSURANCE?

It may be thought that the obvious way to find out about the cost of insurance is to apply directly to the various insurance companies offering this form of insurance. Unfortunately such an approach can prove to be a tedious business, as there are many hundreds of companies selling insurance and the list of companies is growing rapidly as the insurance market becomes more international.

A more popular approach is to consult an insurance broker who has access, via a computer terminal, to the current rates and discounts quoted by the many insurance companies. Insurance brokers are regulated and most brokers are reliable, but some may put the client automatically into the cheapest policy which, as we noted above, may not always be such a good idea. Alternatively the broker may choose an insurance company which pays a high commission, rather than one which offers a low cost (although this is against the statutory SRO regulations, unless the agent is a tied agent with a restrictive set of options. If the broker is an independent agent the broker is required to give 'best advice' – see Chapter 11). The best strategy is for the PFA to ask for a list of the five cheapest policies meeting the requirements and to choose the most suitable from amongst these.

Insurance companies claim that the same insurance from the same insurance company will always cost the same wherever it is bought. However, the PFA is advised to check whether this statement is correct in each particular case, by shopping around.

Insurance can also be bought through other large financial institutions such as banks and building societies. It is unlikely that these policies will be the cheapest on the market, although they may offer other advantages. The client should be advised that just because he or she is dealing with a financial institution on some other matter, they cannot be forced into buying insurance from the company recommended by the institution, unless it is a specific part of the contract.

The PFA should also warn the client against buying insurance on a product or service from the seller of that product or service – for example, buying insurance cover on a hi-fi system from the seller of the hi-fi system. Some of these insurance policies are extremely expensive. The seller cannot force the buyer to buy such insurance, but may sometimes hold out to the naive buyer that this is so. Occasionally, however, a seller of an unusual or foreign product does sell cheaper insurance on the product, to encourage sales.

HOW SAFE IS INSURANCE?

Safety depends on two factors: the precise terms of the insurance contract and the reliability of the insurance company underwriting the contract.

CONDITIONAL CLAUSES

Most insurance contracts contain many pages of small print. These pages need to be read carefully by a PFA who wishes to give a proper service to a client. The insurance claim will only be met if the customer has complied precisely with the terms of the insurance contract. Unfortunately these conditional clauses are not emphasized when the insurance contract is signed, only when the claim comes in!

These conditional clauses impose many limitations on the liability of the insurance company. For example, a life contract requires a precise statement concerning the health of the client at the time the contract is entered into, an annual travel insurance contract requires a statement as to the number of months the insured will spend out of the country during the period when the insurance is in force. The insurance of valuable jewellery will invariably require information on where it is to be stored and for how many days it will be worn in a given year.

Honesty and accuracy are essential requirements when writing an insurance contract. The insurance company will not pay up if any of these carefully drafted questions are answered incorrectly. The number of insurance claims which are refused because of incorrect information being supplied by the insured when entering into the contract is much greater than the public realizes.

THE RELIABILITY OF THE INSURANCE COMPANY

The safety of the insurance contract depends on the reliability of the insurance company underwriting the contract. In recent years a substantial amount of legislation, such as the Insurance Act of 1982, has been passed by Parliament to protect the interests of the insured. However, from time to time insurance companies **do** fail and the customer is left unprotected. It has recently been suggested, for example, that mutual insurance companies could improve their funding position somewhat. The PFA should check the surety rating of the insurance company before placing a contract with them. Exhibit 10.1, set out in Chapter 10, provides a list of some of the insurance-related data bases which contain this type of information. Credit rating agencies, such as Standard and Poor's, may also provide useful information.

In Chapter 11 we will examine the regulatory framework which has been set up to protect those who buy personal financial products and services. Several government-sponsored but independent regulatory bodies, such as the SIB, IMRO and the PIA have been set up to protect the personal investor and the buyer of insurance products.

Until the PIA was set up, most personal life assurance came under the aegis of LAUTRO, the Life Assurance and Unit Trust Regulatory Association, initiated but not controlled by the government. The PFA should check that the insurance company with which his or her client is dealing is a registered member of the PIA or some other regulatory organization who vet membership and set strict standards for the behaviour of registered members. Such information can be accessed through computer terminals.

The PFA should also check that any insurance broker involved in setting up a policy is a member of the British Insurance and Investment Brokers Association. This association lays down strict rules as to how its members conduct their business.

The insurance company itself should be a member of the Association of British Insurers. Again, strict standards are set down for membership. Note that many foreign insurance companies are not members of the ABI.

Complaints against insurers in the UK can be lodged with the Association of British Insurers, the insurance ombudsman and the

Personal Insurance Arbitration Service. Normally the complaints procedure of the individual insurance company must be exhausted before these secondary complaints authorities will take up a case. A listing of the address and telephone numbers of these associations is set out at the end of this book.

Finally, as a very last resort the client could be advised to go to law and take legal proceedings. This is a very expensive procedure and not to be recommended, unless the client is both seriously rich and very determined.

As we noted above, the domicile of the insurance company underwriting the insurance contract is important. If the company is domiciled abroad then the law of that foreign country may apply to any insurance claim arising.[4] Contracts with insurance companies domiciled in small principalities, such as small offshore islands, should be avoided. Several of these companies have gone bankrupt in recent years.

WHAT HAVE WE LEARNED IN THIS CHAPTER?

1. Risk management is the science of handling the uncertainty inherent in human affairs. Insurance is only one of the many devices available for hedging risk.
2. With insurance, if something should occur in the future which inflicts a loss on the insured, that same event will also trigger an equal gain via the insurance policy. Insurance is only a suitable hedge if the event that is insured against is a rare event and the loss is substantial relative to the wealth of the insured.
3. A PFA needs to know how to conduct a 'risk audit' of a client to identify who is at risk, what these risks are and whether or not an insurance contract is the best means of hedging the risk.
4. Insurance is usually divided into the three basic categories of personal insurance, property insurance and special insurance. Personal insurance covers risks to life and health, property insurance covers risk to property owned, or guarded, by the insured, special insurance covers a wide range of potential risky events which seldom occur. The main types of life assurance are designed to cover the risks associated with the death or serious illness of the breadwinner and his or her family. The main items of property to be insured are the family home and car. There is also a wide range of other types of insurance to be considered to cover such possibilities as injury to third parties, libel, holiday cancellation etc.
5. Life assurance can be of the with-profits whole-life variety which provides cover until death but is expensive, or term assurance for a specific period, which is much cheaper. Endowment insurance can

---

[4] The precise application of UK law to foreign-based insurance claims is a legal quagmire, especially since the UK entered the EU. Much seems to depend on where the insurance was bought.

be used to pay off a loan while covering the risk of the non-payment of the debt on the death of the insured.

6. The cost of insurance varies a great deal between insurance companies, and many devices, such as deductibles, are offered by insurance companies to reduce the cost of insurance. The PFA must be aware of these devices if he or she wishes to provide an adequate service to clients.

7. Information about insurance products and costs is available from many sources, including on-line computer data banks which can be linked to a laptop computer via a modem and telephone line.

8. Any insurance taken out in the UK with a UK insurance company is a relatively safe investment, but the PFA must warn the client to be honest and accurate when filling in insurance questionnaires and to take note of the 'conditional clauses' which appear in the small print attached to insurance contracts. Insurance taken out with companies domiciled outside the UK may not be such a safe investment. These companies may not be covered by the extensive UK protective legislation on insurance.

FURTHER READING

Bose (latest edition).
Dickson and Steele (latest edition).
Marshall (1993): an introduction to the basics of life assurance with particular regard to tax aspects.
Stone and Cox (quarterly): provides voluminous information on the products provided by insurance companies. Premiums, special policy conditions, medical requirements, evidence of health required, loan options available, annual bonus declarations, surrender values and much more. A veritable treasure trove of information on insurance products.
Wilson and Wilson (1988): a useful guide to the various types of life assurance and pension schemes available in the UK.

See bibliography on p.311 for a full annotation of these books.

TUTORIAL QUESTIONS: INSURANCE

1. Define 'risk management' and 'hedging'. Suggest four ways of handling risk.

2. Which of the following events can be insured against, and which cannot?

   Rain on a wedding day.
   The birth of twins.
   Failing to pass a university exam.
   The costs of a divorce.

Being sued for slander.
Losing a leg if you are a professional footballer.
Loose slates causing water damage in the room below.
Being hijacked in an airliner.
Losing one's job.

What criteria are used by an insurance company when deciding whether or not they are prepared to underwrite a possible loss (negative event)?

3. Exhibit 6.1 illustrates four ways of avoiding risk of financial loss. Suggest which of these four approaches is best suited to hedging the risks listed below.

Fire caused by very old electrical wiring.
Holiday cancelled because child catches chickenpox.
House damaged by earthquake.
House chimney falls off, injuring passer-by.
Windows smashed frequently by footballers in adjoining field.
Taking six months off work because of serious illness.
Risk of house being destroyed in a war zone.

4. What are the three stages involved in carrying out a risk audit on a client's affairs?
5. What are the three major types of personal insurance?
6. A client who is married with three children approaches you with regard to advice on insurance. Make up a list of five major hazards which you consider might impose costs on your client in the future. Which should be insured against?
7. Why do you think there is such a wide variation in the cost of identical insurance between the various insurance companies?
8. One of your clients, a 28-year-old qualified accountant, enquires about taking out motor car insurance. The General Insurance company quotes an annual premium of £440 for this insurance. The accountant is shocked that the premium is so high and comes to you for advice as to how he might reduce the premium. Advise your client.
9. How safe is an insurance policy? Why might an insurance company not pay out on a policy when a claim comes in? How can the risk of non-payment be avoided?
10. Complaints against practitioners in the insurance industry can be laid before a number of regulatory bodies. Name three of these bodies. What is the procedure which a dissatisfied customer must follow before approaching these regulatory bodies?

Suggested solutions to odd numbered questions are provided at the back of this book.

Pensions

7

THE IMPORTANCE OF PENSION PLANNING

Of all the many different plans a PFA will be asked to design for clients, pension planning is the most important. Nothing can cause more grief to an individual than an inadequate or ill-designed pension plan. The period of retirement now accounts for about one quarter of the lifetime of most individuals, and an inadequate income during this final period can blight an otherwise happy life.

The problem is that an adequate pension cannot be set up and funded in a short period, unless the client is very wealthy. The period required to save up sufficient funds to generate an adequate pension is at least 20 and preferably 30 years. In other words, an employee or self-employed person needs to start saving for a pension at age thirty to enjoy an adequate pension at age 60; yet few persons at age 30 worry about their future pension rights – it is too remote a problem.

The PFA usually finds that clients aged 45 or even 55 come to them asking for an adequate pension to be organized, only to be told that on their income level this will be very difficult to achieve in the time available without substantial financial sacrifice in the period remaining before retirement. There are problems in persuading a client that this is so.

THE THREE FINANCIAL AGES OF MANKIND

Exhibit 7.1 illustrates the lifetime cash flows of an individual who has spent approximately 40 years of his life in employment. The individual's lifetime cash flow can be divided into three 'ages'. During the first age, from birth to 23 years of age, there was a negative cash flow, when he consumed more than he earned. From the age of twenty three until the age of sixty three the individual takes up employment and enjoys a surplus cash flow, when he consumes less than he earns. From the age of 63

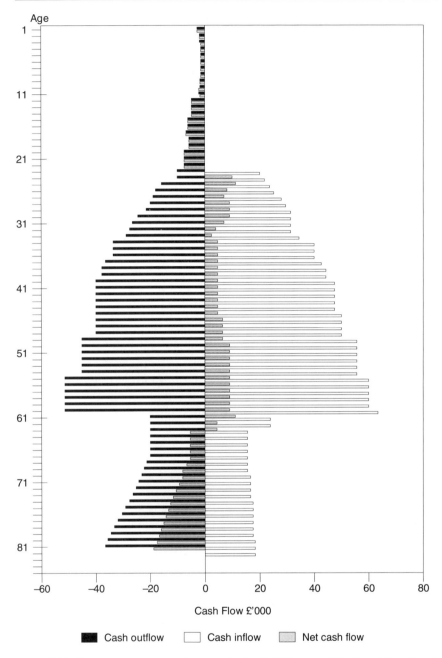

Cash outflow   Cash inflow   Net cash flow

The individual consumes more than he earns for the first 23 years of life. Then his cash flow becomes positive and he earns more than he spends which allows a margin of saving. Part of this saving is invested for a pension which comes on-stream at the age of 63. The individual consumes more than he earns from the age of 63 and so he consumes some capital. This capital is steadily diminished until death at age 81.

Exhibit 7.1   The financial life cycle of the individual.

this individual reverted to a negative cash flow once again, consuming more than he earned.

Note that the positive cash flow covers little more than one half of the lifetime. During the first 20-odd years of his life others have had to accept responsibility for topping up the negative cash flow of this individual. These 'others' are most likely to have been parents, but they could have been other relatives, or representatives of the State. However, the responsibility for funding the last period in the life cycle, the period from around the age of 60 to 80-odd, is very much the responsibility of the individual himself and his financial adviser. Some of the surplus earned during the middle 'earning' period must be invested in some way to produce an income during the later 'retired' period, to ensure that the later negative cash flow can be reduced or even eliminated.

The process of building up a fund sufficient to provide an adequate cash flow in later life is called 'pension planning'. Pension planning is a crucial component of personal financial planning. All PFAs need to acquire a thorough and systematic knowledge of this complex subject.

THE PENSION NUTCRACKER

As our modern industrialized society moves forward towards the twenty-first century, provision of an adequate pension for the retired is posing a serious problem in most countries. The proportion of the total population at work is decreasing, while the proportion of those who are retired is increasing. Exhibit 7.2 illustrates this trend.

From Exhibit 7.2 we can see that the ratio of workers to pensioners in the UK is expected to decrease until well into the next century. Interestingly enough, the situation is expected to be even worse over this period in Germany, USA and Japan.

The British state pension is unfunded; thus if, in the future, the working population is required to fund the pensions of those who are retired, the cost of pension provision will take an increasing and perhaps unacceptably high proportion of the wages of the working population.

Matters are made worse by the fact that workers are retiring at an earlier age than in the past, so the period between retirement and death is increasing, while the number of years at work is decreasing. The average age of retirement of a worker in the UK is now 57. The average length of life is also increasing, although not by much.[1] Thus the average male needs to finance a period of perhaps 15 to 20 years after retirement whereas in the past he only needed to finance a retirement period of 10 years. The situation is much worse for women – they retire earlier, on average, than their male colleagues, and die later. A typical female

[1] In 1950 the average life expectancy of a man was 72 and of a woman 74. By 1994 this had increased to 78 and 82 respectively.

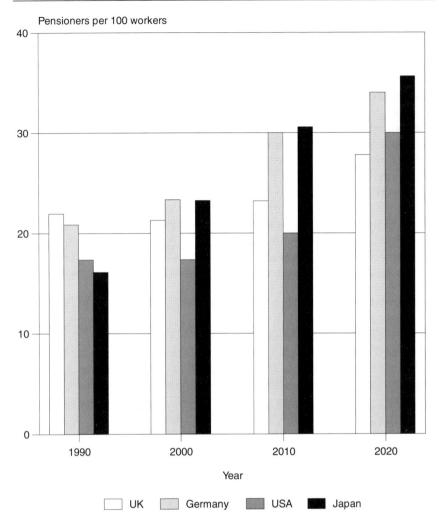

Note how the ratio of retired to working persons increases in every country over the period. The situation is better in the UK than in the other countries. The UK also has lower state pensions than Germany or the USA but not Japan.

Source: Various government publications.

Exhibit 7.2   An estimate of the proportion of working persons to retired persons in the UK and some other countries 1990–2020.

executive will need to finance a retirement period of 20–25 years during her shorter working life.[2] Life expectancy tables for men and women in the UK are provided in Exhibit 2.4 in Chapter 2.

A recent Gallup poll sponsored by Norwich Union found that 56% of persons contributing to pension funds feared that their pension would be inadequate when they retired.[3]

How does all of this effect the PFA? The net effect of all of these changes means that an individual must begin to save for a pension at an early age to ensure that they are saving enough to provide an adequate pension for themselves and, possibly, their spouse for the last quarter of their lives. Because of the pressure on governments, of whatever political hue, to cut taxation rates in the future the real value of the state pension is likely to decline in real terms and the supplementary benefits provided to pensioners on low incomes is also likely to diminish.[4] Relative to the average industrial wage in the country, the UK provides the poorest state pensions in the industrialized world – in 1993 the state pension had a value equal to only 15% of average earnings. If present trends continue, by 2025 this percentage will have fallen to 7%.

Thus a key responsibility of every PFA is to provide sound advice to clients on the adequacy and security of their pension provision. An individual who fails to make proper provision for an adequate pension after retirement can end up in a state close to destitution in later life. This statement is not unduly dramatic – retirees close to destitution are, unfortunately, only too common in the UK at the present moment.

FIVE KEY QUESTIONS IN PENSION PLANNING

In order to devise an adequate pension plan for a client, the PFA needs to ask five key questions.

HOW MUCH INCOME WILL THE CLIENT NEED AFTER RETIREMENT TO MAINTAIN THEIR REQUIRED STANDARD OF LIVING?

This 'required standard of living' will vary a great deal between clients. Some clients will be happy to retire to a country cottage from a town house and grow roses or breed cocker spaniels. Others will envisage an active retirement with frequent cruises to exotic parts and regular visits to

[2] The government has announced a plan to equalize the retirement age between men and women in the UK to 65 in accordance with EU regulations, but this legislation is likely to have a very limited effect on the actual retirement age of women in the UK – it will only affect the age on which the state pension is available to women. In 1994 a 38-year-old woman would need to have made a one-off payment of £10 850 into her pension fund to compensate for equalization of the state scheme. (See *Which Pension*, January 1994.)
[3] *Which Pension*, January 1994.
[4] Michael Portillo, a senior member of the British Treasury team, put forward this view in the TV programme 'House to House' on 14 December 1993.

Name:	John Tyrrel
	Retirement Estimate

Annual Income and Expenditure Account

Income		1994	1995	Ratio	
		Actual	Budget		
	Basic Salary/Pension	42 000	14 000		
	Commission etc.	3000			
	Dividends etc.	1400	9500		
	Other Income	1300			
	Total Income	47 700	23 500	49	%
	Less: Taxation	14 310	4465		
	Other Deductions	2700			
	Net Cash Flow	33 390	19 035	57	%
Expenditure	Mortgage	6800	0		
Household	Gas	690	1100		
	Electricity	330	640		
	Food/Meals out	3300	2400		
	Repairs	231	230		
	House Insurance	240	240		
	Security	220	440		
	Other	744	351		
Transport	Fares	290	120		
	Depreciation (Car)	1000	1000		
	Car Licence	120	140		
	Petrol	1333	720		
	Insurance	220	220		
	Repairs	454	230		
Communication	Postage	287	140		
	Telephone	777	390		
Risk Hedging	Life Assurance	110	110		
	Medical Care Plan	0	720		
Children		1200	400		
Personal	Clothing	2400	1000		
	Holidays	7000	2300		
	Entertainment	1753	800		
	Subscriptions	700	500		
Sundry	Cash Expenses	2000	1200		
	Rates	1000	1100		
Total Expenditure		33 199	16 491	50	%
Net Saving		191	2544		

Exhibit 7.3   An income and expenditure budget before and after retirement.

top London shows. The PFA needs to concentrate the client's mind on expectations which are realistic relative to their expected lifetime income.

The PFA will soon find that few people realize how early one needs to start saving to provide an adequate pension. Twenty-five years is the absolute minimum period.

The first step is to draw up a 'post-retirement' income and expenditure account based on current expenditures adjusted for the various reductions and increases in costs arising from retirement. An example of such an account is provided in Exhibit 7.3.

The exhibit shows that total gross income after retirement is expected to fall by about 51%. However, net cash flow after tax and other deductions will only fall by 43%. Many items of expenditure will be reduced – for example, the mortgage will be paid off and less money will be spent on such things as children, transport, telephone, meals out, clothing and holidays. However, more will be spent on medical care, security, and gas and electricity.

In this case study Mr Tyrrel is budgeted to save more after retirement than he did before! This surplus could be spent on taking out a term insurance policy on the life of Mr Tyrrel if, for example, the pension to his wife should be halved on his death – a common occurrence.

Not all costs will fall after retirement – some will rise by a substantial margin. For example, many executives have most of their car ownership costs and medical care costs met by the firm which employs them. These perks cease on retirement.

WHEN WILL THE CLIENT RETIRE?

The average retirement age is falling year by year. In the 1950s most executives retired at age 65, by the 1980s 60 was a typical retirement age and in the 1990s the typical retirement age for an executive may have fallen to 55 as in the USA and Japan. The earlier the age of retirement the less time is available to accumulate adequate retirement funds. It is best to be conservative with regard to the age of retirement. The more senior the post held, the earlier the retirement age is likely to be. It is best to plan for retirement five years earlier than actually expected, especially if it is still some way off.

If the client is 'invited' to retire early, then additional years of employment are likely to be added to the pension value formula. The PFA should estimate how many years will be added, if any.

HOW SECURE ARE THE CLIENT'S PENSION RIGHTS?

Government pensions are very secure, but the legal security attaching to company 'occupational' pension schemes is still inadequate in the UK.

One company can be taken over by another and the 'surplus' in the pension fund raided. This does not apply to the investments underlying the basic guaranteed pension from the fund – under present legislation these are secure, but the additional benefits, which may cover a substantial part of the pension expectations of the pensioner, can often be clawed back by new, greedy owners of a company. The PFA needs to check up on these matters on behalf of the client. We shall return to this important topic later in the chapter. Anyone who believes that their pension funds are secure is advised to read up on the Robert Maxwell saga.[5]

A greedy or fraudulent management is not the only entity likely to threaten the security of an employee's pension rights. Inflation can destroy the worth of a fixed value pension as effectively as any fraudster. Another threat arises from the possibility of a poor investment strategy being pursued by the managers of the pension fund. Poor fund management can see a pensioner's income expectations eclipsed. The wide range of returns achieved by managed funds – Micropal reports variations as large as 40% over 20 years – shows that the performance of managed funds is very uneven. Some doubts have recently been cast on the future value of personal pension funds monitored directly by the employee. We will return to this topic later in the chapter.

If an employee has worked for many companies during a career there might be a problem in finding out about past pension rights which have been frozen in previous employers' pension funds. In order to assist with this problem the government has set up the Pension Registry and Tracings Service. This organization can trace frozen pensions back to 1975 and possibly even earlier.[6]

IS THE CLIENT EMPLOYED OR SELF-EMPLOYED?

The majority of the clients who approach PFAs regarding pension planning are employed by large companies. The remainder are employed by smaller companies or are self-employed.

The advice provided by the PFA on pension planning will be much affected by the employment situation of the client. In some cases, planning a pension for a client requires that the PFA devise a full pension plan to provide an income after retirement. In other cases it simply involves supplementing an existing pension scheme via an additional pension, which may be a free-standing additional voluntary contribution (AVC) or an AVC added to an existing occupational pension.

---

[5] Read, for example, *Maxwell: The Outsider* by Thomas Bower (1992), published by Viking Press. The financial fallout from this affair has been so severe that we assume it can never be repeated.
[6] The telephone number is 0191 225 6414.

Employees working in large companies usually enjoy generous pension provision, especially if they hold senior positions. In such cases the eventual value of the pension provided will be based on a fraction of the employee's final salary.

Clients employed by small companies are more likely to be participants in a pension plan based on a 'money purchase' scheme. In this case the eventual value of the pension depends on the final value of the fund set up under the scheme. On retirement this fund will be used to buy an annuity, although we should note that, under current tax legislation, 25% of the fund can be taken out in the form of cash if the retiree wishes.

A self-employed client is likely to make pension provision by placing regular contributions into a free standing personal pension fund. The final value of this fund will determine the value of the pension since it will be used to buy an annuity at the going rate for annuities on the retirement date. Some minimum level of pension, usually a very conservative level, may be guaranteed by the insurance company running the fund.

In the case of a client employed by a large company the PFA can advise the client on the security of the company pension scheme and calculate whether the client ought to opt out of the company scheme and set up his or her own free-standing personal pension plan. This is rarely the better option.

It is absolutely essential for any self-employed person to set up a secure and adequate pension fund and to set this fund up as early in life as possible. The British government provides substantial tax concessions to the self-employed to encourage such a course of action.

WHAT BENEFITS DO THE DEPENDANTS OF THE CLIENT GET FROM THE PENSION SCHEME?

Most company pension schemes provide a partial pension, usually one half of the full pension, for the spouse of the pensioner, if the pensioner should die in service or, more likely, after retirement. Young dependant children may also receive a fractional pension for some years until they reach maturity. In addition to a pension for those dependants of the deceased, most pension plans incorporate a life assurance policy held for the benefit of the spouse or other beneficiary of the employee's estate.

The PFA needs to study the likely financial situation of the dependants in the event of the client's death to judge whether the pension rights are sufficient to provide an adequate income for the dependants. 'Top-up' financial provisions in the form of term insurance can be suggested to cover any likely deficiency.[7] A client may have specific addi-

---

[7] For example, currently an employee can make free-standing voluntary contributions to an increased life assurance policy up to a value of 2.5 times salary. This fact is little publicized.

tional problems to contend with if, for example, he has the responsibility of looking after a handicapped child or an elderly parent.

It is not uncommon for a breadwinner to ask a trusted PFA to look after the financial interests of his or her dependants on the breadwinner's death.

MAJOR PROBLEMS IN PENSION PLANNING

Pension planning throws up a number of interesting problems for the PFA. Some of the more important of these problems are listed below.

PRESERVING THE PENSION'S 'REAL' VALUE

Inflation is the traditional enemy of the pensioner. If the pension is fixed in money terms then the real value of the pension diminishes year by year as inflation grinds down its value. Exhibit 7.4 illustrates the annual rate of inflation in the UK over the last 80 years. Note the bursts of high inflation between 1971 and 1981 – this decade alone reduced the value of a fixed value pension by almost 75%. As illustrated in Exhibit 7.5, an annual inflation rate as low as 5% will halve the value of a pension in only 14 years, an inflation rate of 7%, in 10 years.

The state pension scheme is regularly adjusted upwards to allow for inflation and all government pensions make an almost complete upward adjustment for inflation each year. Most final salary based pension schemes run by large private companies increase the pension annually to allow for inflation, but only up to some upper 'capped' limit, say 5%. Many smaller pension schemes, such as money purchase schemes, make inadequate allowance for future inflation and some schemes, where the future pension is based on a fixed value annuity, make no allowance for future inflation whatsoever.

The PFA needs to ensure that the client's pension scheme is designed to provide a reasonable compensation for the falling value of money. However, to obtain full compensation for inflation is exceedingly expensive. As noted above, there is usually an upper 'cap' on the annual maximum increase in value allowed for inflation. Inflation-adjusted government stock can be used to ensure that the pension income keeps up with inflation, but this type of stock pays out a very low rate of interest and so a great deal of the stock would need to be bought to cover for inflation in this way.[8] Inflation-indexed annuities can cost almost double the cost of a normal 'flat rate' annuity paying the same initial income.

As was pointed out in Chapter 5, in the long term, equity shares provide the best buffer against inflation. So equity-based pension funds provide the best security.

---

[8] For example, Indexed Linked Certificates currently pay 3% plus the rate of inflation.

Year	Index Based on 1961	Times 1993 Index	Annual % Inflation	10 Years Averages	20 Years Averages
1914	23.1	47.11			
1915	28.5	38.17	23.4		
1916	33.7	32.30	18.2		
1917	40.7	26.71	20.9		
1918	47.0	23.13	15.5		
1919	48.0	22.68	2.0		
1920	57.5	18.90	20.0		
1921	42.4	25.64	−26.3		
1922	38.6	28.21	−9.1		
1923	38.0	28.63	−1.5		
1924	38.7	28.07	2.0	6.5	
1925	38.0	28.63	−1.9	4.0	
1926	38.2	28.49	0.5	2.2	
1927	36.1	30.16	−5.5	−0.4	
1928	35.9	30.31	−0.5	−2.0	
1929	35.7	30.47	−0.5	−2.3	
1930	33.2	32.76	−7.0	−5.0	
1931	31.6	34.37	−4.7	−2.8	
1932	30.5	35.64	−3.6	−2.3	
1933	30.7	35.42	0.6	−2.1	
1934	30.7	35.42	0.0	−2.3	2.1
1935	31.5	34.57	2.5	−1.8	1.1
1936	32.3	33.72	2.5	−1.6	0.3
1937	34.2	31.82	6.0	−0.5	−0.5
1938	33.2	32.76	−2.9	−0.7	−1.4
1939	41.5	26.22	24.9	1.8	−0.2
1940	52.2	20.84	25.9	5.1	0.1
1941	55.3	19.67	5.9	6.2	1.7
1942	54.7	19.89	−1.1	6.4	2.1
1943	54.3	20.03	−0.7	6.3	2.1
1944	55.3	19.67	1.8	6.5	2.1
1945	56.2	19.34	1.7	6.4	2.3
1946	56.6	19.21	0.7	6.2	2.3
1947	62.0	17.55	9.5	6.6	3.1
1948	65.8	16.52	6.2	7.5	3.4
1949	67.7	16.05	2.9	5.3	3.6
1950	69.5	15.65	2.6	3.0	4.0
1951	77.9	13.96	12.1	3.6	4.9
1952	80.2	13.56	3.0	4.0	5.2
1953	80.4	13.53	0.2	4.1	5.2
1954	83.1	13.09	3.3	4.2	5.4
1955	87.0	12.50	4.8	4.5	5.5
1956	89.2	12.19	2.5	4.7	5.5
1957	93.1	11.68	4.3	4.2	5.4
1958	94.6	11.50	1.6	3.7	5.6
1959	94.6	11.50	0.0	3.4	4.4
1960	96.3	11.29	1.8	3.4	3.2
1961	100.0	10.87	3.8	2.5	3.1
1962	102.3	10.63	2.3	2.5	3.2
1963	104.2	10.44	1.8	2.6	3.4
1964	109.2	9.96	4.8	2.8	3.5
1965	114.2	9.52	4.6	2.8	3.6
1966	118.4	9.19	3.7	2.9	3.8
1967	121.3	8.97	2.5	2.7	3.4

Year	Index Based on 1961	Times 1993 Index	Annual % Inflation	10 Years Averages	20 Years Averages
1968	128.4	8.47	5.9	3.1	3.4
1969	134.5	8.08	4.8	3.6	3.5
1970	145.1	7.50	7.9	4.2	3.8
1971	158.1	6.88	9.0	4.7	3.6
1972	170.2	6.39	7.6	5.2	3.9
1973	188.2	5.78	10.6	6.1	4.4
1974	224.3	4.85	19.2	7.6	5.2
1975	280.2	3.88	24.9	9.6	6.2
1976	322.4	3.37	15.1	10.7	6.8
1977	361.5	3.01	12.1	11.7	7.2
1978	391.9	2.78	8.4	12.0	7.5
1979	459.4	2.37	17.2	13.2	8.4
1980	528.9	2.06	15.1	13.9	9.1
1981	592.6	1.84	12.0	14.2	9.5
1982	624.6	1.74	5.4	14.0	9.6
1983	657.8	1.65	5.3	13.5	9.8
1984	687.9	1.58	4.6	12.0	9.8
1985	727.1	1.50	5.7	10.1	9.8
1986	754.1	1.44	3.7	9.0	9.8
1987	781.9	1.39	3.7	8.1	9.9
1988	835.1	1.30	6.8	8.0	10.0
1989	899.4	1.21	7.7	7.0	10.1
1990	983.1	1.11	9.3	6.4	10.2
1991	1028.3	1.06	4.6	5.7	10.0
1992	1067.2	1.02	3.8	5.5	9.8
1993	1087.4	1.00	1.9	5.2	9.3

Average Inflation % 1914–1993	5.3	4.8	5.0

Sources: 1914–1945 Ministry of Labour Cost of Living Index.
1946–1993 UK Government Retail Price Index.

Exhibit 7.4   Rates of inflation over various periods in the UK 1914–93.

If the pension income or insurance cover is thought to be inadequate to cover future inflation, then additional voluntary pension contributions (AVCs) can be considered. AVCs are allowable against tax at the highest marginal rate of the contributor and can be added to the existing occupational scheme or used to create a 'free-standing' personal pension. We shall expand on this topic later.

PREDICTING THE DATE OF RETIREMENT

Unless the client is self-employed, it is likely that he or she operates in an industry where there is a 'traditional' age for retirement, usually 65 or 60. It has been the case in recent years, however, that executives, and particularly senior executives, have been retiring (or are being retired) at a younger age than in the past. This trend may not continue, or may even

Initial Nominal Value of Pension = £10 000 a year

Inflation Rate %		1	3	5	7	10
Years After Retiral	Year					
0	1995	10 000	10 000	10 000	10 000	10 000
1	1996	9901	9709	9524	9346	9091
2	1997	9803	9426	9070	8734	8264
3	1998	9706	9151	8638	8163	7513
4	1999	9610	8885	8227	7629	6830
5	2000	9515	8626	7835	7130	6209
6	2001	9420	8375	7462	6663	5645
7	2002	9327	8131	7107	6227	5132
8	2003	9235	7894	6768	5820	4665
9	2004	9143	7664	6446	5439	4241
10	2005	9053	7441	6139	5083	3855
11	2006	8963	7224	5847	4751	3505
12	2007	8874	7014	5568	4440	3186
13	2008	8787	6810	5303	4150	2897
14	2009	8700	6611	5051	3878	2633
15	2010	8613	6419	4810	3624	2394
16	2011	8528	6232	4581	3387	2176
17	2012	8444	6050	4363	3166	1978
18	2013	8360	5874	4155	2959	1799
19	2014	8277	5703	3957	2765	1635
20	2015	8195	5537	3769	2584	1486
21	2016	8114	5375	3589	2415	1351
22	2017	8034	5219	3418	2257	1228
23	2018	7954	5067	3256	2109	1117
24	2019	7876	4919	3101	1971	1015
25	2020	7798	4776	2953	1842	923

The table shows the diminishing real value of a pension over 25 years. The real value is the nominal value adjusted for inflation.

On average a woman retiring at 60 lives for 22 years after retirement, while a man retiring at 65 lives for 14 years. The average rate of inflation in the UK over the last 70 years has been around 5%.

The table illustrates the need for a PFA to ensure that the client has made ample provision for inflation in any future pension plan. Note how many years it takes to halve the value of a pension in real terms.

Exhibit 7.5 The impact of inflation on a pension's real value over time.

be reversed if a scarcity of executive talent should arise in the future, but if the trend does continue it poses a financial problem for both the client and the PFA. The value of a pension is often determined by the number of years the employee has contributed to the pension fund, and if the employee retires early the impact on the pension can be quite dramatic. This fact is often ignored by the employee until it is too late.

   Most companies provide some kind of compensation for early retirement, but this compensation is usually much less generous than the
employee supposes. A typical situation is illustrated in Exhibit 7.6; not
only is the pension cut by 16%, but the calculations are almost certainly
based on a lower wage, if the employee retires five years early. In addition, five years' savings are lost. Finally, as illustrated in Exhibit 7.5,
unless inflation is fully compensated for in the pension, the cost of early
retirement can be even greater. Early retirement can do serious damage
to the client's financial health!

Most 'final salary based' pension schemes are based on a formula such as
(n/80) × final salary, where n = the number of years the pensioner has
contributed to the fund.

Example: Final salary = £36 000 gross.
                No of years' contribution = 32
                Expected age at retirement = 65

Normal pension is therefore: 32/80 × 36 000 = £14 400

But suppose this individual is retired at 60 years of age – what effect does this
have on their pension?

$$27/80 \times 36\ 000 = £12\ 150 \text{ at age } 60$$

The pension is cut by (12 150/14 400) × 100 = 16%.

However, this pension is paid for an additional five years. If the individual can
find another job which pays at least £2250 a year he is better off than he would
have been over the age period from 60 to 65, but worse off thereafter.

We have assumed that the real value of the wage is the same on both retirement
dates. However, retirement on the earlier date might be at a lower wage. If the
salary is inflation indexed and the pension is not this could very well be the case.
Also salaries tend to rise faster than inflation, pensions never do.

But what about inflation?
As we noted above, the pension might not be fully inflation indexed. If the
pension is upvalued by 3% a year to compensate for inflation which is actually
6% a year over the period, the real value of the pension will fall by approximately
3% a year. Over five years, calculating in year 0 £s, this amounts to
£12 150 / $(1 + 0.03)^5$ = £12 150 / 0.863 = £10 485, compared to £14 400 in
year 0 £s for retirement five years later if we assume that the salary is fully
inflation indexed over the period. The retiree has lost £3915 a year (27% of his
£14 400 pension) by early retiral. If the company pension plan was not inflation
indexed at all, the situation would be much worse.

Most government pensions are fully inflation indexed. Most company schemes
are not. It might be necessary to arrange an additional 'top-up' pension to
compensate for inflation (or convert a level pension to a lower level pension
which increases at x% a year).

   WARNING: EARLY RETIREMENT CAN DAMAGE YOUR FINANCIAL HEALTH!

Exhibit 7.6   The impact of early retirement on the value of a pension.

If the 'retiree' can find another lucrative job after 'retirement' and save the pension until the original expected date of retirement arrives, he or she may finish off richer than if they had retired at the original date. However, experience suggests that jobs, lucrative or otherwise, are hard to come by for those over the age of 55.

If early retirement is truly voluntary, the PFA should advise the client to think very seriously about it, with all the facts known, before taking this option.

CHECKING ON THE SECURITY OF THE PENSION FUND

Government pensions are safe, and pensions paid out by large well-established companies are reasonably safe. The management of the 'core' pension fund is now tightly controlled and protected by government legislation[9] but, as we have stated previously, this protection applies only to the guaranteed part of the fund.

The law requires that actuarial valuations of the guaranteed part of the pension fund, testing its ability to meet its obligations, be made every few years by a qualified actuary.

If the revaluation of the fund shows a surplus the surplus must be reduced by one means or another. The surplus can be paid back to the contributors or a contribution holiday can be arranged. Large surpluses on pension funds are no longer permitted.

Most pensions are paid out of a fund held by trustees for the benefit of the present and future pensioners. In many cases these funds have a value running into hundreds of millions of pounds.

The company running the pension scheme pays over the monthly contributions into this trust fund and the fund managers invest the money on behalf of the contributors. The fund may be managed by a team of professional investment managers employed by the company; however, an alternative approach is for the management of the company to delegate the running of the fund to an outside organization which specializes in managing investment funds.

The fund manager, whether internal or external, invests the regular pension fund contributions in a wide range of securities. Most UK pension funds are permitted by law to invest their funds in a wide range of financial and real assets. This latitude is not available to fund managers in many other EU countries, where the law requires that pension fund money be invested in a very restrictive set of securities.

How secure are these funds? How easily can the funds be raided by an unscrupulous management board? As we stated above, recent legislation

---

[9] The Pension Law Review Committee Report ('The Goode' Report) sets out the new pension proposals and the thinking behind these proposals. It was well researched and well received by the pension industry.

has greatly tightened the control and supervision of pension funds, but the employees contributing into the pension fund still have far too little say in the running of their own fund, which will in time provide their future pension. The notorious Robert Maxwell case shocked the financial community because of the ease with which Maxwell, a trustee, was able to plunder the fund. Further legislation is promised to protect pension funds against misuse but at the time of writing this legislation is still not on the statute book.

The large financial institutions which hold the majority of pension funds are monitored by watch-dogs such as the SIB, the PIA and IMRO. Several organizations in the private sector, for example Standard and Poor's, measure the performance of privately held pension funds on a regular basis.[10] The Micropal computer-based financial system provides measures of the performance of a wide range of invested funds on a regular basis.

So far as the PFA is concerned, they should be willing to advise on the pension rights of clients. Clients should be asked to obtain a copy of the document setting out the rights of the employee in the pension fund – this information **must** be provided by law to every contributor to a pension fund. The PFA should also try to obtain the latest accounts of the pension fund, assuming that these are available. The latest actuarial report on the fund is also a useful document to check the security of the fund, even if the method of valuation is sometimes a little obscure to the non-expert on pension funding.

Most employees acquire only a very sketchy knowledge of their pension rights, and a competent PFA can be worth his or her weight in gold in this respect. The pension rights should be audited to ensure that no unusual conditions are attached to the pension, that the pension will provide the employee and spouse with an adequate income after retirement and that other important features of pension schemes – such as an adequate life assurance policy and the rights of dependants – are included in the scheme.

'PORTABILITY' OF THE PENSION

Until quite recently the 'portability' of pension rights was a contentious subject. An employee would leave a company after many years of contributing to a company pension fund, and his or her rights in the fund would be 'frozen' until he or she reached retirement age. Thus an employee who held many jobs over a working life could finish up with a bundle of frozen pension rights, which might provide an inadequate income on retirement. This would be especially so if the various pension amounts were not inflation indexed. The pensioner might not know how much his or her pensions were worth until after retirement.

[10] Standard and Poor's provide a grading system for with-profit funds, grading them from AAA to DDD.

Recently the situation in the UK has been much improved, thanks to government legislation.[11] If an employee leaves one company and joins another then the accumulated value of all guaranteed pension rights to date must be evaluated by an actuary and a transfer value notified to the employee. The employee is thus enabled to take the pension transfer value to the next company. In other words the accumulated pension fund value must be portable. Thus employees can now accumulate pension income as they move from one company to another and at any time can calculate with a fair degree of accuracy where they stand with regard to future pension income.

Every employee now has the right to set up his or her own personal pension fund via a free-standing AVC. The company for whom the employee works can pay the additional voluntary contributions into this personal fund.[12] The question of 'portability' does not arise in such a case. When the employee moves from one company to another, the new company or the employee simply continues to make the regular pension contributions into the existing personal pension fund.

TYPES OF PENSION

There are four basic types of pension scheme in the UK. First, the state pension scheme organized by the government, which includes the state earnings related pesnsion scheme (SERPS). Second, those pension schemes run by public bodies such as local government authorities, universities and the Civil Service. The third type are those occupational pension schemes which are run by private companies. The fourth type of pensions are those personal pension schemes which are set up by self-employed persons and employees who decide to opt out of their company pension scheme.

Let us now examine each of these schemes in turn.

THE STATE PENSION SCHEME

In the UK the State runs two schemes. First, the basic state pension scheme, which is available to all who contribute to the scheme for the requisite number of years. A pensioner must have contributed to the scheme for at least 40 years to obtain maximum benefits.

The second state scheme is the SERPS scheme, which is now being phased out, but which can still provide a significant addition to the basic pension if the individual has contributed to the scheme for a good

---

[11] Portable pensions were introduced by UK government legislation in 1987.
[12] ... or not as the case may be. The employee may prefer to keep his or her private pension fund secret. This can be arranged by an insurance company.

number of years in the past.[13] Many employees – 15 000 000 by 1994 – have been opted out of the SERPS scheme in favour of pension schemes run by their employers. A contributor to the SERPS scheme who works for an employer can build up the value of a SERPS pension by paying Class 1 NI contributions at the maximum rate.

It has been estimated that an employee on an average wage who is dependent on the SERPS scheme for a pension will receive an average pension of about £50 a week at 1994 values from SERPS, if he or she retires in 2010.[14]

The basic state pension in the UK is quite inadequate, failing to keep the retired pensioner with no other income above subsistence level. When measured as a percentage of the average industrial wage, the UK pension is the lowest in the industrialized world. Most pensioners whose sole income comes from their state pension also receive supplementary benefits.

These facts suggest that no one should rely simply on the basic state pension, even including SERPS, to provide an adequate income on retirement – certainly no one in the professional class. The basic state pension in the UK, which is currently provided at age 65 for a male and 60 for a female,[15] is no more than a useful supplement to other pension provisions built up over a working life.

FINAL SALARY BASED SCHEMES

Companies are not required by law to run a pension scheme, but most do. Since April 1988 no employee in the UK can be forced to join a company pension scheme; the employee is permitted to set up his or her own personal pension scheme, into which the employer is then obliged to pay the monthly contributions, rather than into the company scheme. Pension contributions are allowable against tax.

The most common form of company pension scheme operated in the UK is the final salary based scheme. Under this type of scheme the value of the pension received by the employee on retirement, usually at age 60 or 65, is based on two factors: a factor based on the final annual salary[16] on retirement, and a factor based on the number of years he has

[13] An individual who has contributed to the SERPS scheme in the past, even many years ago, can find out the additional pension he or she will receive from SERPS by phoning 0800 666 555 and asking for form NP38. Once this form is filled in and sent back to the relevant government department, information on the additional pension will be provided. Currently the maximum to be earned from SERPS is £79 a week.

[14] *Which Pension*, Spring 1994, p.4.

[15] The age at which a woman in the UK receives a state pension will be raised to 65 over the next 20 years.

[16] Based on the highest annual salary ever received, after past annual salaries are adjusted for inflation (or some variant of this).

contributed to the scheme. Normally the employee receives a pension on retirement equal to n/60ths or n/80ths of the final salary, where n equals the number of contributions to the scheme. An example of this type of scheme is provided in Exhibit 7.7. Many large private companies use the n/60 formula, but only compensate partly for inflation. Most government schemes use the n/80 formula but compensate fully for inflation. Whichever is the better scheme depends on the rate of future inflation. The n/80 schemes, which compensate fully for inflation, are the safer schemes but are likely to provide a lower average income to the retiree in the early years after retirement.

The employee usually contributes 5% to 8% of his or her gross monthly salary to the scheme, and the employer contributes an equal or greater amount. If the employee has not worked for a sufficient number of years to gain the maximum possible pension under the scheme, then additional years of contribution can sometimes be bought by the employee in a very tax efficient manner. This 'added years' option may

A Typical Salary Based Pension Scheme

Mr John Tyrrel retires as managing director of Bradford Manufacturing PLC on 31 December 1994. His final salary is £42 000 and he earned an additional £3000 in commission. He has worked for the company for 26 years and 8 months.

Bradford Manufacturing run a final salary based scheme which provides the retiree with n/80ths of their final salary on retiral – n represents the number of years the employee has worked for the company. Commission does not count towards the pension.

The pension partially compensates for inflation. If inflation is 5% or less in any year the inflation will be fully compensated in the next year's pension. If inflation is more than 5% then a 5% increase in the pension will be allowed in the following year.

A capital sum equal to twice the final year's salary will also be paid to Mr Tyrrel on retiral.

Since Mr Tyrrel earned £42 000 in his final year and has worked for the company for 26 years and 8 months, he will earn a pension of:

£ (26.66/80) × £42 000 = £14 000.

He will also receive a lump sum of £84 000.

Final salary based schemes may base the pension not on the final salary but on the highest salary ever received by the retiree when past salary levels are adjusted for inflation.

Exhibit 7.7   An example of a final-salary based pension scheme.

well prove to be an efficient investment outlet for any surplus funds the employee may have accumulated before retirement.

The tax authorities allow a much higher percentage of the employee's gross salary to be paid into his or her occupational pension scheme – up to 15% of salary – if the employee so wishes. If the individual is self-employed, he or she can contribute up to 17.5% of relevant earnings into a pension scheme up to the age of 35. The percentage rises to a maximum of 40% over the age of 60. A maximum cap is placed on relevant earnings – £76 800 in 1994–95.

An employee who opts into a 'final year based salary scheme' will usually retire with a pension equal to between 35% and 60% of his or her final year's gross salary, but between 45% and 75% of the final year's net salary, after all deductions have been made. It is the proportion of net salary that is the relevant figure to consider in pension planning, since this is the amount which is available for spending out of the gross salary. This net figure should be used when a PFA is comparing income before retirement with income after retirement.

If an employee intends to stay with a company for a long period of time, then the final salary based schemes provide excellent value for money. Company-based schemes often provide valuable perks which would be very expensive to purchase under a personal pension plan. Indeed, the cost of these perks is persuading some large companies to move to less expensive 'group personal pension' schemes which are run by insurance companies.

MONEY PURCHASE SCHEMES

Smaller companies usually prefer to organize 'money purchase' pension schemes for their employees, rather than a final salary based scheme. The latter type of scheme can prove to be rather expensive relative to the resources of a small company.

Under a money purchase pension scheme both the employee and the employer contribute an agreed amount each month to the pension fund – usually each party contributes around 5% to 8% of the employee's monthly salary. In addition both the employee and the employer pay a lower rate of NI contribution and this 'saving' is invested in a protected pension for the benefit of the employee.

The total contributions are placed in a fund for the benefit of the employee and spouse. The fund accumulates, with annual income added, until the employee retires. On retirement the amount accumulated in the fund is used to buy an annuity, the income from which will provide the employee with a pension. The future value of the pension is not known under this type of scheme – this will depend on the terminal value of the fund and the annuity rates offered by the insurance companies on the date of retirement. A minimum pension is sometimes guaranteed by the manager of the scheme, usually an insurance company, but this amount is likely to be based on a very conservative estimate.

Money purchase schemes tend to be used by smaller companies as an economical way of providing a pension for their employees at a known, relatively low, cost. The funds are usually administered by an outside organization, such as an insurance company or merchant bank, on behalf of the company.

The problem with annuity-based schemes is that the eventual income to be paid by the annuity is not known until the retirement date, and annuities do not pay out substantial returns until the annuitant is at least 65 years of age, thus an earlier than expected retirement date can leave the retiree with an inadequate pension. Another important factor to consider is that most money purchase schemes do not make allowance for future inflation.[17]

How much does the employee contribute to the fund?

As we noted above, if the employee is expected to retire at the normal age of 60 or 65 then their contribution is likely to be around 5% to 8% of gross monthly salary. There are exceptions to this rule if the employee works in a profession where retirement is at a younger age – for example, firemen, policemen and soldiers retire early. Early retirement can increase the monthly percentage contribution by a substantial amount. On the other hand, some private companies deduct much less than 5% of salary from the employee and occasionally no deduction is made, although this approach might create tax complications for the employee. If a fund is actuarially very sound, contributions to it from the employee may be waived for several years.

We noted above that an employee can opt to pay into a pension scheme a great deal more than the minimum required by the company if they feel that the pension provision at retirement will be inadequate. An additional lump sum pension can also be bought by using up unused tax allowances for up to six years past.

Special pension perks

In a moment we will be discussing personal pension schemes which are organized by the self-employed person or by individual employees who

---

[17] Annuities are available which make annual adjustments to the pension to allow for inflation, but these are very expensive annuities, sometimes costing almost double the cost of a non-inflation indexed annuity.

wish to organize their own pension. These schemes are under the control of the employee rather than of the company for which they work. One of the major deficiencies of such an approach to personal pension planning is the loss of certain perks which may be available for free from a company pension scheme.

Some examples of these 'perks' are as follows.

1. **Inflation compensation**. Most government schemes compensate entirely for inflation. Few private company schemes guarantee total compensation for inflation, but rather provide some limited form of 'capped' inflation compensation, for example a maximum of 5% increase in pension in any one year. The cost of compensating totally for inflation for every future employee who retires is so great that only governments can take this risk. The government can afford this cost because they are using other people's money!

   Money purchase schemes and personal pension schemes will not be inflation indexed unless the employee pays for the indexation, which is expensive.

2. **Early retirement**. What happens if the employee retires early, through ill health or redundancy? Many company pension schemes provide remarkably generous terms for early retirement including topping up the number of years worked to the maximum possible under the scheme. For example, an employee retiring at aged 58 who could have worked until age 65 can be awarded an additional seven years of contributions to the pension fund. Life and health insurance may also be provided after retirement up to the 'normal' retirement age.

   Personal pension schemes may provide no compensation whatsoever for early retirement.

3. **Ill health provisions**. Suppose the employee is off work for an extended period because of ill health. What are the salary implications of this and are the pension contributions paid on his or her behalf by the company while they are off work?

   Company pension schemes may take a more sympathetic approach if the employee is in the company scheme rather than having set up their own scheme independently of the company.

4. **Situation of spouse and children on death of employee**. If the employee dies while still at work or after retirement what portion of the pension, if any, will be paid to the spouse and children? Usually, under a company scheme, the spouse receives 50% of the pension rights which would otherwise have been enjoyed, until death, and an additional 25% for each child until the child reaches the age of 16. The precise conditions can vary a great deal between schemes. The terms need to be checked out by the PFA from the pension documentation.

Money purchase and personal pension schemes may be much less generous than company schemes on the death of the employee in service or after retirement. All benefits to be paid to dependants on the death of the pensioner need to be paid for as an additional cost in a personal pension scheme.

5.   **Transfer value of the pension rights**. When an employee moves from one company to another, the company which he or she is leaving works out a transfer value on the pension rights of the employee.

In this case the personal pension scheme may have an advantage over the company scheme. When the employee decides to transfer from one company to another the employee will ask for an estimate of the transfer value of the occupational pension fund. This value can be placed into the pension scheme of the new employer. However, the transfer value of the pension rights may be much less than the pension rights which would have been enjoyed had the employee remained with the previous employer. It has been claimed that the transfer value of pension rights may be worth no more than one half of the value which would have accrued to the employee had they remained with their first company.

If an employee transfers between companies several times during a working lifetime, these moves can seriously deplete the pension fund.

These problems will not arise if the employee has set up their own pension fund which is independent of the company scheme.

6.   **Other special benefits.** Many other special benefits may be attached to a company pension scheme. For example, in some cases the employee may be allowed to take over the payment of life assurance premiums previously paid by the company, after his or her retirement. Death while at work on company business sometimes results in a doubling of insurance benefits paid to beneficiaries, and so on. Some of these benefits are rarely triggered but they can be very valuable if the unusual event which triggers them should occur.

It often happens that an employee may not even be aware of the importance and value of these additional free perks attached to the company scheme. The PFA should identify these benefits from the pension documentation and inform the client accordingly.

PERSONAL PENSION SCHEMES

If an individual is self-employed or works for a company which has no pension plan, he or she has no option but to set up a personal pension plan in association with a financial institution.

Such schemes operate through the building up of a sufficient fund, via a savings plan, to buy an annuity on or after retirement which will generate the required income.

The individual setting up the pension fund has a choice as to where the monthly contributions into the pension fund will be placed. The contributions can be placed into a with-profits endowment insurance policy, a unit trust fund or a high interest deposit account.

In the case of a salary-related pension scheme, the value of the pension on retirement depends on the final salary of the employee. In the case of a personal pension fund which is used to buy an annuity, the value of the pension on retirement depends on two unpredictable factors: the final value of the pension fund on the date of retirement, and the rate of interest offered on annuities at this or a later date. Both of these variables are subject to wide variation.

If we look at the terminal value of pension funds accumulated over the last 20 years, the value of the best fund is 40% higher than that of the worst fund. While the return offered on annuities halved between 1990 and 1994!

We conclude that it is not easy to estimate the actual pension which will be generated from a personal pension plan.

In April 1988 the government introduced the possibility of an employee setting up his or her own personal pension plan.[18] This alternative is now available to all employees who wish to opt out of their company scheme and set up their own pension plan. Insurance companies are only too happy to arrange private pension schemes for any employee wishing to opt out of their company scheme.

The advantage to the employee of a personal pension plan is that the employee is no longer tied to one company. In the past, many employees felt that they were 'locked in' to employment with a given company by the value of the accumulated pension benefits. If the employee left the company, he or she might lose a substantial part of their future pension rights. Even if the accumulated pension rights were not lost, they might be 'frozen' until retirement, and by reason of inflation the real value of the pension might decline substantially in the intervening period.[19]

The availability of 'portable' pensions and additional voluntary contributions to pension schemes has given employees much greater potential control over their pension planning.

The majority of contributors to personal pension schemes are the self-employed. The government has provided generous tax benefits to the self-employed to encourage them to set up their own pension schemes to

[18] Under chapter IV Part XIV of the Income and Corporation Taxes Act 1988.
[19] Today, frozen pension rights must be upvalued to compensate for inflation up to a maximum of 5% a year.

provide themselves with adequate income on retirement. Indeed, these tax benefits are so generous that the self-employed would be foolish not to take full advantage of them.

However, the financial probity of personal pension schemes is currently a matter of some controversy. The self-employed have no choice but to enter into such schemes but the option is now available to any employee currently contributing to a company scheme. It has been claimed that employees opting out of company schemes into personal pensions are unlikely to benefit by the move. The various valuable perks attached to company schemes will be lost or will have to be paid for separately. These additional benefits are costly if not provided within a group scheme.

Since all pensions are now portable from company to company, personal pensions are somewhat less attractive than they were before portability was introduced.

It has also been suggested by some pension experts that personal pension plans entered into during the period 1988 to 1993 have not provided a very good return on the money invested in them, but this may well prove to be a short-term phenomenon caused by the peculiar financial conditions of this period.[20]

We conclude that it is unlikely that an employee already in a company pension scheme will benefit by transferring funds into a personal pension scheme. The self-employed must set up such a scheme, however – they have no other choice.

ADDITIONAL VOLUNTARY CONTRIBUTIONS (AVCS)

If an employee considers that the pension which will be provided by their company pension scheme is inadequate, probably because they will not be able to contribute to the scheme for a sufficient number of years to generate an adequate pension, they may consider 'topping up' the company pension rather than leaving the scheme. This can be done in one of two ways, both very tax efficient. If the employee works within the public sector he or she may be able to 'buy-in' additional years of contribution to the scheme. If the employee works in the private sector he or she can choose to make additional voluntary contributions (AVCs) to the company scheme. Another alternative is to set up an independent free-standing AVC (FSAVC) with an insurance company. As noted above,

---

[20] Many employees were induced to leave company schemes and the SERPS scheme and enter into personal pension schemes during the period 1990 to 1993 by personal financial advisers who advertised in the national press. In December 1993 a study financed by the SIB and conducted by KPMG found that many of these transfers may have been financially disadvantageous to the employees who chose this option. Compensation may have to be paid to the employees who transferred out. It was claimed in 1995 that the cost of this compensation could reach three billion pounds.

there are limits on the amounts an employee is allowed to contribute to such schemes.[21]

One disadvantage of placing an AVC into a company sponsored scheme is that, if the employee should switch companies, the transfer value is likely to be lower, perhaps significantly lower, than the fund accumulated under the independent FSAVC scheme.

An AVC can only be utilized on retirement, and the minimum age of retirement with an AVC is 50 years of age.

MOVING BETWEEN JOBS

As we noted above, when an employee moves from one job to another the question arises as to how to treat the existing pension rights in the company they are leaving.

If the employee has set up a personal pension scheme no transfer problem should arise – the new company will continue to pay the monthly pension contributions into this fund. But what happens if the employee is contributing to a company pension scheme? In this case the transfer value of the pension fund can be transferred directly into the new employer's pension scheme. An actuarial calculation is made to arrive at the transfer value of the fund.

However, there are several reasons why the employee may prefer not to switch the transfer value of his pension fund to a new company – for example, he or she may have become unemployed, or may be moving to work abroad. Under these conditions the pension rights can be frozen until the employee finds another job, moves back to his home country or reaches retirement age. These events could be some way in the future.

The employee is now faced with a series of possible choices. If the funds are left with the former employer the company must credit interest to the fund and top up the value of the fund each year by a maximum of 5% to compensate for inflation. However, it is unlikely that any employee would choose this option. A better option is to set up a pension transfer plan run by an insurance company. The insurance company will accept the fund and look after it until the employee enters a new pension scheme on finding work or on returning to the UK. Finally, the employee might decide to opt for 'pension independence' and set up a personal pension plan, transferring the existing transfer value of the fund into this plan. If the employee intends to switch jobs frequently in the future, this is likely to be the better option.

---

[21] The limit is 17.5% of net relevant earnings up to age 35, then increasing up to 40% of NRE beyond the age of 60. The maximum NRE was capped at £76 800 in 1995. This latter value is index-linked. The six-year 'carry back' and 'carry forward' provisions on contributions are particularly tax efficient with regard to such schemes.

TAX ASPECTS OF PENSION SCHEMES

In recent years British governments have tried to encourage the growth of private pension plans in order to reduce the burden on the state pension scheme. This encouragement has taken the form of providing substantial tax benefits to the employee or self-employed person who contributes towards a non-state run pension.

The tax provisions are complex and are changed quite frequently. We do not have sufficient space to pursue these matters in detail in this short chapter. Readers are referred to a current edition of Allied Dunbar's *Retirement Planning Guide*, or some other current manual on pension planning.

The basic tax philosophy of the government is to allow the employee's contribution to a pension scheme to be charged against income tax at either the employee's standard or marginal rate. When an income earner sets up a future pension with a lump sum, then so long as this individual enjoys access to a sufficient level of earned income, the reduction in income tax can provide a very substantial benefit to the taxpayer. These tax benefits can be backdated against prior earned income for up to six years. Other tax benefits are also awarded to pension contributions. For example an employer's contribution to an employee's pension fund is not taxable on the employee, and the various lump sums paid out of a pension scheme on retirement are not subject to tax up to a given limit. The pension income itself is taxed as normal income. The earnings of the investments in the pension fund, invested on behalf of the pensioner, are not subject to tax.

The tax treatment of pension mortgages are particularly tax efficient. The mortgage is granted on the security of the endowment insurance policy attached to the pension scheme. The mortgage itself is repaid out of the 25% of the pension fund value which can be encashed on retirement. All of the contributions to the pension fund are allowed against tax at the highest marginal rate of the contributor to the mortgage pension fund.

The tax treatment of pension planning is an extensive and complex subject in its own right. If the PFA is not a tax expert it is advisable, once a pension plan is nearing completion, to ask an expert on the taxation of pension funding to check out the scheme for tax efficiency.

PENSIONS AND ANNUITIES

Most personal pension schemes, in contrast to salary-based schemes, work on the following principles. The contributor pays a series of monthly payments, net of tax, into a pension fund over 10, 20, 30 or even 40 years and at the end of this period, on retirement from work, the money in the fund is used to buy an annuity. The income from this annuity pays the pensioner £x per month until death.

The value of the pension received by the pensioner thus depends on both the terminal value of the pension fund and the rate of interest paid on the annuity at the retirement or a later date. Neither of these factors is known to the employee until the date of retirement, although some pension schemes guarantee a minimum value pension.

We noted above that the contributor to a pension fund has a choice as to the type of fund into which to invest. For example, the fund can be invested in a with-profits endowment policy, a unit trust fund, a high interest deposit account or some other fund. Whatever the fund chosen, at least 75% of the proceeds from the encashed pension fund must, by tax regulation, be invested in an annuity.

The wide variation in the performance of different funds is illustrated in Exhibit 7.8. The difference in performance is influenced by the length of time the fund has been invested. Exhibit 7.8 shows that over an investing period of 20 years, the fund of highest value is 2.75 times the fund of lowest value. Over an investment period of five years the highest value fund is 1.23 times the lowest fund.

Exhibit 7.8 also shows that there is a substantial difference between current estimates of the projected value of unit linked pension funds for five, 15 and 25 years into the future.

Figures such as those set out in Exhibit 7.8 are somewhat misleading, since they ignore the changing value of money. Money fell in value in the UK by about 80% between 1973 and 1993, and is likely to fall in value by 50% to 70% over the next 25 years. The projected values of funds in the future must be adjusted to the present-day value of the pound to make the projections meaningful to the client.

BUYING THE ANNUITY

Only insurance companies are allowed to sell annuities, but the fund holder can select between annuities offered by a wide range of companies. They can also select between a wide range of different types of annuity.

If the pension fund is held by an insurance company the owner of the fund need not buy the annuity from the same insurance company if the fund has an 'open market' option attached to it. Most pension funds have the open market option attached.

At any particular time a significant difference exists between the rate of interest offered on annuities by the many companies operating in this market – it is not unknown for the highest rate offered to be one-third higher than the lowest rate offered. In other words, annuity rates as far apart as 12% and 9% can be offered at one and the same time. It pays to shop around or to approach an annuity broker, such as Annuity Direct, who will have access to the myriad of rates available at that point in time.

Funds Available from Pension Contributions

Personal Pension Funds: With Profit Policies

Sex	Male
Age	65
Premium	£200 a month
Date of retiral	1993
Actual retiral date	1993

Value of Open Market Option Pension Funds: end 1993

Years paid in	20	15	10	5
Performance of Fund	£	£	£	£
Highest	440 000	160 000	60 000	16 000
Average	302 000	136 000	52 000	15 000
Lowest	160 000	90 000	40 000	13 000

Personal Pension Funds: Unit Linked Pensions

Sex	Male	Male		Male
Age	40	50		60
Premium	£200	£200		£200 per month
Date of Retiral	2018	2008		1998

Projected Value of Fund

Years to Retiral	25	15		5
Performance of Fund	£	£	£	£
Highest	208 000	71 000		14 300
Average	190 000	66 000		13 500
Lowest	167 000	59 000		11 700

The above table illustrates the performance of the best, average and worst pension funds resulting from investing in a with-profits policy over five, 10, 15 and 20 years past. The tables are based on a monthly contribution of £200 a month for five, 10, 15 and 20 years ending in 1993.

The second table shows the projected payouts on a unit trust linked pension fund. The table estimates the likely best, average and worst terminal payouts for a male who will pay in £200 a month for the next five, 15 and 20 years. It is assumed he will retire at age 65.

It is most important to beware against the changing value of money in these estimates. For example a monthly payment of £200 in 1973 would be equal to £1143 in 1993 £ value! If inflation averages 5% a year from 1994 until 2018 then £208 000 in 2018 will be worth only £62 000 in 1993 £ values.

A sensible policy would be to increase the monthly premium by the rate of inflation. This policy should keep the terminal value of the fund up with inflation.

Exhibit 7.8   Estimated terminal value of an accumulating pension fund.

As is shown in Exhibit 7.9, age is a key factor in determining the income to be obtained from an annuity. Below the age of 60, annuity rates barely exceed the return on long-term government stock. The return obtainable on annuities rises sharply beyond the age of 65, however, and is a good investment option beyond 70 if the buyer of the annuity is healthy. In 1995 a 95-year-old man can obtain an annuity which pays out at a rate of 25% per annum!

Since women live, on average, four years longer than men, they are offered a somewhat lower rate of return at any particular age – normally around 11% to 13% less than the income offered to a man of the same age.

The various types of annuity on offer were described in Chapter 5. A 'joint annuity' pays the annuitant until his or her death, and then the income is transferred to the surviving spouse until death. As shown in Exhibit 7.9, joint annuities are quite expensive. In late 1993 a 60-year-old

Annuities: Level Rates as at January 1994

1. Based on £100 000 annuity
2. No guarantee or escalation
3. Paid monthly in advance

Age		Male	Index	Female	Index	Female/Male %	Joint
		£		£		%	
50		8450	100	7400	100	88	
55		8700	103	7650	103	88	
60		9600	114	8400	114	88	
70		12 300	146	10 800	146	88	

| M 60, F 57 | | | | | | | 7500 |
| M 65, F 63 | | | | | | | 8100 |

The income available from annuities varies a great deal from period to period. For example the income offered fell by about 25% between 1990 and 1993. There is also a wide variation between the income offered on annuities by the various insurance companies.

The above table illustrates how the income obtainable increases rapidly over the age of 65. Note that the income offered increased by 46% between the ages of 50 and 70. Because women live longer than men they tend to be offered about 12% lower income at any given age. The EU may be about to force a change in this situation.

Note the substantial drop in income offered for joint annuities. A man at age 60 can obtain £9600 a year. If the annuity is extended to both man and wife the income obtainable drops to £7500 a year. A drop of 20% in each year.

Exhibit 7.9 Annuities rates offered to men and women of various ages in January 1994.

man who could buy a flat rate annuity of £9600 a year for £100 000 would only be offered £7500 for a joint annuity – a fall in annual income of 22%.

The average annuity rate offered by the insurance companies is related to the long-term return on gilt-edged securities at that particular time. The return on gilts has varied from 6% to 12% over the last 10 years, so a pension annuitant can be unlucky in the sense that by chance he or she retires when annuity rates are low. An employee in a 'money purchase' scheme who has a choice of retirement date should check out current annuity rates before choosing the date to retire. We shall return to this point later.

So far we have been discussing pension annuities which have been given preferential tax treatment by the Inland Revenue. There are also 'purchased' annuities which are bought with cash out of taxed income like any other investment. Purchased annuities can be bought to top up a pension or to guarantee the availability of funds to pay school fees etc. in the future.

The income from purchased annuities is not taxed like normal income, but is subject to a different tax regime which assumes that the annual 'income' is a partial return of capital.

PHASED PENSION PLANS

We noted above that since the rate of return on annuities varies from month to month, a personal pension fund-holder can be unlucky to retire at a time when the return on annuities is low. Since 75% of the pension fund must be converted into an annuity, the pensioner may suffer from a low pension for the rest of their life simply because, by chance, they retired at the wrong time.[22]

One solution to this problem is to invest in a phased personal pension plan. A phased pension plan fund is divided into segments and each segment can be converted into a small annuity at a time chosen by the contributor to the plan, although the conversions must all take place between the ages of 50 and 75. Thus not all of the pension fund need not be converted into an annuity on the same date. If annuity rates are low, segments can be retained as investments and converted later when annuity rates are high.

A phased pension plan injects a useful degree of flexibility into pension planning. However, phased pension plans are only useful to those retirees who do not need access to all of their pension income immediately.

---

[22] However, if annuity rates are low the value of shares on the Stock Exchange may well be historically high. This will compensate to some extent for the low annuity rate, since the initial pension fund will be higher. Legislation introduced in 1995 now allows the purchase of the annuity to be deferred to a later date if the retiring person wishes to delay the conversion.

Phased plans also incur higher management charges than conventional pension plans.

GUARANTEED ANNUITIES

We stated earlier that an annuity is a gamble between the annuitant and the insurance company selling the annuity. If the annuitant dies early then the insurance company wins since, if an annuitant dies shortly after taking out a conventional annuity, the annuity terminates and nothing from the annuity falls into the estate of the annuitant.

An annuitant who wishes to ensure that part of the annuity value will fall into their estate on early death can buy a guaranteed annuity. Under this form of annuity the income from the annuity is guaranteed for a fixed number of years after it commences. If the annuitant dies within this period the insurance company pays the remaining guaranteed payments to the beneficiaries of the estate. The payment can either be a continuation of the annuity payments, or a discounted lump sum equal to this value.

The guarantee period is usually for five or 10 years. Surprisingly, this guarantee is not expensive. For a 65-year-old man with a life expectancy of 13 years a guaranteed annuity for five years would reduce the monthly payments by about 3% a year; for 10 years, by about 8% a year.

ANNUITIES ON IMPAIRED LIVES

An individual suffering from ill health who applies for a life assurance policy will find that they have to pay a much higher premium than if they were healthy. The reason for this is that their life expectancy is shorter than average, so the insurance company will collect fewer premiums than from a healthy individual.

The reverse of this situation arises when such an individual applies for an annuity. Their poor health means that the insurance company is likely to pay out fewer annuity payments than for a healthy individual, thus the annuity at any given income level will be cheaper.

An unhealthy individual is said to have an 'impaired life' and impaired life annuities can be bought from some, but not all, insurance companies.

Each case is considered individually on its merits and medical assessments are made. A 45-year-old man may receive an annuity income normally granted to a 65-year-old man. This somewhat ghoulish practice is unavoidable. The shorter the life expectancy, the higher the income granted from the annuity. Guaranteed annuities on impaired lives are either unobtainable or very expensive.

ANNUITIES AND INFLATION

Inflation is the major financial threat faced by those who live on annuity income. If the annuitant has invested in a flat-rate annuity the value of the income produced will fall roughly in proportion to the rate of price inflation.

How can the income from an annuity be protected against the impact of inflation?

There are several methods of protecting an annuity from inflation. The first approach is to buy an inflation indexed annuity. The value of the annuity income will be raised each year by the rate of inflation as expressed in a government index of inflation. This approach provides a perfect hedge against inflation. The disadvantage of this approach is the high cost of inflation indexed annuities. These annuities are financed by inflation indexed government stock. When expectations about the future of inflation are low indexed linked annuities are available at a reasonable price but if the future rate of inflation is expected to rise sharply inflation indexed annuities can become exceedingly expensive.

In 1988 when the current UK rate of inflation was 6.5% a £100 000 flat rate annuity would have provided an income of about £11 000 a year to a 65-year-old man. In this same year a £100 000 inflation indexed annuity would have provided an income in the first year of only £7000. By 1993 when the rate of inflation had fallen to just below 2% a year, a £100 000 flat rate annuity would have provided an income of £7500 a year to a 65-year-old man and an indexed linked annuity would have provided an annual income in the first year of only £4800 a year.

However, the index-linked income is safe in real inflation-adjusted terms. The annuitant will never become worse off than they were at the beginning of year one.

A second alternative is to buy an annuity which starts by providing an income well below that of a flat rate annuity, but which includes a built in 'escalator' on annuity income each year. The annuitant can select any rate of escalation, within reason. The rate can be, say, 3% or 6% or 8% or 10% a year.

The higher the escalator percentage, the lower will be the initial income from the annuity.

The income from an escalating annuity must eventually pass the income from a flat rate annuity, so long as the holder lives long enough!

Exhibit 7.10 shows the annual income from three escalator annuities and a flat rate annuity of the same cost. The higher the escalator percentage, the lower the initial income from the annuity. Note that the escalator annuities catch up with the flat rate annuity around years 9 to 12. Then the annual income from the escalator annuities leaps ahead.

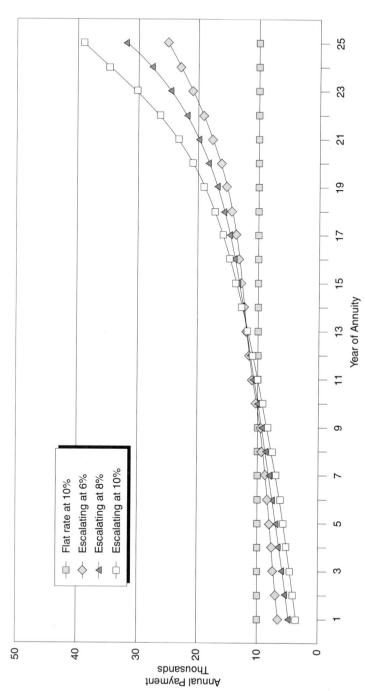

A flat rate annuity bought in year 1 would provide an income of £10 000 for life. If the annuitant wishes he can buy an escalating annuity. The initial income in year 1 will be much less than the flat rate annuity. However, the escalating annuity will increase the income in each year by x%, where x is the rate of annual increase in the annuity.

Notice that the flat rate annuity provides a higher income for about 9–12 years then the escalating annuity provides the higher income.

Exhibit 7.10 The returns on an 'escalating' annuity.

The escalator annuity hedges inflation so long as the average rate of inflation over the life of the annuity is lower than the escalator percentage. The disadvantage of this type of annuity lies in the higher cost or lower initial income.

An alternative shield against inflation is to buy an annuity invested in equity shares, such as a with-profits annuity. The income from this type of annuity depends on the dividends declared on the shares backing the annuity. As we noted in Chapter 5, ordinary shares have proved in the past to be an excellent hedge against inflation. The disadvantage of this type of annuity is that the income is neither constant nor predictable. The income of the annuitant can fall in those years when dividends are low.

Exhibit 7.11 shows some data from Equitable Life Assurance on the performance of a flat rate annuity, a with-profits annuity, an annuity escalating at 5% a year and an index-linked annuity. The profits of companies issuing equity shares did particularly well over this period, so the with-profits annuity is well ahead in 1993, but the escalator annuity will catch up in time.

Which then is the best method of hedging annuity income against inflation?

The index-linked and escalating annuities reduce income for the first 10 years or so after retirement, so an annuitant who retires at the age of 65 is poorer from the age of 65 to 75, but richer thereafter. We suspect that this trade-off would not be selected by the majority of the population.

Both the flat rate annuity and the equity linked annuity are risky. The flat rate risks high inflation, while the equity-based with-profits annuity risks occasional unpredictable dips in income. Despite this, we suspect that an equity-based with-profits or unit-linked annuity provides the package which is best suited to meet the needs of most retirees. The next best package is probably the 5% escalator annuity. As shown in Exhibit 7.4, inflation averaged around 5% in the UK from 1914 to 1994.

The attitude of the client to the taking of risk is the key factor here. Some clients will prefer to sacrifice a substantial part of their initial annuity income for the complete financial security provided by the inflation indexed annuity.

ANNUITIES AND TAX

The income from pension annuities is taxed like ordinary earned income. The fund creating the annuity has benefited from many tax concessions during its accumulation, so the Inland Revenue see no reason to provide additional tax benefits on the income from this fund.

'Purchased' annuities, that is annuities bought with savings which have already suffered tax, are treated quite differently.

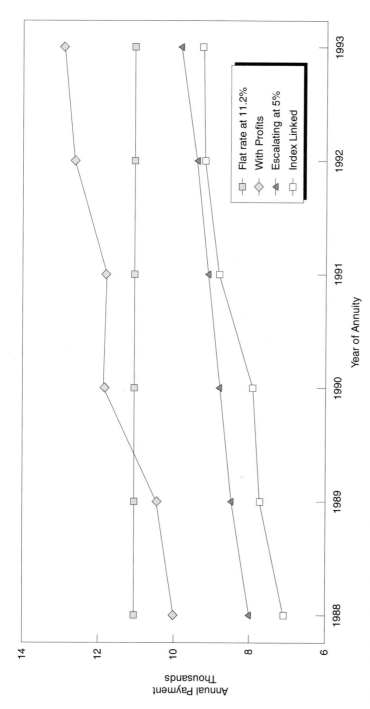

The graph shows the performance of four different kinds of annuity over the years 1988 to 1993. These were good years for equity shares. The income from the 'with profits' annuity beat the flat rate annuity in four of the five years. The index linked and escalating annuity (at 5%) had still not caught up with the flat rate annuity by 1993.

Source: Equitable Life. End of 1993 figures.

Exhibit 7.11   A comparison of the performance of different kinds of annuities 1988–93.

The Inland Revenue consider that the income received from a 'purchased' annuity is partly a return of capital. The capital sum invested in the annuity is being returned over the lifetime of the annuity. The tax treatment of the income from purchased annuities is as follows.

The Inland Revenue approve a set of mortality tables which estimate the life expectancy of any individual at any age. The cost of the annuity, in other words the amount invested in the annuity, is divided by the number of months the individual annuitant is expected to live when he or she buys the annuity. This amount is taken as the capital content of each annuity payment. The balance is taken to be interest and so income. This interest portion is taxed as investment, not earned, income and is added to the other income of the annuitant.

Let us take an example. A woman aged 65 has a personal pension fund valued at £400 000 when she retires. She commutes 25% of this into cash and invests this £100 000 into a purchased annuity which pays £9000 a year. The relevant mortality tables show that she has a life expectancy of 17 years, or 204 months. If we divide £100 000 by 204 we arrive at a monthly capital repayment of £490 a month. Her monthly income is £9000/12 = £750 a month. Thus £(750 – 490) = £260 is the interest portion of the payment. She will pay tax on the £260 at her marginal rate of tax. The £490 is tax-free. The figures are not exact, but they illustrate the method.

Annuities can thus allow a retired person to use up capital in a tax efficient manner without the hassle of selling off assets every year.

A guaranteed annuity left via a will to a beneficiary is taxed as investment income on the trust or on the beneficiary.

ANNUITIES AND GILTS

Annuity rates are closely tied to the rate of return obtainable on medium-dated gilts. Exhibit 7.12 shows the relationship between annuity rates, the return on medium dated gilts and the bank rate over the period 1990 to 1994.

WHAT HAVE WE LEARNED IN THIS CHAPTER?

1. On average a woman will live for a further 20–25 years after she retires, a man for 10–15 years. In order to enjoy a reasonable standard of living during this period, sufficient retirement funds need to be set aside during the preceding income-earning period.

2. The combination of an ageing population and an earlier age for retirement in the UK makes the funding of adequate pensions a major national problem. In the future the value of the state pension is likely to decrease in real terms. An increasing responsibility will thus

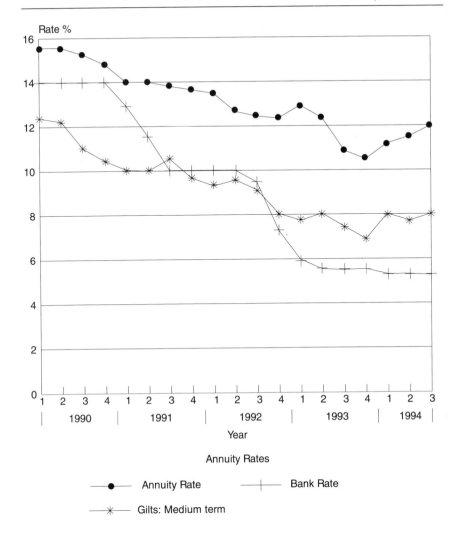

Annuity Rates

● — Annuity Rate   — Bank Rate

✳ — Gilts: Medium term

Note how the average return offered by insurance companies on annuities follows the return on gilt-edged securities.

Over the period from 1990 to 1994 the average return offered on an annuity to a man in normal health retiring at 65 varied from a high of 15.5% in 1990 to a low of 10.2% in early 1994. This represents a difference of £5300 a year on a £100 000 annuity!

It is important that a pension fund is so designed that the conversion of the pension fund into an annuity can be phased over a period of years if the current return offered on annuities is low. Alternatively derivatives can be used to 'lock in' a high return when the terminal date for retiral approaches.

Exhibit 7.12   The average returns on annuities, medium term gilts and base rate of interest 1990–94.

be placed on income earners to fund their own pensions after retirement during their income-earning period.

3. The PFA needs to ask the client five key questions to design a comprehensive pension plan. When will the client retire? How much annual income will the client need when he or she retires? Is the client employed or self-employed? How secure are the client's existing pension rights, and would he or she prefer to switch to a personal pension or add an AVC or FSAVC to the existing pension? What would be the situation regarding the income needs of dependants of the client, should the client die?

4. There are four basic sources of pension in the UK: the state schemes, the schemes run by government departments and public organizations, the schemes run by private companies, and personal pension plans. Most of the pension schemes run by public organizations and companies are based on the final salary of the employee. Smaller companies tend to offer money purchase schemes to their employees. The self-employed are being encouraged to set up tax efficient personal pension plans by the government.

5. All pension schemes in the UK must now be 'portable'. This means that the employee can carry the current transfer value of his or her pension fund from one company to another when he or she changes employer. Alternatively the frozen pension rights must be upvalued for interest and inflation each year. If the employee does not move immediately to another job, or takes up employment abroad, certain problems arise. Each of the options available to deal with this problem need to be carefully evaluated to calculate what should be done with the frozen pension rights in such cases.

6. A PFA who is asked to review a pension scheme must pay particular attention to the security of the scheme and also to the 'special' benefits which are provided by many companies within the pension scheme. These benefits can be expensive to buy-in as part of a personal pension. Examples of such special benefits are early retirement options, cover for dependants, and ill-health benefits. These benefits are particularly worthy of consideration if the employee is considering moving from a company scheme to a personal pension scheme.

7. Taxation is a very important part of pension planning, since the government has provided generous tax allowances to encourage individuals to set up proper pensions for themselves after retirement. The contributions to the pension fund are allowable against tax, the dividends on the pension fund do not pay tax and 25% of the terminal fund can be encashed without incurring a tax penalty. Pensions are treated like earned income.

8. With a personal pension, 75% of the terminal value of the pension fund must be converted into an annuity. Many types of annuity are

on offer. The flat rate annuity is reduced by inflation, so some pensioners prefer to invest in index-linked annuities, share-based annuities or annuities that start with a low income but escalate the value of the annuity by a fixed percentage each year. While pension-based annuities are taxed like earned income, the capital portion of income from purchased annuities is exempt from tax.

FURTHER READING

Anon. (1993) *The Pensions Fact Book.*
Bean *et al.*: a useful collection of facts about pension provision in the UK.
Marshall (1993): a guide to pensions in the UK which pays particular attention to tax aspects of pension planning.
Oldfield (1994): a guide to the current types of occupational pension schemes available in the UK.
Stone and Cox (quarterly) *Individual Pensions Handbook*: these regularly updated tables provide a wealth of information on current pension schemes offered by insurance and other companies. Very useful to the pension consultant.
Williamson (1993): an introduction to the various types of annuities available.
Wilson and Wilson (1988): a useful introduction to the various types of pension schemes offered in the UK.

See bibliography on p.311 for a full annotation of these books.

TUTORIAL QUESTIONS: PENSIONS

1. The financial life cycle of the individual is often divided into three periods. What are these three periods? How long do they last? Which of these periods are likely to have a positive cash flow?
2. Why is it that the real value of the state pension in the UK is likely to fall over the next 50 years, despite the fact that the real national income of the UK will almost certainly rise during this period?
3. What are the five key questions a PFA needs to ask a client before beginning to design a retirement plan?
4. Describe some of the factors which may make the future value of a pension fund insecure.
5. What kind of a pension fund are the following persons likely to enter into: (a) a self-employed builder, (b) a senior executive in a multinational company, (c) the manager of a small textile mill?
6. The dependants of a contributor to a pension fund are likely to derive what kind of benefits from the pension fund?
7. Suggest two methods of ensuring that the value of a pension compensate for the falling value of money in the future.
8. 'Normally one should aim at setting up an indexed pension of about two-thirds of your cash flow in the year before retirement.'
    (a) Explain what is meant by 'cash flow' in this context.

(b) Explain what is meant by 'indexed'.

(c) Why is 66% of the cash flow prior to retirement considered to be enough spending power rather than 100% of cash flow?

9. What is a 'portable' pension?

10. Why are the years between 60 and 65 often 'an awkward time' financially for many men and women who retire between these ages in the UK? What advice could a PFA give to a client who expects to retire at age 65 in 10 years' time but could be retired earlier?

11. Suggest three reasons why a fully funded company pension might prove to be inadequate at the age of 65, even though the employee has made full contribution and the pension plan had seemed to be adequate when it was set up, say, at the age of 40. What advice can a PFA give to a client about covering these risks regarding an inadequate pension?

12. Suggest three benefits which a company pension scheme might provide to an employee which a personal pension scheme might not. Why then is it reported that many employees have opted out of their company scheme and chosen to set up a portable personal pension plan instead?

13. What do you expect the average rate of (consumer) price inflation to be in the UK over the period 1995–2005. (Inflation has averaged out at 5.4% over the period from 1914 to 1993.)

Allocate 100 probability points between the following rates:

1–2.9 %, 3–4.9%, 5–6.9%, 7–8.9%, 9–10.9%, 11–12.9%, over 13%.

What does your weighted average expected inflation turn out to be? (The expected value of inflation.)

14. If average consumer price inflation is 5% a year from 1995 to 2004, by how much will an unindexed pension of £18,000 a year starting on 1.1. 95, be reduced to in real terms by 2004?

15. Explain the difference between a final salary based pension scheme and a money purchase scheme. What kind of company prefers to run a money purchase type of pension scheme? Which type of scheme is best for the employee?

16. A client comes to you with details regarding her company pension scheme. What are the key questions to ask about the scheme regarding (a) early retirement, (b) ill health, (c) spouse, (d) portability, (e) security of the scheme?

17. If an employee who has been contributing to a company pension scheme for 15 years leaves the company and takes a job abroad what options are available regarding the pension rights he leaves behind?

Suggested solutions to even numbered questions are provided at the back of this book.

Housing

8

INTRODUCTION

For most individuals the acquisition of a family home is the most important investment they will ever make in their lives. Living accommodation is essential for everyone, and the ownership of one's own home lays the foundations of a secure life. Most individuals seem to prefer to own their home rather than to rent it, if the finances for home-ownership are available.

The importance of housing within the portfolio of personal investments owned by individuals in the UK is demonstrated in Exhibit 8.1. The figures, which are taken from the CSO Blue Book series, show that the value of housing made up some 42% of the total value of all assets owned by individuals in the UK in 1992, and some 58% of the value of accessible assets.[1]

These statistics demonstrate that the acquisition and maintenance of a family home are a very important part of financial planning for most clients.

In this chapter we will examine four aspects of this complex subject. First we will examine the problem of financing the acquisition of a home. Second we will enquire whether housing is a good investment, as distinct from a necessary investment. Third we will compare the cost of buying a home with the cost of renting a home, and finally we will briefly discuss the importance and cost of maintaining a home in good condition.

FINANCING THE ACQUISITION OF A HOME

The average value of a home in the UK in 1994 was approximately £62 000.[2] In the Central London region the average price was £80 000. These values

---

[1] An 'accessible asset' is an asset which can be sold if a buyer can be found. Examples of such assets are a house, company shares and jewellery. The current value of an employee's pension rights and many whole-life assurance policies are not accessible assets under this definition. It might be more correct to say that these assets are only accessible to the owner at an unacceptably high cost.

[2] Nationwide Anglia quarterly housing report, December 1994.

stand 10% to 15% below the equivalent values for 1989. Despite this fall in the value of housing the cost of the average home still represents a very substantial investment for the average wage-earner in the UK. The average house value stands at 2.9 times the average annual wage. Professional workers, who make up most of the clients serviced by PFAs, will tend to aim at acquiring more expensive properties costing in the region of £150 000 to £400 000 – possibly five to eight times their annual salary.

Were it not for the existence of financial institutions which specialize in providing housing loans (mortgages) to individuals to acquire property the average individual would have to save up for half a lifetime before he or she could hope to acquire a home of their own. This is the situation in Japan, where the financing of privately owned housing is underdeveloped.

Financial institutions in the UK pioneered the process of providing cheap loans to individuals to buy their own homes and the British system of providing mortgage finance to individuals is still the most advanced in

How personal wealth is distributed among assets owned by persons in the UK

Real Assets	**%**
Housing	42
Other real assets	5
% of asset value held in the form of real assets	47

Other assets held by persons

Insurance and pension rights	27
Building society deposits	7
Equity shares	7
Bank deposits and national savings	8
Other assets held	4

% of asset value held in the form of financial assets	53
	100 %

Note that the value of housing makes up over 40% of the value of assets owned by individuals in the UK. Insurance and pension rights are the other major asset owned by persons. The fraction of personal wealth held in the form of building society deposits is almost equal to the value held in the form of equity shares.

Source: Government Blue Book 1992: HMSO.

Exhibit 8.1   The distribution of personal wealth among assets held by persons in the UK.

the world. In no other country of the world is it so easy for an individual on a moderate wage to buy a home.

Building societies are still the main providers of housing loans in the UK but, in recent years, commercial banks and insurance companies have made a determined effort to enter the housing loan market, along with mortgage corporations from the USA and even some foreign financial institutions which offer housing loans denominated in foreign currencies to UK citizens.

The range of institutions offering finance for house purchase in the UK is now so varied that the individual house purchaser is spoilt for choice.

Many types of mortgage are now offered to the potential home buyer. Forty years ago any person wishing to buy a home would be offered only one type of loan, a simple repayment mortgage. Today he or she will still be offered a repayment mortgage, but in addition they are likely to be offered any one of a range of endowment mortgages. These will include the simple endowment mortgage, a unit trust mortgage, a PEP mortgage, or even a tax efficient pension mortgage.

The interest paid on the mortgage might be offered at a fixed rate or a variable rate. The borrower might be asked if he or she wishes to repay the mortgage over 25 years, the usual period, or over a shorter period. They might be offered an interest-only mortgage or a rolled-up interest mortgage. They might even be asked if they wish to have a mortgage denominated in sterling or in some other foreign currency such as Swiss francs.

Thus the finance of housing in the UK has become a much more complicated operation in recent years. This very complexity provides opportunities for the PFA to save a client money and design a financing package best suited to the needs and resources of the client. The job of the PFA is to match the needs of the client to the widening pool of financing opportunities available in the housing market.

TYPES OF MORTGAGE

House mortgages can be divided into two basic types. First there is the simple repayment mortgage, the traditional form of mortgage. The borrower repays the loan over n years in equal instalments, each of which includes a portion of capital and a portion of interest. The payments are usually made once a month, but the interest charge is usually calculated in advance on a yearly basis. Although each payment consists of a portion of interest and a portion of capital, very little capital is repaid during the first two-thirds of the repayment period – most is repaid in the last third of the loan period. Exhibit 8.2 illustrates the portion of capital and interest repaid in each year during the repayment of a 25-year repayment mortgage. Note how high a proportion of the early payments consists of interest.

The lender of the mortgage will insist that the house, which provides the security for the loan, is insured for the full cost of rebuilding it. A 'reducing' term insurance policy is likely to be taken out on the life of the borrower for the benefit of the lender, to cover the risk that if the borrower dies his or her beneficiaries might not be able to repay the mortgage out of the estate.

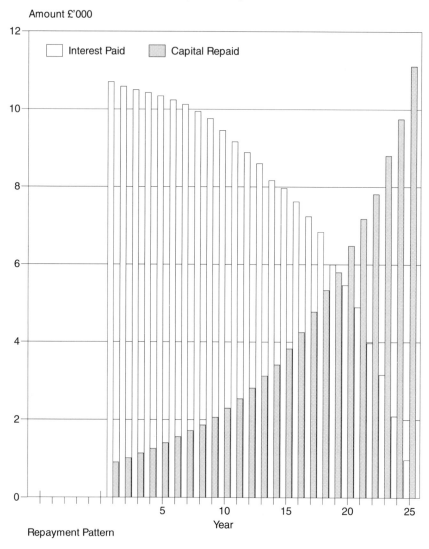

Exhibit 8.2   The proportion of capital and interest in each annual instalment of a 25 year repayment mortgage.

The major alternative to the repayment mortgage is the endowment mortgage. In this case the monthly mortgage payment is again made up of two parts. The first part, as before, consists of the interest payment on the loan, the second part is the premium on a with-profits endowment insurance policy on the life of the borrower.

Under a with-profits endowment policy no capital is repaid over the life of the loan, only interest is paid. However, the terminal value of the with-profits or other type of endowment insurance policy which is taken out is calculated to be sufficient to repay the mortgage at the end of the loan period. If the borrower should die before the loan is fully repaid, the mortgage is repaid out of the proceeds of the life policy, just as it would have been in the case of the repayment mortgage.

The mechanism of repayment is as follows. Under a with-profits endowment insurance policy a part of the monthly payment is invested by the insurance company on behalf of the borrower. These monthly investments accumulate, together with the income on the past invested payments, to create a fund sufficient to repay the mortgage at the end of the loan period.

Since the lending company is dependent on the proceeds of the endowment fund to repay the mortgage, the lending company is very conservative in setting the amount of the monthly insurance premium – it will be set high enough to ensure that sufficient funds will be available at the end of the loan period to repay the mortgage out of these funds. In fact, under a with-profits policy the premium is usually fixed at so conservative a level that a substantial additional sum is likely to be available to the borrower at the end of the mortgage period. That is to say a sum will be available in addition to the amount needed to repay the mortgage. Thus an endowment insurance policy is a 'bundled financial product, a house financing plan plus a savings and investment plan.

Alternative types of endowment policy are also offered. One of these is the 'non-profit endowment policy'. This type of policy is not recommended. A repayment mortgage will usually achieve the same objective as a non-profit endowment mortgage, at lower cost.[3]

Which of these two options, the repayment mortgage or the endowment mortgage, is the better option for the house buyer? The answer to this question depends on the definition of 'better' and the particular circumstances of the client.

---

[3] It depends on the rate of interest, assuming that this is at a variable rate. If the rate of interest in historically low and the tax allowance high, the non-profit policy might be cheaper than the repayment mortgage because it consists entirely of interest whereas the payments on the repayment policy include some capital repayment which is neither variable nor allowable against tax. However, the tax allowances on mortgage interest are currently being reduced, which will reduce the benefit of the non-profit policy.

which are not otherwise available, or the provider of the plan may discount the plan if the products are 'bundled'. Otherwise it is probably more efficient, financially, to structure each need into a separate plan since this approach is likely to provide greater flexibility within each plan.

FIXED OR VARIABLE INTEREST?

Fixed interest loans have always been on offer to the public in the UK, but from a rather limited range of sources. Until quite recently almost all house mortgages on offer were of the variable interest type. This type of

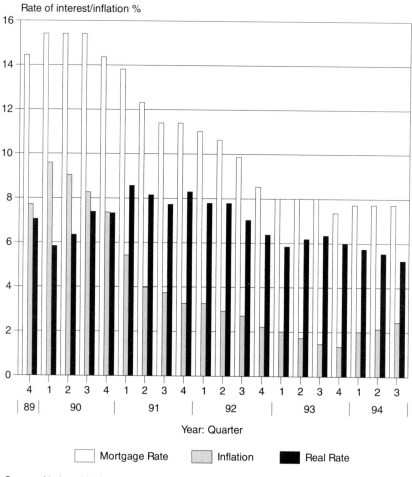

Source: Nationwide Anglia Building Society

Exhibit 8.3   The average mortgage rate of interest in the UK 1989–94, before and after allowing for inflation.

mortgage provides more security to the lender, since, as the market rate of interest changes, so the rate charged on the mortgage changes and the lender's profit margin is secure. Exhibit 8.3 shows that the mortgage rate, which is heavily influenced by government policy, changes frequently in the UK.

In recent years fixed interest mortgages have been offered by most lenders in the housing market in the UK. Thus the borrower is able to choose between a variable rate loan and a fixed rate loan. The fixed rate mortgage is usually offered for shorter periods than the variable rate, although there are exceptions to this rule.

A fixed rate home mortgage is seldom offered for the full mortgage term of 25 years – usually it is offered for a period of two, three or five years and is renewable, as another fixed rate loan, at the end of this period. The level of the new interest rate on offer at the end of the initial loan period is decided by the mortgage lender at that time. The borrower need not accept this offer of a new fixed rate loan at the end of the loan period, and can negotiate a new loan with another company.

How does a PFA decide whether to put a client into a variable or a fixed rate mortgage? The decision depends on the level of the fixed rate of interest offered on the loan compared to expectations as to the trend of future interest rates on the open market over the period. The expectation as to the trend of future open market rates, in its turn, is much influenced by expectations as to the trend of future inflation. The decision is not an easy one to make!

The average nominal rate of interest, gross of tax and inflation, on variable interest mortgage loans over the period from 1970 to 1993 in the UK was around 9%. If this rate can be taken as a guide to the future, then if a fixed rate loan is offered significantly below 9% it would seem prudent to take the fixed rate mortgage rather than the variable rate. Unfortunately the past is no sure guide to the financial future, and the long-term real rate of interest seems to be stabilizing in the UK at a lower rate than in the past. This is not true in the EU as a whole.

We conclude that accepting a fixed rate loan for a good number of years ahead, say five years, at a gross rate below 7% would seem to be safe unless the market rate of interest should collapse, which is most unlikely. Accepting a fixed rate above 9% would seem to be unwise.

The decision will also be influenced by the PFA's expectations about future inflation rates and by the tax rate at which mortgage interest can be charged against tax. Expectations as to the future rate of inflation over various periods ahead can be estimated from the difference between the current return on inflation indexed bonds for a given period compared to the current return on unindexed bonds of the same type for the same period.

In this case we also consider the cost of maintaining the house and the fee to the renting agent.

We see that if we ignore the capital appreciation in the value of the house then the return on a large house, treated simply as an investment, is very poor. In other words a large house in the UK is only a worthwhile investment if it is expected to attract a substantial tax-free capital gain during the period of ownership. Over the long period from 1945 to 1993 the average increase in detached house prices in the UK was under 2%

		£200 000 5-bedroom house	£100 000 3-bedroom house	£50 000 2-bedroom flat
Monthly			£	
Maintenance cost		167	100	63
Mortgage cost		1561	781	390
Renting agency cost		120	72	48
Assumed tax assessed		0	0	0
Total monthly cost		1848	953	501
Capital appreciation	7%	1167	583	292
(in nominal terms)	3%	500	250	125
	0%	0	0	0
Assumed monthly rent £		1000	600	400
Total monthly income	at 7%	2167	1183	692
Appreciation at:	at 3%	1500	850	525
	at 0%	1000	600	400
Monthly surplus	at 7%	319	231	191
Appreciation at:	at 3%	-348	-103	24
	at 0%	-848	-353	-101
Nominal return	at 7%	1.91	2.77	4.58
(% per annum)	at 3%	-2.09	-1.23	0.58
	at 0%	-5.09	-4.23	-2.42

The return on rented accommodation is highly sensitive to the current rate of interest on the mortgage used to finance the purchase. However, the above figures show that it is difficult to make an adequate return on rented accommodation.

Rent is not a constant proportion of the market value of the house. Low-value flats and houses can be rented for a much higher proportionate rent than expensive houses, except in large cities. The data used are taken from the renting book of a large estate agent.

Exhibit 8.10(b)   An estimate of the nominal rate of return on an investment in rented accommodation of various sizes.

mortgage provides more security to the lender, since, as the market rate of interest changes, so the rate charged on the mortgage changes and the lender's profit margin is secure. Exhibit 8.3 shows that the mortgage rate, which is heavily influenced by government policy, changes frequently in the UK.

In recent years fixed interest mortgages have been offered by most lenders in the housing market in the UK. Thus the borrower is able to choose between a variable rate loan and a fixed rate loan. The fixed rate mortgage is usually offered for shorter periods than the variable rate, although there are exceptions to this rule.

A fixed rate home mortgage is seldom offered for the full mortgage term of 25 years – usually it is offered for a period of two, three or five years and is renewable, as another fixed rate loan, at the end of this period. The level of the new interest rate on offer at the end of the initial loan period is decided by the mortgage lender at that time. The borrower need not accept this offer of a new fixed rate loan at the end of the loan period, and can negotiate a new loan with another company.

How does a PFA decide whether to put a client into a variable or a fixed rate mortgage? The decision depends on the level of the fixed rate of interest offered on the loan compared to expectations as to the trend of future interest rates on the open market over the period. The expectation as to the trend of future open market rates, in its turn, is much influenced by expectations as to the trend of future inflation. The decision is not an easy one to make!

The average nominal rate of interest, gross of tax and inflation, on variable interest mortgage loans over the period from 1970 to 1993 in the UK was around 9%. If this rate can be taken as a guide to the future, then if a fixed rate loan is offered significantly below 9% it would seem prudent to take the fixed rate mortgage rather than the variable rate. Unfortunately the past is no sure guide to the financial future, and the long-term real rate of interest seems to be stabilizing in the UK at a lower rate than in the past. This is not true in the EU as a whole.

We conclude that accepting a fixed rate loan for a good number of years ahead, say five years, at a gross rate below 7% would seem to be safe unless the market rate of interest should collapse, which is most unlikely. Accepting a fixed rate above 9% would seem to be unwise.

The decision will also be influenced by the PFA's expectations about future inflation rates and by the tax rate at which mortgage interest can be charged against tax. Expectations as to the future rate of inflation over various periods ahead can be estimated from the difference between the current return on inflation indexed bonds for a given period compared to the current return on unindexed bonds of the same type for the same period.

A fixed rate loan provides one considerable advantage to the borrower. The borrower knows exactly how much cash they will have to find to pay the fixed rate loan over that period. This allows for accurate cash budgeting – no small advantage when we consider that the nominal cost of a variable rate mortgage swung between a low of 5% and a high of 16% over the period between 1970 and 1993, and that even the real rate swung between 5.5% and 8.5% during the short period between 1989 and 1993 – see Exhibit 8.3.

HOW MUCH TO BORROW?

Cash budgeting is a key activity in financial planning. The monthly payment on a mortgage is likely to be the largest single regular payment made by a client. The amount of the monthly mortgage payment is determined by several factors – the amount of the loan, the interest rate on the loan, the tax allowed on the interest payment and the length of the repayment period.

The PFA needs to ensure that this regular payment will not cause financial distress to the client now or at some point in the future. Thus the PFA needs to calculate the monthly net of tax cost of the mortgage under various assumptions, and ensure that the client's future income can cope with these payments. For example, what will be the impact on the family cash flow if a wife becomes pregnant and gives up work; what happens if a breadwinner falls ill or unexpectedly loses his or her job?

Exhibit 8.4 sets out the annual charge on a £100 000 repayment mortgage under various assumptions about interest rates and repayment periods. These figures take no account of the fact that interest on a mortgage up to £30 000 is currently allowed to be charged against tax at the 15% rate in the UK. This allowance is likely to be phased out.[9]

Figures such as these can be used to calculate what fraction of the regular monthly net cash flow of an individual or a family can be safely committed to mortgage repayment.

Lenders themselves limit the size of the mortgage they are prepared to offer to a multiple of the individual or family annual gross income. Twenty years ago this multiple was two, and it was only applied to the income of the main breadwinner. The years following 1985 witnessed a dramatic increase in the multiple offered by lenders. In some cases lenders offered three times the income of the breadwinner plus another fraction of a multiple for the spouse if he or she was a wage-earner. These multiples subsequently proved to be much too high and many who borrowed in the late 1980s ran into severe financial difficulties in the early

---

[9] Budget speech by the Chancellor of the Exchequer, Kenneth Clarke, November 1993.

Repayment Period (Years)	Mortgage Loan	Interest Rate	Monthly Payment	Total Amount Paid	Additional Interest Paid
5	£100 000	12	£2224	£133 467	
10	£100 000	12	£1435	£172 165	£38 698
15	£100 000	12	£1200	£216 030	£82 564
20	£100 000	12	£1101	£264 261	£130 794
25	£100 000	12	£1053	£315 967	£182 501

Repayment Period (Years)	Mortgage Loan	Interest Rate	Monthly Payment	Total Amount Paid	Additional Interest Paid
25	£100 000	15	£1281	£384 249	
25	£100 000	12	£1053	£315 967	(£68 282)
25	£100 000	10	£909	£272 610	(£111 639)
25	£100 000	8	£772	£231 545	(£152 704)
25	£100 000	6	£644	£193 290	(£190 959)

The normal repayment period for a mortgage in the UK is 25 years. When inflation was high, say above 10%, it made financial sense to repay a mortgage over a long period and allow the rate of inflation to destroy the real value of the debt. Under current conditions, when inflation in the UK is under 4%, it is worth considering repaying a mortgage over a much shorter period of 20 or 15 years if the cash is available to do so.

Note from the above table the additional interest saved on a mortgage of £100 000 repaid over 15 rather than 25 years; the saving is close to £100 000!

The rate of interest also has a degree of influence on the total interest paid which might come as a surprise to some clients. A drop in the rate from 12% to 6% on a 25-year mortgage of £100 000 saves around £122 000 over the 25 years.

Exhibit 8.4 Monthly cost of a repayment mortgage under various repayment schemes (ignoring tax allowance).

1990s. The ratio of average house price to average earnings reached 4.65 in June 1989,[10] against a long-term average of 3.

The gross earnings of the breadwinner is the wrong measure of income to use. The correct measure of income to use is the net monthly cash flow from all sources of the breadwinner and spouse after tax and other compulsory deductions have been subtracted. A family should not commit more than one-third of this net cash flow towards mortgage payment, unless there is strong evidence that the cash flow will increase in the near future. If the borrower is in the top quartile of professional earners this proportion can, perhaps, be increased to 40%. The current level of house prices is also a key factor (see below). If the current level of house prices is well below the long-term trend line the percentage might be increased somewhat, but it is not wise to commit a client to an excessive

[10] Nationwide Anglia Building Society house price index, June 1989.

mortgage if he or she can be persuaded otherwise. The one-third of net cash flow rule is a sound basis for a decision.

The estimated future net cash flow of the family over the next decade is also an important factor, as is the job security of the breadwinner and spouse.

How much will one-third of net cash flow allow a client to borrow at an average gross rate of interest of 9%? A gross family income of £30 000 a year – a substantial income which would have placed the household in the top 10% of family incomes in the UK in 1994 – will only allow the borrower to take out a loan of £70 000 over 25 years using this rule. The average value of a new mortgage taken out in 1993 in the UK was £50 000.

In the late 1980s it became fashionable to take out a mortgage costing much more than one could afford in order to buy an expensive house as an investment which would appreciate in value in the future. The value of the mortgage, it was assumed, would be destroyed by inflation. Between 1989 and 1994 nominal house prices in the UK dropped on average by 12%, and inflation fell to an annual rate well below 4% – we know better now. Two million households in the UK were enjoying the fruits of 'negative equity' by the end of 1993. Negative equity occurs when the loan on a house exceeds the current market value of the house. There should be a notice on all house sale contracts warning the buyer that house prices can go down as well as up!

PFAs should discourage their clients from confusing the accommodation decision with the investment decision. Clients should be encouraged to buy property at a price they can afford. Inflation no longer destroys the value of a mortgage, and housing, as we shall see later in this chapter, has proved to be a rather poor investment at most times in the past in most of the countries of the world. The PFA should always be very cautious in giving advice on property finance.

THE DOUBLE MORTGAGE PROBLEM

A final caution on limits to borrowing. A client who is selling a home and finds a new 'dream home' before the original house is sold may well decide to negotiate a temporary bridging loan from a bank, which allows him or her to own both homes until the old home is sold. This is a very dangerous course of action to pursue, although, alas, it is all too common. In some sad cases it has even led to the bankruptcy of the dual owner. The problem of the double mortgage is often not obvious to the house seller who lacks financial sophistication.

A dual owner must pay interest on the original mortgage plus the interest, usually at a higher rate, on the entire cost of the new home. This monthly joint interest bill can easily exceed the entire monthly cash flow of the dual owner. See Exhibit 8.5.

Loans	Repayment Period (Years)	Mortgage Loan	Interest Rate	Monthly Payment
Loan 1	25	30 000	6	193
Loan 2	25	100 000	8	772
Total		130 000		965

During the late 1980s many house-buyers fell into the 'mortgage nutcracker'. They found a new house before they had finalized the sale of the old. They bought the second home with an additional bridging mortgage and then the sale on the first home fell through. Thus they were left with a substantial double mortgage, which could well exceed their entire monthly cash flow.

Exhibit 8.5   The double mortgage 'nutcracker'.

If the dual owner sells the original house within a reasonable period, say within three months, the additional interest charges to the bank can be rolled up and paid off out of the proceeds of the surplus on the house which is sold. But suppose there is a failure to sell within three months, or six months, or a year? A financial catastrophe will be building up, month by month. This happened many times during the 1989–90 period in the UK, when the bottom fell out of the housing market. Amateur house speculators found themselves saddled with a rapidly depreciating and unsaleable asset, their old home, and an exponentially mounting debt burden on the new one.

So far as the PFA is concerned the moral of this cautionary tale is, 'Don't let your client buy a new house before he or she has sold the old one.' Sophisticated methods are available for holding on to the right to purchase a new home until the old home is definitely sold.

WHAT LOAN REPAYMENT PERIOD?

The conventional period for repaying a mortgage on a house in the UK is 25 years. Most borrowers accept this period of repayment without question, but a mortgage can, within reason, be repaid over any period the borrower wishes, although the maximum period offered is likely to be 30 years.

Twenty-five years need not be the optimal repayment period for every borrower. Two important factors to consider in choosing a repayment period are the number of years to retirement, and the monthly cash flow available to the borrower.

In certain circumstances there are good reasons for advocating a period of repayment of much less than 25 years. A borrower who enjoys a sufficiently large regular cash flow should consider making a higher regular payment over a shorter period. When inflation is high, say over 8% per annum, it is likely that the real rate of interest will be relatively low,[11] and sometimes even negative, after allowing for inflation and tax. Under such circumstances, which prevailed in the UK between 1973 and 1981, a long repayment period allows inflation to destroy the real value of the mortgage. On the other hand, when the real rate of interest is high, as in the UK in the early 1990s, the PFA should consider advising the client to repay the mortgage over a much shorter period, to save on interest charges. Exhibit 8.4 showed the net cost of repaying a £100 000 mortgage over 25, 20, 15, 10 and five years respectively. Note the substantial saving in interest charges that can be achieved by early repayment. If sufficient cash flow is available, the PFA should consider advising the client to adopt the shorter repayment option when the real rate of interest is high.

The general rule should be that the higher the real rate of interest and therefore, quite probably, the lower the rate of current and expected inflation, the quicker the mortgage should be repaid if the client's cash flow is sufficient to finance this option.

SHOULD A MORTGAGE BE REPAID EARLY IF FUNDS BECOME AVAILABLE?

It often happens that a client with a large mortgage suddenly finds that he or she has access to considerable funds, possibly inherited funds on the death of some relative. Should they be advised to repay all, or part, of an existing mortgage with these new funds?

This is a difficult question to answer, as it depends on so many factors. Interest on mortgage finance on a first home up to £30 000 is still available net of tax at the 15% rate. This is a cheap source of funds. Even that portion of a mortgage above £30 000 is still one of the cheapest forms of finance available to a borrower because of the excellent quality of the security, namely the house, backing the loan.

If a client believes that he or she will need further finance in the future it would be foolish to repay the mortgage and then subsequently have to seek additional funding at a cost substantially above the net cost of mortgage finance. The estimated future funding needs of the client will decide the issue here.

If the mortgage is a repayment mortgage, then most of the payment made near the end of the loan period consists of capital repayment which

[11] The real rate of interest is the nominal rate adjusted for inflation. For example, if the nominal rate is 12% after tax and the rate of inflation is 5%, the real rate is approximately 7.4%. Academic studies have shown that over long periods of time the nominal rate has not risen sufficiently to compensate for **unexpected** bursts of inflation, therefore the real rate tends to fall when inflation is high. See Laidler and Parkin (1975).

is not allowed against tax. For this reason it has been advocated by some financial advisers that repayment mortgages should be repaid a few years early, if the funds are available, since the tax benefits attached to a repayment mortgage diminish rapidly over the last few years of the repayment period.

Another somewhat arcane factor relates to health. If the client has taken out a life policy to repay the mortgage while he or she was healthy, and has subsequently developed a serious condition such as cancer or a bad heart, then the mortgage should not be repaid, since the benefit of the life policy would be lost. The precise conditions differ between policies, but if the loan were repaid thus terminating the life policy, the client would be likely to find that taking out another life policy of equivalent value would be either very expensive or impossible.

But the ultimate deciding factor is what economists call the 'opportunity cost' of the interest payments on the mortgage. What opportunity, that is what net cash flow, is forgone if the inherited money is used to repay the mortgage rather than being invested in some other venture? If the cash inflow on the venture, net of tax, is likely to be higher than the cash outflow, net of tax, on the mortgage then the advice should be not to repay the mortgage, as the client can generate a higher income by investing the money elsewhere.

The final factor to consider is a psychological one. Some people do not like to owe large debts. The mortgage hangs like an albatross around their neck, making life a misery. In these circumstances, even if the future financial position of the client is sound and better investment opportunities exist elsewhere, it might be wise to advise the client to repay a substantial part of the mortgage, no matter what the opportunity cost of this decision might be.

SWITCHING MORTGAGES

During the late 1980s it became fashionable in some quarters to switch home mortgages from one company to another as new, more flexible or cheaper mortgages came on to the market. Is it sensible to advise a client to follow this course of action if the opportunity should arise?

There can be no doubt that as circumstances change, so the best mortgage for those circumstances can also change. The situation of the client may change – for example, he may move abroad and rent his property, or, if he has a variable interest mortgage and takes a view on future rates, he may decide to switch to a fixed rate mortgage.

The trouble with switching mortgages is the cost of the switch. The house will have to be resurveyed and there are additional legal costs. These can exceed £1000 a switch. Thus the benefits derived from switching to a new mortgage which better matches the needs of the client are often cancelled by the switching costs. It may be, however, that the new lender will pay these switching costs on behalf of the client. The decision to switch depends on the net benefit or cost of the switch.

The PFA has a duty to keep up to date on new financial products, and if some new mortgage product comes onto the market which better suits the needs of the client, then during the annual financial audit of the client's affairs the PFA should carry out a cost–benefit analysis on the net benefit to the client of switching to a more suitable type of mortgage.

The old idea, popular prior to 1985, that a mortgage taken out with one company is a mortgage for life, is no longer valid. If a mortgage provider becomes uncompetitive, the mortgage should be switched to another company, just as a car owner switches from an unsatisfactory model to a better one. The increase in mortgage switching after 1985 has greatly improved the competitiveness and therefore the efficiency of the mortgage market in the UK.

FOREIGN CURRENCY MORTGAGES

The abolition of exchange control regulations in the UK in October 1979 opened up the UK mortgage market to foreign competition and in recent years the mortgage market has become more international.

Few foreign institutions have taken advantage of this opportunity, however. Those that have are mainly offering sterling mortgages – foreign currency mortgages make up a very small part of the total mortgage market in Europe, less than 0.5%. However, in the future, as the countries within the EU draw closer together, the option of taking out a mortgage denominated in a currency other than the home currency must be considered. The introduction of a single European currency would simplify matters and would truly open up the entire EU mortgage market to any financial institution operating within it. Interesting as the implications of this move might be, such a possibility is too remote to be worth considering at present.

The statistical pages of the *Financial Times* show the rate of interest charged on identical loans denominated in different currencies; these rates are not the same. Substantial differences in interest rates exist at any one time. Exhibit 8.6 illustrates a typical spread of base interest rates in different currencies.

The financially naive home-owner might consider reducing the interest burden by taking out a mortgage denominated in that currency offering the lowest rate of interest. From Exhibit 8.6 we see that this currency would have been the Japanese yen in December 1993. This minimum-cost strategy suffers from one serious snag, however. If the loan is taken out in Japanese yen, the loan and the interest on the loan will have to be repaid in Japanese yen. This raises the question: 'What will the cost of

	Rate of Interest %	Cost % Difference
Greek Drachmas	19.00	13.5
Portuguese Escudos	13.40	7.9
Spanish Pesetas	9.50	4
Danish Krone	8.75	3.25
Italian Lire	8.00	2.5
Swedish Krone	7.00	1.5
French Francs	6.50	1
German DM	5.75	0.25
Belgian Francs	5.50	0
UK £	5.50	0
Dutch Guilders	5.25	–0.25
Swiss Francs	4.25	–1.25
USA $	3.00	–2.5
Japanese Yen	1.75	–3.75

Exchange controls were abolished in the UK on 19 October 1979. Since then, residents have been able to raise loans in any foreign currency they choose, so long as the central bank in the foreign country approves the removal of funds for investment in a foreign country. The nominal cost of funds varies a great deal between countries. The difference between the highest and lowest cost in the above table is 17.25%.

The difference in cost represents the market's estimate of the likely future rate of inflation in the two countries. In other words, the markets believe that over the next few years the difference in the rate of inflation between Greece and Japan will be 17.25% a year.

The cost of housing loans is likely to be 3% to 9% above the base rates quoted. Whether a UK house buyer should take out a loan in a 'cheaper', or 'more expensive', foreign currency depends on their estimate of future inflation rates in the two countries. This is a sophisticated financial decision which is best left to the experts. Foreign interest payments can be hedged using derivatives called 'futures' and 'options', but these only apply for short periods of a few years.

Exhibit 8.6   The base rate of interest in 14 currencies on 7 December 1993.

Japanese yen be in terms of sterling in one year's time, or five years' time, or 25 years' time?' No one knows the answer to this question.

Unless the borrower has access to Japanese yen, or Swiss francs etc. from some foreign source of income, he or she might be faced with a loan and interest repayment in terms of sterling which is 10% or 30% or even 50% higher than if the loan had been taken out in sterling.

Loans denominated in a foreign currency are subject to foreign exchange risk. Loans denominated in the local currency, that is the currency in which the borrower receives his or her income, are not subject to foreign exchange risk. The difference in interest rates between otherwise identical loans denominated in different currencies represents the capital market's best guess as to the likely changes in future exchange and inflation rates in the two countries in the months and years ahead (see Buckley, 1993).

Further discussion of this subject would lead us into the choppy waters of international finance, a topic much too complex to be pursued here. Financial products called 'derivatives', devices such as forwards, futures, options and swaps, are available for hedging the exchange rate risk attached to foreign loans, but only experts on derivatives are qualified to advise on their use. Unless the PFA intends to become a foreign loans expert, it is advisable to steer clear of foreign currency loans. Venturing into this market would require the PFA to burn a good bit of midnight oil before being able to advise a client on taking out a mortgage in a foreign currency, since it would also be necessary to advise the client on how to hedge the foreign exchange risk involved.

There is also the question of whether the interest on a personal mortgage denominated in a foreign currency would be allowed against UK income tax.

However, if at some time in the distant future a single European currency becomes a possibility, then opportunities might exist prior to this changeover to gain access to cheap mortgage money from currencies offering rates of interest lower than that obtainable in sterling.[12]

IS HOUSING A GOOD INVESTMENT?

Everyone in this life needs to acquire some sort of accommodation, so everyone must find a house or a flat to live in. The major benefit derived by the owner of a home from the home is its role as accommodation. However, a house also provides its owner with other useful benefits. For example, a home can be a prestige symbol, an index of creditworthiness and last, by no means least, an investment.

Is a house a good investment? In other words, how accurate is the popular expression 'safe as houses'? In Chapter 5 we discussed the role played by real assets in the portfolio of an investor. We commented that most real assets are acquired for reasons other than cash flow. This comment applies to an investment in a house just as much as it does to any other real asset. A house is bought primarily to provide adequate accommodation for the owner and family; the investment aspect of house purchase is usually a secondary consideration. At least it was a secondary consideration until around 1982, when many home-owners in the UK began to look upon their homes as an important component in their overall wealth portfolio.

One consequence of this change in attitude to housing was the spending spree on consumer goods that occurred in the late 1980s as some home-owners watched their homes double in value in nominal terms

---

[12] We assume that the mortgage repayment period would extend far beyond the date of the introduction of the single currency.

over two years. This apparent increase in wealth reduced their perceived need for saving. See Exhibit 3.6 in Chapter 3 for the relevant figures.

As demonstrated in Exhibit 8.7, over the period from 1974 to 1989 the real, inflation-adjusted, value of houses rose by anything from 100% in Greater London to 50% in the East Midlands. This rise in value was followed by an equally dramatic fall. House prices in the UK fell, on average, by 12% between 1989 and 1994. In Cambridge, for example, nominal house prices fell by a dramatic 20% over this five year period. So much for 'safe as houses'!

We now return to the original question posed: 'Are houses a good investment?' We need to look at house prices over a much longer period of time to answer this question. The booms in house prices in 1971–74,

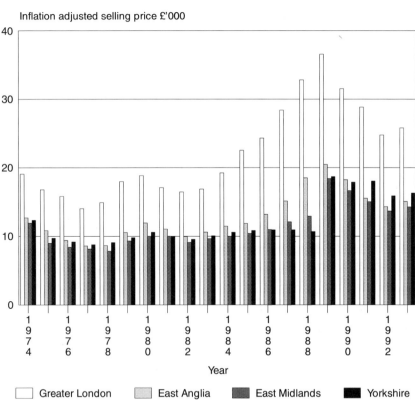

The selling value adjusted for inflation

Source: Nationwide Anglia Building Society

Exhibit 8.7   The movement in real house price values in four regions of the UK between 1974 and 1993 (1974 pound values).

1976–78 and 1984–89, and the busts in the intervening years, are no suitable basis for a logical discussion of this question.

The first thing to understand when discussing house prices is that it is not the house that alters in price, but the land on which the house is built. House prices act as a proxy for land prices. In July 1989 the average house price in London cost 2.3 times the nominal value of the same size of house in Yorkshire, yet the cost of building the house was only 30% more in London than in Yorkshire.[13] The real difference lay in the cost of buying the land on which the house was built. It is scarcity of land that drives up house prices not the cost of building houses.

Exhibits 8.8(a) and (b) show the price of the average house in London and Yorkshire over the period from 1969 to 1993. Exhibit 8.8(a) shows the

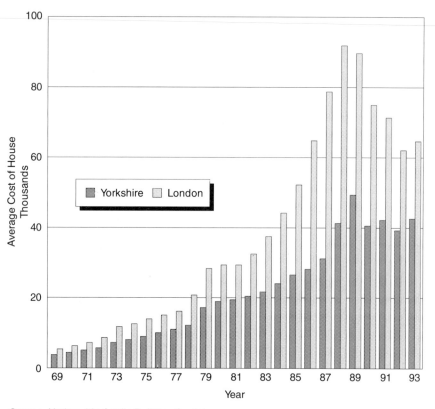

Source: Nationwide Anglia Building Society

Exhibit 8.8(a)   The market price of the average house in Central London and Yorkshire between 1969 and 1993.

[13] Source: Nationwide Building Society Quarterly Bulletin, December 1989.

actual selling price and Exhibit 8.8(b) the inflation-adjusted price. Exhibit 8.8(a) shows why so many home-owners in the UK believed themselves to be seriously rich by 1989 – the nominal value of their homes had risen by a factor of 12 over the period since 1969. However, as Exhibit 8.8 (b) shows, this belief was based on an illusion. A substantial part of this increase in value simply reflected a fall in the value of money over the period. Exhibit 8.8 (b) shows that the real average value of a house in both London and Yorkshire in 1993 was below the real value in 1973!

Thus an important factor in understanding the true trend in house price change is to understand the impact on house values of inflation, the falling value of money. Exhibit 8.9 illustrates the nominal value and the real, inflation-adjusted, value of the average house in Yorkshire over the period 1970 to 1993. Note that the nominal value of the average house rose from £3000 in 1970 to £52 000 in 1990 – a rise of almost 17 times. Yet once the figures are adjusted for inflation the rise is a mere 30% and by

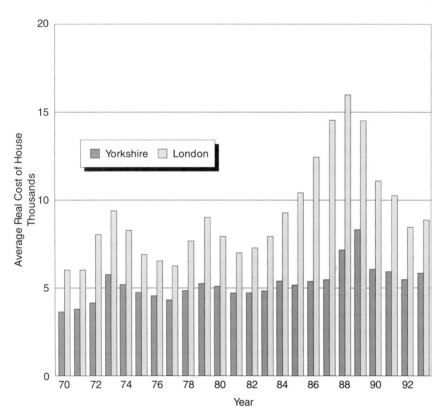

Source: Nationwide Anglia Building Society

Exhibit 8.8(b)   The inflation adjusted price of the average house in Central London and Yorkshire between 1969 and 1993.

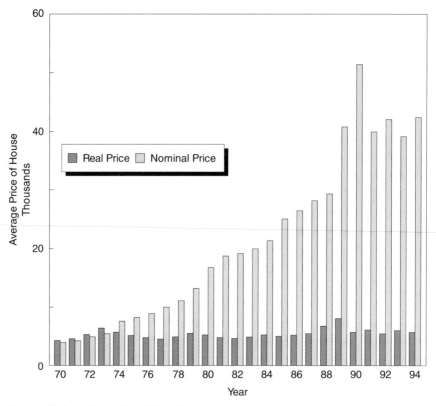

Source: Nationwide Anglia Building Society

Exhibit 8.9 The market price of the average house in Yorkshire compared to the inflation adjusted price 1970 to 1994.

1993 this rise in real value had fallen to 20% and was actually below the 1973 value.

Inflation in recent years has done much to propagate the myth of housing as a golden investment. In fact the real benefit to home-owners in Britain during the 1970s and 1980s was not the rise in house values, but the destruction by inflation of the value of the mortgage which financed the purchase of the house in the first place. The ratio of the nominal value of housing in the UK to the nominal value of UK mortgages financing those houses rose dramatically between 1970 and 1990 because of the fall in the real, inflation-adjusted, value of the mortgages.

We have already discussed the impact of high inflation on interest rates. Mortgage interest rates fail to compensate fully for high inflation, so the real interest rate tends to fall in inflationary periods, dragging down the real value of the mortgage with it.

We repeat that, although land prices did rise in real terms during the period from 1971 to 1988, the major benefit to home-owners over the period was not the rise in the value of the land or the house, but the fall in the real repayment value of the fixed value mortgage financing the purchase of the home. Mortgage interest rates rose, but not sufficiently to fully compensate for this fall in the value of money.

CALCULATING THE RETURN ON HOUSING AS AN INVESTMENT

The best way to evaluate housing as an investment is to look at the return on a house which is rented out and yet continuously maintained in its original condition by the owner.

Exhibit 8.10(a) shows the real return, after stripping out the effects of inflation, on the average value home in five regions of the UK over the two periods 1973–89 and 1973–93. This calculation assumes that the cost of maintaining the home is identical to the rent, net of tax, received from the home. In other words, the only income accruing to the owner arises from the increase in the capital value of the house over the period.

Exhibit 8.10(b) sets out the estimated return on a series of houses of various sizes in the North of England in 1992. The return on the house is calculated by estimating the rent received from the tenant plus or minus the capital increase or decrease in the value of the house during the year.

Average real values after adjusting for inflation

	Greater London	East Anglia	East Midlands	Yorks and Humber	Scotland
Average value of house 1973	19 480	12 619	11 253	11 875	11 814
Average value of house 1989	36 864	20 346	18 410	16 918	12 780
Average value of house 1993	27 648	15 260	13 808	12 689	9585
Return on real values 1973–89	3.30%	2.50%	2.70%	1.70%	0.50%
Return on real values 1973–93	1.80%	1.00%	1.10%	0.35%	–0.11%

The table shows the real return on an investment in a house in five regions of the UK if (a) the effect of the falling value of money is removed from the house value and (b) the cost of maintenance is assumed to be exactly equal to the revenue from rent.

The return over the period from 1973 (top of housing boom) to 1989 (top of housing boom) is reasonable, except in the case of Scotland. When the real return is measured from 1973 to the bottom of the housing trough in 1993, the real returns are poor.

Exhibit 8.10(a)   An estimate of the real, inflation adjusted, rate of return on an investment in a home which is rented out to a tenant. Maintenance cost is assumed equal to the rent net of tax.

In this case we also consider the cost of maintaining the house and the fee to the renting agent.

We see that if we ignore the capital appreciation in the value of the house then the return on a large house, treated simply as an investment, is very poor. In other words a large house in the UK is only a worthwhile investment if it is expected to attract a substantial tax-free capital gain during the period of ownership. Over the long period from 1945 to 1993 the average increase in detached house prices in the UK was under 2%

		£200 000 5-bedroom house	£100 000 3-bedroom house	£50 000 2-bedroom flat
Monthly		£		
Maintenance cost		167	100	63
Mortgage cost		1561	781	390
Renting agency cost		120	72	48
Assumed tax assessed		0	0	0
Total monthly cost		1848	953	501
Capital appreciation	7%	1167	583	292
(in nominal terms)	3%	500	250	125
	0%	0	0	0
Assumed monthly rent £		1000	600	400
Total monthly income	at 7%	2167	1183	692
Appreciation at:	at 3%	1500	850	525
	at 0%	1000	600	400
Monthly surplus	at 7%	319	231	191
Appreciation at:	at 3%	−348	−103	24
	at 0%	−848	−353	−101
Nominal return	at 7%	1.91	2.77	4.58
(% per annum)	at 3%	−2.09	−1.23	0.58
	at 0%	−5.09	−4.23	−2.42

The return on rented accommodation is highly sensitive to the current rate of interest on the mortgage used to finance the purchase. However, the above figures show that it is difficult to make an adequate return on rented accommodation.

Rent is not a constant proportion of the market value of the house. Low-value flats and houses can be rented for a much higher proportionate rent than expensive houses, except in large cities. The data used are taken from the renting book of a large estate agent.

Exhibit 8.10(b)   An estimate of the nominal rate of return on an investment in rented accommodation of various sizes.

per annum in real terms.[14] Even when the net of cost return on renting the house is added to this figure, the return is far short of the return of 7% to 9% gross of tax achieved by ordinary shares over the same period. Only the small two-bedroomed flat provides an adequate return. The return is superior because rental returns show that a small flat can be rented at a higher fraction of its market value than can a larger detached house in most regions of the UK.

We conclude that so far as financial return is concerned, housing is a poor investment, easily surpassed by many other types of financial and real assets.

But what about those other characteristics of investment discussed in Chapter 5? How does housing shape up? Housing is illiquid, it generates high buying and selling costs, the protection and maintenance costs are also high, except for the insurance cost which is low relative to the value invested. A house is not transportable and it is geographically fixed on one site. We see that these attributes of a house, except for insurance cost, are all negative.

The only positive characteristics associated with housing as an investment are the many tax perks attached to housing, plus the possibility of a stable cash flow if the owner finds a good tenant.

We conclude that housing is a poor investment. This opinion is shared by financial analysts in most other countries of the world. There are a few exceptions to this rule, such as property sited in some city centres and property on islands with limited space available for housing – Singapore and Hong Kong spring to mind – but such prime housing sites are few and far between.

The PFA should direct clients away from investing in housing if the house is to be treated solely as an investment. The acquisition of a house for the purpose of accommodation is obviously essential, but the house need not be bought, it could be rented.

BUY OR RENT?

The proportion of persons who own their own homes in the UK, at 67% in 1994, is higher than in almost all the other countries of the world. There are several reasons for this high proportion of home-ownership in the UK but the limited availability of rented accommodation is, without doubt, a major reason. The lack of private rented accommodation – only 10% of homes in the UK are privately rented – stems from the poor legal treatment of those who own and rent property, and the poor image presented of such persons by the media. If we add to these negative aspects of renting the fact that housing is a poor investment compared to the

---

[14] Calculated by the author, in association with Ms Fang Dong, from data supplied by the Nationwide Anglia Building Society.

many alternatives available, then it is not surprising that so few houses are privately rented[15] in the UK compared to other countries. The fault lies in the limited supply of rented property, rather than the lack of demand for such property.

The lack of rented accommodation in the UK is unfortunate, since there are many situations where renting a home is a superior option to buying a home. If a person moves job location frequently, particularly if he or she moves abroad, renting is the better option. If a house-seeker lacks capital for a deposit on a house, then acquiring a rented property is a simple solution. Many older people would benefit financially if they could release capital by selling their home and renting a similar property. Much too high a proportion of the wealth of many retired persons is tied up in their homes.

The major advantage of renting a home is that the occupier is not required to invest a high proportion of their total wealth in a single asset, a home. In Chapter 5 we noted the financial advantages flowing from diversifying a wealth portfolio between different kinds of assets. Diversification removes the specific risk attached to holding one particular asset. Renting also passes the cost of maintaining the property on to the owner of the home and away from the occupier.

We noted above that investment in property provides a poor return to the investor unless substantial profits are made from capital gains. If we return to Exhibit 8.7, which illustrates the rise in real house prices in four regions of the UK from 1974 to 1993, we find that capital gains on house values in the UK are less spectacular than is popularly supposed. If the opportunity cost of the investment in property is taken into account, then renting is the cheaper option in many cases. What we mean by this is that if the return on the money the renter is not investing in the property he occupies is deducted from the rent he pays to the owner of the property, then the occupier is paying remarkably little for the privilege of living in the property. The current levels of rent charged in many regions of the UK do not include a proper charge for the cost of the funds invested by the owner in the home that is being rented out.

All of these curious anomalies in the UK housing market stem from the unsubstantiated belief that housing values are sure to outpace inflation in future years. All of the evidence available at present suggests quite the contrary. The proportion of young people in the population, those who buy homes and are entering the housing market, is falling. As shown by Exhibit 7.2 in Chapter 7 the proportion of older people in the population, that is those who sell homes and leave the housing market, is rising. A study by the Joseph Rowntree Foundation published in July 1994 found that by the year 1999, around 200 000 homes a year will be

---

[15] Some 21% of homes in the UK were rented out by local authorities in 1993.

coming on to the UK housing market each year to be sold by the inher-
itors of property from deceased parents. The value of these homes will be
in the region of £20 billion a year.

We appear to be facing a diminishing demand for homes and an
increasing supply of homes in the future – not a recipe for rising prices.

Renting should not be dismissed as an inferior option to buying. In every
case where home acquisition is being considered the cost of renting should
be compared to that of buying in the context of the client's situation.

PROPERTY AND CREDIT

In Chapter 9 we will be discussing the question of raising short-term
credit. Ownership of a home is a most important determinant of creditworthiness. In order to gain access to credit the borrower needs to persuade the lender that he or she is a good credit risk. If the potential
borrower owns rather than rents a home, credit is easier to come by. The
cost of credit based on the security of a house or flat is likely to be
cheaper than credit loaned without such sound security. This is one of
the benefits flowing from home-ownership which is often overlooked.

BUY–RENT SWITCHING

As we noted above, there were some wild oscillations in the nominal
value of houses in the UK between 1970 and 1994. These swings in house
value have persuaded some sophisticated investors to switch from renting to buying and then back again every few years. If house prices are
depressed, as in 1994, they buy. When house prices move above the long-
term trend, as in 1989, they sell at a profit and rent.

We suspect that few householders, particularly the married variety,
would be willing to take this trouble just to maximize their property
income. Also the cost of switching can be quite high, some £3000 to £7000
a switch, and these switching costs may well cancel out the capital profits
arising from the switch. However, it is claimed that substantial profits can
be made by following this strategy.

MAINTAINING THE HOME

We noted in Chapter 5 that the cost of maintenance and protection may
be an important attribute of an asset.

The annual cost of insuring a house against fire, landslip etc. is very
low, normally well below 1% of the current market value of the house.
However, the cost of maintaining a house in good condition can be very
high, relative to the cost of maintaining other assets. The annual maintenance cost of a house is determined by many factors – climate, type of

soil on which the house is built, behaviour of the occupants, pollution levels, neighbourhood characteristics, etc.

This cost is almost invariably overlooked when personal financial budgets are being constructed. The maintenance costs are irregular, but very substantial when they do arise. The best solution to this problem is to set up a maintenance equalization fund, into which a regular payment is made and out of which the maintenance costs will be paid.

If a house is not regularly maintained the quality of the fabric can deteriorate to a point where a second mortgage may have to be raised to bring the house back to good condition.

How much does it cost to maintain a house in as good condition as when it was bought? A realistic figure is very substantial and will shock many home-owners. The figure cannot be expressed as a percentage of current market value of the house since, as we noted above, this figure varies a great deal from year to year while the cost of maintenance rises steadily with inflation, always upwards!

An approximate estimate of the annual cost of maintaining an older house or flat with a given number of rooms in good condition in 1994 is as follows:[16]

5 bedrooms	£2000 per annum
4 bedrooms	£1500
3 bedrooms	£1200
2 bedrooms	£ 750
1 bedroom	£ 500

Thus if the owner of a four-bedroom house wishes to set up a maintenance fund to ensure that he or she can afford to pay out the irregular maintenance costs when they become due, a fund must be accumulated which will produce £1500 a year, net of tax. If the owner pays tax at a marginal rate of 25% on investment income, the fund needs to earn £2000 a year gross of tax. If the fund can earn 8% gross of tax the value of the fund would need to be 2000/0.08 = £25 000 to meet these requirements.

We suspect that most owners of four-bedroomed houses would be shocked if they realized that after buying and financing the house and contents for, say, £150 000 they will need to set aside an additional amount of this magnitude just for maintenance. But this is the only safe policy. Otherwise financial pressures are likely to persuade the home-owner to let the fabric of the house deteriorate – a policy which, in the long run, will cost him or her a good deal more than the annual £2000 cost of maintaining the fund intact.

---

[16] The figures are calculated by the author in consultation with a leading firm of Yorkshire Estate Agents who rent and maintain homes for clients.

ADVICE ON INVESTING IN HOUSING

What advice should a PFA give to a client about acquiring a home?

The prime consideration in acquiring accommodation is to find a suitable home at a price the client can afford without putting undue strain on their financial resources. The next step is to select a financing policy suited to the client's future cash flow. Investment considerations, that is the risk–return mix on housing as an investment, should be treated as a secondary consideration. However, the client should be advised to avoid tying up too high a proportion of their total wealth (equity) in this one asset, a house. Such a lopsided wealth portfolio will breach the diversification principle discussed in Chapter 5.

Contrary to popular belief housing is a poor investment. The returns available in the UK over the last 50 years or so do not justify the risks involved in investing in housing. Renting out a second home is simply not an economic proposition. Although there may be good reasons for owning a second home, investment is not one of them.

Investment in housing has proved to be a reasonably good hedge against inflation over the years, but no better than many other investments. It would be unwise to assume that substantial capital profits can be made on an investment in housing in the future. Current socio-economic trends do not support this hypothesis; they suggest relatively stable house prices in real inflation-adjusted terms for many years ahead.

At current levels of rent, renting a home is a cheaper option than buying, if the capital invested in the rented house is taken into the calculation. Renting is only an inferior option if the large capital profits flowing to home-owners in the 1980s are repeated in the future, which is most improbable. The rent/buy decision depends primarily on the likely future lifestyle of the client and their desire for security; the investment return on the purchase of a house is a secondary consideration and would probably favour renting. Renting is the favoured option in Europe and may well be adopted as the favoured option in the UK, if housing law in the EU is standardized.

In the recent past the only real economic advantage accruing to housing as an investment has arisen from the attached tax benefits, such as the fact that the interest on housing loans up to £30 000 is paid net of tax at 15%, and capital gains on the sale of a first home are not subject to tax. How many of these benefits will survive a more integrated EU tax system remains to be seen. The allowance on mortgage interest is already being phased out.[17]

A house provides many benefits to its owner – benefits such as security, prestige and creditworthiness – but a good investment return is not high on this list.

[17] See note 9 above.

WHAT HAVE WE LEARNED IN THIS CHAPTER?

1. For most individuals the investment in a home is far and away the most important one they will ever make in their lives.
2. The value of housing in the UK has fluctuated widely in recent years. The expression 'safe as houses' may need to be discarded.
3. Most houses in the UK are financed by a mortgage. Many different kinds of mortgage are now available to the house buyer. The two basic types of mortgage are the repayment mortgage and the with-profits endowment mortgage. The endowment mortgage 'bundles' house finance with a saving and investment scheme. Whether or not 'bundling' of financial products is a financially efficient technique is a matter of some controversy.
4. In the past, most loan providers charged the borrower a variable rate of interest, linked to the current market rate of interest. In recent years, in addition to the variable rate mortgage, most loan providers have offered mortgages at a fixed rate for shorter periods of time. If the current market rate is well below the historical trend line for interest rates, the fixed rate might be advantageous. A fixed rate mortgage allows for accurate cash budgeting.
5. In the past, high inflation in the UK destroyed the real value of a mortgage over a few years. This, and the associated tax benefits, encouraged many house buyers to take on a housing loan well in excess of what they could actually afford. Actual inflation and expectations about inflation have now fallen to a much lower figure. House buyers should not be encouraged to take on a mortgage if the cost of the mortgage exceeds a third of their monthly net cash flow.
6. Many of the old conventions on housing finance are changing. The conventional period of 25 years to repay a mortgage may be much too long a period under current conditions. Fixed interest mortgages are now widely available. Switching mortgages from one lender to another is common, and 'covered' mortgages denominated in a foreign currency are now available to house buyers in the UK. Housing finance has become much more sophisticated in recent years, providing profitable consulting opportunities for the PFA.
7. Apart from a few exceptional years between 1970 and 1990, housing has seldom proved to be a good investment in the UK, although it may be a necessary one. If house prices simply match inflation in the future, renting rather than buying a home may become the norm in the UK, as it was in the nineteenth century and is currently in Continental Europe.
8. The full cost of maintaining a house in good condition is high and is often overlooked by the owner. Home-owners should be encouraged

to set up a 'maintenance equalization fund' to equalize the cost of house maintenance over the years.

FURTHER READING

Barr, A. and Barr, R. (1994).
Buckley, A. (1993).
Burgess (1991).
Nationwide Anglia Building Society, quarterly bulletins on house prices in the various regions of the UK.

See bibliography on p.311 for a full annotation of these books.

TUTORIAL QUESTIONS: HOUSING

1. What proportion of the value of assets owned by individuals in the UK is invested in housing? What proportion of the assets of individuals in the UK could be quickly turned into cash?
2. Explain the key differences between a repayment mortgage and an endowment mortgage. What are the benefits flowing from each type of mortgage? What kind of client would benefit from taking out a repayment mortgage to buy a house, rather than an endowment mortgage?
3. Why is an endowment mortgage sometimes described as a 'bundled' financial product? Do you approve of such products?
4. What is a unit trust linked endowment mortgage? How does it work? Are there any disadvantages associated with holding a unit linked mortgage compared to a conventional with-profits endowment mortgage?
5. Why do lenders usually prefer to offer variable rate mortgages to fixed rate mortgages? Why are fixed rate mortgages usually offered for shorter periods than variable rate mortgages?
6. What are the advantages flowing to a borrower from a fixed rate mortgage compared to a floating rate mortgage?
7. What is 'negative equity' in housing finance? Why do you think that in the UK in December 1993 two million home-owners were in a negative equity situation?
8. How does the expected future rate of inflation affect the period over which a mortgage should be repaid?
9. A client who has being paying off a 25-year repayment mortgage over the last 10 years comes to you to ask advice about switching to a fixed rate mortgage over the next 10 years with a built-in option to switch again in 10 years' time. What advice would you give the client?

10. It has been claimed that investment in housing enjoys an unfair tax advantage over other types of investment in the UK, and that this advantage explains the very high cost of housing relative to average wages in the UK compared to most other European countries.

    Do you agree with this prognosis? What advantages does investment in housing currently enjoy over other forms of investment in the UK?

10. A house costing £200 000 in Leeds, Yorkshire can be rented for £700 a month plus rates. Your client is posted to a job in the Leeds area for five years. Would you advise your client to rent or buy a house there?

11. The average household income in the UK in 1994 was approximately £19 000 a year. Net of all deductions this gross income provides, on average, a cash flow of £15 000 a year. The average house price in 1994 in the UK was £55 000 and in London it was £66 000.

    Calculate whether the average household could afford to buy the average house assuming a net of tax interest rate of 6% per annum. (Assume that the annual cost of food and clothing is about £5000, heat and light about £1200 and other basic expenses are around £2000 for the average family.)

12. An unmarried client comes to you who is a marketing manager in the City of London. He would like to buy an upmarket two-bedroomed flat in North London for £200 000. You discover that he has a gross income of £36 000 a year – £26 000 net of all deductions. He tells you that he will need a £180 000 mortgage to buy the flat. You calculate that the interest on this mortgage, net of tax on the first £30 000, plus life assurance, is £1800 a month. You explain that he cannot really afford this amount unless he has other assets to sell. He tells you he has no other assets, but that he is still very keen to buy his 'dream' flat.

    The Boomtime Property Company, which is having difficulty selling these new high-tech flats, makes your client the following offer:

    'You pay half the flat cost now and take half the equity. In three years' time you buy the remaining half as valued by an independent valuer. Meanwhile you pay us £500 a month rent for the half of the flat we own.'

    Discuss the merits and risks of this deal. Would you advise your client to take it on?

13. We heard a great deal in the 1980s about the advantages of investing in property in London. Do you think this advice was justified? What are the disadvantages of investing in property in a major city such as London in the future?

    Over the last 15 years some 'City types' have moved between buying and renting property every few years. What criteria would you use for deciding when to sell and move to rented property, and when to buy back the property?

14. If you are advising a client on the maximum amount they should borrow to buy a house, what factors would determine this amount?

15. If building costs in London were only 30% higher than in Yorkshire in 1989, why were London house prices 75% higher than Yorkshire prices?

16. A five-bedroomed detached house was bought in Yorkshire in 1971 for £20 000. The purchase was financed with a 100% mortgage. In 1989 this house was sold for £200 000. If the value of money fell by 82% over this period, what was the ratio of house value to mortgage value in 1972 and 1989? What were the nominal and real profits on the sale of the house? What would the average mortgage interest rate have had to have been to fully compensate for inflation?

17. Mr William Steel owns a house in Cambridge which cost £200 000 in 1985 and is now worth £250 000. It was valued at £350 000 in 1989. He has taken out a £150 000 variable interest repayment mortgage on this house the current cost of which is 8% per annum gross of tax.

    Mr Steel reads in the *Investors Chronicle* that 10-year fixed interest mortgages in Swiss francs are now offered to UK residents by a Swiss bank in Zurich at a gross rate of 4% per annum. The interest, up to a limit of £30 000, would still be allowable against his income tax as with a UK loan.

    Mr Steel approaches you as his financial adviser. Advise him on whether or not he should switch from the current variable interest sterling loan at 8% to the 10-year Swiss franc fixed rate loan at 4%.

18. How do the various attributes of an investment set out in Chapter 5 apply to housing? How would investing £200 000 in a house in London for rent compare to investing £200 000 in fixed interest government stock?

19. Is the dramatic rise in house prices seen in the UK during the period from 1984 to 1989 likely to be repeated in the future? If not, why not?

20. What would be the value of a maintenance equalization fund needed to keep a two-bedroomed flat in mint condition?

Suggested solutions to several odd and even numbered questions are provided at the back of this book.

Consumer credit 9

THE AVAILABILITY OF SHORT-TERM CREDIT IN THE UK

Personal financial advisers are seldom asked to provide advice on consumer credit, but sometimes they are asked to advise on rescheduling a client's debt position, and this debt position may well include a substantial portion of short-term consumer credit.

The main problem with consumer credit is that it is much too easy to come by. Lending institutions spend vast sums of money offering credit to potential borrowers about whom they know very little. This can lead to problems for both the borrower and the lender.

The problem of taking on excessive personal debt occurs because there is a mismatch between the generous lending policies pursued by many financial institutions on the one hand, and their tough pursuit of borrowers who are in debt, on the other. The law in the UK should be altered to require some kind of symmetry between the lending policy and the debt recovery policy of financial institutions. If institutions pursue an irresponsible lending policy, a brake should be imposed on their powers of debt recovery.

The volume of short-term credit granted to individuals in the UK increased substantially in real terms between 1960 and 1980, but has declined since then as a proportion of total personal financial liabilities.

The per capita volume of personal credit is lower in the UK than in many other industrialized countries.

CREDITWORTHINESS

A good credit rating is a valuable asset. This fact is often not appreciated by clients. Many sources of short-term credit are available to individuals in the UK; the difference between the cost of credit offered by each of these sources is very substantial. Clients with a good credit rating can borrow at a rate of interest which is often 10% p.a. or more below the rate charged to a borrower with a poor credit rating.

A good credit rating is determined by many factors. Some lenders use a purely subjective form of assessment when offering credit. Other lenders use something called a 'credit rating scale' to determine the creditworthiness of a potential borrower. Some of these credit rating scales are quite sophisticated and apply statistical techniques such as discriminant analysis to past credit data to identify the key attributes of a sound borrower.[1]

Some of the key attributes which appear to differentiate a good from a poor credit risk include past credit record, income, age, state of health, job security, owning own home, length of time in present job and home, and marital status.

A client who has a good past credit record and a high income, who is married and middle-aged with good job security and who owns his own home will enjoy a high degree of creditworthiness with any lender. He should be advised to use this valuable asset and find a lender who will appreciate these attributes and, in consequence, provide cheap short-term credit funds to the borrower. Oddly enough, many borrowers fail to follow this course of action and accept the first source of credit offered, often by the seller of the goods they are about to buy.

CREDIT RATING AGENCIES

Most sellers of consumer goods who sell on credit subscribe to one or more of the five large credit rating agencies in the UK who offer a credit evaluation service. These agencies keep the court records of individuals who default on credit repayments. Once an individual is on the books of one these agencies it can be difficult to find further credit; at best, the credit offered will cost more than it otherwise would.

Some credit data bases hold a formidable amount of information. The credit agency Infolink, for example, keeps 44 million records in its data base and can be accessed by on-line computer during 80 hours a week. Infolink produces regular reports on the overall financial behaviour of those of the population logged into its data base.

If an individual is refused credit, he or she is permitted by law to ask if a credit rating agency has been consulted. If the answer is 'yes', then the individual can ask for the name of the agency. The person refused credit can then write to the agency within 28 days enclosing a fee of £1 and asking for a copy of the relevant credit rating report. This must be provided by the agency on request. If the file is incorrect or misleading in some respect, the individual can force the agency either to make a correc-

---

[1] See Edwards (1990) for a discussion of the use of statistical credit scales.

tion or to include an explanation of the reasons for the credit default in the file.[2]

SOURCES OF CREDIT IN THE UK

Sources of credit can be classified as either open-ended credit or specific credit. The provider of an **open-ended** source of credit will initially agree some upper credit limit with the borrower. The borrower can then borrow and repay loans within this credit limit. The lender does not keep a record of how the borrower spends his or her money, the lender simply checks that the upper spending limit on the credit has not been exceeded.

A **specific** source of credit is usually targeted at acquiring some specific asset, such as a car or a dishwasher. The loan is related to the value of the asset. A fixed repayment term, the rate of interest charged and other loan conditions are agreed between the lender and the borrower. These conditions must be strictly adhered to by the borrower.

The more common forms of open-ended credit are a bank overdraft, a bank or other credit card, and the revolving credit schemes offered by some large multiple stores. Common forms of specific credit include bank loans, insurance company loans secured on assurance policies, and hire purchase agreements.

Bank credit tends to be cheaper than the other sources of credit listed above but, in recent years, the gap between the cost of bank credit and other forms of credit has narrowed considerably as the relative cost of bank credit has risen. The providers of bank credit and 'gold' credit cards tend to pay more attention to the creditworthiness of the borrower than do the other sources of credit listed above. Thus a creditworthy client should be advised to seek short-term credit from these sources, since the cost of credit will be much less than from other less discriminating lenders.

Most insurance companies will, if asked, provide the insured with a loan secured on a life assurance policy. The maximum value of the loan available from this source depends on the paid-up value of the policy. This cheap source of credit is not advertised and is often overlooked by individuals with substantial life policies.

Hire purchase credit is easy to come by and for that very reason is usually the most expensive form of credit on offer.

THE COST OF CREDIT

The provision of short-term credit is a very simple and profitable business activity, thus the sources of short-term credit in the UK are legion.

---

[2] See the leaflet entitled 'No credit? Your right to know what credit rating agencies are saying about you'. This can be obtained from the Office of Fair Trading, Field House, 15 Breams Buildings, London EC4A 1PR. Tel.: 0171 242 2858.

There is a great variation between the cost of credit offered by these various sources. It is not uncommon for the most expensive credit on offer to be two to three times the cost of the cheapest!

A client should be persuaded to take time to shop around among these various sources of credit, using his or her credit worthiness to find the cheapest source. It is a foolish and expensive practice to accept credit from the first source of credit offered.[3]

Loans from insurance companies normally provide a cheap source of credit. If the client has a with-profits whole-life assurance policy or some suchlike, it is likely that he or she can borrow at relatively low cost against the security of this policy.

The key point to keep in mind is that the more discriminating the lender is in accepting borrowers, the cheaper is the credit provided. A lender who loans money indiscriminately takes on many poor credit risks who fail to repay their loans and so run up heavy legal costs for the lender. Thus the interest rate charged by such a lender must be increased to all borrowers, to cover these costs. The discriminating lender does not bear these costs. The astute borrower needs to find the most discriminating lender who will accept him or her as a client!

CALCULATING THE TRUE RATE OF INTEREST ON CREDIT: THE APR

The problem of calculating the true rate of interest on a loan has been much improved in recent years in the UK by the provisions of the Consumer Credit Act. Since the Consumer Credit Regulations were introduced, the true rate of interest, called the annual percentage rate (APR), must be stated in adverts offering loans, in addition to any other interest rate advertised. In other words, whatever rate is advertised, this rate must be converted to its APR equivalent for the period of the loan.

The APR on a loan allows the potential borrower to compare the true interest cost of various loans offered.

In the past, the rate of interest advertised as the cost of a loan could be very misleading to a naive borrower. A good example of this misrepresentation was the 'flat add-on' rate of interest much favoured by sellers of consumer goods who offer loans to buy these goods on hire purchase.

Suppose, for example, that a customer wanted to buy an expensive hi-fi system for £1000. If he couldn't afford to pay cash, the seller might offer a £1000 loan to buy the item with a repayment period of four years at a 'flat rate of 20% a year'. The lender made the calculation as follows: 20% a year = £200 a year for four years = £800. The total to be paid by the

---

[3] It might be argued that the 'opportunity cost' of the time spent searching for the cheapest credit could outweigh the benefit in finding it. This is unlikely to be the case. The current cost of credit can be checked out with a few phone calls to banks and credit card companies.

borrower was thus £1000+£800=£1800 and if this was repaid over 48 monthly instalments the monthly instalment was £1800/48=£37.50 a month.

The rate of interest was stated to be 20%; in fact the true rate was close to double this at 38%. The reason for the discrepancy is that the capital of £1000 was being continuously repaid over the four-year period of the loan repayment, so the average value of the loan outstanding over the four years was not £1000, but just over £500.

The Consumer Credit Act was introduced to prevent lenders from misleading borrowers in this way. Under the Act a true rate of interest, or APR, needs to be published along with the 'flat' rate, or any other rate which is not the APR rate, when loans are offered to the public in the UK.

Calculation of the APR can be a rather complex process in certain cases, but this is not a problem for the PFA. The PFA need simply ensure that an APR is provided by the lender. The UK government has published a booklet on the subject.[4]

As we noted above, the calculation of the true APR can be rather complex. However a simpler method of approximating the APR is available in some, but not all, cases. An illustration of this simpler method is provided in Exhibit 9.1. The method is applied to calculating the APR on a 'flat rate add-on' interest loan of £2000 at a flat rate of 10% per annum. The exhibit provides a formula for making a rough estimate of the APR.

ADJUSTING THE NOMINAL RATE OF INTEREST

The PFA might occasionally have to adjust a nominal rate of interest in certain ways to arrive at a more accurate rate.

For example, a PFA may wish to convert a rate based on a period of less than a year to an annual rate, or an annual rate to a rate based on a period of less than a year

Another possibility is that a PFA may wish to adjust a nominal rate of interest to a real rate after adjusting for the effects of past or expected inflation.

Exhibit 9.2 illustrates the sensitivity of the rate of interest to the compounding period used. The table shows the true rate of interest being charged if a loan is being compounded annually but is being paid monthly or at some other fraction of a year. Building society interest is calculated this way. Notice that the difference is small in absolute terms at low rates of interest, but significant at high rates of interest.

MEASURING THE DEBT CAPACITY OF A CLIENT

The debt capacity of a client is determined by several factors, the more important of which are (a) the amount and stability of the periodic net

---

[4] See *Calculating the APR*, HMSO (1982).

The precise calculation of the APR is rather complicated but the following formula provides a good approximation to the true APR rate.

Let us suppose that a merchant offers to sell a microcomputer costing £2000 sterling on the following credit terms. A loan of £2000 over two years at a flat rate of interest of 10% per year. Payments to be made monthly.

The seller makes the following calculation:

£2000 × 10% = £200

The borrower to repay £2000 + 2 × 200 = £2400 over the two years.

Therefore the monthly payment is £2400/24 = £100.00

Thus the capital = £2000   Finance charges = £400

QUESTION: What is the APR on the loan?

SOLUTION:

Let:

APR = Annual percentage rate
P = Number of loan payments per year
N = Number of loan payments to be made over entire life of loan
C = Finance charges
L = Loan amount

The requisite formula for approximating the APR is:

$$P \times (95 \times N + 9) \times C / 12 \times N \times (N + 1) \times (4 \times L + C)$$

Substituting in the formula:

$$(12 \times ((95 \times 24) + 9) \times 400) / 12 \times 24 \times (24 + 1) \times ((4 \times 2000) + 400)$$

Therefore: APR = $\boxed{18.17}$ %

Since: P = 12 periods
N = 24 periods
C = £400.00
L = £2000.00

The true rate of interest is not 10% a year but 18.17% a year.

It is often quite difficult to make a precise calculation of the APR but the above formula provides an approximation which is likely to be close enough to the true rate for this type of calculation.

Exhibit 9.1   An approximate method of calculating the APR.

Annual	Quarterly	Monthly	Weekly	Daily	Continuous
%	%	%	%	%	%
5.00	5.09	5.11	5.12	5.12	5.13
10.00	10.38	10.47	10.50	10.51	10.52
15.00	15.86	16.07	16.15	16.17	16.18
20.00	21.55	21.93	22.09	22.13	22.14
30.00	33.54	34.48	34.86	34.96	34.98
40.00	46.41	48.21	48.95	49.14	49.18
50.00	60.18	63.20	64.47	64.81	64.87
75.00	98.85	106.98	110.56	111.53	111.70
100.00	144.14	161.30	169.25	171.45	171.82

The table illustrates the effect of compounding the rate of interest more than once a year. For example if the annual rate is stated to be 20% but it is paid monthly in advance, not annually, then the true annual rate is 21.93%.

As can be seen the difference is quite substantial once the rate exceeds about 10% a year. So long as the rate is expressed as an APR this difference will be brought to the notice of the debtor.

Exhibit 9.2 The true rate of interest when an amount compounded at the end of the year is paid in advance over several payments during the year.

cash flow received by the client, (b) the value of this net cash flow after deducting all legally committed and essential expenditures – we shall call this latter figure the 'discretionary' net cash flow, (c) the expected **future** net cash flow of the client, and (d) the market value and composition of the wealth (equity) of the client, with particular regard being paid to the state of liquidity (speed into cash) of this wealth.

Thus calculating the debt capacity of a client is not a simple assignment, since several of these factors are not easy to measure with any degree of certainty. The PFA will be wise to err on the side of safety if asked to make an estimate of the debt capacity of a client.

THE INCOME AND EXPENDITURE ACCOUNT

The left-hand column of Exhibit 9.3 illustrates a typical monthly income and expenditure account for an individual client.

The major part of the net cash inflow is likely to be represented by the gross cash inflow from salary, reduced by personal tax and other mandatory and contractual payments deducted by the employer on behalf of the employee. This net cash flow will normally be paid into the employee's bank account on a monthly basis.

In additional to the net cash flow from salary there may well be other regular cash inflows from interest, dividends, royalties etc.

THE DISCRETIONARY NET CASH FLOW

The discretionary net cash flow is represented by what is left over once the essential and legally committed expenditures are deducted from the monthly gross cash flow. The right-hand column of Exhibit 9.3 segregates the monthly expenditures between essential, important and discretionary expenditures.

RANKING EXPENDITURES IN ORDER OF IMPORTANCE

In order to calculate the true 'opportunity cost' of taking on additional debt for a period, it is necessary to allocate future budgeted expenditures in this way. The total monthly expenditures must be segregated into several slices. Each 'slice' of expenditure will then be ranked in order of importance, from essential to inessential.

The key to measuring future debt capacity is to calculate what additional expenditure on top of existing expenditures can be undertaken without impinging on the important or essential and legally committed expenditures.

Expenditures are likely to fall into three classes. First the essential expenditures like basic food, gas, electricity, local rates, insurance premiums etc. which cannot be avoided. Second, other important but not essential expenditures like motoring costs, telephone and repairs. The third slice will list all the inessential 'discretionary' expenditures which can be avoided, like holiday costs, theatre tickets and meals out. If the total of these slices does not exhaust the net cash flow available to the client, then a final slice is created called 'involuntary savings'.

Once this ranking of expenditures and savings on a spectrum of relative importance is complete it is easy to calculate the 'opportunity cost' of taking on additional debt of a given amount. If a loan is to be taken out at £x a month for n months, it is now possible to calculate the effect of the repayment of this loan on current spending and saving. It might be found that the monthly cost of this additional expenditure will simply reduce 'involuntary saving' for the period of the loan. Alternatively it might reduce voluntary saving plus cash available for some inessential expenditures like theatre and meals out. Once the cost of the debt has eliminated these inessential expenditures its opportunity cost becomes a more serious matter. The cost of the debt will then force a reduction in important but not essential household expenses like clothing and transport. This provides the upper limit to debt capacity, since the borrower will not wish to cut into essential contracted monthly expenses like health insurance or mortgage interest.

A ranking of expenditures in this way allows a client to gauge both the 'opportunity cost' and the degree of risk he or she is taking when entering into a consumer finance contract involving regular additional cash outlays for a given period.

Name:	John Wilson		
Occupation:	Shop Manager		
Marital Status:	Widower	Children	2
Assumed Inflation: (1994–2004) %	4	Per annum	
Currency Unit:	£		

	Age	45	Date of Birth	1949
	Year	1994	Actuarial Life Expectation	33 Years

Income	Classified Ranking		Ranked by Importance
Salary	24 500		24 500
Dividends	4000		4000
Other Income	400		400
Total Income	28 900		28 900
Less:			
Tax	5780		5780
Other Deductions	920		920
Total Deductions	6700		6700
Gross Cash Flow	22 200		22 200

Expenditure		Ranked Expenditure	
Classification		Essential	8370
Accommodation	550	Accommodation	550
Clothing	1500	Food	1000
Food	2200	Gas and Electricity	1200
Gas and Electricity	1700	House Insurance	340
House Insurance	340	Medical and Health	480
Medical and Health	480	Rates	1100
Children	500	Telephone	200
Rates	1100	Transport	1000
Recreation	1500	Clothing	1100
Repairs	1200	Repairs	900
Subs and Gifts	500	Children	500
Telephone	330		
Transport	1900	Important	1700
Other	1200		
		Food	500
		Gas and Electricity	300
		Telephone	100
		Transport	500
		Repairs	300
		Discretionary	4930
		Food (meals out)	700
		Gas and Electricity	200
		Telephone	30
		Transport	400
		Recreation	1500
		Subs and Gifts	500
		Clothing	400
		Other	1200

Total Expenditure	15 000	Total Expenditure	15 000
Surplus for Saving	7200	Surplus for Saving	7200

The left-hand column shows a conventional income and expenditure account. The right-hand column ranks the expenditure into three categories with respect to their importance. Each item of expenditure is allocated to the 'Essential', 'Important' and 'Discretionary' category. Such a classification allows the 'opportunity cost' of the credit to be calculated.

Exhibit 9.3   A personal expenditure account ranked by the relative importance of the expenditure.

The initial question posed has now been answered – 'What are the financial consequences if my regular cash inflows remain constant and the outflows increase by £x a month because of additional credit commitments?' – in other words, what is the opportunity cost of taking on this additional credit?

We should note that taking on additional debt for the purpose of consumption provides no additional investment which will, in its turn, provide additional income. Additional consumer credit provides no 'leverage' effect on income, such as there would be if the debt were invested in shares or some other form of income-producing assets. Additional leverage, in this case, simply increases the risk attached to the existing cash outflows.

Clearly, additional debt should not be allowed to put either contracted payments or essential household expenditures at risk. The degree to which the client is willing to put other expenditures at risk is up to the client, who will have to compare the benefits derived from the object acquired with the opportunity cost of what has to be given up to repay the loan. The job of the PFA is to provide a numerical framework within which this choice can be made.

THE EXPECTED FUTURE CASH FLOWS OF THE CLIENT

The above discussion assumes that the client will enjoy a constant future cash flow. If the client expects a substantial, permanent and steady increase in his or her cash flow in the future, then the risk attached to each 'slice' in the above schedule will be affected. If other expenditures remain constant, the 'involuntary saving' portion will increase. This will reduce the risk factor attached to each of the 'more important' slices in the expenditure statement, and so allow the client to absorb a higher debt capacity.

But how certain is the client that this future increase in his or her cash inflow will actually materialize? Securing certain cash outflows today against uncertain cash inflows due tomorrow is not a wise policy to follow at any level of finance.

There is also the possibility that the current net cash flow might decline suddenly and unexpectedly by reason of unemployment, illness or pregnancy. What is the chance of this happening? What can be done about it? As we noted in Chapter 6 on personal insurance, medical and permanent health insurance (PHI) can be taken out to hedge against risks such as these.

THE VALUE AND LIQUIDITY OF THE CLIENT'S ASSET BASE

Another important factor in determining the debt capacity of a client is the value and composition of the existing wealth of the client. The marketable assets owned by a client will provide security to a lender which may increase the potential debt capacity of the client well beyond the level supported by his or her cash flow. Lenders will usually provide credit up to a value equal to about two-thirds of the market value of the assets pledged in security for the loan. However, it is not wise for a borrower to pledge marketable assets as cover for an inadequate cash flow.

A substantial tranche of liquid assets ensures that even if the client's cash flow proves inadequate to service the debts at some future time, these liquid assets can be used to cover, at least temporarily, for a shortage of cash to meet the regular instalments on the debt. Measures of the value and liquidity of the client's assets can be derived from the client's personal balance sheet. The construction of a personal balance sheet is described in Chapter 2.

Thus a 'discretionary' cash flow statement and a personal balance sheet provide the basic framework for deciding on the 'safe' volume of personal debt that can be raised by a client. However, the ultimate ceiling on personal credit is determined by the attitude of the client towards accepting financial risk and the strength of the client's desire to acquire the good or service in question. As always, the PFA can advise and warn, but cannot decide.

CONSUMER CREDIT AND THE LAW

The consumer credit industry is a favourite abode of confidence tricksters, so it is not surprising to find that the government and the law both take a great deal of interest in this area of business activity. The government department responsible for supervising consumer credit is the 'Office of Fair Trading' (OFT).[5]

The legal constraints applied to providing consumer credit have been much tightened in recent years. The most important legislation which controls credit operations in the UK is the Consumer Credit Act. Some of the more important restrictions placed on the behaviour of the providers and monitors of consumer credit are listed below.

1. As we noted above, those credit rating agencies which provide personal information about potential borrowers to potential lenders must, if asked, send a copy of the credit report supplied to the lender to any individual who believes they have been denied credit because of the contents of the report. If an individual finds that he or she has been denied credit because of a negative credit agency report the applicant can request the credit agency, as detailed above, to submit a copy of their credit report. If this is found to be inaccurate it must be changed; if it is thought to be misleading, the applicant can write

---

[5] See note 2 above.

an explanation and insist that the explanation be included with the credit report if the report is supplied to a customer of the agency in the future. Severe penalties are imposed by the Office of Fair Trading on any credit agency which fails to comply with this procedure.

2. Several rules regarding consumer credit contracts are set down in law. For example, if a contract is signed on the premises of the seller, the contract has immediate effect unless fraud or deception can be proved. However, if the potential buyer has a face-to-face chat with the seller of the goods and then takes the contract away from the premises of the seller before signing it and sending it back to the buyer, the buyer may have a right to cancel the contract. A copy of the signed contract will be sent back by the seller to the buyer, and the buyer has five days from receipt of this contract to cancel it. The law of contract is complex, and legal advice is needed if the buyer feels he or she has been misled by the seller on the terms of credit offered.

3. A borrower who finds that his or her cash flow is insufficient to service their debts has three options: (a) to try to do a deal with the creditors, (b) to apply for an administration order, (c) to file for bankruptcy. Options (b) and (c) apply in England and Wales only.

So far as the debtor is concerned the first of these three options is by far the best, since the other two options, particularly option (c), can blight their creditworthiness for years to come, if not for ever.

Since options (b) and (c) will entail the involvement of a third party, the courts, in the dispute, many lenders are willing to renegotiate a deal if the borrower can persuade them that he or she can repay the debt over a longer period of time. At this point the lenders may agree to suspend any further interest charges on the debt – the court would probably enforce this condition anyway, if it went to law.

An 'award of administration' will only be made if the debtor fills in form N92 detailing his or her various debts and current income and expenditure. The debts must total at least £5000 and a judgment by the County Court must already have been made against the debtor. Under these circumstances the courts will take it upon themselves to administer the debt repayment. The court will write to all the creditors involved, checking that the debt schedule is accurate, and then fix an amount which the debtor will pay to the courts each month. Additional interest payments will be stopped. The courts will decide how to distribute the monthly payment from the debtor between the various creditors.

If the total debt amounts to less than £5000 but the court believes that it is still too large, relative to the current and expected income of the borrower, to ever be repaid, the borrower can apply to the courts for 'composition', which means that the courts may set aside a substantial part of the debt. This procedure is sailing very close to bankruptcy but is not actual bankruptcy, thus credit can still be obtained by the borrower in the future.

If the total debt exceeds £5000 the debtor can file for bankruptcy. If the debtor has substantial assets the courts might refuse to grant this and force the debtor to set up an **individual voluntary arrangement** whereby he or she must sell assets and distribute them pro rata to the debts owing to creditors.

The law of bankruptcy is very complex and legal advice is essential. A mishandling of bankruptcy by a debtor can result in imprisonment for a long term.[6]

The financial consequences of bankruptcy are severe. The bankrupt client must declare him- or herself to be a discharged bankrupt for the rest of his or her life when applying for credit (if he or she remains in the UK). Any form of credit will be extremely hard to come by in the future. A debtor who ignores this legal condition faces a gaol sentence.

PFAs should always advise their clients to avoid bankruptcy at all costs.

It should be noted that mortgage and tax arrears are not written off by bankruptcy proceedings. A home-owner in a 'negative equity' situation cannot cancel the mortgage debt by simply handing the home over the building society which granted the loan (and which now exceeds the market value of the home). The building society will simply sell the property for what it can get, deduct this amount from the outstanding value of the mortgage, and bill the client for the balance. The client is now worse off than before – he or she still owes money and now has no home![7]

4. The law provides some useful back-up cover for credit card holders who buy goods or services with their credit card. If the goods cost more than £100 and are not delivered to the buyer or do not come up to scratch or the seller goes bankrupt, the credit card holder can sue the credit card company in addition to the seller of the goods. This 'joint liability' is a useful and free additional benefit provided to the users of credit cards.

5. The law regarding disclosure of the annual percentage rate (APR) on loans offered to borrowers has been discussed earlier in this chapter. Note that the APR must be clearly displayed on the offer of the loan and must be displayed using the same size of font as the other rates quoted (but a **different** font of the same size may be used for representing the two rates).

---

[6] For a short introduction to bankruptcy proceedings see the booklet entitled 'The Insolvency Act 1986: A guide to bankruptcy law' from the Insolvency Service organization, 2 Burnhill Row, London EC1Y 8LL.
[7] Study the Sally Bryant case study in part B of this book for an example of this problem.

WHAT HAVE WE LEARNED IN THIS CHAPTER?

1. Short-term credit is too easy to come by in the UK at present. This can lead to severe financial problems for unwary borrowers.

2. Good creditworthiness is a valuable asset which should be exploited by the borrower when seeking credit, but which is often ignored. Borrowers with a good credit rating can obtain cheaper credit.

3. The key factors in achieving a good credit rating are a high regular income, a steady job, a reasonable length of time in the job, a stable marriage, ownership of a home, good health and an excellent past credit payments record.

4. Credit rating agencies keep records on borrowers with poor past payment records. If a client is denied credit he or she can ask why, find the name of the credit agency involved and demand to see a copy of the credit record, which must be corrected if wrong.

5. Credit can be supplied on open account up to a set limit or provided for a specific purpose. The former form of credit is usually cheaper than the latter.

6. The cost of credit varies a great deal between credit providers. A client should be encouraged to shop around. The more discriminating the supplier of credit, the cheaper is the credit provided by that supplier.

7. The cost of all credit advertised must be expressed as an annual percentage rate (APR). This rate is consistent between different forms of credit offered. The APR can be used by a borrower to compare the true cost of each source of credit offered.

8. The debt capacity of a client depends on many factors, such as the regularity of the client's cash flow, the clients discretionary expenditure, volume of involuntary saving, and the value and composition of his or her wealth. A ranking of regular expenditures in order of importance will allow a client to estimate the volume of additional credit he or she can take on and the true opportunity cost of any additional credit.

9. The government and the common law impose strict rules on those who provide consumer credit. Credit rating agencies must disclose copies of their individual files to persons listed on these files. The law also provides some protection to individuals against the machinations of unscrupulous credit providers. Borrowers who cannot fulfil their financial obligations have several choices as to how to proceed, but bankruptcy should be avoided at all costs.

10. Purchasing goods or services with a credit card from a UK-based seller provides the buyer with some useful additional protection and benefits, compared to buying the same goods or services with cash.

FURTHER READINGS

Burgess (1991): A legal compendium and discussion of the law relating to borrowing money and other goods.

Elkington (1988): a useful introduction to the rights of the individual with regard to dealing with personal credit and other financial matters.

Jones (1989): all you will ever want to know about the law relating to the issue and use and abuse of credit cards.

Spears (1993): useful collection of facts about credit and the raising of personal loans.

See bibliography on p.311 for a full annotation of these books.

TUTORIAL QUESTIONS: CONSUMER CREDIT

1. Why is debt recovery currently a serious problem in the UK?
2. What are the key factors involved in gaining a high credit rating score from a lender? Why is a high credit rating a valuable asset?
3. How does a credit rating agency operate?
4. What is the difference between an 'open ended' source of credit and a 'specific' source? Give an example of each source.
5. Why is bank credit and credit from a 'gold card' source usually cheaper than other sources of credit?
6. Why is a loan obtained from an insurance company, based on the security of a whole-life assurance policy, usually a cheap source of credit?
7. 'The astute borrower needs to find the most, discriminating lender who will accept him as a client!' Explain.
8. What is the APR on a loan? Why is this calculation of the cost of credit important to a potential borrower?
9. A merchant offers to sell a client a dishwasher for £500. The client does not have this amount of cash available so the merchant offers to loan the client the £500 repayable over three years at a 10% flat rate of interest added on to the capital sum. How much interest is the merchant going to charge the client? What is the APR rate in this case?
10. A borrower is paying interest on a loan in monthly instalments at a nominal interest rate of 20% per annum. He decides that he would now like to pay the interest in a single annual instalment at the end of each year. How much interest does he save by making this change from monthly to annual payment?
11. In company finance the income of the shareholders of a profitable company can be improved by taking on additional debt via the 'leverage' effect. Why is this not the case when an individual raises a loan to buy a car?

12. A credit card company charges a card holder 1.8% interest monthly on a £1000 loan repaid over one year. The £18 payment is charged to the account at the end of each month. The credit card company claims that the annual interest rate charged is 1.8 × 12 = 21.6% per annum. What is the true annual rate being charged?

13. The cost of a loan is the interest charge on the loan plus any additional charge for 'arranging' the loan. What is the 'opportunity cost' of a loan?

14. Describe how a conventional monthly expenditure budget can be reorganized to find the true opportunity cost of taking on a loan.

15. What is the 'discretionary cash flow' of a client? How is it measured?

16. Suggest two attributes of the assets owned by a client which would be of some interest to a potential lender?

17. What two financial schedules need to be prepared to estimate the 'debt capacity' of a client?

18. What is the name of the government department which monitors consumer credit in the UK?

19. How can a client who has been refused credit because of a report from a credit agency find out about the contents of the credit report? If the report is inaccurate or misleading, what can he or she do about it?

20. Under what conditions can a buyer withdraw from a credit contract he or she has signed with the seller?

21. What is an 'award of administration'? How can such an award be obtained? Why should a creditor apply for an administration order? How does it benefit the creditor?

22. Why should PFAs advise their clients to avoid bankruptcy at all costs?

23. If a good is purchased using a credit card, what additional benefits does the credit card holder enjoy over someone who pays for the same good in cash?

Suggested solutions to even numbered questions are provided at the back of this book.

Computers in personal finance
10

BENEFITS DERIVED FROM USING A COMPUTER

Computers can be of considerable assistance to the personal financial adviser. Detailed files on every client can be stored very compactly on the computer, and the computer allows the PFA to make complex financial calculations very quickly and very accurately. The computer, when attached via a modem to the telephone network, allows the PFA to access a wide variety of on-line data bases containing up-to-date information on financial and other matters. Finally, certain programs called 'decision support systems' or 'expert systems' are currently available which can be run on a computer to produce basic financial plans for clients at a low cost per plan.

Let us now examine these benefits in more detail.

STORING INFORMATION ABOUT CLIENTS

The PFA can store all of the available information about every client in a set of files held on a laptop microcomputer. Computers are able to store vast amounts of information – five hundred million characters can be stored on the hard disk of a quite modest microcomputer, and some of these hard discs are removable, a facility which provides the machine with, in effect, an infinite storage capacity.

Clients' files can be stored in a general purpose software storage package such as 'DBase IV' or 'Paradox", or the PFA can use a specialist personal finance software package such as 'Microsoft Money' or Intuit's 'Quicken' – packages which have been specifically designed for storing personal financial information. The general package provides the PFA with greater freedom of design, but is more expensive to set up, in both money and time.

THE DATA PROTECTION ACT 1984

Client information held on a computer comes under the jurisdiction of the UK's Data Protection Act of 1984.[1] In particular the Act requires that the PFA should devise a reasonably secure system to protect clients' files – unauthorized access must be made difficult. A password system restricting access to the files plus a system which encrypts the data on entry and decrypts on exit should suffice to meet these requirements of the Act.

The Data Protection Act also requires that any information about a client stored on a computer must be available for checking by the client, if the client should so wish. This requirement should pose no problems for the PFA, since the data stored are likely to be a copy of data already supplied by and in the possession of the client.

QUICK AND ACCURATE CALCULATION

The speed and accuracy of calculation of the computer are legendary. Once the PFA has installed a suitably programmed data base and loaded clients' files into the data base the computer allows the PFA to carry out a wide range of 'what if' analyses on the data with a minimum of time and effort.

The wide range of options and scenarios which can be explored on a computer are not economically feasible using any other processing method.

The experienced PFA soon finds that the analyses required in designing investment plans or pensions plans or mortgage finance plans are very similar for all clients. Thus a spreadsheet 'template' or other model designed to study the financial situation of one client can be stored, empty of data, and used for designing plans for other clients. The PFA will gradually build up a portfolio of such analytical tools.

Once a PFA becomes accustomed to processing client data on a computer, he or she will soon conclude that any alternative approach to storing and analysing data is obsolete.

ACCESS TO ON-LINE DATA BASES

A major development has been introduced into the business world over the last 10 years. Electronic data bases holding vast quantities of information have become accessible to the business world at reasonable cost. These data bases are accessible on-line, often for 24 hours a day, through

[1] The Data Protection Act of 1984 requires that any information stored on the computer must be of the type specified to the Registrar in the registration of the data base and must be accurate and up-to-date. The data must only be disclosed to those who are registered as expected recipients of the information.

the conventional telephone network to millions of potential users throughout the world. The information is available to anyone who owns a computer and a modem and has access to a direct telephone link to the country holding the host mainframe computer which stores the data base.

The 'publisher' of the data base, which is usually stored on a host computer by another company, is required to keep the information in the data base up to date. Customers, for example PFAs, can now access this current information via their own computer and modem[2] at the cost of an access fee plus the price of a local telephone call.

Computer-based trading devices such as the 'Common Trading Platform'[3] developed by the Stock Exchange and introduced in 1994 for electronic trading on the London exchange will give PFAs direct access to a wide range of financial information and services. For example, one system which has already been developed by a company called FAME/LSD can link the adviser directly into an analytic package which will analyse pensions and other financial products for the benefit of clients.[4]

The access fee charged for using such facilities can be either a substantial annual fee linked to a very low charge for each individual interrogation, or a low annual fee linked to a much higher charge for each individual interrogation. The PFA can choose the fee structure suited to his or her needs.

The enquirer can access the data base through a general 'gateway' such as MAID, Compuserve, Data Star, Telecom Gold, Dialog, Profile, PSS, Prestel or Reuters, or through a specialist gateway specifically designed for use by one specific group. No specialist gateway is offered to PFAs at present, but several software companies such as FAME are working towards this objective.

Exhibit 10.1 lists a selection of on-line data bases and CD-ROM-based[5] data bases which are currently available to any PFA possessing a computer and a modem or CD-ROM drive. Once the PFA has subscribed to a gateway service the protocols for extracting information from the data base are not complex, but it is advisable for the PFA to attend a short

[2] Once data sent over a telephone line become fully digitized, computer users will be able to dispense with modems since there will be no need to convert between digital and analogue modes.
[3] The 'Common Trading Platform' which has been developed by the Exchange will provide an electronic system to allow PFAs and others to communicated directly with product providers. Information will be available on new products, commission rates, policy enquiries and so forth. The system is designed to provide a data highway between financial product providers and financial intermediaries.
[4] Information from FAME/LSD software, Fame House, Ashted Lock, Aston Science Park, Birmingham B7 4AZ. Tel: 0121 606 6600.
[5] A CD-ROM is simply a conventional compact disc containing information in place of music.

course on the subject of on-line networking, to be able to extract maximum benefit from a given data base at minimum cost. For example, a high-speed modem allied to a sophisticated data capture system can greatly reduce the cost of the telephone calls.

Several update services held in loose-leaf binders are also available to the PFA. These updating systems use conventional printing and the postal services to keep users abreast of current developments in their field. They usually update the data held monthly, quarterly or annually.

The data bases of most interest to the PFA are likely to be financial data bases on such things as share and bond prices, currency rates, interest rates, tax data, mortgage finance products, pension products and insurance products. There are, however, a wide range of data bases on other subjects which the PFA might also find useful. For example, data bases are provided on such things as the legal restrictions imposed on certain activities like retrenchment, the current value of 'collectables' and backnumbers of newspapers and journals. The data bases currently available are legion and yet their numbers are growing at an exponential rate. A PFA will find that it is difficult to keep track of what is available.

A PFA who buys the hardware required and subscribes to a data base gateway service will find that they can access thousands of data bases held world-wide on every conceivable subject under the sun. They can browse or 'surf' through these information sources at relatively low cost to keep up to date on financial developments and to extract material relevant to constructing financial plans for clients.

The cost of interrogating data bases stored on host computers in distant countries such as Switzerland, the USA or even South Africa or Australia is remarkably low – often no more than a few pence per minute, provided the user has a sophisticated extraction system to store data 'off-line' as quickly as possible.

The use of electronic data bases is a very recent development in personal finance, a development which is not as yet fully explored. Cheap access to such a wealth of data should allow a diligent PFA working in a small practice in a remote part of the country to compete with the giants of the industry, if they so wish. The work involved in acquiring the skills necessary to utilize this powerful new tool efficiently is not negligible, but there can be little doubt that in the long term the returns will justify the effort involved.

COMPUTER-BASED FINANCIAL PLANNING PROGRAMS

Most personal financial plans are hand-crafted. The plan is carefully designed piece by piece by the PFA in consultation with the client. Hand-crafted plans take a good deal of time to develop and so are expensive to produce. An average 'comprehensive' plan may take around 10 hours to

On-line and other financial data bases

On-line Data Bases

Name of Data Base	Host	Publisher	Subject Matter
ABI/INFORM	Many	ABI	Abstracts of 800 journals in Finance and Economics etc.
ACTUARIAL DB	Many	I.P. SHARP	National and international mortality tables and projections
BANK OF ENGLAND	Many	DRI	800 financial indicators about the UK economy
BANKING DB	TEXTLINE	Reuters	Information on UK banks. Run by Reuters
BLISS	Many	GBI	Citational data base on articles on business and management
BRAIN	Many	Brain	Information about mortgages. Types of, rates of interest etc.
CEEFAX FINANCE	BBC	BBC	A wide range of financial statistics from TV screen
CNN	CNN	CNN Systems	Credit ratings on individuals and companies
COMPANIES HOUSE	Many	Govt	Company accounts, registration data etc.
CSO	Govt	DRI etc.	17 500 time series on the UK economy
DATASTREAM	Datastream	Datastream	Stock prices, dividend yields, p/e ratios etc. for 30 000 companies. Interactive system
FIND	Pergammon	MCC	Financial institutions data base
FINIS	Dialog	MC	Finance industry information service. Products and services available
FT PROFILE	FT Profile	FT	Company information etc. 200 sectors covered
ICC BUSINESS RATIOS	Dialog/ICC	ICC	Information on all UK companies registered at Companies House
ICC Financial Data sheets	Dialog/Viewdata	ICC	Information on 100 000 UK companies
ICC Stockbroker research	Dialog/Data-star	ICC	Analysts reports on UK companies and industries
INFOCHECK	Data-star	Infocheck	A wide range of information on 420 000 companies
INFOLINK	Data-star	Infolink	Credit rating agency for individuals and companies
INSURANCE COs. DB	FIND	Tektron	Accounts of UK Insurance Cos. plus news on same
JORDANWATCH	Pergamon	Jordan's	Financial information on all registered UK companies
LEXIS	Dialog	Butterworth	On line Legal data base. Cases. Acts etc.
LEXIS Finance	Pergamon	Mead Data	International finance and business information
MEDIAT	Many	BT INS SERVICE	Life, pensions and motor insurance, price feeds, performance. On viewdata
MICROPAL	Many	Micropal	Facts about performance of financial institutions and funds. Unit trusts, investment trusts etc.
MINTEL	Many	Mintel	Financial news indexing service
PROFILE	Many	FT	Full text of newspapers, journals, stockbroker reports etc.

Name of Data Base	Host	Publisher	Subject Matter
On-line Data Bases			
STONE & COX	Many	S & C	Comprehensive Life tables
TELESURE	Many	Telesure	Insurance rates and other data
TEXTLINE	Reuters	Reuters	Vast array of newspapers, journal articles etc. Full text
COMPANYLINE	Maid	Maid	Financial reports on 4.5 million companies in 40 countries
Data Bases on CD-ROM			
C-TEXT	CD ROM	C-Text	Rules and regulations arising out of the Financial Services Act 1986
BLAY's GUIDES	CD ROM	Blay	Venture capital, factoring, leasing, grants and incentives
FAME	CD ROM	Jordan	Jordan's analysis of UK and other companies' financial data
MICROEXTAT	CD ROM	Extel	Financial information on companies etc. 3500 companies updated each week
Update Services in Looseleaf Binders			
GEE & CO	The compliance fact book		SRO rules and regulations
BLAY'S	Moneymaster		Personal finance products from banks and building societies
GEE & CO	Financial Intermediaries Factbook		Factual information for PFAs
IDS PENSIONS SERVICE	Pension information update		Update on all matters concerning pensions
LAFFERTY PUB.	EU Financial Industry Monitor		Update on developments in the Finance Industry in the EU
MONEY MANAGEMENT	Rate update		Weekly guide to life assurance rates etc.
STONE & COX	Life Assurance Handbook (Pub. Buckley Press)		Premium guide, policy conditions, health evidence needed, loan options, bonus declarations and much else
STONE & COX	Individual Pensions Handbook (Pub. Buckley Press)		Details re the many pension schemes offered on the financial market in the UK

Several thousand data bases are now accessible to a personal financial adviser who owns a micro-computer and a modem linking the computer into one or other of the telephone networks. The number of on-line data bases are expanding at such a speed that it is difficult to keep track of them. Information is also stored on CD-ROMs and looseleaf updating services. These are both updated on a regular basis.

The above list provides no more than an illustrative sample of the vast range of information sources now available to a personal financial adviser.

Exhibit 10.1 A listing of some information sources which might be of use to a personal financial adviser.

produce. If the PFA is fee-based and charging £50 to £150 an hour, then a comprehensive plan will cost the client from £500 to £1500 in fees.

Some clients are not prepared to pay this amount of money for a plan, and so a great deal of effort has gone into devising alternative, more automated, methods of designing personal financial plans.

One solution, instigated in the USA, is to hand over a great deal of the basic financial analysis and planning to a computer. A number of computer-based financial planning tools have been developed in the USA which can be used to speed up the design of a personal financial plan.

A computer-based planning program (CBPP) is produced, often at considerable cost, by a software publisher who sells the program, or more likely, leases it to a PFA at an agreed fee. The publisher contracts to keep the program up-to-date by regularly incorporating into the program any new developments which occur in the personal finance field, developments such as new tax legislation. Regular updated copies of the planning program are issued to the purchasers of the program. Users who run into operating problems can seek advice from the publisher via a 'hotline'.

A CBPP system works as follows. The PFA asks the client to fill in a comprehensive questionnaire. This information is keyed into the input module of the CBPP program stored in the computer. The financial planning programme stored in the computer then analyses this input information and produces a series of financial plans on such things as investment, insurance, pensions, housing finance, educational finance and so on. Each plan is specifically crafted for the benefit of an individual client.

The PFA reviews the plans suggested by the CBPP and if these plans seem reasonable offers them to the client. A computer-based financial planning program will cut the cost of preparing a financial plan by half to one-third – a substantial saving.

These computer-based personal financial planning programs are sometimes called 'expert systems' (ES) (see Phillips, Brown and Nielson, 1990), but this is a misnomer. An expert system is a computer program which encapsulates a set of rules for taking complicated decisions. The difference between an expert system and the many other computer based decision support systems (DSSs) currently available on the market is that within a true expert system the rules are objectively deduced from the behaviour of experts by an expert systems engineer using a rule derivation computer program. The computer-based personal financial planning programs currently on offer would not seem to have been designed using this method. This does not mean to say that they are not useful decision support systems of high quality.

Phillips et al. (1990) claim that, based on their experience in using such programs, computer-based planning programs make the planning process more consistent between clients while at the same time reducing by a substantial margin the costs involved in preparing a plan.

As with all plans produced by computer, the PFA needs to review the plan before offering it to a client. As everyone with an extensive knowledge of computers knows, computers lack common sense and can occasionally produce nonsense.

A CBPP offers two major advantages to the PFA. First it speeds up the analysis, so long as the client is facing standard financial problems. Second it ensures that the analytical procedures and facts used in the preparation of the plan are kept up to date. For example, investment products, pension products, tax, law and other matters are frequently changed by the product providers, the government and market regulators. These matters can be regularly updated by the publisher. The publisher employs a team of experts in law, personal taxation, government regulation, new financial products and suchlike to keep the CBPP up to date. This updating process reduces the chance of a PFA missing out on some important development in personal finance.

One of the limitations on the use of CBPPs is that they cannot tackle non-standard problems, while a hand-crafted personal finance plan will almost certainly be more efficient than a computer-produced plan; however, if the former is beyond the financial resources of the client, the latter is available as a cheaper alternative.

The legal responsibility for any loss incurred by a client resulting from an incorrect plan produced by a computer program has not yet been decided by a British court, although the PFA would almost certainly be held responsible since they should have reviewed the plan prior to offering it to the client.

The PFA will also need to ensure, before relying on the output produced by a CBPP, that the regular updating of the computer-based planning program is conducted by persons who are truly expert in their particular field.

CBPPs can be targeted at specific areas of personal finance such as pension planning, estate planning, educational financing or personal tax, or they can be comprehensive, producing a fully comprehensive personal financial plan for the client.

CBPPs are more likely to be hired than bought, since the full cost of producing a comprehensive CBPP can be in the region of £100 000 to £1 000 000. The hire cost may be based on an individual charge per use, or alternatively based on an annual leasing charge with unlimited use. The program may be provided to the PFA on a computer disk, or it may be stored on a mainframe host computer and interrogated via a modem attached to the PFA's computer. In the former case a series of computer disks updating the CBPP program are sent to the user on a regular basis.

Sophisticated CBPPs will incorporate direct links via a telephone line to an on-line financial data base such as the Common Trading Platform provided by the Exchange. The plans will thus incorporate up-to-date financial values.

Properly designed CBPPs will also allow the PFA or her client to modify the assumptions and some of the parameters built into the planning program. Examples of such factors are the attitude of the client towards risk and assumptions about the future rate of inflation.

The complexity of some CBPP programs is formidable. They can employ as many as 10 000 decision rules in generating their output. The output reports themselves can run to 100 pages. Such a plethora of information introduces the danger of swamping the client with an excess of facts, scenarios and options. The sensible PFA will simplify such an excess of information before presenting it to the client.

SOME QUESTIONS A PFA SHOULD ASK ABOUT A CBPP SYSTEM

If a PFA is considering buying or leasing a computer-based personal planning system, it would be wise to ask the following questions of the publisher.

Who wrote the system? Using what software language? What are the qualifications of the team who wrote the system?

How long has the system been operating? How many PFAs are using it? The system has been used to prepare how many client plans? Are current or past users happy with the results?

How expensive is the system? Can it be hired or must it be bought? If it can be hired, what is the basis of the hiring charge? Is the charge based on the number of client plans produced or is it hired on a time basis?

How often is the system updated? What are the qualifications of those who update the system?

Is the planning system comprehensive? If not, which particular financial plans does it cater for?

How user-friendly is the system? Does it crash easily?

Can the system be modified by the PFA to incorporate the particular wishes, assumptions and preferences of the client? Is 'what-if' analysis available within the program to allow the PFA to produce a range of scenarios?

What is the presentational quality of the plans produced by the system? Are the recommendations of the plan set out clearly? Can the data output format be easily modified by the user?

Do the publishers of the system provide a 'hotline' to answer questions on running the system? How accessible and reliable is this hotline, and is it free?

THE 'PLANMAN' SYSTEM

Planman is a typical personal finance planning system which has been in use in the USA since 1988 and since 1990 in the UK. The system incorporates 7500 decision rules and was written by the Sterling Wentworth Corporation from Salt Lake City, Utah.[6]

Cash flow projections, investment plans, life assurance plans, disability income plans, retirement and pension plans, educational funding and inheritance plans are all personal financial plans that can be generated by the system, either singly or as a comprehensive package.

The aspirations and attitudes of the client can be built into the system. A 'what-if' analytic tool is available to the user to test out assumptions. A graphics facility is incorporated into the system.

The accounting firm Arthur Andersen has used the system to assist in producing personal financial plans for its clients.

THE INTERNET

The Internet is a communication system which uses telecommunications and computers to link millions of computer users into a vast global network of over 10 million people.

The system was designed by the US military in the 1960s against the possibility of a nuclear attack knocking out a substantial section of the US telephone system.

No one controls the Internet, it just grows and grows. The cost of using it is astonishingly cheap – usually little more than the cost of a local phone call.

The Internet is best known as a means of sending electronic letters via E-Mail. Messages can be sent around the world to another user of the Internet at the cost of a local phone call.

Internet can be of interest to PFAs, since it is linked to data bases which hold lots of financial information. Many of these data bases provide free access, since the information is supplied and updated by governments as a public service. Internet also provides discussion groups or 'forums' for users. There are several discussion forums on personal finance. Some 'bulletin boards' on the Internet also log information on personal finance.

If a PFA already has a computer and modem, and few will not have such essential tools, then accessing the Internet is simply a matter of subscribing to a gateway provider such as CIX or Compuserve.

Finding one's way around the Internet is quite another matter. The system has no owner or controller, is virtually free, and so is anarchic in

---

[6] Sterling Wentworth Corporation, 57 West 200 South, Suite 510, Salt Lake City, UT 84101. Tel: US (800) 752 6637.

structure. Search tools such as 'Gopher', 'Mosaic' and 'Netscape' are available, and Krol (1994) provides a useful best selling introduction to the Internet.

Collecting useful information from the Internet is so difficult that several companies collect information on specific topics and write it to CD-ROM discs. These are then sold to computer users who can study the data at leisure by using their CD-ROM. 'Instant investor' listed in the readings at the end of this chapter, is one such disk.

Apart from the difficulty of access, the major limitation on the usefulness of the Internet for British users at the time of writing is the strong US bias of the data which can be accessed. Most of the interesting data assumes a US readership.

However, we have no doubt that this immensely powerful system will become a major instrument in the PFA's toolkit in the near future.

WHAT HAVE WE LEARNED IN THIS CHAPTER?

1. Computers can be of considerable assistance to the personal financial adviser.
2. The computer can store client files very economically, make accurate and fast calculations on client data, access financial and other data bases to find up-to-date information for financial planning and run computer based personal financial planning systems which can cut the cost of preparing a financial plan by a substantial margin.
3. Computer packages specifically designed to store and process personal financial data are available at a reasonable cost.
4. If a PFA stores client data on a computer the PFA is subject to the Data Protection Act which insists on the setting up of adequate security measures to protect the confidentiality of the data. The use of passwords and encryption should be sufficient to achieve this objective. Clients must be given access to their own data on request.
5. The PFA will probably devise a set of spreadsheet 'templates' for analysing financial problems which are common to many clients.
6. If the PFA buys a modem plus a 'gateway' program which links his or her computer to the telephone network, they can gain access to many thousands of electronic data bases around the world at relatively low cost. This facility should allow a PFA working in a small practice in a remote part of the country to compete with the larger firms.
7. Personal financial plans can now be prepared automatically by using one or other of the computer based personal planning systems, sometimes called 'expert systems' offered on the market. Such systems are expensive to design but can be hired at a reasonable cost. CBPPs can speed up the production of financial plans and cut the cost of producing personal plans by a substantial margin.

8. Before acquiring such a system the PFA needs to ask the publisher of the system a series of questions regarding the quality of the product, its user-friendliness and how often the program is updated and who updates it.
9. The Internet provides access to a world-wide communication system at very low cost. E-Mail, 'forums' and 'bulletin boards' on personal finance should be of interest to the PFA. Although the access cost to the Internet is low, navigating the Internet is currently exceedingly complex. Navigation tools such as Gopher are now available to help and in the near future finding what one wants on the Internet is likely to become much simpler. The potential of the Internet to a PFA is 'mind-blowing', to use current jargon.

FURTHER READING

CD-ROM disk, 'Instant Investor", Market Data Centre: a compilation of lots of free information about economics and finance. Mostly compiled from US government sources. Includes the CIA World Fact Book. Updated quarterly.

Johnson Fry: this booklet provides a useful list of the larger on-line data bases, world-wide and country specific, accessible via a modem and a telephone line. Publisher, host, telephone, fax, company address and contents provided.

Krol (1994): the best-selling book on the subject. Comprehensive.

Schofield (1994): a British book on the subject, very clearly written! Most other books on computers and communications are almost all heavily biased towards the USA.

Investment advisers interested in collecting financial and other information from the Internet computer communication network should join the BBC's 'Networking Club' (£25 a year) or the more sophisticated IP GOLD run by CityScape[7] (£50 to join plus £180 a year). IP GOLD includes the very useful search package 'Mosaic', which has been designed to access the increasingly important 'World Wide Web' network

See bibliography on p.311 for a full annotation of these books.

TUTORIAL QUESTIONS: COMPUTERS IN PERSONAL FINANCE

1. Suggest three benefits available to a PFA if the client's records are stored on a computer.
2. If the PFA keeps client records on a computer the rules set out in the Data Protection Act apply to those records. What are the key requirements?
3. Explain how a password entry system works on a computer. What does 'encryption' of data mean?

---

[7] BBC Networking Club Tel: 0181 576 7799; Cityscape Tel: 01223 566950.

4. Give an example of 'what-if' analysis applied to a pension plan prepared for a client. Suggest four variables which might be altered one at a time to provide four different scenarios.

5. What is a spreadsheet 'template'? Give an example of a template which might be used for analysing a common problem faced by many clients.

6. What is an electronic data base? What is a 'host'? What is the role of the publisher of a data base? Give three examples of electronic data bases that could be of help to a PFA in preparing personal financial plans for clients.

7. What equipment does a PFA need to extract information from an electronic data base?

8. Why is a high-speed modem so important in extracting information from an electronic data base? Describe a sophisticated extraction system with reference to electronic data bases.

9. What is a computer-based personal planning program? What work does it take off the shoulders of the PFA?

10. What is an expert system? Why are the computer-based personal planning programs now on offer not really expert systems?

11. How is the CBPP program made available to the PFA?

12. Why are CBPPs more likely to be hired by a PFA, rather than bought outright?

13. Suggest five questions a PFA should ask before hiring or buying a CBPP.

14. With regard to the CBPP called 'Planman': what kinds of plans can Planman generate? How many decision rules are incorporated in the package? What other useful facilities are built into the package?

15. What exactly is the Internet? In relation to using the Internet, what is the difference between a 'gateway', a 'network' and a 'data base'?

16. Why do some companies sell data stored in data bases attached to the Internet on CD-ROMs? Why should anyone pay, say £25 for a CD-ROM when they can find the same information for themselves on the Internet?

Suggested solutions to odd numbered questions are provided at the back of this book.

Regulation of the personal financial adviser

11

THE NEED FOR REGISTRATION AND REGULATION

In recent years a number of financial scandals have occurred in Britain which have damaged the reputation of the financial markets in general and personal financial advisers in particular.[1]

Prior to the 1986 Financial Services Act which introduced legislation to regulate financial advisers, the qualifications required to practise as a PFA were almost non-existent. The result was that some individuals with a very limited knowledge of finance entered the industry, and by providing poor advice to their clients lost them a great deal of money. Even worse, some individuals entered the personal finance profession with the sole objective of stealing their clients' money. Some other equally discreditable incidents occurred in other branches of the financial services industry during this period. The Robert Maxwell pension fund affair and the heavy losses imposed on 'names' attached to various underwriting syndicates at Lloyd's are well documented. The personal financial adviser has not been the only financial adviser in the dock.

The aim of the Financial Services Act of 1986 was to control and monitor the efficiency and honesty of the financial services industry in the UK. The government opted for self-regulation rather than government con-

---

[1] For example, the Barlow Clowes affair and the Dunsdale and Levitt saga. The collapse of many home income plans in 1991 is another example of a failed scheme which attracted much bad publicity. Prior to 1990, many PFAs advised their elderly clients to take out a mortgage and invest the money so gained in securities. These home income plans had unfortunate consequences for clients when house prices plunged below mortgage valuations following 1989. Again many employees contributing to a company occupational pension plan were persuaded by PFAs, during the period 1989 to 1993, to leave their company scheme and switch their pension contributions into a personal pension plan run by an insurance company. Subsequent analysis has shown that the PFAs who advised such persons to switch did not collect sufficient information to properly assess the advice given. There is talk of government compensation.

trol, and the main self-regulatory organizations (SROs) set up under this Act and later legislation are shown in Exhibit 3.3 in Chapter 3.

The regulatory bodies which currently have responsibility for regulating the PFA are the Securities and Investments Board (SIB) and the Personal Investment Authority (PIA).

The SIB is a private limited company financed by members of the investment industry in the UK. Its chairman reports annually to the Chancellor of the Exchequer who, in turn, lays his report before Parliament. The SIB enjoys regulatory powers which are backed by statute. The ultimate responsibility for regulation lies with the Treasury. The SIB is empowered to instigate criminal prosecution against any person who is found to be acting as an unauthorized investment adviser in the UK. The SIB maintains a list of firms which are authorized to act as investment advisers.[2]

The PIA, an amalgam of two former bodies known as FIMBRA and LAUTRO, is the arm of the SIB which monitors those advisers who advise on personal investment planning and associated matters. Since implementation of the Act, no adviser operating in the UK has been allowed to advise on, sell or manage personal investments unless they are authorized to do so by one or other of the regulatory bodies set up under the Act. It is now a criminal offence to do any of these things without authorization.

The current scheme of regulation has set itself two objectives, first to monitor entrants to the investment profession by checking that they are competent, honest and solvent, second to provide a set of 'rules of correct conduct' which must be followed by investment advisers when dealing with their clients.

In addition to setting up the regulatory bodies, legislation was introduced which set up the Investor's Compensation Scheme (ICS). This scheme compensates the clients of investment advisers up to a fixed maximum amount, currently £48 000.[3] The clients of PFAs can claim under the scheme if they lose money because of the negligence, incompetence or fraud of an **authorized** adviser. The scheme is run by an independent company, ICS Limited. The SIB supervises the scheme and compensation is paid out by the SIB, but paid for by way of a levy on members of the particular SRO, such as the PIA or IMRO, involved in the loss.

Members who are registered indirectly via a recognized professional body (RPB), such as solicitors or accountants, are excluded from the scheme. These organizations run their own compensation schemes.

---

[2] The public can consult this list by phoning 0171 929 3652 or keying into Prestel (key *301# or *SIB#).
[3] The actual amount of compensation is 100% up to £30 000 and 90% on the next £20 000 – £48 000 in all.

The scheme to regulate investment advisers came into force on 29 April 1988, but the results have not been very satisfactory. The entire system of financial regulation which flowed from the setting up of the Securities and Investments Board and the other regulators, set out in Exhibit 3.3, has been subject to a great deal of criticism by the regulated, the regulators and the public who use the services of the finance industry: 'The single most significant observation anyone poking below the surface of financial services regulation is likely to make is its apparent lack of logical structure and cost effective organization.'[4]

The concept of self-regulation has come under particularly strong attack. It 'has not worked and will not work because of the inherent conflicts of interest within it'.[5]

The second part of the control apparatus, the Investor's Compensation Scheme, has been subject to no less stringent criticism. The ICS was inadequately funded from the start and has staggered from one funding crisis to another, as several large firms providing financial advice have collapsed into bankruptcy.

The SIB was so worried by these developments that in 1990 it commissioned Sir Kenneth Clucas to report on the regulation of the personal finance services industry in the UK, paying particular attention to the funding crisis on compensation. Sir Kenneth's excellent report was published in March 1992. The Clucas report was very critical of the regulatory system and suggested several major changes in the structure of control and compensation. The most important change suggested was that the various sections of the self-regulating bodies purporting to be looking after the interests of the small private investor, bodies operating mainly within the SROs which were at that time called LAUTRO and FIMBRA, should be unified with certain members of IMRO into one single regulatory body called the Personal Investment Authority (PIA).

After much argument a modified version of these recommendations was introduced in July 1994; the PIA is now the regulatory body authorized to look after the interests of the small investor.

The crux of the disagreement between the large institutions and the government is that the large institutions believe that the small independent financial adviser should be regulated by a different organization and set of rules to those regulating the advisers working for the large financial institutions.

HOW DOES ALL OF THIS AFFECT THE PFA?

These various attempts to regulate the personal finance industry have important consequences for every PFA.

[4] Quoted from Harper (1992) 'Watching their own', *CA Magazine*, May, p.10.
[5] Ibid.

The first and most important consequence is that the independent PFA must register with the PIA or some other SRO if they wish to operate as an independent investment adviser in the UK. The PIA will audit the background and competence of applicants; if they are found to be honest, competent and solvent, the PIA will register them as members. This registration allows the PFA to advise clients on investment and other related matters. The PFA can now inform clients on a letterhead that he or she is a registered member of the PIA. Some of the more important qualifications required before an individual will be accepted for registration with the PIA are set out in Exhibit 11.1.

In order to prove their competence to act as an investment adviser, the PFA must pass the Financial Planning Certificate of the Chartered Insurance Institute as an absolute minimum educational standard and, in addition, must have accumulated at least two years' practical experience in the field; three years if they wish to act as a principal. It is likely that many aspiring PFAs will have already gained a more advanced financial qualification than the FPC before applying for PIA membership.[6]

Both the SIB and the PIA have devised rule books to control the relations between a PFA and his or her client, and the organization of the work of the PFA. A PFA who is registered with the PIA and who ignores these rules could find themselves subject to criminal prosecution; any contracts which he or she has persuaded the client to sign would be void.

Every member registered with the PIA is visited from time to time by a representative of the PIA to see that he or she is complying with the recommended rules.[7] The rules vary somewhat, depending on whether the registered member is a sole trader, a partnership or a company.

SOME OF THE MORE IMPORTANT SIB RULES

The only sure way to check out the rules of the SIB and the PIA is to read the rule book, and the associated guidelines, issued by the organization. These rule books can be obtained at a charge of around £60 from the information department of these organizations.

Some of the more important rules set out in the SIB rule book are listed below.

WHO MUST REGISTER?

If an independent PFA is dealing in, managing or advising on investing in shares, debentures, government securities, unit or investment trusts,

[6] The topics listed in the syllabuses of the exams set by financial institutes in the UK contain very limited material on personal finance. The SIB is asking the accounting institutes to introduce more training in personal finance into their educational syllabuses. Thirteen UK universities provide undergraduate courses in Financial Services. These courses include some training in personal financial matters.
[7] About half the registered membership of FIMBRA were visited in 1993.

Registering with the PIA

The PIA is a self-regulating organization set up under the Financial Services Act of 1986. The objective set for the PIA is to ensure that those who advise on or manage investments in the UK are fit and proper persons to do so. The PIA regulates both firms and individuals who operate in the investment industry. The PIA replaced two prior regulators FIMBRA and LAUTRO in July 1994.

Any person or firm who advises on investments, deals in investments or operates collective investment schemes will come under the aegis of the PIA or one of the other regulatory authorities.

The types of investment covered are shares, debentures and bonds, government securities, unit and investment trusts and long term insurance contracts. Warrants, options and any other rights or interest in investments are also covered.

The entity registered with the PIA can be a sole trader, a partnership or a limited company.

Before an individual is registered with the PIA the organization must ensure that the applicant is honest, competent and solvent. The question of honesty is monitored by requiring the applicant to present references from reliable referees.

The question of competence is addressed by requiring the applicant to have, at the very least, passed the Certificate in Financial Planning set by the Chartered Insurance Institute. Many applicants will hold other financial qualifications which support their claim to competence in handling personal financial matters.

With regard to a sole trader or a partnership, solvency is addressed by requiring the applicant to provide a statement of personal assets and liabilities. An opening balance sheet is required plus a forecast profit and loss account for the first year of trading. If the applicant is a company, Form 88(2) must be supplied to the PIA showing the issued and fully paid share capital of the company plus a statement proving that shares are in issued not bearer form.

If the applicant has a criminal record the PIA must be told of the nature of the offence.

Every applicant applying for authorization by the PIA must have arranged professional indemnity insurance of a value acceptable to the PIA.

All members registered with the PIA must submit annual reports to the PIA. The nature of these reports depends on the category under which the member is registered. Category 1 covers all members who act as principals and handle clients' money. Category 2 covers members who handle clients' money but do not act as principals in buying and selling shares etc. Category 3 covers those members who neither act as principals nor handle clients' money.

Category 1 members must supply the PIA with an audited balance sheet, profit and loss account and statement of financial resources each year. A monthly unaudited balance sheet and profit and loss account and resource statement must also be supplied.

Category 2 members must supply the same statements annually plus management accounts quarterly. They must also fill in a questionnaire on various aspects of their dealings annually.

Category 3 members need only fill in a questionnaire and a statement of solvency once a year.

Special activities such as discretionary portfolio management and transacting options and warrants requires specific authorization from the PIA.

The PIA requires applicants for membership to supply detailed information on their personal attributes and financial status. The requirements imposed on members who intend to handle their clients' money and act as principals in transactions are particularly rigorous.

Exhibit 11.1   The conditions which must be fulfilled before an investment adviser can register as a member of the Personal Investment Authority.

options (but not futures), warrants or any other right or interest in investments, or if they are arranging long-term insurance contracts related to investment, then the PFA must be registered with an appropriate regulator.

There are one or two specific exemptions to this blanket rule. For example, those who provide financial advice in newspapers or journals need not register, those providing advice on shares in private companies are also excluded, as are those providing advice on employee share schemes. Those providing casual financial advice, at a party for example, but not acting in the specific role of a financial adviser, are also exempt from the rules.

Note that those who arrange mortgages and loans for clients, or who provide advice on or sell futures contracts, are specifically excluded from control by the PIA.

SOME ORGANIZATIONAL RULES

The PFA must declare him- or herself to be either an independent financial adviser or a tied agent. This is called the 'polarization' rule. This declaration has important implications for the PFA. A 'tied agent' can only sell the products of the company to which they are tied. This company, in its turn, will probably be registered with an SRO. If a PFA is 'tied' the job of the PFA is simplified somewhat, since the possible investment choices to be considered are much reduced.

The SIB rule book states that there must be 'integrity and fair dealing' between a PFA and client. This clause has caused some anguish among PFAs, since the precise meanings of 'integrity' and 'fair dealing' might be subject to various interpretations.

The independent PFA must also give 'best advice' on selecting an investment plan for a client. This means that the advice must be competent and impartial, and must place the interests of the client before those of the PFA. The PFA must not bias their advice towards one organization or one product and must, to the best of their ability, choose that product best suited to the needs of the client. In other words, they must not simply choose that product which provides the highest commission! For example, gilts generate no commission for the PFA but might well suit the investment needs of a risk-averse client. However, the PIA itself admits that a certain subjectivity will enter into the selection of investment products: 'There is an element of subjective judgement in most recommendations'.[8]

The rules are very strict on 'packaged' products provided by a group associated in some way with the PFA. In such circumstances the pack-

[8] FIMBRA Guidance note no.9, section 1.

aged product 'must be better at securing the client's objectives than all other products from other sources'.[9]

The PFA must make a reasonable attempt to find out about a client's affairs before providing financial advice to the client. For example, is the client married? Are they employed? When, if employed, do they retire? What form of pension will be provided on retirement? What other investments are held? What is the condition of their health? What insurance is held, and so on. In summary, every PFA must enquire into the background of his or her client – advice must not be given in a vacuum.[10] If the client refuses to divulge to the PFA information which might be important, the PFA should record this fact and confirm it in writing to the client.

The PFA must also agree a set of investment objectives with the client, discuss the degree of risk involved in any investment and assess the client's ability to maintain regular payments on any long-term contracts.

If the PFA is authorized to hold clients' money, the PFA must keep this in a separate account. Interest must be credited to this account at the current rate paid on commercial bank deposits and the PFA's accounts must be audited at least once a year by a qualified auditor.

If a PFA is authorized by the PIA to manage a client's portfolio of securities, then an up-to-date statement of investment performance must periodically be provided to the client. An annual report must provide information to the client on such things as the sales and purchases of stock during the year, the income from and the costs of running the portfolio and the specific charges made by the PFA for managing the portfolio.

With regard to the sale of investment-linked life policies, 'best advice' must again be given. If forecasts are made as to the future value of the fund on the termination of the policy, or forecasts are made of future profits to be earned from the fund, then both 'optimistic' and 'pessimistic' forecasts must be provided in the light of past experience. An estimate must be provided of how much money the insured would receive if the policy is stopped within five years of taking it out.

The contents of advertisements by members registered and authorized by the PIA are strictly controlled. For example, warnings on the volatility and marketability of shares must be clearly stated.

The basis of the relationship between the PFA and the client must be set out in a customer agreement letter. This letter will set out the services

[9] FIMBRA Guidance note no.9, section 5.

[10] In December 1993 the SIB commissioned a pilot survey to test the amount of information which PFAs collected about the clients before giving them advice on pension switching. KPMG Peat Marwick carried out the survey. The results were disappointing. Only 9% of the sample showed 'substantial compliance' with the regulation that a PFA must collect full information about the client before giving advice on switching into a personal pension: *C.A. Magazine*, February 1994, p.12.

to be provided, the responsibilities of the adviser and the basis of the charges to be levied by the PFA.

Proper records must be kept of all transactions between a PFA and client. These records must include the facts and information relied on by the PFA in arriving at recommendations to the client. The records must show that each recommendation was appropriate in the light of the client's investment objectives, attitude to risk and any special instructions which may have been given to the PFA by the client.

SOME TECHNICAL RULES

In addition to the above rules the SIB rule book sets out some technical rules on investment advice and management.

Contracts signed during a 'cold call' are not enforceable at law. There are, however, a few exceptions to this rule such as when a salesman is selling unit trusts or certain life policies.

When a PFA is advising a client on investing in financial products the PFA must provide written answers to the set of questions set out in Exhibit 11.2. These answers are intended to inform the client about the true cost of the product he or she is about to buy.

If the investments are 'high-risk investments', for example if the PFA suggests to the client that they should invest part of the portfolio in such things as writing options, reverse tracker funds or high-risk (high beta) shares, the PFA must inform the client that such investments are 'high-risk–high-return' investments and describe the particular risks involved, even if the risks are hedged.

The Financial Adviser must answer these questions in writing

1. How much am I due to pay to enter this scheme?

2. How much am I likely to get back as a return?

3. Re mortgage: Is the repayment of the mortgage guaranteed under this mortgage scheme?

4. Re mortgage: Can I move house and retain the mortgage?

5. What deductions are made from my payments into the scheme and what are these deductions for?

6. How much commission is deducted from my payments into the scheme?

7. Are there any bonuses paid to me under this scheme?

The SIB requires all financial advisers registered with them to provide written answers to the above questions. These answers must be provided to all clients who buy financial products based on the advice of the financial adviser.

Exhibit 11.2   Questions which must be answered by financial advisers.

If a PFA is asked by a client to manage a portfolio of the client's securities the PFA must ensure that he or she is specifically authorized to conduct this activity by the PIA, and must not 'churn' the shares of the client simply to earn commission on the churning process.

If the PFA has privileged access to a desirable stock , this must be allocated equitably between clients – the PFA must not channel all the best stock to favoured clients.

A proper complaints procedure must be set up to deal with complaints from clients. The complaint and subsequent action on the complaint must be recorded.

SOME RULES FROM THE PIA RULE BOOK

In addition to the rules set out in the SIB rule book the PFA must also obey some additional rules set out in the PIA rule book. It is required by the SIB that the rules set out in the PIA rule book must be at least as strict as those set out in the SIB rule book.

Most of the additional PIA rules are supplements to the SIB rules. The PIA and its predecessors FIMBRA and LAUTRO have issued several 'Guidance Notes' which help to clarify the meaning of some of these rules.

Every adviser working for a firm which is not itself regulated must be registered with a regulatory organization such as the PIA as one who can act as an investment adviser or as a supervisor of an investment adviser.

A PFA must organize an information system to ensure that they know about both those investment products currently available on the market and the product providers, so that they are adequately qualified to give 'best advice' to clients on selecting between investments and other financial products. This information must be kept up to date.

A wide range of information sources is currently available to assist a PFA in this task. Exhibit 10.1 in Chapter 10 set out a list of computer based and other sources of financial information. Many financial publications and 'updating services' are available to the PFA at relatively low cost.

PFAs 'should avoid making any suggestion that cash or percentage returns achieved in the past are any indication of the returns which may be achieved in the future.' When using statistical information, 'members should be especially careful to compare like with like and draw the correct inferences.'[11] PFAs should only advise on subjects on which they are competent. A PFA who is uncertain in this regard should pass the client on to another PFA who is competent to advise on the particular product or service.

[11] FIMBRA Guidance note 9, section 3.

PFAs 'are expected to consult authoritative financial journals, to be aware of the technical aspects of the various products available, and to be knowledgeable about the nature and past performance of the investments they may recommend.' With regard to product providers, the PFA is expected to be aware of 'the solvency or financial strength of the product providers, the quality of the investment teams, specialisation within the product range, contract features and terms, overall quality of service and level of charges or expenses.'[12] These conditions impose a formidable set of research requirements on the PFA.

Any bias or self-interest which might influence the advice a PFA gives to a client must be revealed to the client. This does not mean that a PFA cannot recommend products in which he or she has an interest, but simply that they must inform the client that this is so.

An additional requirement of 'best execution' is added to the previous requirement of giving 'best advice' on investment. 'Best execution' means that the deal must be executed at the lowest price or the best terms available to the client at the time. The deals must not be executed through a high-charging network which feeds high commission to the PFA.

The SIB rule book requires that any clients' funds which are held by the PFA must be audited. The PIA rule book adds to this requirement the rule that the PFA's accounts must be audited at least once a year by a qualified auditor.

Every PFA registered with the PIA must have arranged professional indemnity insurance against the consequences of negligence or misconduct sufficient to satisfy the PIA.

When a PFA provides advice to a client or handles the client's investments, they are required to hand the client a summary of the more important SIB and PIA rules which are pertinent to these transactions.

Finally, every member registered with the PIA must be willing to submit to interrogation and possible warning or reprimand by the PIA disciplinary panel if evidence is provided to the panel regarding negligent conduct.

If a PFA should knowingly break any of the rules set out in the SIB or the PIA rule books, he or she could be warned or reprimanded or fined or suspended. The ultimate sanction is that the member can be expelled from the SIB or the PIA and legal action may be taken against him or her. In effect, the adviser would no longer be able to give advice on a wide range of personal financial matters to his or her clients and would have to take up other employment.

As from 1 January 1995 all investment advisers must declare any commission or fee or other reward received from a product provider on the sale of a product to their client, whether or not the client asks for this

---

[12] Ibid., section 5.

information. Previously only independent advisers were required to provide this information, and only if asked to do so by the client.

AN ALTERNATIVE SCHEME FOR PIA REGISTRATION

An alternative method of registering with a regulator is available to members of certain professional organizations such as the Institute of Chartered Accountants in England and Wales (ICAEW), the Insurance Broker's Registration Council or the Law Society. Members of a recognized professional body (RPB) can register with the PIA etc. as institutional members. This does not mean that all the members of that organization can consider themselves qualified to act as independent financial advisers. They must notify the relevant RPB that they intend to provide advice on personal investment to their clients. Such members may have to prove their competence on these matters to their institute, pass an additional examination and pay an additional fee to their institute for receiving this privilege.

A PFA registered in this way must act as an independent financial adviser and not as a 'tied agent'.

THE INVESTOR'S COMPENSATION SCHEME

One of the most heavily criticized facets of the new regulatory regime is the 'Investor's Compensation Scheme' which has been set up by the SIB to compensate clients who lose money because of the incompetence or dishonesty of their investment adviser. The maximum amount of compensation which can be claimed by a client is currently £48 000. The claim must be lodged by the client with the relevant regulatory authority within six months of the claimed loss.

The scheme is run by the SIB but the costs and charges are analysed each year and passed on by the SIB to the appropriate regulatory body, such as the PIA or IMRO. The PIA, in its turn, recovers this cost from a levy imposed annually on the registered members of the PIA. The annual individual cost to each member depends on the calls on the fund in the previous year. Unfortunately a few incompetent and dishonest members cost the fund a very large amount of money in the early years of the scheme. As noted above, all PFAs are required to take out personal indemnity insurance to cover negligence claims by clients, but despite this, the annual charge has reached a level which is considered excessive by many registered members. The net effect of all of this is that the honest and competent members have to pay for the errors of their incompetent and dishonest colleagues. A much more sensible system would be to insist that adequate indemnity insurance is taken out by each member to cover the maximum amount of their clients' money that they could lose. The incompetent PFA would then be driven out of the industry by the high annual insurance premiums he or she would be required to pay to continue to practise.[13]

CURRENT CRITICISM OF THE REGULATORY MECHANISM

The current regulatory mechanism for controlling the UK personal financial services industry has come under attack in recent years from several different directions. First from the media, second from the users of the system and third, and by no means least, from those who are regulated. The efficient regulation of financial services at an economic cost is clearly a major problem facing all advanced industrial societies.[14]

Some of the criticisms which have been levelled at the personal financial sector of the financial services industry in the UK are discussed below.

QUALIFICATIONS

Since PFAs are handling and advising on the investment of substantial amounts of their clients' money, it has been persuasively argued that PFAs should be required to pass a tough examination demonstrating their competence in personal finance. Even those PFAs who are professionally qualified in some branch of finance other than personal finance are often not particularly well qualified to advise on personal finance. For example, qualified accountants must pass demanding examinations to gain membership of their institute, but only a small part of these examinations, the examination paper on personal taxation, is concerned with personal finance. Tough qualifying exams need to be passed to enter the Chartered Institutes of Bankers and the Chartered Insurance Institute, but again only limited parts of these exams are directly concerned with personal finance.

There is a need for a properly organized Institute of Personal Finance which, hopefully, could gain a Royal Charter. Entry would be by a carefully designed and externally monitored set of examinations which would cover the entire field of personal financial planning, including investment, insurance, pensions, personal tax, raising credit and long term housing finance. The exams would also cover the law relating to personal finance and the rules imposed by the SIB and the PIA on the personal financial adviser.

---

[13] The total levy attributed to FIMBRA members in 1992–93 was £15.5 million. The life assurance companies agreed to pay half of this levy. Thus the charge in 1993 was £375 per firm for category three member firms, plus £290 per registered individual member. Category 1 members paid £1140 per firm and £290 per individual member.

[14] In 1991 the budgets for FIMBRA and IMBRO were both £10.8m., and for LAUTRO £8.2m.

Two organizations in the UK[15] are attempting to set up such an institute but neither has, as yet, gained substantial recognition from the general public. The situation is rather better in the USA.

EARNINGS BASED ON COMMISSION

One of the most difficult problems faced by the personal finance industry in the UK relates to fact that most personal financial advisers or the organizations which employ them obtain most of their income from commission received from selling financial products. A few PFAs derive their income exclusively from charging for advice, but these truly independent financial advisers are few in number.[16] The term 'Independent Financial Adviser' does not mean that the adviser receives no commission on the products he or she sells. Some independents hand back this commission to the client.

If any individual is dependent on commission from sales for most of his or her income, that person is primarily a salesperson and not a professional adviser. The low esteem into which the PFA profession has fallen in recent years is a direct consequence of this dependence on commission attracting the wrong sort of person into the industry.

It is rumoured that in the near future certain insurance companies and other sellers of financial products intend to sell their products net of any commission to the financial advisers, and leave the adviser to negotiate an advisory fee with the client. If this scheme is implemented it will go a long way towards solving a very serious problem for the industry.

DECLARATION OF FEES AND COMMISSION RECEIVED

Up until January 1995 a PFA who was a tied agent did not need to divulge to the client the amount of fee or commission received from selling financial products to the client. An independent adviser, on the other hand, was required to supply this information if asked.

This anomaly has now been rectified. All financial advisers registered with an SRO must declare to the client any commission, fee or other reward he or she has received from selling the financial product.

---

[15] These organizations are the Society of Financial Advisers (MSFA) and the Institute of Financial Planning (AIFP). In the USA financial planners need to be certified by the state. One of the best-known certifying organizations in the USA is the International Board of Standards and Practices for Certified Financial Planner Incorporated. This organization was set up in 1985. It has a membership of 27 000 persons and allows the designation CFP to be used by its members. Tel: USA (303) 830 7543.

[16] The list of addresses at the end of this book provides the name, address and telephone number of two organizations which will provide the name of five local registered financial advisers to enquirers for free.

GIVING 'BEST ADVICE'

The guidance notes provided by the PIA and its predecessor attempt to define 'best advice', but the precise meaning of the term is still not clear to many advisers. Does 'best advice' simply mean that the PFA must not place his or her own financial interests before those of the client, or does it have a much wider meaning? If the former, then the meaning is clear and most right-thinking people would accept that any professional person who is not simply a salesperson should obey this rule. However, if 'best advice' means that a PFA must know all the investment options available to a client in every circumstance in order to select the best possible plan available at that time, the rule seems to be too demanding. Only a large organization employing many specialists could hope to meet this requirement. The sole practitioner or small-scale PFA firm would be eliminated by this interpretation of the 'best advice' rule.

Guidance note no. 9 published by FIMBRA stated that 'there is an element of subjective judgement in most recommendations'. It would be useful if the SIB or PIA could provide some clarification of this comment.

WHO IS A PERSONAL FINANCIAL ADVISER?

A good deal of personal financial advice is given by professional workers who are not regulated by the SIB. For example, estate agents, auctioneers and dealers in many real assets such as gold coins give financial advice to their clients. These advisers are not covered by either the SIB or the PIA rules. If the intention of current legislation is to protect the public against poor financial advice then something should be done to monitor the advice provided by these 'indirect' investment advisers.

PERSONAL FINANCIAL ADVERTISING

The rules regarding the advertising of personal financial products need to be tightened up. The definition of personal financial advertising is not clear. What exactly is a financial advert? What exactly can be said about a product in a financial advert? What numbers can be used and how exactly does the advertiser of a financial product calculate an 'optimistic' and 'pessimistic' forecast on investment returns and future investment values? How should the impact of inflation on past and future values be introduced into financial advertising?

The rules on advertising, particularly regarding adjustment for inflation, need to be clarified and expanded.

PERSONAL FINANCIAL ADVICE FROM ABROAD

The rules of the SIB and the other regulatory bodies apply to PFAs operating in the United Kingdom. PFAs also operate in most other countries of the world, including those in the European Union.

How can a PFA who is resident and operating abroad be regulated by the SIB or the PIA? The answer is simple – he or she cannot be regulated! Foreign-based advisers can currently sell products from abroad to British residents via 'cold calling' by phone from Brussels or Barcelona, or simply by meeting the British resident abroad. Currently work is being done to standardize the rules regarding the provision of financial services in the EU, but this work is still at a preparatory stage and governments in Continental Europe seem to be much less concerned about the exploitation of investors than is the UK government.[17]

It may be that PFAs operating from within the UK will find themselves at a disadvantage compared to their competitors operating from other countries in the EU. These latter may be able to sell financial products to British residents under less stringent rules than would be applied if they were based in the UK. PFAs operating from 'offshore' financial centres, such as Guernsey, Gibraltar, Bermuda, or even the Isle of Man present another similar problem. We are not suggesting that PFAs operating out of these centres are dishonest, simply that their conduct may well be less tightly monitored than their counterparts in the UK.

The regulations applied to financial advisers by these offshore centres vary a great deal in quality. Guernsey and the Isle of Man have instituted strict controls over financial institutions, but such regulations are not universal in all offshore centres.

There is a clear conflict of interest here between protecting the financial rights of the British citizen and constraining the freedom of operation of the UK personal financial services industry within the EU.[18]

The subject is currently under review by the SIB and calls for further investigation.

KNOWLEDGE OF THE SIB AND PIA RULES

Although the rule book published by the SIB has been around for quite some time, there is an astonishing ignorance about the rules among both PFAs and the general public. It is not simply that the clients of PFAs do not know their rights, but it seems that many registered PFAs do not know the rules under which they are supposed to operate!

A research study financed by the SIB in 1993 found that 90% of the PFAs approached by the researchers acted in such a way as to breach one or more of the rules set down in the SRO rule books as applying to them at that time!

---

[17] See the EU *Financial Industry Monitor*, published by Lafferty Publications.
[18] See *Information About Financial Services*, OECD (1992) for a discussion of personal financial services in the wider context of the EU. The SIB has drawn up a list of designated investment exchanges operating outside the UK. These are deemed to operate procedures close to those applying in the UK. This list is available from the SIB.

A good deal more needs to be done to ensure that the rules are being followed and that clients of PFAs know about their rights. The abbreviated list of rights which are currently required to be handed out to clients during a consultation are inadequate. Despite the fact that in 1993 FIMBRA made compliance visits to 2826 member firms, about half the total membership at that time, compliance still appears to be inadequate.

A reduction in the cost of the PIA rule book from its current cost of £60 for members and £90 for non-members might help to disseminate its requirements more widely among the community. For example, the rules could be made available to enquirers on a floppy disk and so sold at a fraction of the present price. Even better, the rules could be placed on a data base accessible through Internet or Compuserve.

THE FUNDING OF THE PIA

FIMBRA suffered from a severe lack of funds from its foundation in 1988 to its termination in 1994. While most of the other regulatory bodies are funded by large and very rich organizations like banks and insurance companies, FIMBRA, the Cinderella of the regulatory family, was funded for the most part by around 5500 personal financial advisory firms, most of which were small firms. Thus that regulatory body saddled with the duty of monitoring by far the largest number of members was also the one with the poorest source of funding.

It is also likely that the PIA will be required to handle more complaints than the other regulatory bodies because so many of its members are less well qualified than the membership of the other regulatory bodies.

Unless the government of the day is prepared to put more money into the PIA, it is difficult to see how this regulator can perform its monitoring function effectively. Many advisers registered with the PIA are smaller and less well organized than advisers registered with the other regulators, thus they need to be monitored more frequently. Yet a substantial increase in the frequency and depth of audit of members registered with the PIA would be an expensive operation which might well be beyond the current financial resources of the new expanded regulatory organization.

Between 1988 and 1993 FIMBRA investigated 193 fraud cases, 93 of which were criminal in nature; 77 members were brought to trial. Of those found guilty 90% were sent to prison. The longest sentence handed down was Peter Clowes's 10 years.

The personal finance industry does not enjoy a good public image in the UK, following the financial scandals of recent years. A properly funded organization is needed to monitor standards. This could be achieved by the PIA if it were adequately funded, but a better solution would be to set up a self-regulating institute on the lines of the Institute of Chartered Accountants in England and Wales to control the personal finance profession.

WHAT HAVE WE LEARNED IN THIS CHAPTER?

1. Several financial scandals rocked the world of finance in the 1980s. These scandals persuaded the government to introduce various self-regulating bodies to monitor the financial markets in the UK.
2. The regulator which monitors most personal investment advisers in the UK is the PIA, which is itself monitored by the SIB. The PIA took over responsibility for monitoring personal investment advisers from FIMBRA and LAUTRO in July 1994.
3. All persons providing advice on, selling or managing investments in the UK must be registered with the PIA or some other SRO.
4. The SIB and the PIA publish rules regulating the qualifications and conduct of PFAs who advise on or manage investments.
5. All PFAs must declare themselves to be either independent PFAs or tied agents selling the products of one company. PFAs must also declare the type of work they will be doing with regard to investment. Are they simply advisers, or will they actually manage investments on behalf of clients?
6. The SIB rules regulate both the organization of the practice of the PFA and the PFA's method of operation. There must be 'fair dealing' between the PFA and the client, and the PFA must give 'best advice' on investment matters. The PFA must make a reasonable attempt to find out about a client's affairs before giving advice. The client must be warned about risky investments, the PFA must not 'churn' shares to earn commission and must allocate scarce stock equitably between clients.
7. In addition to the SIB rules there are the PIA rules. These state that the PFA must be knowledgeable about the financial products on which she is giving advice; any bias or self-interest must be revealed to the client, 'best execution' of contracts is added to 'best advice', clients' funds must be kept separate from those of the PFA and these funds must be audited on a regular basis. Every PFA must take out professional indemnity insurance. PFAs must be willing to submit to interrogation by the PIA disciplinary panel. If found guilty of fraud or negligence the PFA might be warned, reprimanded, fined or imprisoned.
8. There has been much criticism of the present regulatory set-up in the UK as it affects the personal finance profession. In particular, the cost of the Investor's Compensation Scheme to compensate clients who have lost money by reason of the fraud or negligence of a PFA has

caused much heartache in the profession. It is hoped that the new Personal Investment Authority will solve many of these problems.

FURTHER READING

Anon. (latest edition) *The Financial Adviser's Handbook*: instruction on the authorization required, the forms needed and the procedures to act as an investment adviser in the UK following the recent legislation.

Anon. (latest edition) *The Financial Intermediary's Handbook*: a regularly updated service of information relevant to PFAs. With particular emphasis on the changing compliance rules.

Gower (1984): the key report which persuaded the government to act to protect investors in the UK.

Hindle (1990): provides information to PFAs on the regulatory bodies, the rules they have promulgated, administration of the rules and the dealing rules on securities.

Lumnicka and Powell (1990).

Miller (1990): this book defines the regulations applying to a wide range of financial institutions.

SIB (1993).

The SRO rule books.

Tolley's Compliance Monitor: an update service for PFAs on how to comply with the latest regulations from their SRO.

See bibliography on p.311 for a full annotation of these books.

TUTORIAL QUESTIONS: REGULATION OF THE PERSONAL FINANCIAL ADVISER

1. A client asks you, 'How can I be sure that I am being given safe, impartial advice on my financial affairs by an expert?' How would you respond? Pay particular attention to defining the words 'safe', 'impartial', and 'expert'.

2. Some financial advice on investment is not covered by the regulations set up under the Financial Services Act 1986. What are these exclusions? Why is this type of advice excluded?

3. Describe one recent financial scandal which has forced the government to set up a tighter regulatory system to control the UK financial system.

4. Name three of the self-regulatory bodies set up by the government to monitor the qualifications and conduct of PFAs in the UK.

5. What is the 'Investor's Compensation Scheme'? How does it work? What is the limit to the maximum claim under the scheme? Why do so many PFAs consider the scheme to be unfair?

6. What are the four key conditions an investment adviser must satisfy before being authorized by the PIA to act as an investment adviser?

7. How can a PFA find out about the regulations to obey as set down by the SIB and the PIA?

8. An individual or organization must register with a regulatory organization if they wish to perform which activities relating to investments in the UK?

9. 'Advice to a client must not be given in a vacuum.' What does this mean? Suggest five important facts about a client which must be discovered before advice can be given to the client on investment matters.

10. If you, as a PFA, are authorized by the PIA to manage a portfolio of shares etc. on behalf of a client, what rules apply to the information that you must supply on a regular basis to the client regarding the portfolio of shares?

11. A PFA must inform a client about the risks attached to any 'high-risk investment' made on the client's behalf. How would you define a 'high-risk investment' in this context? Give two examples, along with the risks involved.

12. There must be 'integrity and fair dealing' between a PFA and his client. How would you interpret the words 'integrity and fair dealing' in the context of advising on a choice between taking out either a repayment or an endowment mortgage to buy a house?

13. Explain the difference between the PIA regulations as they apply to a 'tied agent' and an 'independent financial adviser'.

14. The words 'best advice' are not explicitly defined in the context of the Financial Services Act 1986. How do you personally interpret them?

15. What restrictions on the rules set out in the PIA rule book are imposed by the SIB rule book?

16. What is meant by a PFA 'churning' the stocks and shares in the portfolio of a client? Why is this action specifically prohibited by the SIB rule book?

17. With regard to investment-based life policies offered by insurance companies and sold by PFAs to clients, what is meant by the rule that both 'optimistic and pessimistic predictions' must be provided on the future returns from the investment? What can be said about past performance of the investment? Suggest two future events which might strongly influence the terminal value of such policies.

18. Why has it been claimed by some financial journalists that the necessity to disclose commission on the sale of financial products to a client has almost eliminated the existence of truly independent financial advisers not attached to large organizations?

19. What are the possible consequences for an authorized PFA if he or she is found guilty of conducting the affairs of his or her client negligently?

20. Explain how a PFA might become registered with the PIA by reason of being a member of a recognized professional body (RPB). What limitations, if any, does such a registration process place on the actions of a PFA compared with registering in the usual way?
21. Why has the PIA been described as the 'Cinderella' of the family of regulatory bodies in the finance industry.
22. Much criticism has been aimed at the present regulatory mechanism which purports to protect the personal investor. Suggest four criticisms which you think are valid. What do you think could be done to improve the situation in each of these cases?

Suggested solutions to even numbered questions are provided at the back of this book.

Case studies

MS SALLY BRYANT BSC (MATH.), MBA

Ms Sally Bryant is a bond dealer with Shearson and Bevan, a merchant bank in the City of London. She has held this position for seven years and enjoys a large but widely fluctuating annual income. She claims that she has no fear of redundancy since she is very good at her job.

Sally was born 32 years ago in Ripon, a town in North Yorkshire. She took a degree in maths at the University of Warwick and subsequently read for an MBA degree at the City University where she won the Finance prize.

She entered the corporate finance department of ICA PLC from City University and worked there for three years before being invited to join Shearson and Bevan as a bond dealer.

Sally enjoys excellent health, collects nineteenth-century glass artefacts, loves travelling, and her scarlet Porsche is the apple of her eye. Her parents are both in good health. Her father retired last year on an adequate pension at the age of 62. She has a sister, Anna, who is at University College, Cardiff reading for a degree in biology.

Sally comes to you for advice on reorganizing her personal financial affairs. Although Sally works in the financial market in the City, her knowledge of personal finance is very limited. She appreciates the benefit of specialist knowledge in the financial field. She tells you that because of her rather hectic business life she has ignored her financial affairs until recently, since her income has been substantial. Now she suspects that her personal finances are in a 'bit of a mess' and she is seeking objective, impartial advice.

Sally lives in a three-bedroomed modern high-tech flat, which she shares with her friend John. The flat cost £300 000 seven years ago. When Sally and John bought the flat they took out a £300 000 variable interest repayment mortgage shared equally between them. The flat is situated in a modern block on the Isle of Dogs in London's Docklands, near the City of London financial centre. In 1988 the block won an architectural prize for its originality. John Wilson, with whom she shares ownership of the flat, works as a programmer-designer with Norland PLC, an international software company. Sally and John have lived together for seven years but, when asked, Sally states that she doubts if she will marry John: 'I have other friends.'

The rate of issuing international bonds varies from year to year and Sally's income is highly dependent on the sale of bonds. Her basic income is only £22 000 but she can earn £100 000 or more from the commission on the sale of bonds in a good year.

Sally contributes 6% of her basic salary to a company pension scheme. The company contribute a further 6%. The pension fund is run by the company itself. The pension is a 'money purchase' scheme type which buys an annuity at the end of the pension period at age 55 or 60. She has taken out insurance cover on her flat and contents and her car, and has medical insurance via BUPA of £300 a year. She was required to take out a diminishing term insurance to cover the repayment of her mortgage in the event of her death.

Sally and John bought the flat when their joint income was very high and flats in the Isle of Dogs were very expensive. Unfortunately house prices have fallen in this part of London by around 30% since the flat was bought, and the flat is currently only worth about £200 000, if a buyer can be found, which is not certain since several similar flats are currently lying empty and on the market at a price of around £195 000.

Sally asks for your advice on the following matters.

1. Should I redistribute my assets? I'm prepared to accept quite high risk to gain a high return on my assets.
2. What risks do I face in the future, and how can I hedge these risks?
3. Is my pension adequate? If not, what should I do to build up a reasonable pension? I hope to retire at 55 years of age.
4. What can I do about the jointly owned flat? I would like an independent assessment of my investment in this flat in the Isle of Dogs. Is this a good long-term investment and are the current financing arrangements satisfactory? Should I sell my share of the London flat if this is possible, even at a loss?

Other personal details are set out in the following documents.

CLIENT INFORMATION SHEET

Name	Ms	Sally Bryant
Address	Street	Flat 14.7 Thatcher Tower
	Town	The Isle of Dogs
	District	London E14
	Postal Code	E14 1FT
Tel No.		071 6549
Fax No.		071 6448
Sex		Female
Date of Birth		16.9.62
Marital Status		Unmarried
Children		None
Occupation		Bond Dealer
Company		Shearson and Bevan,
		11 The Cakewalk,
		City of London
Parents still living		FATHER Yes MOTHER Yes
Special responsibilities		Nil

Client Name: Ms Sally Bryant

Inventory of Client's Assets: June 1994

Financial Assets	At Cost Price £	At Current Market Value £
Liquid Assets		
Cash	420	420
Building Society	5427	5427
Total Liquid Assets	5847	5847
Fixed Interest Stocks		
Govt. Stocks	0	0
Commercial Bonds	5000	4200
Other	0	0
Total Fixed Interest Stocks	5000	4200
Equity Stocks		
Shares (Exhibit D)	14 200	17 300
Total Financial Assets	25 047	27 347
Real Assets		
50% Share of Flat (Mortgaged for £150 000)	150 000	100 000
Land	0	0
Other Real Assets Porsche car 1989	25 000	12 000
Total Real Assets	175 000	112 000
Total Value of Assets	200 047	139 347

Client: Ms Sally Bryant

Inventory of Client's Liabilities

Mortgage

Original amount	£150 000
Date acquired	6 June 1988
Amount outstanding	£142 000
How many years to pay off?	18
Current monthly amount: net of tax	£834

Loans Contracted

	Second-hand Porsche 1	Hi-fi 2
Original loan amount	£20 000	£2000
Date acquired	April 1989	June 1992
Amount outstanding	£6000	£1200
How many months to pay off?	24	14
Current monthly payment	£333	£83

Other Contracted Monthly Payments

Item	£
Health Insurance	25
Property Insurance	35
Term Insurance	50
Rates	100
Subscriptions	40
Total	£250

Other Important Non-Contracted Monthly Payments

Item	£
Electricity	30
Gas	55
Telephone	50
Food	100
Transport	50
Security	84
Clothing	100
Total	£469

Ms Sally Bryant

Annual Income and Expenditure Account

Income		1992 £	1993 £	1994 £	Budget 1995 £
Basic salary/Pension		15 000	20 000	20 000	22 000
Commission etc.		52 000	93 000	44 000	30 000
Dividends etc.		1200	1300	1400	1300
Other income					
Total income		68 200	114 300	65 400	53 300
Less:	Taxation	23 870	40 005	22 890	17 589
	Other deductions	1400	1500	1800	1500
Net cash inflow		42 930	72 795	40 710	34 211
Expenditure					
Mortgage		12 500	11 250	10 000	10 000
Household	Gas	429	528	572	660
	Electricity	298	327	350	370
	Food/Meals out	1842	2294	1852	1200
	Repairs etc	543	668	246	512
	House insurance	420	420	420	420
	Security	600	700	800	1000
	Other	943	2321	1765	511
Transport	Fares	420	480	560	600
	Loan on car	4000	4000	4000	4000
	Car licence	100	120	140	140
	Petrol	583	974	523	480
	Insurance (car)	1500	1800	2000	2200
	Repairs (car)	400	800	1000	1500
Communication					
	Postage	120	140	150	160
	Telephone	553	939	831	600
	Computer costs	821	879	731	344
Risk hedging	The company provides no medical aid plan				
	Term insurance	600	600	600	600
	Medical care plan	200	240	270	300
Personal	Clothing	840	2400	1500	1200
	Holidays	2500	7500	2400	1200
	Entertainment	1300	4500	2000	1000
	Subscriptions	600	800	800	500
Sundry	Cash expenses	3200	5000	2500	2000
	Poll Tax/Rates	450	1200	1200	1200
Total expenditure		£35 762	£50 880	£37 210	£32 697
Net saving		£7168	£21 915	£3500	£1514

WILLIAM STEEL, SENIOR EXECUTIVE

Mr William Steel BSc (Eng.) is a senior executive with Axel Excavations, a medium-sized British company which manufactures excavating equipment and exports 70% of its output. William is the production director and sits on the board of the company. He has worked for the company for 10 years, following five years with Brown Boveri as a project manager.

William, who is 45 years of age, is married to Janet (37) and has three children, Robert (10), Clare (8) and Katherine (7). Clare is handicapped – she suffers from epileptic fits and goes to a special, publicly funded, school.

William owns a house in Cambridge which cost £200 000 in 1985 but is now worth £250 000 (it was worth £350 000 in 1989!). The house is partly financed with a £150 000 25-year variable interest repayment mortgage from the Mortgage Corporation.

William enjoys a substantial income, currently £50 000 a year plus a profit-related annual bonus which last year amounted to £12 000. He owns a portfolio of equity shares currently valued at £75 000 plus £50 000 in a joint building society account. He has an option to buy 10 000 shares in Axel for £5 a share in 1998. The current market price of Axel shares is £4 a share. He enjoys the use of a two-litre company car, all costs paid by the company.

William would like to send his son, Robert, to a public school (Uppingham), where the fees are currently £12 000 a year, for five years in two years' time.

The company contributes an amount equal to 10% of William's gross income into a company pension fund. William contributes 5%. This will provide a pension on retirement equal to n/80ths of retirement income, where n = the number of year's contribution to the fund. Ten years of contribution have already been made into this fund. After retirement the pension will be upvalued each year by a maximum of 4% to allow for inflation. A life insurance policy of 2.5 times final salary will be paid if William dies while employed by the firm. If he should die, his wife Janet would be paid half the pension that would have been paid to William. No additional pension is paid for the children.

The Steels' house is insured for £300 000 and its contents for £20 000. William has a life assurance mortgage cover policy for £150 000.

Janet Steel has no assets of her own except for a building society deposit of £5500. William does not want his wife to work – he considers that with his substantial income his wife is better employed looking after the children. The children have no assets of their own. The parents of both William and Janet are deceased.

You are asked to give the Steel family advice about the following.

1. Their assets: are they suited to meeting the risk/return profile of the family? Should the asset portfolio be changed? If so, how?
2. The major risks the family may face in the future: are these risks adequately hedged? If not, what should be done about it?
3. William Steel's pension position: is this adequate to cover himself and the family?
4. The investment in the family home: is it likely to be a good investment in the future? Are the financing arrangements of the home acceptable? Should these be altered? If so, how?
5. Some special problems, particularly with regard to Clare's future and the cost of financing Robert's schooling at Uppingham.

Further personal details are set out on the following documents.

CLIENT INFORMATION SHEET

Name   Mr   William Steel

Address   Street   67 Bacon Grove
                   Town   Cambridge
                   District   Cambs.
                   Postal Code   CM34 7FU

Tel No.   054 6723
Fax No.   054 6499

Sex   Male

Date of Birth   23.2.1949

Marital Status   Married
Wife   Janet (37)

Children   Name   Sex   Age
                                            1. Robert John   M   10
                                            2. Clare Patrice F   8
                                            3. Katherine   F   7

Occupation   PD of Excavation Company

Company   Axel Excavations PLC,
                                               Cams Industrial Estate

Parents still living   FATHER   No   MOTHER   No

Special responsibilities
                   Handicapped Relative   Clare is epileptic
                   Aged Parents   None
                   Other   Cost of schooling for Robert

Client: William Steel

Inventory of Client's Assets

Financial Assets	Cost Price £	Current Market Value £
Liquid Assets		
Cash	570	570
Building Society	50 000	50 000
Total Liquid Assets	50 570	50 570
Fixed Interest Stocks		
Govt. Stocks		
Commercial Bonds		
Other		
Total Fixed Interest Stocks	0	0
Equity Stocks		
Shares (Exhibit D)	48 000	75 000
Total Financial Assets	98 570	125 570
Real Assets		
House and Land	200 000	250 000
Land		
Other Real Assets Timeshare	14 000	17 000
Total Real Assets	214 000	267 000
Total Value of Assets	312 570	392 570

Client: William Steel

Inventory of Client's Liabilities 1994

Mortgage

Original amount	£150 000
Date acquired	1985
Amount outstanding	£110 000
How many years to pay off?	15
Current monthly amount: net of tax	£930

Loans Contracted

Loans	Modern Kitchen 1	Timeshare France 2
Original loan amount	£12 000	£15 000
Date acquired	1990	1986
Amount outstanding	£9600	£11 400
How many months to pay off?	94	72
Current monthly payment	£100	£110

Other Contracted Monthly Payments

Item	£
Property Insurance	57
Term Insurance	25
Rates	100
Covenants	50
Subscriptions	40
Total	£272

Other Important Non-Contracted Monthly Payments

Item	£
Electricity	55
Gas	90
Telephone	62
Food	240
Transport	170
Security	40
Clothing	200
Total	£857

Name: | William Steel |

Annual Income and Expenditure Account 1992–1994 + Budget

| Budget |

Income	1992	1993	1994	1995
	£	£	£	£
Basic salary/Pension	45 000	48 000	50 000	52 000
Commission etc.	2000	5000	12 000	14 000
Dividends etc.	4300	5500	6000	6200
Other Income	540	720	870	900
Total income	51 840	59 220	68 870	73 100
Less: Taxation	15 552	17 766	22 038	24 123
Other deductions	4500	4700	5000	5500
Net cash inflow	31 788	36 754	41 832	43 477

Expenditure

Mortgage (net of tax)	13 000	12 500	11 160	11 000
Household Rates	800	1100	1200	1200
Gas	900	980	1080	1100
Electricity	582	603	660	700
Food/Meals out	2386	2456	2880	3000
Repairs	561	448	549	600
House insurance	550	597	684	684
Security	480	480	480	480
Other	593	619	631	700
Total household	6852	7283	8164	8464

(Mr Steel has a company car but pays for private petrol)

Transport Fares	1800	1875	2040	2000
Petrol	385	402	420	500
Total transport	2185	2277	2460	2500

Communication

Postage	55	65	60	70
Telephone	611	688	744	800
Computer	311	750	320	500

Risk hedging (company pay for family health plan under PPP)

Term Insurance	300	300	300	300

Children	1800	2000	2100	3000

Personal Clothing	2300	2000	2400	2400
Holidays	3200	5334	4000	5000
Entertainment	1788	1889	2000	2000
Subscriptions	500	500	500	600

Sundry Cash expenses	2400	2400	2500	2500

Total expenditure	£35 302	£37 986	£36 708	£39 134

Net saving	−£3514	−£1232	£5124	£4343

MARK WESTLAND: RETIRED SURGEON

Before he retired Mark Westland was, for 20 years, a distinguished cardiologist at Norwich Hospital; he also lectured at the local university. He was forced to retire at the age of 57 (three years before normal retirement age) because of ill health. He has been diagnosed as suffering from cancer of the pancreas and is not expected to be able to undertake further work. His current life expectancy is around 10 years.

When Mark retired on the grounds of ill health he was awarded an inflation-indexed pension of £12 000 a year plus a capital sum of £90 000. He invested this £90 000 in £40 000 worth of 8% government stock and the remaining £50 000 in a Woolwich Building Society high interest account. He owns a charming house on the seafront in Southwold, currently worth £200 000, which was partly financed by a £70 000 repayment mortgage. In addition Mark owns equity shares having a current market value of £60 000, a building plot in Devon recently valued at £40 000 and a sketch by the artist Whistler valued at £20 000 which he inherited from his father who was an avid art collector.

Mark admits that in the past he has never paid much attention to money, 'So long as I had enough of it.' He had paid no attention to long term financial planning, assuming that his house, his investments, his pension and the lump sum at 60 would cover the needs of himself and his wife quite adequately. Until Mark fell ill some 12 months ago he had enjoyed a robust constitution. He tells you: 'Until last year I had never had a day off work or university because of ill health in 40 years!'

If Mark dies Mrs Westland will receive a pension equal to 60% of the pension Mark would have received.

Mark is married to Susan (age 50) and they have two children Denise (27) and Hallam (24). Susan does not work but is a qualified physiotherapist. She has not practised since she married Mark some 28 years ago.

Denise, Mark's daughter, is married to an insurance executive, they live in Walthamstow, London and have two children. Hallam believes that all work is exploitation and lives on a commune in California which is pioneering an 'alternative lifestyle for the future of humanity'. Hallam has obtained a second class degree in fine arts from Sunderland Polytechnic.

Three months after his retirement from Norwich Hospital Mark comes to you for advice on planning his financial future. He admits that he has paid less attention to this aspect of his life than he ought to have done. As noted above, his financial assets are currently invested in equity shares and building society deposits.

You find that Mark has taken out the following insurance policies:

House £ 150 000 (cost of rebuilding).
House contents £20 000.

£70 000 whole-life policy with Commercial Union (taken out 15 years ago). Car insurance.

Mark contributes to a family health insurance plan run by PPP. He inherited this plan from his job at Norwich Hospital; it costs £32 a month. This covers all hospital bills up to £10 000 a year for Mr Westland. Mrs Westland does not believe on principle in contributing to a private health plan.

Mrs Westland owns shares currently worth £12 000 paying around £600 a year in dividends. Hallam, so far as Mark is aware, has no assets of his own.

You are asked to give the Westland family advice on the following matters.

1. The asset base: how should the assets be best invested to provide a proper risk/return profile for the family under their present circumstances?
2. The risks the Westland family face in the future: how should those be hedged?
3. Is the current income of the family adequate for the future? What alternative income profiles are available?
4. The house: what should be done about it? Should the balance of the mortgage be paid off? Should the house be sold and a smaller home purchased or rented?
5. What is the financial situation facing Mrs Westland? Is her financial future properly protected?

Further personal details are set out on the following documents.

You have put together the income and expenditure account from documents supplied to you by Mr Westland. You found this to be a somewhat difficult task since Mr Westland did not keep proper records.

CLIENT INFORMATION SHEET

Name   Mark Westland

Address   Street   211 Seaview Drive
                 Town   Southwold
                 District   Suffolk
                 Postal Code   SW54 Y33

Tel No.   0455 7620
Fax No.

Sex   Male

Date of Birth   23.11.37

Marital Status   Married
Wife   Susan (50)

Children   Name   Sex   Age
                                  1. Denise   F   27
                                  2. Hallam   M   24

Occupation   Retired cardiologist

Company

Parents still living   FATHER   No   MOTHER   No

Special responsibilities

                 Handicapped Relative   None
                 Aged Parents   None
                 Other   Client has an impaired life

Client: Mark Westland

Inventory of Client's Assets

Financial Assets	Cost Price £	Current Market Value £
Liquid Assets		
Cash	−274	−274
Building Society	50 000	50 000
Total Liquid Assets	49 726	49 726
Fixed Interest Stocks		
Govt. Gilt-Edged Stocks	40 000	36 000
Total Fixed Interest Stocks	40 000	36 000
Equity Stocks		
Equity Shares	45 000	60 000
Total Financial Assets	134 726	145 726

Real Assets		
House and Land Mortgage of £40 000	80 000	200 000
Land	14 000	40 000
Art Works	8000	20 000
Car	12 000	5000
Total Real Assets	114 000	265 000
Total Value of Assets	248 726	410 726

Client: Mark Westland

Inventory of Client's Liabilities

Mortgage

Original amount	£70 000
Date acquired	1979
Amount outstanding	£40 000
How many years to pay off?	7
Current monthly amount: net of tax	£500

Other Contractual Monthly Payments

Item	£
Health Insurance	32
Property Insurance	20
Life Assurance	22
Rates	102
Covenants	10
Subscriptions	42
Total	228

Other Important Non-Contractual Monthly Payments

Item	£
Electricity	30
Gas	60
Telephone	32
Food	192
Transport	200
Security	20
Clothing	84
Total	618

Name:　　　│ Mark Westland ▊

Annual Income and Expenditure Account

Income		1992	1993	1994	Budget 1995
		£	£	£	£
Salary/Pension		45 000	50 000	12 000	12 000
Consultancy etc.		13 500	12 000		
Dividends etc.		1300	1400	7500	8000
Other Income		1700	1300	800	350
Total income		61 500	64 700	20 300	20 350
Less:	Taxation	18 450	19 410	3248	3256
	Other deductions	2300	2300		
Net cash inflow		43 050	45 290	17 052	17 094
Expenditure					
Mortgage		7200	6800	6000	6000
Household	Gas	680	690	720	720
	Electricity	302	330	360	360
	Food/Meals out	3700	3900	2400	2400
	Repairs	456	231	230	230
	House Insurance	240	240	240	240
	Security	200	220	240	240
	Other	629	744	351	351
Transport	Fares	270	290	120	120
	Depreciation (car)	1000	1000	1000	1000
	Car Licence	120	120	140	140
	Petrol	1231	1333	720	720
	Insurance	220	220	220	220
	Repairs	1004	454	230	230
Communication					
	Postage	267	287	140	140
	Telephone	673	777	390	390
Risk hedging					
	Life Assurance	264	264	264	264
	Medical Care Plan	384	384	384	384
Children		2600	1200	400	400
Personal	Clothing	2100	2400	528	528
	Holidays	5300	7000	2300	2300
	Entertainment	1256	1753	340	340
	Subscriptions	700	700	500	500
Sundry	Cash expenses	2500	2500	1200	1200
	Rates	800	1000	1100	1100
Total expenditure		£34 096	£34 837	£20 517	£20 517
Net saving		£8954	£10 453	−£3465	−£3423

Note: Dr Westland's pension is low because he worked abroad from 1964 to 1974.

STELLA MASON, DIVORCEE

Mrs Stella Mason is 45 years of age. She divorced her husband John Mason (50) six months ago on the grounds of infidelity. She has two children, Mark aged 11 and Jenny aged 8 who will stay with her; both are in good health. Mrs Mason has an elderly mother, Janet Dobbs (78), who is living in rented property on a small pension of £4000 a year provided from her deceased husband's pension fund. Mrs Mason tells you that she has no immediate intention of remarrying.

The divorce settlement was agreed as follows:

1. Mrs Mason will receive alimony of £12 000 a year indexed for inflation from her husband until Jenny reaches the age of 16, when the annual payment will fall to £6000 until Mrs Mason reaches 60 years of age, when it will cease. If Mrs Mason should remarry the alimony will fall immediately to £6000 a year and cease entirely when Jenny reaches 16 years of age.
2. Mrs Mason will be granted full ownership of the family home and contents in Oxford; previously it was in joint ownership. The house and contents are currently valued at £220 000. Mrs Mason will take over the payments of £150 a month on the £20 000 repayment mortgage (variable interest) on this property which still has 15 years to run before it is paid off. She will also retain the family car.

In addition to the alimony Mrs Mason was also granted a final settlement of £80 000 in cash. This she has invested in a Halifax Building Society high interest account, currently paying 8% p.a. gross. Her only other valuable assets are a set of German Expressionist drawings by Otto Dix, inherited from her father (a similar set was sold in 1993 for £50 000) and a three-year-old Ford Sierra car, currently worth £4000 according to a car valuation manual.

Currently Mrs Mason holds term insurance cover for a £20 000 'bare' life policy to cover the loan on the house. This policy was taken out on her ex-husband's life. She has also taken out insurance cover on the house and contents. The premium on this policy is £350 a year.

Mrs Mason is a qualified speech therapist who, since her divorce, has taken up a job in a local government medical facility in Oxford and is currently earning £20 000 a year. Her employer runs a pension fund and Mrs Mason will receive a pension of $n/60$ths of final salary at age 60 (n = the number of working years) plus a lump sum of twice her final year's salary. However, Mrs Mason tells you that she hopes to set up her own private practice in Oxford, since there is a shortage of qualified speech therapists in the region. She estimates that the set-up costs of such a practice would be approximately £20 000 for the equipment plus an annual rent of £12 000 for suitable premises.

Mrs Mason states that, next year, she would like to send her son to Rugby School, which would initially cost £12 000 a year for five years. She is not sure whether this is financially feasible. Her father went to Rugby.

Mrs Mason comes to you, as her personal financial adviser, to ask for advice on reorganizing her financial affairs. You ask Mrs Mason a series of questions which allows you to prepare the schedules set out in the four exhibits attached.

Required:

1. What key questions would you still have to put to Mrs Mason regarding her future? What additional information would you need before you can prepare a set of financial plans? What do you consider to be Mrs Mason's key financial problems?
2. Write a report to Mrs Mason setting out your advice on: (a) reorganizing her investments, paying particular attention to the house; (b) taking out additional insurance, if this is needed; (c) looking after the future interests of her children; (d) arranging an adequate pension for her old age.

What would Mrs Mason's income and expenditure account look like once your financial plans have been fully implemented?

CLIENT INFORMATION SHEET

Name   Mrs Stella Mason

Address   Street   23 Keynes Road
                   Town   Oxford
                   District   Oxon

Tel No.   021 667 834
Fax No.

Sex   Female

Date of Birth   18.6.49

Marital Status   Divorced

Children   Name   Sex   Age
                              1.   Mark   M   11
                              2.   Jenny   F   8

Occupation   Qualified speech therapist

Parents still living   FATHER   No   MOTHER   Yes

Special responsibilities
                   Handicapped Relative   None
                   Aged Parents   Mother aged 78
                   Other   Schooling of children

Client: Mrs Stella Mason

Inventory of Client's Assets

Financial Assets	Cost Price £	Current Market Value £
Liquid Assets		
Cash	549	549
Building Society	80 000	80 000
Total Liquid Assets	80 549	80 549
Fixed Interest Stocks		
Total Fixed Interest Stocks	0	0
Equity Stocks		
Shares	0	0
Total Financial Assets	80 549	80 549
Real Assets		
House and Contents (£20 000 mortgage)	120 000	220 000
Car	6000	4000
Other Real Assets Paintings	5000	50 000
Total Real Assets	131 000	274 000
Total Value of Assets	£211 549	£354 549

Client: Mrs Stella Mason

Inventory of Client's Liabilities

Mortgage

Original amount	£20 000
Date acquired	1987
Amount outstanding	£17 000
How many years to pay off?	15
Current monthly amount: net of tax	£150

Loans Contracted

Loans	Ford Cortina 1	2	3	4
Original loan amount	£6000			
Date acquired	April 1988			
Amount outstanding	£2000			
How many months to pay off?	24			
Current monthly payment	£168			

Other Contracted Monthly Payments

Item	
Life Assurance (Ex-husband)	21
Rates	75
House Insurance	22
Subscriptions	40
Total	158

Other Important Non-Contracted Monthly Payments

Item	
Electricity	27
Gas	75
Telephone	53
Food	200
Transport	50
Security	20
Clothing	130
Total	555

Name: **Mrs Stella Mason**

Annual Income and Expenditure Account

Income		1992 £	1993 £	Budget 1994 £	1995 £
Basic Gross Salary		0	0	20 000	20 000
Husband: Allowance/Alimony		2400	2400	12 000	12 000
Building Society Interest		250	200	4000	4000
Total income		2650	2600	36 000	36 000
Less:	Taxation	0	0	5760	5760
	Other deductions			1480	1480
Net cash inflow		2650	2600	28 760	28 760

Expenditure					
Mortgage/Rent				1800	1800
Household	Gas			880	900
	Electricity			310	324
	Food/Meals out	200	220	2400	2400
	Repairs			340	340
	Gardening	89	127	321	428
	Security			600	600
	Other	100	100	1600	1800
Transport	Fares			550	600
	Loan Payment (car)			2016	2016
	Car licence			140	140
	Petrol			500	520
	Repairs			350	400
Communication					
	Postage	50	50	100	110
	Telephone			570	600
Risk hedging					
	Insurance			516	516
Children		450	400	1600	1800
Personal	Clothing	500	500	1100	1200
	Holidays			1000	1000
	Entertainment	250	200	800	900
	Subscriptions	40	40	500	480
Sundry	Cash expenses	450	500	800	780
	Sundry costs	230	200	1000	1200
Total expenditure		£2359	£2337	£19 793	£20 854
Net saving £		£291	£263	£8967	£7906

Note: Alimony is not taxed.

JOHN SILVERS WEBB BSC (ENG.), INST. MECH. ENG.

Mr John Silvers Webb, a British citizen, has been recently 'headhunted' by an executive placement service to become Managing Director of Armalite Engineering PLC. Armalite are specialist bridge-builders, currently working in 17 different countries. The HQ of Armalite is in Newcastle upon Tyne. In the year to 31 December 1994 the company had a turnover of £830 million and a profit of £93 million. The company is standing on a price earnings ratio of 17 on the London Stock Exchange.

Previous to his appointment at Armalite Mr Webb had been MD of the Bridgcor Corporation, a medium-sized US company operating out of San Diego, California. On leaving Bridgcor Mr Webb cashed in all his pension rights, converted the US dollars into sterling which allowed him to bring back £300 000 of capital to the UK. He invested £100 000 of this money in a range of unit trusts which provide him with additional investment income of around £5000 a year. The remainder he has put into buying a £250 000 house just outside Newcastle, the balance of the purchase price coming from a mortgage. Property and contents insurance of £280 000 has been taken out.

Mr Webb is a 50-year-old widower. His wife Ethel was tragically killed in a plane crash in California in 1991. John has two children, Sally, aged 15, and Andrew, aged 12, both in good health. The parents of Mr and Mrs Webb passed away some time ago. Mr Webb states that he has no immediate intention of remarriage, but that this is a possibility in the future.

Mr Webb is very keen on providing a good education for his children – he tells you that he gives this objective 'top priority'. He wishes to send both his children to private day schools in Newcastle, for three years in the case of Sally and six in the case of Andrew. The current cost of this education will be £3000 a year for Sally and £6000 a year for Andrew. However, private school fees are increasing at 10% a year in England.

Mr Webb's negotiated salary is £80 000 a year plus a prestige car. In the future the salary will normally be expected to increase with the rate of inflation, but by no more than this. He has negotiated a five-year contract with Armalite which is renewable at age 56 to age 60 so long as his performance with the company is thought by the board to be 'satisfactory'.

Mr Webb has entered into the Armalite company final salary based pension plan, which provides the following benefits.

1. A pension at retirement age of 60 equal to $n/60 \times$ final salary, where n equals the number of years Mr Webb will have worked for the company. The pension after retirement will be inflation-adjusted upwards, but only to a maximum of 3% per annum. Also, on retirement at age 60, a capital sum equal to twice his final year's salary will be paid to Mr Webb. Mr Webb contributes 6% of his gross salary

towards this pension plan while the company contributes an amount equal to 14% of his gross salary.

2. Mr Webb has also entered into a company-sponsored private health plan, called PHP, which covers Mr Webb and his family while he is with the company. The plan provides medical benefits of up to £20 000 a year in total for the Webb family in any one year.

3. If Mr Webb should fall seriously ill during his term of office then his full salary will be paid for three months then half salary for a further three months, then a pension equal to $n/60$, as above, assuming retirement after the six months. The capital sum due on retirement will be reduced proportionately, by 10% a year, for each year short of 10 years that Mr Webb works for the company. On his death in service an amount equal to 25% of his pension would be paid to each child up to the age of 17 years.

4. A life assurance policy is also in force which will pay an amount equal to twice the final year's salary to his beneficiaries on the death of Mr Webb. This amount is not subject to reduction for early loss of office.

Mr Webb earns a small royalty on two books he has written on the techniques of bridge-building. These books are updated every two years to incorporate new techniques.

Mr Webb has taken out a variable interest mortgage of £50 000 on his £250 000 detached home in a prestigious Newcastle suburb. He currently pays £7800 a year, net of tax, on this repayment mortgage which is repayable over 10 years.

Required: After extensive discussions with Mr Webb regarding his current needs and expected post-retirement lifestyle, you work out the set of schedules appended to this case study.

During these discussions you discover that Mr Webb currently spends a great deal of time abroad reviewing the progress of foreign contracts.

Study the financial data provided below.

What additional questions would you need to put to Mr Webb before designing a set of financial plans for him? Identify his key financial problems. What financial risks are faced by the Webb family? How would you suggest that Mr Webb hedges these potential risks? What investment portfolio would suit Mr Webb? Do you consider Mr Webb's pension position to be satisfactory? If not what do you suggest should be done about it? How should the school fee planning be organized?

CLIENT INFORMATION SHEET

Name   John Silvers Webb

Address   Street   The Rectory, Smailes Road
                   Town   Newcastle
                   District   Northumberland
                   Postal Code   NW56 9TT

Tel No.   088 5209
Fax No.   088 5227

Sex   Male

Date of Birth   28.11.43

Marital Status   Widower

Children | Name | Sex | Age |
|---|---|---|
| 1. Sally | F | 15 |
| 2. Andrew | M | 12 |

Occupation   Managing Director

Company   Armalite Engineering, Newcastle

Parents still living   FATHER   No   MOTHER   No

Special responsibilities

                   Wife Deceased   Nanny for children
                   Aged Parents   None
                   Other   School fees of children

Client: John S. Webb

Inventory of Client's Assets: June 1994

Financial Assets	Cost Price £	Current Market Value £
Liquid Assets		
Cash	1324	1324
Total Liquid Assets	1324	1324
Equity Stocks		
Shares in 10 unit trusts	100 000	120 000
Total Financial Assets	101 324	121 324
Real Assets		
House (Mortgage for £50 000)	250 000	240 000
Book Royalty	0	4000
Furniture	20 000	10 000
Total Real Assets	270 000	254 000
Value of Total Assets £	371 324	375 324

Client: John Silvers Webb

Inventory of Client's Liabilities

Mortgage

Original amount	£50 000
Date acquired	15 March 93
Amount outstanding	£49 000
How many years to pay off?	9
Current monthly amount: net of tax	£650

Other Contracted Monthly Payments

Item	£
Nanny and Cook	1000
Health Insurance	54
House and Cont. Insurance	40
Life Assurance	120
Rates	100
Covenants	50
Subscriptions	12
Total	£1376

Other Important Non-Contracted Monthly Payments

Item	£
Electricity	52
Gas	95
Telephone	95
Food	330
Transport	85
Security	84
Clothing	170
Total	£911

Name: | John Silvers Webb |

Annual Income and Expenditure Account

	1992 £	1993 £	1994 £	Budget 1995 £
Income				
Salary			80 000	81 600
Bonus	ABROAD	ABROAD	5367	6500
Interest etc.			5000	5500
Book Royalties			874	1022
Total income			91 241	94 622
Less: Taxation			31 934	33 118
Other deductions			6200	6380
Net cash inflow			53 107	55 124
Expenditure				
Mortgage/Rent			7800	7800
Household Nanny and Housekeeper			12 000	12 000
Gas			1140	1200
Electricity			624	700
Food/Meals out			3960	4000
Repairs etc.			653	700
Insurance			480	480
Security			1008	1000
Other			2000	2200
Transport Fares			1020	1200
Taxis			264	250
Car Licence			140	140
Petrol			240	250
Insurance (nanny's car)			370	370
Repairs (car)			452	500
Communication				
Postage			280	300
Telephone			1140	1200
Computer Costs			2300	2500
Risk hedging				
Health Insurance			648	670
Children			2300	2600
Personal Clothing			2040	2400
Holidays			5000	5000
Entertainment			2500	2500
Covenants			600	600
Subscriptions			140	140
Sundry Cash expenses			2000	2500
Rates			1200	1300
Total expenditure			£52 299	£54 500
Net saving/Deficit			£808	£624

MRS MARGARET GEE, AN ELDERLY WIDOW

Mrs Margaret Gee, an elderly widow, has a financial problem on which she is seeking advice from you, as her personal financial adviser.

Mrs Gee is 73 years of age; she has been a widow for 12 years. Her husband was self-employed and had not arranged a pension, although he saved regularly and had built up a considerable portfolio of investments when he died.

Mrs Gee has one son, Robert, aged 38, who is married with two daughters, Helen and Shirley. Robert is a marketing manager with a large pharmaceutical firm in Manchester, earning around £40 000 a year with commission. Mrs Gee gets on very well with her son Robert, who pays his mother a generous allowance of £300 a month. Some three years ago Robert had a minor heart attack. He has fully recovered from this setback and the doctors have told him that he can now lead a normal life.

Mrs Gee's problem is that she does not get on very well with her daughter-in-law, Jenny, whom she considers to be a bit of a spendthrift. Mrs Gee is of the opinion that if Robert should die Jenny would immediately cut the £300 a month allowance that Robert is currently paying her. At the moment Mrs Gee is living very comfortably with her three sources of income from state pension, dividends from her former husband's estate and Robert's £300 monthly allowance. However finance would be tight if Robert's allowance were discontinued.

Mrs Gee's major asset is the family home. The mortgage of £7000 on this home was paid off out of a life assurance policy when her husband died. The house, in Knutsford, Cheshire cost £8000 in 1972 but by 1989 the value had risen to £200 000. Its current value is estimated to be in the region of £170 000. The maintenance cost of the house is quite high and is growing year by year. Mrs Gee asks about a scheme she has heard of whereby a charity called 'Home for Life' will maintain a house in excellent condition free of charge until the owner dies, if the owner will pass the ownership of the house to the society in the owner's will.

Mrs Gee's other assets of significant value are the stocks and shares left to her from her husband's estate. These consist of £20 000 of 5% government stock with a current market value of £12 000, and a portfolio of equity shares with a current market value of £42 000. The shares currently earn Mrs Gee annual dividends of around £2500 gross of tax.

Mrs Gee has reached an age when she wants to ensure her financial future. She is quite healthy and believes she could well live on for another 10 to 15 years. She wants to ensure that if Robert should die her income will be maintained at its present level in real terms until she dies. In addition she does not want her estate to pass to her daughter-in-law Jenny if Robert should pass away after her own death. If she leaves anything when she dies she would like the money to be divided equally between her two grandchildren.

Required: Mrs Gee asks you to work out a set of financial plans, the primary objectives of which are to ensure that her standard of living will not fall in the future and that Jenny will not get her hands on her, Mrs Gee's, estate.

After consultation with Mrs Gee you work out the attached balance sheet and long term cash flow statement to assist with your analysis. You assume an inflation rate over the next 13 years of 4% per annum.

CLIENT INFORMATION SHEET

Name   Mrs Margaret Gee

Address   Street   33 Fletcher's Close
                     Town   Knutsford
                     District   Cheshire
                     Postal Code   CH43 8EQ

Tel No.   081-65-6631
Fax No.

Sex   Female

Date of Birth   5.4.1921

Marital Status   Widow

Children

Name	Sex	Age
1. Robert Gordon	M	38

Occupation   Housewife

Parents still living   FATHER   No   MOTHER   No

Special responsibilities

          Handicapped Relative   None
          Aged Parents   None
          Other   Inheritance

Client: Mrs Margaret Gee

Inventory of Client's Assets: June 1994

Financial Assets	At Cost Price £	At Current Market Value £
Liquid Assets		
Cash	87	87
Building Society	1230	1230
Total Liquid Assets	1317	1317
Fixed Interest Stocks		
Govt. Stocks	20 000	12 000
Commercial Bonds	0	0
Other	0	0
Total Fixed Interest Stocks	20 000	12 000
Equity Stocks		
Shares: in 7 major UK companies	17 532	42 000
Total Financial Assets	38 849	55 317
Real Assets		
House Unmortgaged	8000	170 000
Land	0	0
Other Real Assets Antique Thimble collection	200	2000
Total Real Assets	8200	172 000
Value of Total Assets	£47 049	£227 317

BUDGETED ANNUAL LIFETIME CASH FLOW

Name:	Margaret Gee		
Occupation:	Retired		
Age:	73	Widowed	Children 1
Assumed inflation:	4% per annum		
Currency unit:	£		

Age	73	74	75	76	77	78	79	80	81	82	83	84	85
Year	1995	1996	1997	1998	1999	2000	2001	2002	2003	2004	2005	2006	2007
Income	£	£	£	£	£	£	£	£	£	£	£	£	£
Pension	2500	2600	2704	2812	2925	3042	3163	3290	3421	3558	3701	3849	4003
Dividends	3700	3885	4079	4283	4497	4722	4958	5206	5467	5740	6027	6328	6645
Allowance	3600	3816	4045	4288	4545	4818	5107	5413	5738	6082	6447	6834	7244
Total income	9800	10 301	10 828	11 383	11 967	12 581	13 228	13 909	14 626	15 380	16 175	17 011	17 891
Less:													
Tax	1960	2060	2166	2277	2393	2516	2646	2782	2925	3076	3235	3402	3578
Total deductions	1960	2060	2166	2277	2393	2516	2646	2782	2925	3076	3235	3402	3578
Gross cash flow	7840	8241	8663	9106	9574	10 065	10 583	11 127	11 701	12 304	12 940	13 609	14 313
Expenditure													
Accommodation	500	525	551	579	608	638	670	704	739	776	814	855	898
Repairs	800	840	882	926	972	1021	1072	1126	1182	1241	1303	1368	1437
Utilities	600	624	649	675	702	730	759	790	821	854	888	924	961
Food	1920	1978	2037	2098	2161	2226	2293	2361	2432	2505	2580	2658	2737
Transport	500	510	520	531	541	552	563	574	586	598	609	622	634
Clothing	500	500	500	500	500	500	500	500	500	500	500	500	500
House insurance	300	315	331	347	365	383	402	422	443	465	489	513	539
Rates	990	1030	1071	1114	1158	1204	1253	1303	1355	1409	1465	1524	1585
Recreation	900	909	918	927	937	946	955	965	975	984	994	1004	1014
Medical and health	300	330	363	399	439	483	531	585	643	707	778	856	942
Subs and gifts	200	200	200	200	200	200	200	200	200	200	200	200	200
Other	200	208	216	225	234	243	253	263	274	285	296	308	320
Total expenditure	7710	7968	8238	8521	8817	9127	9452	9792	10 149	10 524	10 918	11 332	11 766
Net surplus/deficit	130	273	424	586	757	938	1131	1335	1551	1780	2022	2277	2546
Total surplus/deficit	130	403	827	1412	2169	3108	4239	5574	7125	8905	10 927	13 204	15 750

Assumptions:

It is assumed that the cash flow will remain constant after the age of 85

Margaret Gee: Most likely cash flow scenario assuming no serious illness or other disasters

DAVID BALDRICK, POP STAR

David Baldrick is lead singer with the Skullcaps, a successful pop group which has performed in some 20 countries over the last seven years. David has made a great deal of money during this period, but he has also spent a great deal and is now in trouble with the Inland Revenue. His tax advisers have agreed that an amount of £135 000 is due to the Inland Revenue to clear his tax arrears. David admits to you that 'I just don't know where all the money has gone to, but you get lots of hangers-on, especially girls, in this business.'

The Skullcaps are still drawing audiences in the UK, but most of their foreign work has dried up and David's income from performing and records has fallen from a high of £274 000 in 1990 to a mere £103 700 in 1994. David reckons that his singing career might last for another two to three years, if he is lucky.

David took a fine arts degree at the Slade during the years 1983 to 1985 but was unemployed from 1985 to 1987 before the Skullcaps took off as a very successful 'heavy metal' group in 1988. The group was recently described in *Pop Record* as 'another of these shooting stars which illuminate the firmament for a few years and then burn out completely'.

David Baldrick is now seeking financial advice. He asks you to act as his personal financial adviser, since his finances are in 'a bit of a mess' and he wants to ensure a good future income for himself while he still has some money left to invest. He admits that he finds it difficult to hold on to money if it is there to spend. He has never kept accounts in his life and has never even studied his bank statements, except to look at the end of month balance. He states that 'Over the last few years there has always been loads of money around, so why should I have bothered to save?'

On other matters David is more stable. He is not into drugs or alcohol and has what he describes as 'a steady girlfriend'. He says that they 'May get hitched one day, if it becomes fashionable again.'

David has taken out no insurance whatsoever except third party car insurance and cover for his musical equipment. He has never even considered the question of a pension: 'At my age! You must be kidding! That's for civil servant types.' He lives in a three-bedroomed furnished flat in a trendy section of Chelsea, on the Thames embankment. The flat costs £36 000 a year to rent. He has had trouble with his neighbours recently because of complaints to the police with regard to excessive noise.

The only investments that David has ever made are a deposit with the Nationwide Building Society of £440 000 plus £34 000 on instant access deposit in a bank account with Lloyds Bank earning 3% a year. He has also run up an overdraft of £12 340 with the same bank. He has recently agreed an overdraft limit of £30 000 with the bank.

David owns a Mercedes Benz which cost him £170 000 new in 1989. He also owns 12 000 shares in Skullcaps Ltd, a private unquoted company which owns the Skullcaps pop group. These shares were estimated by an independent accounting firm to be worth about £20 each in December 1992, but the same firm warns that such shares can vary sharply in price from month to month depending on the group's forward bookings.

In July 1994 the sudden collapse of forward bookings for the Skullcaps, especially from the USA, has spread panic in the ranks. In 1992 the forward bookings for 1993 were worth around £1 500 000 for the group. In 1993 the forward bookings for 1994 had fallen to £1 000 000, and the projection for 1995 is a mere £600 000. David's net income share of the gross bookings is usually about 10% of the gross bookings.

Thus David has decided that the time has come to ensure his financial future. He asks you to set up a series of forward financial plans on the assumption that his income from the Skullcaps will fall to zero by 1996. David is very firm in his demands. He is used to ordering people around – his nickname in the group is 'the sergeant major'. He wants you to arrange for him to have a gross income of at least £50 000 a year in the future, adjusted for future inflation (he is not so financially unsophisticated as he seems). He considers this amount will provide him with a comfortable living for the rest of his life. He tells you that he is thinking of setting up an 'adult comic' publishing company based in a warehouse in Walthamstow, London, when he retires in 1996. He has always had a talent for cartoon drawing. He claims that financing this venture will be no problem since he has a pal who comes to his parties in Chelsea who is a well-known merchant banker.

David only wants you to handle his personal financial affairs 'and leave the big stuff to the merchant banker'.

After a brief examination of David's financial affairs you point out to David that he seems to have been living beyond his means for the last two years. David claims that this opinion is 'rubbish'. 'I have been cutting my spending to the bone' he says, 'Look I have spent almost nothing on holidays and entertainment in the last two years. I have become a virtual monk. I only throw one party a month now. I used to throw one a week. And since I have been going steady with Cindy C. I am spending nothing on the other birds.'

Required: Advise David on his financial position. What additional questions should you put to David before preparing a set of financial plans? What are his key problems? Design a set of financial plans for David Baldrick. These should include at least (a) an investment plan, (b) an insurance plan, (c) a pension plan.

The following documents include an information sheet, a statement of assets and liabilities as at 6 June 1994 and an income and expenditure account for the years 1992 to 1995; the 1995 figures are a best estimate 'budget' after consultation with David Baldrick.

CLIENT INFORMATION SHEET

Name   David Baldrick

Address   Street   5.45 Murchiston Tower
                      Town   Chelsea
                      District   London
                      Postal Code   SW3 5GR

Tel No.   071 554 7777
Fax No.   071 554 4205

Sex   Male

Date of Birth   28.10.64

Marital Status   Unmarried

Children   None

Occupation   Musician, singer

Company   The Skullcaps Ltd

Parents still living   FATHER Yes (61)   MOTHER Yes (58)

Special responsibilities

            Handicapped Relative   None
            Aged Parents   In the future?
            Other   None

Client: David Baldrick

Inventory of Client's Assets: June 1994

Financial Assets	At Cost Price £	At Current Market Value £
Liquid Assets		
Overdraft: Lloyds Bank (14%)	−12 340	−12 340
Bank Deposit (3%) Lloyds	34 000	34 000
Building Society Deposit 4% net	440 000	440 000
Total Liquid Assets	461 660	461 660
Equity Stocks		
Shares in Unquoted Co: Skullcaps Ltd	1000	240 000
Total Financial Assets	462 660	701 660
Real Assets		
Mercedes Benz Car 1989 model	170 000	60 000
Total Real Assets	170 000	60 000
Value of Total Assets £	632 660	761 660

Client: David Baldrick

Inventory of Client's Liabilities

Debt to Tax Authorities

Original amount	£135 000
Interest thereon to date	£5400
Amount outstanding	£140 400
How many years to pay off?	?

Other Contracted Monthly Payments

Item	£
Flat content insurance	63
Equipment insurance	100
Car insurance (3rd party)	30
Rates	92
Rent	3000
Total	3285

Other Important Non-Contracted Monthly Payments

Item	£
Electricity	110
Gas	88
Telephone	170
Food	583
Transport	167
Security	240
Clothing	600
Total	£1958

Name:　│　David Baldrick　█

Annual Income and Expenditure Account

Income		1992	1993	1994	Budget 1995
		£	£	£	£
Dividends from Skullcaps		210 000	125 000	103 700	60 000
Advertising etc.		30 000	15 000	1200	1000
Interest etc.		10 400	12 000	18 960	20 000
Other income		800	1750	2200	2500
Total income		£251 200	£153 750	£126 060	£83 500
Less:	Taxation	87 920	53 813	44 121	27 555
	Other deductions	3400	3100	3700	3500
Net cash inflow		159 880	96 838	78 239	52 445
Expenditure					
Rent		36 000	36 000	36 000	36 000
Household	Gas	1230	1185	1056	911
	Electricity	967	1520	1320	1100
	Food/Meals out	8450	7743	6996	2000
	Repairs etc.	1323	780	740	500
	Contents insurance	800	800	756	600
	Security	8000	8000	2880	2000
	Other	6000	4000	4000	3000
Transport	Fares	2500	2200	2004	1500
	Car licence	100	120	140	140
	Petrol	2600	2700	2300	2000
	Insurance (car)	1500	1800	2000	2200
	Repairs (car)	600	800	1700	2000
Communication	Postage	880	1000	780	550
	Telephone	2711	2100	2040	900
	Equipment costs	3400	3000	2300	2000
Risk hedging	Equipment Insurance	2000	1700	1200	800
Personal	Clothing	12 000	8000	7200	2000
	Holidays	15 000	12 000	5000	5000
	Entertainment	5700	3500	2500	2500
	Subscriptions	120	120	140	140
Sundry	Cash expenses	9000	10 000	4000	3000
	Rates	450	1100	1104	1100
Total expenditure		£121 331	£110 168	£88 156	£71 941
Net saving		£38 549	−£13 331	−£9917	−£19 496

Appendix A: Discounting and personal finance

INTRODUCTION

A great deal of the financial analysis conducted by a PFA requires the PFA to move money about in time. He or she needs to be able to answer such questions as: 'What is the terminal value of a series of contributions to a pension fund likely to be on the date of retirement of the client?', or 'What annual payment is needed to repay a loan of £12 000 over three years if the interest rate on the loan is 18%?', or 'What will the revised annual payment be and how much interest will a client save if a housing mortgage is repaid over 20 years rather than 25 years?'

All of these questions require a PFA to have a good grasp of **discounting** procedures.

DISCOUNTING

Discount tables can be used to calculate:

the future value of a present amount which earns a given rate of interest over a period
the present value of a future amount discounted at some given rate of interest over a period
the future value of a series of payments earning a given rate of interest over a period
the present value of a series of payments discounted at a given rate of interest over a period
the periodic payment needed to repay a loan over a given number of periods at a given rate of interest.

There are several other discounting calculations which are useful to a PFA, but the above five will cover most of the situations likely to be encountered in practice. Several excellent textbooks are available which provide a relatively painless introduction to these more complex discounting procedures.

THE FUTURE VALUE OF A SINGLE PRESENT AMOUNT

Exhibit A.1 provides the actuarial formula required to calculate the future value of a single amount of £x earning a rate of r% over n periods.

For example, if a single payment of £867 is invested in a bond which earns interest at 7% a year for 10 years and the interest is reinvested in the bond, what is the terminal value of the investment at the end of the 10-year period?

$$£867 \times (1.07)^{10} = 867 \times 1.9672 = £1706.$$

THE PRESENT VALUE OF A SINGLE FUTURE AMOUNT

Exhibit A.1 provides the relevant formula. For example, if £13 962 is due in seven years' time and the recipient can earn 7% on an investment over this period, what is this right to a future payment of £13 962 worth at present at the beginning of year one?

Discounting Formula

Future value of present single payment	$(1 + r)^{n}$
Present value of future single payment	$1/(1 + r)^{n}$
Terminal value of future stream of payments	$(1 + r)^{n} - 1/r$
Present value of future stream of payments	$(1 - (1 + r)^{-n}) / r$
Periodic payment needed to repay a loan	$r(1 + r)^{n} / (1 + r)^{n} - 1$
Periodic payment needed to set up a sinking fund	$r / (1 + r)^{n} - 1$
Adjusting the nominal rate of interest for inflation	$(1 + r) / (1 + f) - 1$
Converting nominal annual rate of inflation to effective rate	$(1 + j/m)^{m} - 1$
Calculating the yield to maturity of a bond	$(R + D/N) / ((P + V) / 2)$

Where:

r	= rate of interest
n	= number of periods
f	= expected rate of inflation
j	= nominal rate of interest for period
m	= number of times interest is paid during period
R	= absolute amount of interest received on bond
D	= amount of discount on bond i.e. $V - P$
N	= number of periods (years) to maturity
V	= maturity value of the bond
P	= current market price of the bond

Exhibit A.1   Some formulas commonly used in discounting.

The present value of £13 962 discounted at 7% over seven years is:

£13 962 × 1/(1.07)^7 = 13 962 × 0.6227 = £8694.

THE FUTURE VALUE OF A SERIES OF PAYMENTS OVER N PERIODS

Again, referring to Exhibit A.1, if an investor pays £800 a year for 20 years into a fund which earns 7% on the money invested, we can calculate how much this fund is worth at the end of the 20 years:

800 × (((1.07)^20 − 1)/0.07) = 800 × ((3.87 − 1)/0.07) =
800 × 41 = £32 800.

THE PRESENT VALUE OF A SERIES OF PAYMENTS OVER N PERIODS

An investor is offered the opportunity to invest in a project providing £527 a year at the end of each year for a period of 10 years. How much should they pay for this investment? If the investor can earn 7% a year in alternative projects, then they should pay a maximum of:

527 × (1 − (1/(1.07)^10)/ 0.07) =
527 × (1 − 0.5083) / 0.07 =
527 × 7.0236 = £3701.

Exhibit A.1 provides the relevant formula.

THE PERIODIC PAYMENT REQUIRED TO REPAY A LOAN

A loan of £50 000 at 16% interest cost is to be repaid in five instalments at the end of each year over five years. What is the annual payment required to repay the loan over this period? Using the formula in Exhibit A.1:

£50 000 / (0.16 / 1 − (1 / (1.16)^5)) =
£50 000 / (0.16 / 1 − 0.4761) =
£50 000 / 3.2743 = £15 270 a year.

THE PERIODIC PAYMENT REQUIRED TO SET UP A SINKING FUND

A sum of £3500 is needed at the end of 15 years to repay the capital portion of a bullet loan. How much money must be set aside each year to provide this sum after 15 years, if interest can be earned at 7% on the sum so invested? Exhibit A.1 again provides the relevant formula.

3500 × (0.07 / ((1.07)^15) − 1)
= 3500 / 25.13 = £139.27.

ADJUSTING THE NOMINAL RATE OF INTEREST FOR INFLATION

If a rate of interest contains an allowance for expected inflation the nominal rate needs to be adjusted to arrive at the real, inflation-adjusted rate.

The formula needed to achieve this objective is shown in Exhibit A.1.

The nominal annual rate of return on a government bond is 12%. The expected inflation rate over the next year is estimated to be 5%. What is the real rate of return on the bond over the next year?

Real rate % = (1 + 0.12) / (1 + 0.05) – 1

= 1.067 – 1 = 0.067 = 6.7 %.

CONVERTING NOMINAL YEARLY RATE TO EFFECTIVE RATE

If the nominal rate of interest on a loan is paid in instalments several times a year, the effective annual rate of interest is higher than the nominal rate.

The formula to convert a nominal to an effective rate is given in Exhibit A.1.

The nominal interest on a loan at 12% per annum is paid four times a year. What is the effective rate?

$(1 + 0.12 / 4)^4 – 1 = (1.03)^4 – 1 = 1.1255 – 1 = 0.1255 = 12.55\%$.

THE YIELD TO MATURITY OF A BOND

A bond can be bought today for £8000. The maturity value in five years' time is £10 000. The bond pays an annual rate of interest of 8% – £800 a year. What is the yield to maturity of the bond? Exhibit A.1 provides the relevant formula.

Yield to maturity is :

(800 + (2000 / 5)) / ((8000 + 10 000) / 2)

= (800 + 400) / (18 000 / 2)

= (1200) / (9000)

= 13.3%.

THE USE OF DISCOUNTING TABLES

Most textbooks on finance provide a set of discounting tables to assist with these calculations. Usually the tables provide the factors to use when calculating the first four of the formulas set out above – the present value of a single future payment or series of future payments, or the future value of a single present payment or the terminal value of a series of future payments.

A simplified set of discounting tables is set out at the end of this appendix.

DISCOUNTING AND COMPUTER CALCULATION

All computer spreadsheets and many word processing programs provide facilities for calculating discount values. The spreadsheet user simply tells the computer the range of values to process and the calculation formula to use, and the computer does the rest.

Some of the more powerful spreadsheets provide such a wide range of discount formulas that the user needs to be careful to use the right one. He or she is advised to calculate one example by hand and then check the result against the spreadsheet answer to ensure that the correct formula has been chosen.

Many hand-held calculators can process sophisticated discount calculations or can be programmed to achieve this end.

TUTORIAL QUESTIONS: DISCOUNTING AND PERSONAL FINANCE

The following questions can be answered using either (a) the formula provided, (b) a spreadsheet, or (c) the discounting tables provided.

1. Calculate the present value of the following future payments:
    £2400 due in five years' time discounted at 10%.
    £25 000 due in 17 years time' discounted at 15%.
    £780 due in two years' time discounted at 7%.
2. Calculate the future value of the following amounts:
    £100 000 invested in a bond at 15% for five years.
    £17 000 invested in a bond at 3% for 20 years.
      A self-employed person pays £27 000 into a pension fund which is estimated to earn 12% net of all tax for the 20-year period up to retirement. How much will the pension fund be worth in 20 years' time?
      Assume in all cases that the interest can be reinvested at the same rate.
3. What is the present value of an annuity of £12 000 a year for 10 years, discounted at 8%?
      A payment of £2400 a year is to be paid to a landlord for renting premises for five years. If the landlord can earn 6% on capital invested, what single sum could be paid to the landlord at the beginning of the rental period in lieu of the rental?
4. What is the terminal value of an annuity of £3600 a year for 10 years which can be invested at an interest rate of 5% a year?

Discounting Tables

Present value of £1 discounted back n periods of time at r% interest.

Percentage %

Period	1	2	3	4	5	6	7	8	9	10	12	14	16	20	25	30	40	50
1	0.9901	0.9804	0.9709	0.9615	0.9524	0.9434	0.9346	0.9259	0.9174	0.9091	0.8929	0.8772	0.8621	0.8333	0.800	0.7692	0.7143	0.6667
2	0.9803	0.9612	0.9426	0.9246	0.9070	0.8900	0.8734	0.8573	0.8417	0.8264	0.7972	0.7695	0.7432	0.6944	0.6400	0.5917	0.5102	0.4444
3	0.9706	0.9423	0.9151	0.8890	0.8638	0.8396	0.8163	0.7938	0.7722	0.7513	0.7118	0.6750	0.6407	0.5787	0.5120	0.4552	0.3644	0.2963
4	0.9610	0.9238	0.8885	0.8548	0.8227	0.7921	0.7629	0.7350	0.7084	0.6830	0.6355	0.5921	0.5523	0.4823	0.4096	0.3501	0.2603	0.1975
5	0.9515	0.9057	0.8626	0.8219	0.7835	0.7473	0.7130	0.6806	0.6499	0.6209	0.5674	0.5194	0.4761	0.4019	0.3277	0.2693	0.1859	0.1317
6	0.9420	0.8880	0.8375	0.7903	0.7462	0.7050	0.6663	0.6302	0.5963	0.5645	0.5066	0.4556	0.4104	0.3349	0.2621	0.2072	0.1328	0.0878
7	0.9327	0.8706	0.8131	0.7599	0.7107	0.6651	0.6227	0.5835	0.5470	0.5132	0.4523	0.3996	0.3538	0.2791	0.2097	0.1594	0.0949	0.0585
8	0.9235	0.8535	0.7894	0.7307	0.6768	0.6274	0.5820	0.5403	0.5019	0.4665	0.4039	0.3506	0.3050	0.2326	0.1678	0.1226	0.0678	0.0390
9	0.9143	0.8368	0.7664	0.7026	0.6446	0.5919	0.5439	0.5002	0.4604	0.4241	0.3606	0.3075	0.2630	0.1938	0.1342	0.0943	0.0484	0.0260
10	0.9053	0.8203	0.7441	0.6756	0.6139	0.5584	0.5083	0.4632	0.4224	0.3855	0.3220	0.2697	0.2267	0.1615	0.1074	0.0725	0.0346	0.0173
11	0.8963	0.8043	0.7224	0.6496	0.5847	0.5268	0.4751	0.4289	0.3875	0.3505	0.2875	0.2366	0.1954	0.1346	0.0859	0.0558	0.0247	0.0116
12	0.8874	0.7885	0.7014	0.6246	0.5568	0.4970	0.4440	0.3971	0.3555	0.3186	0.2567	0.2076	0.1685	0.1122	0.0687	0.0429	0.0176	0.0077
13	0.8787	0.7730	0.6810	0.6006	0.5303	0.4688	0.4150	0.3677	0.3262	0.2897	0.2292	0.1821	0.1452	0.0935	0.0550	0.0330	0.0126	0.0051
14	0.8700	0.7579	0.6611	0.5775	0.5051	0.4423	0.3878	0.3405	0.2992	0.2633	0.2046	0.1597	0.1252	0.0779	0.0440	0.0254	0.0090	0.0034
15	0.8613	0.7430	0.6419	0.5553	0.4810	0.4173	0.3624	0.3152	0.2745	0.2394	0.1827	0.1401	0.1079	0.0649	0.0352	0.0195	0.0064	0.0023
20	0.8195	0.6730	0.5537	0.4564	0.3769	0.3118	0.2584	0.2145	0.1784	0.1486	0.1037	0.0728	0.0514	0.0261	0.0115	0.0053	0.0012	0.0003
25	0.7798	0.6095	0.4776	0.3751	0.2953	0.2330	0.1842	0.1460	0.1160	0.0923	0.0588	0.0378	0.0245	0.0105	0.0038	0.0014	0.0002	0.0000
30	0.7419	0.5521	0.4120	0.3083	0.2314	0.1741	0.1314	0.0994	0.0754	0.0573	0.0334	0.0196	0.0116	0.0042	0.0012	0.0004	0.0000	0.0000
40	0.6717	0.4529	0.3066	0.2083	0.1420	0.0972	0.0668	0.0460	0.0318	0.0221	0.0107	0.0053	0.0026	0.0007	0.0001	0.0000	0.0000	0.0000
50	0.6080	0.3715	0.2281	0.1407	0.0872	0.0543	0.0339	0.0213	0.0134	0.0085	0.0035	0.0014	0.0006	0.0001	0.0000	0.0000	0.0000	0.0000
100	0.3697	0.1380	0.0520	0.0198	0.0076	0.0029	0.0012	0.0005	0.0002	0.0001	0.0000	0.0000	0.0000	0.0000	0.0000	0.0000	0.0000	0.0000

Discounting Tables

Future value of £1 at the end of n periods of time at r% interest.

Percentage %

Period	1	2	3	4	5	6	7	8	9	10	12	14	16	20	25	30	40	50
1	1.0100	1.0200	1.0300	1.0400	1.0500	1.0600	1.0700	1.0800	1.0900	1.1000	1.1200	1.1400	1.1600	1.2000	1.2500	1.3000	1.4000	1.5000
2	1.0201	1.0404	1.0609	1.0816	1.1025	1.1236	1.1449	1.1664	1.1881	1.2100	1.2544	1.2996	1.3456	1.4400	1.5625	1.6900	1.9600	2.2500
3	1.0303	1.0612	1.0927	1.1249	1.1576	1.1910	1.2250	1.2597	1.2950	1.3310	1.4049	1.4815	1.5609	1.7280	1.9531	2.1970	2.7440	3.3750
4	1.0406	1.0824	1.1255	1.1699	1.2155	1.2625	1.3108	1.3605	1.4116	1.4641	1.5735	1.6890	1.8106	2.0736	2.4414	2.8561	3.8416	5.0625
5	1.0510	1.1041	1.1593	1.2167	1.2763	1.3382	1.4026	1.4693	1.5386	1.6105	1.7623	1.9254	2.1003	2.4883	3.0518	3.7129	5.3782	7.5938
6	1.0615	1.1262	1.1941	1.2653	1.3401	1.4185	1.5007	1.5869	1.6771	1.7716	1.9738	2.1950	2.4364	2.9860	3.8147	4.8268	7.5295	11.3906
7	1.0721	1.1487	1.2299	1.3159	1.4071	1.5036	1.6058	1.7138	1.8280	1.9487	2.2107	2.5023	2.8262	3.5832	4.7684	6.2749	10.5414	17.0859
8	1.0829	1.1717	1.2668	1.3686	1.4775	1.5938	1.7182	1.8509	1.9926	2.1436	2.4760	2.8526	3.2784	4.2998	5.9605	8.1573	14.7579	25.6289
9	1.0937	1.1951	1.3048	1.4233	1.5513	1.6895	1.8385	1.9990	2.1719	2.3579	2.7731	3.2519	3.8030	5.1598	7.4506	10.6045	20.6610	38.4434
10	1.1046	1.2190	1.3439	1.4802	1.6289	1.7908	1.9672	2.1589	2.3674	2.5937	3.1058	3.7072	4.4114	6.1917	9.3132	13.7858	28.9255	57.6650
11	1.1157	1.2434	1.3842	1.5395	1.7103	1.8983	2.1049	2.3316	2.5804	2.8531	3.4785	4.2262	5.1173	7.4301	11.6415	17.9216	40.4957	86.4976
12	1.1268	1.2682	1.4258	1.6010	1.7959	2.0122	2.2522	2.5182	2.8127	3.1384	3.8960	4.8179	5.9360	8.9161	14.5519	23.2981	56.6939	129.7463
13	1.1381	1.2936	1.4685	1.6651	1.8856	2.1329	2.4098	2.7196	3.0658	3.4523	4.3635	5.4924	6.8858	10.6993	18.1899	30.2875	79.3715	194.6195
14	1.1495	1.3195	1.5126	1.7317	1.9799	2.2609	2.5785	2.9372	3.3417	3.7975	4.8871	6.2613	7.9875	12.8392	22.7374	39.3738	111.1201	291.9293
15	1.1610	1.3459	1.5580	1.8009	2.0789	2.3966	2.7590	3.1722	3.6425	4.1772	5.4736	7.1379	9.2655	15.4070	28.4217	51.1859	155.5681	437.8939
20	1.2202	1.4859	1.8061	2.1911	2.6533	3.2071	3.8697	4.6610	5.6044	6.7275	9.6463	13.7435	19.4608	38.3376	86.7362	190.0496	836.6826	3325.2567
25	1.2824	1.6406	2.0938	2.6658	3.3864	4.2919	5.4274	6.8485	8.6231	10.8347	17.0001	26.4619	40.8742	95.3962	264.6978	705.6410	4499.8796	25251.1683
30	1.3478	1.8114	2.4273	3.2434	4.3219	5.7435	7.6123	10.0627	13.2677	17.4494	29.9599	50.9502	85.8499	237.3763	807.7936	2620.00	24201.43	191751.06
40	1.4889	2.2080	3.2620	4.8010	7.0400	10.2857	14.9745	21.7245	31.4094	45.2593	93.0510	188.8835	378.7212	1469.7716	7523.1638	36118.86	700038	11057332
50	1.6446	2.6916	4.3839	7.1067	11.4674	18.4202	29.4570	46.9016	74.3575	117.3909	289.0022	700.2330	1670.70	9100.44	70064.92	497929	20248916	637621500
100	2.7048	7.2446	19.2186	50.5049	131.5013	339.3021	867.716	2199.76	5529.04	13780.6	83522.3	490326	<<<<VERY LARGE NUMBERS!>>>>					

Discounting Tables

Present value of a series of future payments of £1 discounted back *n* periods of time at *r*% interest.

(Present value of an annuity of £1 per period)

Percentage %

Period	1	2	3	4	5	6	7	8	9	10	12	14	16	20	25	30	40	50
1	0.9901	0.9804	0.9709	0.9615	0.9524	0.9434	0.9346	0.9259	0.9174	0.9091	0.8929	0.8772	0.8621	0.8333	0.8000	0.7692	0.7143	0.6667
2	1.9704	1.9416	1.9135	1.8861	1.8594	1.8334	1.8080	1.7833	1.7591	1.7355	1.6901	1.6467	1.6052	1.5278	1.4400	1.3609	1.2245	1.1111
3	2.9410	2.8839	2.8286	2.7751	2.7232	2.6730	2.6243	2.5771	2.5313	2.4869	2.4018	2.3216	2.2459	2.1065	1.9520	1.8161	1.5889	1.4074
4	3.9020	3.8077	3.7171	3.6299	3.5460	3.4651	3.3872	3.3121	3.2397	3.1699	3.0373	2.9137	2.7982	2.5887	2.3616	2.1662	1.8492	1.6049
5	4.8534	4.7135	4.5797	4.4518	4.3295	4.2124	4.1002	3.9927	3.8897	3.7908	3.6048	3.4331	3.2743	2.9906	2.6893	2.4356	2.0352	1.7366
6	5.7955	5.6014	5.4172	5.2421	5.0757	4.9173	4.7665	4.6229	4.4859	4.3553	4.1114	3.8887	3.6847	3.3255	2.9514	2.6427	2.1680	1.8244
7	6.7282	6.4720	6.2303	6.0021	5.7864	5.5824	5.3893	5.2064	5.0330	4.8684	4.5638	4.2883	4.0386	3.6046	3.1611	2.8021	2.2628	1.8829
8	7.6517	7.3255	7.0197	6.7327	6.4632	6.2098	5.9713	5.7466	5.5348	5.3349	4.9676	4.6389	4.3436	3.8372	3.3289	2.9247	2.3306	1.9220
9	8.5660	8.1622	7.7861	7.4353	7.1078	6.8017	6.5152	6.2469	5.9952	5.7590	5.3282	4.9464	4.6065	4.0310	3.4631	3.0190	2.3790	1.9480
10	9.4713	8.9826	8.5302	8.1109	7.7217	7.3601	7.0236	6.7101	6.4177	6.1446	5.6502	5.2161	4.8332	4.1925	3.5705	3.0915	2.4136	1.9653
11	10.3676	9.7868	9.2526	8.7605	8.3064	7.8869	7.4987	7.1390	6.8052	6.4951	5.9377	5.4527	5.0286	4.3271	3.6564	3.1473	2.4383	1.9769
12	11.2551	10.5753	9.9540	9.3851	8.8633	8.3838	7.9427	7.5361	7.1607	6.8137	6.1944	5.6603	5.1971	4.4392	3.7251	3.1903	2.4559	1.9846
13	12.1337	11.3484	10.6350	9.9856	9.3936	8.8527	8.3577	7.9038	7.4869	7.1034	6.4235	5.8424	5.3423	4.5327	3.7801	3.2233	2.4685	1.9897
14	13.0037	12.1062	11.2961	10.5631	9.8986	9.2950	8.7455	8.2442	7.7862	7.3667	6.6282	6.0021	5.4675	4.6106	3.8241	3.2487	2.4775	1.9931
15	13.8651	12.8493	11.9379	11.1184	10.3797	9.7122	9.1079	8.5595	8.0607	7.6061	6.8109	6.1422	5.5755	4.6755	3.8593	3.2682	2.4839	1.9954
20	18.0456	16.3514	14.8775	13.5903	12.4622	11.4699	10.5940	9.8181	9.1285	8.5136	7.4694	6.6231	5.9288	4.8696	3.9539	3.3158	2.4970	1.9994
25	22.0232	19.5235	17.4131	15.6221	14.0939	12.7834	11.6536	10.6748	9.8226	9.0770	7.8431	6.8729	6.0971	4.9476	3.9849	3.3286	2.4994	1.9999
30	25.8077	22.3965	19.6004	17.2920	15.3725	13.7648	12.4090	11.2578	10.2737	9.4269	8.0552	7.0027	6.1772	4.9789	3.9950	3.3321	2.4999	2.0000
40	32.8347	27.3555	23.1148	19.7928	17.1591	15.0463	13.3317	11.9246	10.7574	9.7791	8.2438	7.1050	6.2335	4.9966	3.9995	3.3332	2.5000	2.0000
50	39.1961	31.4236	25.7298	21.4822	18.2559	15.7619	13.8007	12.2335	10.9617	9.9148	8.3045	7.1327	6.2463	4.9995	3.9999	3.3333	2.5000	2.0000
100	63.0289	43.0984	31.5989	24.5050	19.8479	16.6175	14.2693	12.4943	11.1091	9.9993	8.3332	7.1428	6.2500	5.0000	4.0000	3.3333	2.5000	2.0000

Discounting Tables
Future value of a series of payments of £1 for n periods of time at r% interest.
(Future value of an annuity of £1 per period).

Period	Percentage %																	
	1	2	3	4	5	6	7	8	9	10	12	14	16	20	25	30	40	50
1	1.0000	1.0000	1.0000	1.0000	1.0000	1.0000	1.0000	1.0000	1.0000	1.0000	1.0000	1.0000	1.0000	1.0000	1.0000	1.0000	1.0000	1.0000
2	2.0100	2.0200	2.0300	2.0400	2.0500	2.0600	2.0700	2.0800	2.0900	2.1000	2.1200	2.1400	2.1600	2.2000	2.2500	2.3000	2.4000	2.5000
3	3.0301	3.0604	3.0909	3.1216	3.1525	3.1836	3.2149	3.2464	3.2781	3.3100	3.3744	3.4396	3.5056	3.6400	3.8125	3.9900	4.3600	4.7500
4	4.0604	4.1216	4.1836	4.2465	4.3101	4.3746	4.4399	4.5061	4.5731	4.6410	4.7793	4.9211	5.0665	5.3680	5.7656	6.1870	7.1040	8.1250
5	5.1010	5.2040	5.3091	5.4163	5.5256	5.6371	5.7507	5.8666	5.9847	6.1051	6.3528	6.6101	6.8771	7.4416	8.2070	9.0431	10.9456	13.1875
6	6.1520	6.3081	6.4684	6.6330	6.8019	6.9753	7.1533	7.3359	7.5233	7.7156	8.1152	8.5355	8.9775	9.9299	11.2588	12.7560	16.3238	20.7813
7	7.2135	7.4343	7.6625	7.8983	8.1420	8.3938	8.6540	8.9228	9.2004	9.4872	10.0890	10.7305	11.4139	12.9159	15.0735	17.5828	23.8534	32.1719
8	8.2857	8.5830	8.8923	9.2142	9.5491	9.8975	10.2598	10.6366	11.0285	11.4359	12.2997	13.2328	14.2401	16.4991	19.8419	23.8577	34.3947	49.2578
9	9.3685	9.7546	10.1591	10.5828	11.0266	11.4913	11.9780	12.4876	13.0210	13.5795	14.7757	16.0853	17.5185	20.7989	25.8023	32.0150	49.1526	74.8867
10	10.4622	10.9497	11.4639	12.0061	12.5779	13.1808	13.8164	14.4866	15.1929	15.9374	17.5487	19.3373	21.3215	25.9587	33.2529	42.6195	69.8137	113.3301
11	11.5668	12.1687	12.8078	13.4864	14.2068	14.9716	15.7836	16.6455	17.5603	18.5312	20.6546	23.0445	25.7329	32.1504	42.5661	56.4053	98.7391	170.9951
12	12.6825	13.4121	14.1920	15.0258	15.9171	16.8699	17.8885	18.9771	20.1407	21.3843	24.1331	27.2707	30.8502	39.5805	54.2077	74.3270	139.2348	257.4927
13	13.8093	14.6803	15.6178	16.6268	17.7130	18.8821	20.1406	21.4953	22.9534	24.5227	28.0291	32.0887	36.7862	48.4966	68.7596	97.6250	195.9287	387.2390
14	14.9474	15.9739	17.0863	18.2919	19.5986	21.0151	22.5505	24.2149	26.0192	27.9750	32.3926	37.5811	43.6720	59.1959	86.9495	127.9125	275.3002	581.8585
15	16.0969	17.2934	18.5989	20.0236	21.5786	23.2760	25.1290	27.1521	29.3609	31.7725	37.2797	43.8424	51.6595	72.0351	109.6868	167.2863	386.4202	873.7878
20	22.0190	24.2974	26.8704	29.7781	33.0660	36.7856	40.9955	45.7620	51.1601	57.2750	72.0524	91.0249	115.3797	186.6880	342.9447	630.1655	2089.2064	6648.5135
25	28.2432	32.0303	36.4593	41.6459	47.7271	54.8645	63.2490	73.1059	84.7009	98.3471	133.3339	181.8708	249.2140	471.9811	1054.7912	2348.8033	11247.20	50500.3366
30	34.7849	40.5681	47.5754	56.0849	66.4388	79.0582	94.4608	113.2832	136.3075	164.4940	241.3327	356.7868	530.3117	1181.88	3227.17	8729.99	60501.08	383500.1185
40	48.8864	60.4020	75.4013	95.0255	120.7998	154.7620	199.6351	259.0565	337.8824	442.5926	767.0914	1342.0251	2360.7572	7343.86	30088.66	120392.88	1750092	22114663
50	64.4632	84.5794	112.797	152.6671	209.3480	290.3359	406.5289	573.7702	815.0836	1163.9085	2400.0182	4994.5213	10435.65	45497.19	280255.69	1659760.7	50622288	1275242998
100	170.481	312.232	607.288	1237.62	2610.03	5638.37	12381.7	27484.5	61422.7	137796	696011							

<<<<VERY LARGE NUMBERS>>>>

5. What is the annual payment needed to pay off a mortgage of £100 000 over 20 years if the fixed rate of interest on the mortgage is 9%? Ignore tax.

6. Calculate the annual payments needed to repay a loan of £10 000 at 7% p.a. interest charge over 10 years, the repayment to start in five years' time, interest charges to commence immediately.

7. Convert a nominal annual rate of interest of 16% a year on a £10 000 loan to an effective rate if the annual interest charge of £1600 is paid in four instalments of £400 a quarter.

8. A bond pays £10 000 a year in the first year and increases this amount by 5% a year. The bond has a 10-year life. What is the present value of this bond if the rate of discount (alternative use of funds to the bondholder) is taken as 7%?

9. What rate of discount equates £5000 a year for four years to a present value of £17 000?

10. A bond with a maturity value of £100 000 can be bought today for £93 000. The bond is due to be repaid in seven years' time at par. The interest earned on the bond is £8000 a year. Calculate the yield to maturity on the bond.

11. A car is bought for £20 000. The car is bought with an interest-only loan at 17% p.a. The loan must be repaid in full in five years' time. The buyer decides to set up a sinking fund to provide £20 000 to repay the loan in five years' time. How much must the buyer set aside each year over the next five years to ensure that she has a fund of £20 000 available in five years' time? She can invest her fund at 12%.

Appendix B:
Financial products

A wide range of financial products are available to an investor in the UK. Some of the more popular of these financial products are described below.

UNITARY PRODUCTS

ORDINARY SHARES

Ordinary shares are issued by companies. The holder of an ordinary share certificate owns a part of the company issuing the share. The owner of an ordinary share has certain rights:

1. the right to a dividend, if a dividend is declared by the board of directors of the company (but dividends need not be declared by the directors – some companies pay no dividends);
2. the right to a vote at any general meeting of the company shareholders (this allows the shareholder to change the board of directors if he or she can gain enough support from other shareholders);
3. the right to a portion of the residue of the value of the company if the company is liquidated, but only after all prior debts are paid.

The shares of large UK companies are called 'blue chip' shares. These are considered to be very safe investment vehicles.

CUMULATIVE PREFERENCE SHARES

Cumulative preference shares are issued by companies. The holder of a cumulative preference share has a right to:

1. a fixed rate of interest payment each year
2. a priority claim over the ordinary shareholders as to rights to dividend – ordinary dividends cannot normally be paid if the preference

dividend is in arrears; the preference dividend is accumulated until paid;

3.   normally, priority rights to capital over the ordinary shareholders in a winding up of the company.

DEBENTURES

A debenture is a loan to a company, for a fixed period of time at a fixed rate of interest. The owner of a debenture has a right to receive a fixed amount of interest each year, and repayment of the loan at the end of the loan period. If the interest is not paid, debenture-holders can take legal action to acquire and sell the security supporting the debenture. During a liquidation the debenture-holder has a priority claim on the assets providing the security to the ordinary and preference shareholders. However, the company may be able to claim a moratorium on interest payments for one or more periods. Debenture-holders normally have no vote at meetings of the company shareholders, except when interest payments are in arrears. Interest on debentures is allowable against company tax.

BONDS

So many different kinds of bonds are offered on the market that no single definition can hope to cover the entire field.

Technically a bond is a whole of life assurance policy paid for by a single premium. Life cover of 101% of the value of the selling price of the 'units' is usually written. However, the life assurance aspect is not very important.

The funds underlying the bond can be invested in a wide range of assets such as ordinary shares, fixed interest securities, indexed linked gilts and so on.

Investment bonds are designed to run for a fixed period of time like term insurance. Therefore the terminal date might be important for tax reasons. There is usually a penalty for early surrender – 6%, falling to 1% after n years.

With a distribution bond, income is distributed as dividend. The dividend buys units in a separate cash fund, from which income payments can be made to bond-holders. Distribution bonds can be a useful tax avoidance vehicle if placed in trust for children.

The guaranteed equity bond is an interesting variant. In this case the fund is invested in the SE FT 100 Index of large companies. If the index rises over a period, usually a quarter year, then a proportion of the profit is locked in to the bond (usually 27% to 53% of the profit before tax, 20% to 40% after tax). If the SE FT 100 Index falls, however, the bond price is not reduced.

Property bonds, 'with-profit' bonds, fixed interest bonds, cash bonds and a host of other types of bonds are also on offer to the investor.

Bonds can be encashed at any time, but there may be a penalty to pay.

Up to 5% can be taken out of the fund each year before any tax is paid by the investor. The tax treatment of income above 5% when taken out by a higher-rate taxpayer is rather complicated, and a recent tax case has also complicated the previous exemption of bonds from capital gains tax.

The annual management charge on bonds is usually around 1%. There may be a 5% spread between the buying and selling price of the bond.

ANNUITIES

An annuity is a contract whereby an annuitant pays a fixed sum of money to an insurance company, which in its turn guarantees to pay the annuitant a certain sum of money for life. A wide range of annuities are offered.

A flat rate annuity pays a fixed sum for life. An escalating annuity increases the sum paid by $x\%$ a year. An index-linked annuity increases the annual payment by the cost of living index. A guaranteed annuity pays out some capital into the deceased annuitant's estate if he or she should die soon after the annuity is taken out (usually within up to five years). A joint annuity is one taken out on the lives of two persons. A managed annuity allows the annuitant to vary the amount paid, and possibly the nature of the investment supporting the annuity. A phased annuity allows the annuity to be taken in 'slices' over several years.

WARRANTS

A warrant is a highly geared derivative. It is the right to buy a share at a fixed price in the future. If the share price stands below the 'right to buy' price, the warrant is worthless except as a gambling chip. As the share price rises above the warrant price, however, the profit on the warrant is geared upwards, since the profit on the share and on the warrant are identical, but the warrant is only a fraction of the cost of the share. Several warrant portfolios are offered for the investor who likes to take a big risk in the hope of making a big profit.

TRADED OPTIONS

A traded option is another highly geared derivative. It offers the right, but not the obligation, to buy a block of shares (usually 1000) or any other asset at a fixed price in the future. Buy (call) options and sell (put) options are available on the shares of certain large companies and various commodities. Options are also available on interest rates. The most popular option is the FT All-Share Index Option, which allows the investor to hedge against movements in the FT All-Share and some other indices. Options are traded in the LIFFE exchange, London.

Buying a traded option must not be confused with 'writing' an option. This is a much riskier business. In this case, the writer of the option underwrites the promise to buy or sell the share etc. and must implement this contract if the option buyer wishes to take it up. Not for widows and orphans.

SECOND-HAND 'WITH-PROFITS' INSURANCE POLICIES

Companies such as Securitised Endowment Contracts PLC will buy second-hand with-profits endowment and whole-life assurance policies, and then sell them on to potential investors. Policies must have been in force for at least seven years. In 1992 £4 billion worth of assurance policies were surrendered early, that is before they matured. Only £80 million worth of these policies were sold to buyers of policies such as SEC. These 'second-hand' policies can make useful investments which do not fluctuate in value as much as ordinary shares, yet which provide equivalent protection against inflation. Profits on the sale of these policies are subject to capital gains tax if they are 'qualifying' policies. Profits on 'non-qualifying' policies are subject to tax 'top-slicing' but only for higher rate taxpayers.

GILTS

'Gilts' are securities which are issued by the government. Most of these securities offer a fixed rate of interest to the investor, but some securities offer a variable interest rate. Index-linked gilts are a particularly useful investment vehicle. These securities provide a base guaranteed rate of interest plus additional income to compensate for inflation. The real value of the income to the investor will thus remain constant, no matter what the rate of inflation may be.

CASH FUNDS

Banks and building societies provide convenient repositories for surplus cash. The basic funds are the instant access accounts and the three-month notice of withdrawal accounts. Since these funds are safe and very liquid investments, the returns offered are low.

The government's National Savings accounts provide a wide range of repositories for longer-term cash funds. The gross income offered on many of these accounts, such as income and capital bonds, is very competitive. On these latter two, interest can be paid gross of tax if required.

Some of these products are free of tax. Gilts are free of capital gains tax. Examples of tax-free products are National Savings certificates, the yearly savings plan, the children's bonus bond and index-linked certificates. The index-linked certificates currently pay 3% a year to holders plus an addition to compensate for inflation, all tax-free. They are a very competitive product if inflation is expected to rise over the life of the investment.

More use would be made of these products were it not for the fact that no commission is paid to investment advisers for recommending them!

TRACKER FUNDS

A tracker fund mimics the performance of a given stock exchange index such as the FT 100 index. An investment in a tracker fund thus has the advantage of being well diversified among many large companies. The manager of the fund needs only to buy or sell a few shares each period to keep the fund in line with the composition of the given index, thus the management fee is very low – sometimes no more than 0.5% per annum. The beta of the fund will, by definition, be 1 – that is, an investment in a tracker fund is an investment of average market risk. Specific risk is almost entirely eliminated and tracker funds are a very safe investment, with low running costs. Most stock markets in developed countries offer a tracker fund to mimic the index.

COLLECTIVE INVESTMENT FUNDS

The substantial reduction in risk which can be effected by diversifying a portfolio among many shares has encouraged the development of what have come to be called 'collective investments', such as unit trusts and investment trusts. Note that tracker funds and many types of bonds are, in effect, also collective investments.

UNIT TRUSTS

The managers of a unit trust buy a portfolio of shares and then offer units of this portfolio to the general public. The value of the units are directly correlated to the value of the portfolio of shares. The units can be bought from or sold back to the managers of the fund at any time – buying and selling prices are published daily in the newspapers. A unit trust offers an investor a professionally managed, well-diversified investment medium. When they were first started in the 1960s unit trust portfolios were widely spread among many types of shares, although in recent years many specialized unit trusts have been offered on the market which only invest in certain types of assets. Examples are trusts which invest in one country such as Japan or North America, trusts which invest exclusively in 'convertibles', or money market instruments, or commodity and energy shares or smaller companies. The choice is very wide. Unit trusts cannot be geared, unlike investment trusts.

There are over 500 unit trusts, divided into 22 different categories.

INVESTMENT TRUSTS

Investment trusts are much older than unit trusts. Investment trusts which invested in South American shares were being offered in the nineteenth century.

The managers of an investment trust set up a company to buy a portfolio of shares. The shares in this company are, in turn, offered to the general public. Thus the shares in an investment trust are quoted on the Stock Exchange just like any other quoted company.

An investment trust can be geared. This means that the trust raises money via debt to acquire more shares. If the return on the shares is higher than the annual cost of the debt then the holders of the investment trust shares receive a higher return than they otherwise would. The reverse also applies!

An investment trust portfolio, like a unit trust portfolio, can be invested generally or in some specialized field.

Split level investment trusts have raised a good deal of interest among investors in recent years. The basic idea here is that the income from the shares held in the investment trust is separated from any changes in the capital value of the shares in the trust. Some investors who want high income buy the split level income-shares. Investors who prefer capital gains but no income buy the split level capital-shares. Highly geared ordinary shares and zero dividend preference shares can achieve the same objectives. Zero income shares which provide capital gains can offer tax advantages to high income investors and also to the beneficiaries of certain types of trusts.

The market values of the shares of many investment trusts often stand at a discount to the market value of the shares held in the trust – this reflects the administration cost of the trust plus the likely costs involved in breaking up the trust.

Some 250 investment trusts are quoted on the UK market. These are classified into 24 sectors.

PERSONAL EQUITY PLANS

Shares held in PEPs are not subject to either income tax or capital gains tax. Only a limited amount, currently £6000, can be invested in a PEP each year and not all shares quoted on the London Stock Exchange are

PEPable! Generally the shares must be the shares of UK or EC companies. Unit trusts and investment trusts are PEPable if at least 50% of the funds are invested in UK or EC shares. In addition to the basic PEP, a further £3000 may be invested in a single company share so long as the company is British. Up to £1500 may be invested in a non-qualifying trust, for example in an emerging company fund.

PEPs are set up on behalf of the investor by banks and investment companies. The management fee is usually a 5% initial fee plus around 1.5% a year – rather expensive! More competitive fees have been introduced recently by some investment companies, however.

ENTERPRISE INVESTMENT SCHEME

In 1994 the government introduced an 'Enterprise Investment Scheme', to replace the 'Business Expansion Scheme'. Companies can raise up to £1 million of capital through the scheme, which is intended to encourage rich investors to invest in small to medium-sized companies and thereby receive some considerable tax benefits compared to conventional investment in such companies. These investors can become fully paid directors of the companies in which they invest.

A free booklet on the scheme is available from the small firms division of the DTI.

TESSAS

TESSAs are tax exempt savings funds, set up mainly by banks and building societies. In 1995 the maximum amount that can be invested in a TESSA by one individual is £9000 – up to £3000 in the first year and £1500 a year thereafter for the following four years. Income accumulates tax-free in the fund each year, so long as no income or capital is withdrawn. Any income withdrawn during the five-year period is treated as income of that year and taxed accordingly. The maximum amount that can be withdrawn is usually the amount of interest accumulated net of the basic tax rate.

Funds can be transferred from one TESSA fund to another fund of the same or another group. A transfer charge may be imposed – usually around £20–£25 if the fund is transferred to another group.

The amounts involved are so small and the procedures so complicated that the system is treated as a bit of a joke by some PFAs, but it is useful perk for higher-rate taxpayers and investors with limited wealth and income.

Appendix C:
Beta and market risk

The total risk attached to the future earnings from a share can be segregated into two types of risk.

First there is 'specific' risk. This includes all of those risky factors which apply exclusively to the individual company. A lawsuit or a factory fire are examples of specific risk.

The second type of risk is 'market' risk. This includes all those risky factors which will affect all of the shares quoted on a given stock exchange. A rise in the market rate of interest is an example of a market risk.

Specific risk can be almost eliminated from a share portfolio by simply diversifying the total wealth invested over 20 or 30 shares chosen at random from all the shares quoted on the stock exchange.

Market risk cannot be eliminated but it can be measured. Every share quoted on a given stock exchange is not affected equally by market risk. If the average return on all of the shares quoted rises by, say, 15%, the return on some shares will rise by more than 15%, others by less than 15%.

The beta measures the impact that a given rise or fall in the market return has on the return of any individual share. For example, if a share has a beta of 1.7, then the return on this share is likely to be around 70% more risky than the average share, while a share with a beta of 0.90 is around 10% less risky than the average share. The 'risk' we are considering here is market risk, not specific risk.

The beta values of most of the shares quoted on the London Stock Exchange are calculated regularly by the London Business School Risk Service.

The beta measures the co-variance[1] between the market return and the return on any individual share over many periods in the past. The beta of

---

[1] The co-variance is a sort of amalgam of the variance on the returns and the autocorrelation of the returns.

a share is relatively stable over time. The beta concept is only useful if the stock market processes information efficiently.

Once the beta of a share is known, the management of a quoted company can find out the return that the market expects from the share in the next accounting period.

The required equation, somewhat simplified, is:

$$R = G + B \times (A - G)$$

Where:

R = The return required by the market from this share in the next period
G = The return on a very safe, riskless, investment.
B = The beta of the share
A = The current return on a share of average risk.

For example if the shares of Teleware PLC have a beta of 1.7 and the return on a share of average risk is 22% and a riskless government stock returns 10% per annum, then the required return for Teleware PLC in the coming year is:

$$R = 10\% + 1.7 \times (22 - 10) = 30.4\ \%$$

Similarly, if Surewater PLC has a beta of 0.7, the required return is:

$$R = 10\% + 0.7 \times (22 - 10) = 18.4\ \%.$$

Appendix D:
Some useful addresses and telephone numbers

SIB
Securities and Investments Board
Gavrelle House
2–14 Bunhill Row, London EC1Y 8RA
Tel. 0171 638 1240

PIA
Personal Investment Authority
Hertsmere House, Hertsmere Road, London E14 4AB
Tel. 0171 538 8860

IMRO
Investment Managers Regulatory Association
Broadwalk House, 5 Appold Street, London EC2A 2LL
Tel. 0171 628 6022

ICS
Investor's Compensation Scheme
Tel. 0171 638 1240

ABI
Association of British Insurers
51 Gresham Street, London EC2V 7HQ
Tel. 0171 600 3333

The Insurance Ombudsman
135 Park Street, London SE1 9EA
Tel. 0171 928 7600

Personal Insurance Arbitration Service
Chartered Institute of Arbitrators
24 Angel Gate, London EC1V 2RS
Tel. 0171 837 4483

Insurance Brokers' Registration Council
Tel. 0171 588 4387

SFA
Securities and Futures Authority (Complaints Department)
The Stock Exchange Building,
London EC2N 1EQ
Tel. 0171 256 9000

Association of Investment Trust Companies
Park House, 16 Finsbury Circus, London EC2M 7JJ
Tel. 0171 588 5347

Society of Pension Consultants
Tel. 0171 353 1688

Unit Trust Association Information Unit
65 Kingsway, London WC2B 6TD
Tel. 0171 831 0898

Banking Ombudsman
Citadel House
5–10 Fetter Lane, London EC4A 1BR
Tel. 0171 583 1395

Building Society Ombudsman
Grosvenor Gardens House
35–37 Grosvenor Gardens, London SW1X 7AW
Tel. 0171 931 0044

Office of Fair Trading
Field House, 15–25 Breams Building, London EC4A 1PR
Tel. 0171 242 2858

Micropal (computer-based financial information source)
Tel: 0181 741 4100

The Annuity Bureau
Tel: 0171 495 1495

Registry of Fee-based Advisers
FT Business Information 'Money Management'
Tel. 0171 405 6969

Registry of Financial Planning
Tel. 01432 274 891

These organizations supply the addresses of several financial advisers near to an enquirer.

Law Society
113 Chancery Lane, London WC2A 1PL
Tel. 0171 242 1222

Institute of Chartered Accountants in England and Wales
Moorgate Place, London EC2P 2BJ
Tel. 0171 920 8100

Most of the above organizations either monitor a section of the financial system or provide advice to users of the system. Several, such as the ombudsmen, provide a mechanism for handling complaints from users of the financial system.

Bibliography

REFERENCES

Anon. (latest edition) *The Financial Adviser's Handbook*, PBI.

Barlow, J.S. *et al.* (latest edition) *Wills, Administration and Taxation*, Sweet & Maxwell.

Barr, A. and Barr, R. (1994) *Which Way To Buy, Sell And Move House?*, Which Consumer Guides.

Bean, B. *et al.* (latest edition) *Retirement Planning Guide* Allied Dunbar/Longman

Begg, P. (1994) 'In the money: personal finance software', *Personal Computer World*, August, pp. 422–429.

Buckley, A. (1993) *Multinational Finance*, Prentice Hall.

BZW (1992) *Gilt Equity Study*, Barclays de Zoete Wedd Research Limited.

Chamberlain, G. (1990) *Trading In Options*, Woodhead Faulkner.

Cheney, J.M. and Moses, E.A. (1993) *Fundamentals Of Investments*, West Publishing Company.

Dickson, G. and Steele, J. (latest edition) *Introduction To Insurance*, Pitman.

Edwards, B. (ed.) (1990) *Credit Management Handbook*, Gower.

Gray, B. (1993) *Beginner's Guide To Investment*, Investor's Chronicle/Century Business Books.

Johnson Fry (latest edition) *European Information Pocket Book*, NTC Publications.

Krol, E. (1994) *The Whole Internet. User's Guide And Catalogue*, O'Reilly.

Laidler, D. and Parkin, J. (1975) 'Inflation: a survey', *Economic Journal*, vol. 85.

McHattie, A. (1992) *The Investor's Guide To Warrants*, FT/Pitman.

Marshall, C.(1993) *Introduction To Life Assurance And Pensions*, Taxbriefs.

Oldfield, M.(1994) *Understanding Occupational Pension Schemes*, Tolley.

Phillips, M.E., Brown, C.E. and Neilson, N.L. (1990) 'Personal financial planning with expert systems', *Management Accounting*, September , pp. 29–33.

Schofield, S. (1994) *The PC Plus Modem And Communications Guidebook*, Future Business Books.

Slevin, K.(1993) *Capital Gains Tax*, CCH Editions.

Sinclair, W.I. and Silke, P.D. (latest edition) *Capital Taxes And Estate Planning Guide*, Allied Dunbar/Longman.

Tingley, K.R. (latest edition) *Daily Mail Income Tax Guide*, Chapmans Publishers.

FURTHER READING

Anon. (latest edition) *Directory of the PIA*, Pitman.

Anon. (latest edition) *The Pensions Fact Book*, Professional Publishing.

Anon. (latest edition) *The Financial Intermediary's Fact Book*, Gee.

A regularly updated service of information relevant to PFAs, with particular emphasis on the changing compliance rules.

Anon. *The Personal Finance Pocket Book*, Johnson Fry Plc / NTC Publications.

A treasure trove of statistics on personal finance. A useful reference work.

Block, S.B., Peavy, J.W. and Thornton, J.H. (1990) *Personal Financial Management*, Harper & Row.

One of the standard academic texts on personal financial planning used in US business schools. A useful text but has a strong US bias.

Bose, M. (1988) *Insurance: Are You Covered?*, Allied Dunbar.

A guide to the different forms of personal insurance which are offered by insurance companies.

Burgess, R. (1991) *The Law Of Borrowing*, Sweet & Maxwell.

Information on the legal side of credit management.

Butterworth's (1993) *International Tax Guide*, Butterworth.

A guide to the international tax scene.

Daily Mail Income Tax Guide (annual).

A simple introduction on how to you calculate a personal tax liability. Introduction to income tax, capital gains tax and inheritance tax. Some advice is given on reducing the tax burden.

DTI (1985) *Financial Services In The UK*, Cmnd. 9632, HMSO.

A detailed and impartial report on the state of the industry in 1985. The basis for much of the later legislation.

Elkington, W. (1988) *Abbey Financial Rights Handbook*, Roster Ltd.

A useful introduction to the rights of the individual with regard to dealing with financial institutions, personal financial advisers and investment managers.

Frost, A. and Hager, D. (1990) *Debt Securities*, Heinemann.

A careful study of the nature of the various debt securities which are available for investment. Written in a technical style but very informative.

Galitz, A. (1994) *Financial Engineering*, Financial Times/Pitman.

An introduction to most of the high-powered tools which can be used by financial advisers for hedging financial risk – such tools as options, futures, swaps etc. Only for the brave.

Gitman, L.J. and Joehnk, M.D. (1990) *Personal Financial Planning* (revised edn.), The Dryden Press.

Possibly the best US academic text on personal financial planning, very comprehensive. Strong US bias.

Gower, L. (1984) *Review of Investor Protection in the UK*, Cmnd. 9125, HMSO.

The key report which persuaded the government to act to protect investors in the UK. Still very relevant, despite its vintage.

Hindle, J. (1990) *The Compliance Handbook*, Longman.

Provides information to PFAs on the regulatory bodies, the rules they have promulgated, administration of the rules and the dealing rules on securities.

Ingledew, S. (1994) *Identifying And Satisfying Client Needs*, CII/LIA.

This useful and practical book is designed for students sitting paper 3 of the FP certificate of the CII.

Jones, S. (1989) *The Law Relating To Credit Cards*, Blackwell.
All you will ever want to know about the legal aspects of the issue and use and abuse of credit cards.

Kay, W. (1986) *A-Z Guide to Money*, Constable.
A dictionary providing explanations of many of the terms used in financial transactions.

Littlefair, H. (1993 – updated regularly) *Allied Dunbar Investment And Savings Guide*, Longman.
Another book from this reliable stable.

London Business School (1993) *The Cost And Effectiveness Of The UK Financial Regulatory System*, London Business School.
A study of the costs of regulating the UK financial system, including a comparison with the cost of regulation in some other countries such as the USA and France.

Lumnicka, E. and Powell, J. (1990) *An Encyclopaedia Of Financial Services Law*, Sweet & Maxwell.

Marshall, C. (latest edition) *Life Assurance And Pensions Handbook*, Taxbriefs.

Matatiko, J. and Stafford, D. (1985) *Key Developments In Personal Finance*, Basil Blackwell.
A rather old book now but unique in presenting developments in the UK economy which have impacted on personal saving, spending and investment.

Mellows, D. (1992) *Taxation For Executors And Trustees*, Butterworth.
A useful reference book on a very tricky subject.

Miller, J. (1990) *Dictionary Of Financial Regulation*, Stock Exchange Press.
This book covers the regulations applying to a wide range of financial institutions.

Mitchell A. (1993 and regular updates) *Guide To Personal Finance*, Viking: Penguin Books.
An excellent introduction to the basics of personal finance. Not a textbook, but packed with useful information for the DIY enthusiast in financial planning. Strong on the legal side.

Morris, S. (1989) *Financial Services*, Longman.
A synopsis of the legal regulations applying to financial advisers in 1989.

Pawley, M. *et al.* (1994) *UK Financial Institutions And Markets*, Macmillan.
An introduction to the financial institutions and markets operating in the UK.

PBI (1991) *The Financial Adviser's Handbook*, PBI.
Instruction on the authorization required, the forms needed and the procedures to act as an investment adviser in the UK following the recent legislation.

Popplewell, K. (latest edition) *Financial Services And Their Regulation*, CII/LIA.
A very clear guide to the regulations currently imposed on those working in the personal finance industry. Aimed at students sitting part 1 of the FP certificate.

Robson Rhodes (1993 and regular updates) *Personal Financial Planning Manual*, Butterworths.
A rather dry but informative listing of what one should do on a regular basis to arrange one's personal financial affairs.

Shim, J. and Siegel, S. (1991) *Personal Finance*, Schaum.
An American textbook. The book supplies the reader with hundreds of simple calculations to test the user's ability to make personal finance calculations in investment, insurance, housing, pensions and many other areas.

SIB (1993) *SIB Principles And Core Rules For The Conduct Of Investment Business*, Securities and Investment Board.

Sinclair, W.I. (latest edition) *Allied Dunbar Tax Guide*, Longman.

A readable yet comprehensive guide to UK personal and company taxation. Lots of tips about reducing the personal tax bill.
Spears, J. (1993) *Money Costs Money*, Spears.
A most useful collection of facts about credit and the raising of loans.

SRO rule books
The SIB rule book from the SIB
The PIA Rule Book from the PIA
The IMRO rule book from IMRO
The 'Guidelines' are also essential reading.
Stillerman, B. (1992) *Stoy Hayward Guide To Personal Financial Planning*, Century Business.
Another listing of actions to be taken by DIY enthusiasts in the personal finance field. Strong on taxation.
Stone and Cox (quarterly) *Life Assurance Handbook*, Buckley Press.
The bible of the insurance salesman. The regularly updated tables give a wealth of information about current insurance policies, premiums, policy conditions, medical requirements, loan options on policies, etc.
Stone and Cox (quarterly) *Individual Pensions Handbook*, Buckley Press.
These regularly updated tables provide a wealth of information on current pension schemes offered by insurance and other companies. Very useful to the pension consultant.
Travers, S.A. (1990) *The Investor's Guide To Coin Trading*, John Wiley.
A comprehensive guide to the market in trading valuable coins. Useful advice on buying, selling and getting coins properly certified as genuine.
Tolley's (1993) *Tolley's Compliance Monitor*, Tolley Publishers.
An update service for investment advisers and others on complying with the latest regulations from the financial regulators.
Vaitilingam, R. (1993) *The Financial Times Guide To Using The Financial Pages*, Pitman.
A useful guide to the jargon of the financial world plus explanations as to how to read the voluminous statistical tables in the Financial Times.
Williamson, G.K. (1993) *All About Annuities*, John Wiley.
A guide to the different kinds of annuities offered by insurance companies.
Wilson, J. and Wilson, C. (1988) *A Guide To Pensions And Life Assurance*, Kogan Page.

MAGAZINES AND JOURNALS

The personal financial adviser operating in the UK is fortunate in having access to a number of excellent magazines on personal finance. Most of these are published on a monthly basis.
The first six magazines listed below are targeted at personal financial advisers. The others are targeted at their clients.

Money Management
Planned Savings
Financial Adviser
Mortgage Finance Gazette
Money Marketing
Money Week

Investors Chronicle
Money Observer
Money Wise
Prospect
The CII Journal
What investment
What Mortgage?
What Pension?
Money Which
Private Investor
Financial Times Quarterly Review of Personal Finance.

Answers to selected tutorial questions

THE PERSONAL FINANCE PROFESSION

1. Substantial personal saving, much of it contractual, by many wage earners became possible after the Second World War as real incomes rose allowing the majority of wage earners to save a surplus over basic expenditure. These savings were channelled through intermediary financial institutions such as pension funds, investment/insurance companies, collective investment funds and building societies. This huge increase in personal saving created the dramatic growth witnessed in the size of UK financial institutions since 1945.

3. If the income of a financial adviser is based solely on commission earned from the products he or she sells then there must be a big temptation to sell products providing the highest commission. Products such as government stocks and investment trusts which provide no or low commission will tend to be overlooked.

   A salesperson attempts to maximize sales; a financial adviser attempts to provide a viable set of financial plans for his or her client. The latter is a professional worker like a doctor or an architect and operates under a different set of ethics from those motivating a salesperson.

5. A pension plan, an investment plan, an insurance (risk hedging) plan, a tax plan (including an inheritance plan), a house financing plan, a school fees plan.

7. In order to be registered with the PIA an individual must have passed the Financial Planning Certificate of the Chartered Institute of Insurance or have a higher qualification. Two years practical experience as an assistant adviser is also required. Proven honesty and solvency are other requirements.

9. The ICAEW set and mark examinations which test the quality of entrants to the profession. General standards of conduct and perfor-

mance are monitored and a disciplinary panel can rebuke poor performance and even revoke membership of the Institute. An extensive library is maintained covering all accounting matters. The ICAEW is often consulted by the government on matters affecting the profession. The status of the profession of personal financial planners could be much improved if it were able to set up a similar institute which achieved public recognition.

11. The Personal Investment Authority (PIA) monitors most small scale investment advisers in the UK (and many very large ones).

13. The ICS is a compensation scheme set up by the SIB to compensate investors who have lost money through the negligence or fraud of their registered financial adviser. The maximum amount which can be claimed by a client under the scheme is currently £48 000 per claim. The cost of the scheme has been resented by competent small-scale investment advisory firms, since they are being asked to cover for their incompetent colleagues in the profession.

PERSONAL FINANCE RECORD KEEPING

1. Income and expenditure account, balance sheet, long-term cash flow statement, tax documents, insurance cover, pension rights.

3. The financial 'equity' of an individual is the market value of the assets owned by that individual less the debts owing. Another word for equity is wealth.

5. A sale catalogue on antiques, stamps, collectables and suchlike tells the reader the price at which the dealer will sell the goods, not the price at which the dealer will buy them. The buying price is likely to be at least 30% below the selling price, except for very high quality goods.

7. Housing cost, food and clothing, risk hedging, transportation, communication, children.

9. A record of the purchase is automatically logged. This makes personal book-keeping much easier and can provide useful evidence in later legal proceedings.

11. Woman: 35 years 3 months. Man: 10 years 9 months.

13. (a) To arrange an adequate bank overdraft or loan. (b) To arrange the sale of an existing liquid asset. (c) To shift the timing of expenditures. (d) To generate additional income.
    The option chosen depends on the cost of each of these options. Each must be individually evaluated.

15. (a) P 2 (T) The latest PAYE notice of coding (P2).
    (b) P 60 Certificate of pay, income tax and NI contributions.
    (c) 300 (CODA) Latest Schedule D tax assessment.
    (d) 46A Latest accounts and agreement of accounts.

(e) Certificates of loan interest paid.

(f) Certificates of dividend tax credits.

17. Ease of use, ease of entry of data, good security, simple and rapid analysis of the data, low cost of package, a helpful hotline to publisher to enquire about problems in running the package, a wide choice of output formats, customization of the package possible to meet special needs of specific clients.

THE UK FINANCIAL SYSTEM

2. Raising capital...building society

   Managing funds... investment trust

   Payments mechanism...cheque system

   Absorbing risk...insurance

   Providing markets... stock exchange

   Financial services...personal financial advisers

4. A unit trust is 'open ended' – it can buy and sell shares. It trades units in the fund it administers.

   An investment trust holds a fixed portfolio of shares (unless it makes a new rights issue). Investment trusts can be 'geared' with debt finance. Unit trusts cannot take on debt to expand the fund. IT shares are quoted and traded on the stock exchange. UT units are bought from and sold to the fund managers. IT shares usually stand at a discount to the market value of the shares. UT units are quoted at current market value. An IT can split income from capital gain to create two IT funds.

6. The Bank of England is the government's banker and provides finance for government spending. It also monitors the entire UK financial market. It acts as a lender of last resort to the UK money market if funds are scarce and influences the bank rate.

8. Telecommunications linking computers can provide a very rapid access to financial information so most financial markets now operate within electronic 'networks' rather than on a specific physical site. Networks provide more rapid access to information and allow many more operators to use a market over a wider geographic area.

10. (a) If the good or service bought is not supplied the buyer using a credit card may be able to sue the provider of the credit card as well as the supplier of the good or service. (b) A longer period of credit is made available compared to payment by cash or cheque.

12. 'Networking' in personal finance means regular contacts with experts on a particular subject – tax experts, annuity experts, legal experts on trusts etc.

14. The ratio of total house loans to value of houses in the UK has risen in recent years: 1976 (20%), 1992 (31%). Although the total of house

loans has risen in recent years, the very substantial rise in house prices since 1984 has put a great deal of potential credit into the hands of the general public. This is claimed to have increased consumer demand and depressed saving over the period 1984–89.

The reason for the very large rise in house prices in recent years is a matter of much debate. Clearly it is the result of shifts in various demand and supply schedules. The baby-boomers of the 1960s entered the housing market. The supply of land is limited in certain areas of the UK so the rise in real personal incomes in the 1980s allowed sellers to ask for higher real house prices. The building societies allowed higher multiples to wage earners when raising loans. The banks also became flush with cash in the early 1980s via the very liquid Eurobond markets. Conclusion: too much money chasing too few houses.

16. Around £2200 billion, as per Exhibit 3.5.
18. (a) There has been a dramatic rise in expenditure on cars (which were actually cheaper in real terms in 1993 than in 1979).
   (b) A doubling of expenditure on durable goods ('You never had it so good').
   (c) The spending on food (excluding meals out) and liquor was steady over the period but it fell as a percentage of total income. There was a rise in expenditure on clothing and footwear and 'other consumer expenses'.
   (d) There was a huge rise in spending on 'other services', that is such things as 'holidays abroad', 'meals out', 'Security', 'car maintenance', etc. Note the rise in the amount spent on 'services provided' (38% to 43%) against 'personal consumption' of goods (53.7% to 46%).

PERSONAL TAXATION

2. Tax avoidance is legal and means reducing tax bills by utilizing tax allowances provided by current tax legislation. An example occurs if a husband passes income producing assets to his wife who is not utilizing all her tax allowances. Tax evasion means concealing income, on which tax is due from the Inland Revenue. This activity is illegal. An example is 'moonlighting' income not declared in the annual tax return. Tax 'avoision' refers to the many ingenious tax reduction techniques which lie on the borderline between legality and illegality.
4. Casual gambling: on average you lose more than you win.
    Premium bonds winnings: again average cost of the investment exceeds average winnings.

Educational grants, income support: if these grants were taxed the grants would have to be increased proportionately. This would be a waste of government clerical resources.

If the state is providing a minimum grant to support life there is no point in taxing it. Gambling is a net losing activity.

Compensation for loss of office: no very obvious reason. However, it would be unfair to tax the compensation at the highest marginal tax rate of the recipient all in one year.

6. The marginal rate of tax is the highest rate paid on any slice of income. Allowances can often, but not always, be set off against this highest marginal rate of tax. Thus if allowances can be found to set off against taxed income, the benefit can be maximized if these allowances are set off against the highest 'marginal' rate. For example the income from various bonds is not taxed if the income is less than 5% of the value of the bond. This provides a higher benefit if the marginal rate of the taxpayer is 40%, rather than just 25% or 20%. Many allowances, such as the allowance against mortgage interest, can no longer be offset against the highest marginal rate but only against some lower rate.

8. CGT is charged on the profit from the sale of assets – for example, the profit on the sale of equity shares bought for £100 000 and sold in the same year for £120 000. Currently £5800 of capital gains can be earned in any one tax year before CGT becomes due and payable. An asset which is divisible, like 100 Krugerrands, can be sold off over several years in such a way that no more than £5800 of capital profit is made in any one year, thus no CGT is payable. A single gold ornament cannot be so divided, it must all be sold in the same year. Thus CGT is payable on (sale price – inflation adjusted cost price – £5800).

10. The capital gain in both cases is £400 000 – £120 000 = £280 000. However, an allowance is made for inflation so the original value can be upvalued by £120 000 × (130/100) = £156 000. Therefore if the wine or the painting were sold the profit of £400 000 – £156 000 = £244 000 less £5800 = £238 200 would be taxed at the individual's marginal tax rate of 40%.

However, Ms Mitford has the option of selling her wine in small batches over many years, thus spreading and reducing her CGT tax liability. Mr Wiles does not have this option with the painting.

12. Mr Witherspoon lives for over four years after making the gift to his son. Thus inheritance tax is due on 80% of the value of the gift at the IT 40% rate. Thus the tax bill will be for 80% × 40% × £200 000 = £64 000.

14. Inheritance tax payable by Jameson family
  (a) No inheritance tax is paid on the assets left by Mr Jameson to his wife. However when his wife dies two years later, at current

rates, inheritance tax is paid at £330 000 – 150 000 = 180 000 × 40% = £72 000.

(b) Under the second option the stock and shares left to his son are worth £150 000. Inheritance tax allowance of £150 000 can be offset against this liability, so no inheritance tax is payable

When his mother dies her estate is worth £165 000. The inheritance tax payable is £165 000 – £150 000 = £15 000 × 40% = £6000.

By leaving half his shares to his son Mr Jameson has saved his son £72 000 – £6000 = £66 000.

PERSONAL INVESTMENT

1. To balance income and risk. Higher income implies higher risk. Safety of income and capital is very important for older clients.

3. A few examples:

   10 000 shares in Glaxo PLC
   Variable but growing income, positive capital growth, some insecurity but not much, very liquid, good divisibility, low transaction costs, very low maintenance cost, little tax flexibility.

   A 200-ounce bar of gold ($370 × 200 = $74 000)

   No income, possible capital growth but recent history makes this unlikely, value rather unstable, very liquid anywhere in the world (best attribute), very divisible (can be melted down), low transaction costs, no maintenance costs, useful tax aspects (can be transported and sold anywhere, no income to tax). High security cost.

   Vintage car

   No income, possibly good capital growth (but fashion products always risky), not very secure in value, not too liquid, not divisible, high transaction cost (15%), high maintenance costs, little tax flexibility.

   Warrant to buy 10 000 ordinary shares in Glaxo PLC
   No income, very good prospects of capital growth, good security in value, good liquidity, good divisibility, very low transaction costs, no maintenance costs, little tax flexibility but may not be taxed.

5. *Age*: low risk investment with high safety needed.
   Gender: research suggests probably more conservative.
   Health: good health = high risk, poor health = low risk.
   Existing wealth: The wealthier the individual the greater the risk he/she is prepared to take with marginal investment. The new investment must be fitted into the existing portfolio.

Shape of future income flow: the income/capital growth of investment chosen will be influenced by the client's likely future cash flow. For example, if the client is retiring at 55 years of age his cash flow will fall and so must be topped up with AVC pension paying off after 55 but not before.

Dependants: The financial needs of dependants can strongly influence current investment plans. For example, future income for wife on death of husband, school fees for child, trust for handicapped child etc.

7. *The three variables*: (1) R = Return on riskless investment. (2) S = Surplus income on share of average risk. (3) B = Beta providing a measure of the market risk added to an existing portfolio of shares.

Expected return	=	$R + B \times (S - R)$
Con Gold Fields		$13 + 0.4 \times (20 - 13) = 15.8\%$
Intel corporation		$13 + 1.8 \times (20 - 13) = 25.6\%$
Unilever		$13 + 1.05 \times (20 - 13) = 20.35\%$
British Gas		$13 + 0.8 \times (20 - 13) = 18.6\%$

Only Intel will suit this client, assuming he is willing to invest in a company carrying such a high risk attached to the cash flow. Perhaps you should explain to him the relation between income and risk and the existence of specific risk.

9. The decision depends on the client's:

expected date of retirement
state of health
current wealth and pension prospects
dependants
attitude to risk.

If the client is in good health and need not retire for many years then the equity shares are definitely the best option (using maximum PEPs). However, if the client is due to retire shortly and is in poor health, he needs income and the commercial bond looks a good choice (8%). The annuity income at his age is too low (6%), the building society deposit income is rather low (4%) but the capital is safe (which it might not be with the bond or shares).

A mix of 20% BS, 30% bonds and 50% equity would be the conventional mix at his age, assuming good health.

11. (a) Buy a portfolio of high beta shares with average beta of 1.5. (b) Borrow another 50% of initial value and put total amount into a portfolio of average beta shares (average beta of 1).

13. **A PEP investment**: can provide a high untaxed return if held for five years but it can be risky. Many PEPs have crashed. The investor must

check out the scheme very carefully. Professional advice is essential. Long-term investor.

A block of gold: the key factor here is portability. A block of gold can be converted to cash almost everywhere in the world. The current value is easily found. It is divisible, with zero maintenance cost. On almost all other aspects of investment, however, a block of gold is a poor investment. There is no income and the capital growth of gold in recent years has not been high. For the investor moving capital internationally.

A Victorian painting: these have very high transaction costs (15%) and high maintenance cost (security and/or insurance). The value is variable but they have provided a reasonably high return in recent years (1981–89 = 4.3, same as UK share index). Inflation over same period 1.56. A painting is not divisible. Art lovers only.

A time-share apartment in Acapulco: an investor who likes to holiday abroad. Otherwise a poor investment.

A box of Krugerrands: useful for releasing capital gains slowly for tax efficiency. Can switch wealth around the world quickly.

100 'bearer shares': useful for storing illegally gained wealth (tax evasion) – ownership cannot be traced. Can be sold privately. Very popular in France, Italy and Belgium.

15. The return on a share is made up of the dividend or interest on the investment for the period plus any gain or loss on the capital value.

$$
\begin{array}{llllll}
X & 15 + & (110-100) & = & 25p & 25/100 & = & 25\% \\
Y & 2 + & (180-120) & = & 62p & 62/120 & = & 51.7\% \\
Z & 20 + & (55-100) & = & -25p & -25/100 & = & -25\% \\
\end{array}
$$

The above gives return per period, assuming annual return. If the return is for a longer period, say, three years, obviously the annual return is reduced.

17. (a) It is not possible to invest the money at zero risk against all risks including inflation. A suitable investment medium to protect income is indexed linked government bonds (e.g. 7th issue). This will provide a certain income of 3% plus inflation for the year. Building society deposits protect capital value but not against inflation, income is variable. Certain insurance bonds guarantee both income (low return) and capital but not against inflation.

   (b) Around 20 to 30 randomly selected shares. The specific (company) risk is diluted by spreading it around 20 or so different companies.

19. Least risky to most risky: annuity, government bond, shares, silver, Impressionist painting. (See Exhibit 5.12.)

21. The BZW chart Exhibit 5.11 shows that an amount invested in equity shares in 1951 would have earned around 6% net of inflation but gross of tax annually over the period 1951 to 1991. The same amount invested in government stock would have earned barely one half on one per cent per year over the same period. However the same amount invested in shares and stock over the period 1981 to 1991 would have earned over 12% annually on shares and over 8% annually on stock over this period.

23. So long as the retirement fund rules allow it, he should only convert a portion of the retirement fund into an annuity if he can afford to forgo the income. The fund income will be reinvested in the fund until converted but it will not be available to the pensioner until converted into an annuity. The annuity will be converted in slices. Hopefully annuity rates will rise in the future. It may be worthwhile to borrow funds to delay the conversion process. As the pensioner gets older, the return on annuities offered rises.

INSURANCE

1. Risk management is composed of a set of techniques for reducing risk. Hedging is one form of risk management where a 'hedge' is set up which eliminates any loss from a possible future negative event. The event which triggers the future loss also triggers the hedge.
   Self-insure, change the system, leave the system, insure.

3. Alter the system, self-insure (absorb the risk yourself), leave system, insure. Re examples given:

   Fire: alter system.
   Holiday cancelled: you can insure.
   House damage from earthquake: difficult! Insurance may not be available since this is an 'Act of God'. Move house to another region?
   House chimney: you can insure.
   Windows smashed: alter system. Use the law. Insurance difficult if it happens often.
   Serious illness: insure.
   House in war zone: leave system.

5. Life and health assurances, property insurance, general insurance against other hazards.

7. Some insurance companies try to expand their business by cutting premiums others expand via motivating agents with high commission. This causes large variations in cost between companies.

9. Few insurance companies in the UK go bankrupt. A client is covered up to an amount of £48 000 if an insurance company should go bust. Foreign-based insurance companies are more risky. One of the jobs

assigned to a loss adjuster is to ensure that the insurance company will not pay a claim if the insured has not followed the rules of the insurance contract. The insured must read the small print and follow the contract rules precisely.

PENSIONS

2. Since the working population is falling in proportion to the number not working, the Conservative government feels it cannot afford to fully fund pension needs as this policy would substantially increase taxation on the working population in the future. An alternative government might take another view.

4. The investment skills of those managing your pension funds. The honesty of the organization managing your pension funds. Your date of retirement. The future return on investments. The future rate of inflation.

6. The dependant(s) will be likely to receive (a) 50% of the pension due to the contributor on the original date of retirement of the pensioner or earlier. (b) A lump sum life insurance payment related to the salary of the pension contributor. (c) Some additional perks related to school fee payment, child benefit (additional pension), possibly health cover for a few years until children grown up.

8. (a) Net cash flow: the amount of cash any employee receives is well short of his/her gross income.

    (b) 'Indexed' means that the pension is increased by an amount to compensate for inflation during the previous period. The real value is held constant. Normally full indexation is only available to ex-government and other state employees.

    (c) There are such things as tax, national health insurance, superannuation etc. The net income received in cash each month is usually between 60% and 75% of the gross income. It is the net cash income received which is important in pension planning for retirement purposes.

10. Most pensions are structured (for men) to begin paying out at age 65 and for women, until recently, at age 60. If the employee leaves because of ill-health, redundancy or free choice before this expected retirement age his/her pension will be reduced.

    The normal state pension is not paid until a man reaches 65 years of age (a woman 60 at present). Thus if a man retires at 60 his income could fall substantially even if he is in a pension plan. His pension will be reduced by 5/80 or 5/60 and he will not receive the state pension until the age of 65. This is the 'awkward time' mentioned in the question.

A client should be advised to build up an investment fund to cover this period, possibly via a free-standing additional voluntary contribution scheme. The fund should be sufficient to release an amount equal to the state pension for the five years.

12. Three possible advantages of a company occupational pension scheme over a personal pension plan:
    (a) Company pension funds are usually more generous particularly with regard to the unexpected event, i.e. treatment of dependants on early death, 'top up' for early retirement, inflation proofing etc.
    (b) A company 'final years based' pension is usually based on best three years of previous earnings, rather than on terminal value of invested contributions. This can be the safer option in times of economic upheaval or when annuity rates are low. The personal pension may have no inflation proofing; most occupational schemes have some inflation proofing.
    (c) If employee is ill or temporarily incapacitated for some other reason, the company will invariably continue to pay the pension contributions at the usual rate until the employee returns to work. This may not be the case with a personal pension.

14. £11 050. See inflation table in chapter.

16. (a) Is early retirement penalized or are additional pension years granted?
    (b) Are pension contributions still paid if the employee is off work because of ill health? If so, for how long are they paid? If employee loses job because of ill health, what happens to the pension rights? At how early an age will pension be paid because of leaving by reason of ill health?
    (c) What are the rights of the spouse on death of employee? Pension rights, child pension? Life assurance lump sum payment? Health insurance?
    (d) Is the pension portable? How is the transfer value calculated? What penalties are imposed, if any?
    (e) Who are the trustees? Are they independent of management? Are there any employee trustees? Who manages the pension fund? How often does the scheme have an actuarial valuation? Is this valuation available to the scheme members?

HOUSING

2. A repayment mortgage is repaid over the lifetime of the loan. An endowment mortgage is repaid out of an insurance fund at the end of the loan period. The EM is also a life assurance policy and a saving scheme. The RM is much more flexible. The EM forces a house owner

to save and to insure his/her life, who might not otherwise do so. The RM is cheaper and so might appeal to a potential house buyer who is short of cash. Also it might appeal to an individual who prefers to do his/her own investing and life assurance.

4. The periodic insurance premium is invested in a unit trust selected by the mortgagee. At the date of repayment of the mortgage the fund is liquidated and the mortgage paid out of the fund. Yes, the mortgagee has the responsibility for ensuring that the value of the fund exceeds the mortgage value at the terminal date.

6. If the current rate of interest is below the long-term trend in the UK (10.1%), as in 1993, it may well pay to take out a fixed rate mortgage for many years ahead. In 1993 Lloyds Bank were offering a fixed rate mortgage for 25 years at 9.7%. The variable rate is currently 7–8%. There are advantages in being able to budget your cash flows ahead which you cannot do with a variable rate mortgage.

8. Inflation destroys the value of a mortgage. If inflation is expected to be high in the future, take out a mortgage for repayment many years away. Let inflation do its job of reducing the real value of the mortgage. If low inflation is expected, repay over a shorter period and save interest charges.

10. Yes, but the benefits are now diminishing. CGT is not paid on capital profits from selling a first home. Mortgage interest on a loan of up to £30 000 is allowable against tax at a 15% rate.

12. If your client can sell the flat in three years' time, this is a bargain offer. You are only paying half the mortgage but have the use of the entire flat for three years. You are only paying £500 a month for a £100 000 loan. Can he bring in a paying guest at no tax cost?

Questions to ask: 'Can you rent half the flat over the three years?', 'Can you sell the other half or your own half in the intervening three years?', 'What happens if you don't, or can't, buy the other half in three years' time?', 'Who is the independent valuer to be ?'

It is a risky but potentially profitable venture.

13. Property in London, except for a few choice areas, has provided a low real return, on average, over the last 30 years (1–2%); however, over short periods (1983–89), property in London has proved to be a very profitable investment. However, property has high maintenance and transaction costs, is illiquid and also indivisible.

Some City types buy property when it is at the bottom of the value cycle (as in 1993), sell near the top (1989) and then rent. There is a distinct property value cycle in the UK, particularly in London. There have been booms – 1971–74, 1976–79 and 1983–89, and slumps – 1974–75, 1980–83 and 1989–94.

15. The real difference in house prices in the different regions of the UK is caused by differences in land prices. Land in London costs three to four times the cost of land in Yorkshire.

17. There is a strong argument in favour of taking out a fixed rate loan, at present, with interest rates currently below the long-term trend. However, the Swiss franc loan must be repaid in Swiss francs in 10 years' time. What will be the £–Swiss franc exchange rate in 10 years' time? No one knows, it cannot be predicted. Thus Mr Steel must go to a mortgage broker who can arrange exchange rate cover via options or futures. The cost of this cover must be added to the cost of the loan. (Currently the SF loan would still be cheaper.)

19. It is very unlikely. The immense cash surplus and high inflation of the early 1980s are unlikely to be repeated for many years. There are fewer young house buyers and an increasing number of older house sellers.

CONSUMER CREDIT

2. A good past payments record, a steady job, a high salary, owning one's own home, and age have been found to be the best indicators of a good credit risk in the UK.

   A high credit rating allows a borrower to borrow from discriminating lenders who provide credit at lower cost than other credit providers.

4. An 'open-ended' source of credit provides credit up to some agreed limit, say £2000. The borrower can borrow or repay credit up to this limit. A bank overdraft is a good example of an open-ended source of credit.

   A 'specific' source of credit is credit extended to purchase a specific object, such as a computer or a washing-machine. The credit is limited to a fraction of the value of the object bought. Any additional specific credit must be renegotiated with the lender.

6. A whole-life assurance policy is a very sound form of security. The risk of default by the borrower is almost zero, thus the cost of credit offered from such a source is low.

8. The annual percentage rate (APR) on a loan is a technique for measuring the cost of credit in such a way that interest charges on a loan presented in different ways can be accurately compared. The cost of credit is set down in different ways by different lenders. Since the introduction of the APR, credit providers have been unable to mislead naive borrowers by representing the cost of credit to be lower than it actually is.

10. $21.93\% - 20\% = 1.93\%$ per annum (see Exhibit 9.2).

12. If the APR formula is used, the rate is close to 38%.

14. Classify the monthly expenditures of the client into 'essential', 'important' and 'discretionary' spending. The value of the benefits

from the least important 'discretionary' expenditures forgone, that is the savings which provide the money to pay for the loan, furnishes an estimate of the opportunity cost of the loan.

16. The market value and the degree of liquidity of the assets offered as security for a loan.

18. The Office of Fair Trading.

20. If the buyer discusses the credit contract with the seller on the seller's premises but then takes the contract away, signs it elsewhere, then returns it to the seller, the buyer has five days to withdraw from the contract once it is returned by the seller.

22. Bankruptcy can blight the creditworthiness of a person for a lifetime. A bankrupt may never be able to gain access to credit again – a severe penalty in the modern world.

COMPUTERS IN PERSONAL FINANCE

1. Compactness, ease of analysis of data, security.

3. Before a file stored on a computer can be interrogated the interrogator must know the 'password' which gives him or her access to the file. 'Encryption' means that the individual numbers and letters are coded by the computer, as they are placed in the file by an encryption algorithm. The data cannot be read until it is decrypted by using another algorithm.

5. A 'spreadsheet' is a software package much beloved by accountants. A spreadsheet allows numbers to be processed very quickly and accurately. A spreadsheet 'template' is a pre-programmed spreadsheet designed to solve a specific problem.

   Almost every type of personal finance plan can be aided by using a pre-programmed spreadsheet. Examples are investment (portfolio) planning to reduce risk, pension planning (what contributions needed for how long), house mortgage selection (length of mortgage period) and school fee planning (how long to save before school fees start).

7. A computer, probably a micro-laptop, and a modem to connect the computer to the telephone system.

9. Several computer programs have been written which can produce personal financial plans for clients. Such programs can be either hired or bought by a PFA. So long as the client has 'standard' problems, a computer generated plan is viable. A CBPP can reduce the cost of producing a plan by a substantial margin. The publisher of the CBPP can relieve the PFA of the burden of keeping up-to-date if the program is regularly updated by a team of experts. Personal tax software programs are currently used by accountants to service clients with standard problems.

11. CBPP programs are very expensive to produce. Thus they are expensive to buy. Most CBPP programs are hired from the publisher. The payment is based either on a given period of use or per application of the program.

13. (a) What is the overall cost of the system, including help from publisher?
    (b) How long has the system been in operation. How many PFAs use it?
    (c) Can the system be customized by the user?
    (d) Who wrote and who maintains the system? How much experience do these people have?
    (e) How user friendly is the system? Does a help hotline exist?
    (f) How often is the system updated?

15. The Internet is a world-wide communications system which uses modems and telephone lines to connect millions of computer users. The Internet actually consists of thousands of interlinked smaller nets.

    A gateway is a computer program plus some hardware which simplifies the link between a user, the Internet and the accessing of data contained in an electronic data base linked into the Internet. A network is a group of computers linked via telephone or cable or radio. A data base is a classified collection of facts which can be quickly searched using a computer and a suitable search program.

REGULATION OF THE PERSONAL FINANCIAL ADVISER

2. If **all** financial advice came under the control of the FA Act of 1986 the receiver of financial advice at a dinner party could sue the innocent provider of advice, if it proved to be incorrect!

   Some specific exclusions: advice provided by financial journalists in newspapers etc., casual advice (e.g. at a dinner party), Estate Agents, advice provided by dealers in real assets, advice to employees re an employee share scheme etc.

   Either the advice is generic and not specific, or the provider is not claiming to be a professional financial adviser to a specific individual.

4. The SIB, The PIA and IMRO.

6. The adviser must prove himself or herself to be competent, honest and solvent and also have the requisite two or three years' practical experience required.

8. Any person or entity which advises on, deals in or manages investments or collective investments in a professional capacity. The entity can be an individual, a partnership or a limited company.

10. The fee charged to the client for the service, commission earned on selling and buying securities, the current composition and market value of the portfolio, shares bought and sold during the period.

12. 'Integrity' means that the PFA's advice is based entirely on benefiting his client. He does not have some secondary motive, such as high commission, which benefits the adviser at a cost to the client.

'Fair dealing' means that the adviser tells the client all the relevant facts about his role.

The client should be appraised of the simplicity of the repayment scheme as against the complexity of the endowment mortgage. The latter is a complex 'bundled' financial product comprising a loan scheme, a savings scheme and an assurance scheme.

14. No one is quite sure what the expression, 'best advice' actually means! The SROs have issued several 'guidance notes' on the subject. Presumably it means that the advice must always put the client's interest first. Commission rates must not influence the advice given. The PFA must be competent at financial analysis and have a good knowledge of the financial products available to her client.

16. 'Churning' means that the PFA buys and sells shares on behalf of a client not to improve the return on the client's portfolio but to make additional commission for the adviser! It breaches the 'integrity' rule.

18. All financial advisers must now disclose to a client the commission and any other benefits he or she receives from the sale of a financial product. It has been argued that advisers working for the large financial institutions will enjoy a great advantage over independent advisers in this environment. The cost of advice is seen to be high and so the clients may prefer the security of advice from a large well established institution. However fee-based independent advisers may now be in a stronger position *vis-à-vis* commission-based advisers.

19. The adviser may be warned by the SRO, reprimanded by the SRO, fined by the SRO or, ultimately, deregistered. A charge may be laid against the adviser by the SIB in a court of law. A few advisers have been imprisoned for the fraudulent misconduct of clients' affairs.

20. Many PFAs are members of professional organizations such as the Institute of Chartered Accountants in England and Wales (ICAEW) or the Law Society. In such cases the individual member can be registered with the PIA as a member of a registered group. Such members must convince their institute that they are qualified to act as investment advisers, and pay an annual fee to their institute who in turn register with the PIA.

The limitations placed on a member registered in this way are that the PFA must not be a tied agent and, like all other registered advisers, must disclose the fee or commission to the client.

22. Criticisms:

(a) The qualifications required of members of the PIA are not demanding compared to other professions. A proper Institute of

Personal Financial Planning needs to be set up to examine and discipline PFAs.

(b) The PIA is underfinanced relative to its responsibilities. The PIA has more registered members but has much lower funding and resources compared to the other SROs. Some government funding needed here.

(c) The rules governing the behaviour of PFAs are not clear in all cases. Case law is needed to clarify matters.

(d) The financing of the Investor's Compensation Scheme is insecure. A properly funded scheme needs to be set up.

DISCOUNTING AND PERSONAL FINANCE

1. (a) £1 490
   (b) £2 323
   (c) £681

2. (a) £201 136
   (b) £30 704
   (c) £260 450

3. (a) £80 521
   (b) £10 110

4. £45 280

5. £10 955

6. The value of the loan at the end of the five years is £14 025.

   The amount to be repaid annually over the 10 years is £1997.

7. 16.99%

8. £85 976   The adjusted discount rate is found by using the formula $(r - g)/(1 + g)$
   Where r is the discount rate and g is the growth rate.
   $(0.07 - 0.05)/(1 + 0.05) = 1.9\%$
   $A_{n/1.9\%}/1.05 = £85\ 976$

9. Close to 7% $(17\ 000/5000 = 3.4)$
   Look up 3.4 for 4 years in the annuity table.
   The answer is close to 7%. (6.84%)

10. 9.33%

11. £3148.22

Author and title index

Subject index